THE STAGE IS SET

LEE SIMONSON

THE
STAGE
IS SET

THEATRE ARTS BOOKS

NEW YORK

COPYRIGHT, 1932, BY HARCOURT, BRACE & COMPANY
COPYRIGHT RENEWED, 1960, BY LEE SIMONSON
© COPYRIGHT, 1963, BY THEATRE ARTS BOOKS

Library of Congress Catalog Card Number: 62-12338

To Carolyn

Sixth printing, revised and amended, 1963

Published by Theatre Arts Books
333 Sixth Avenue, New York 14

Published simultaneously in Canada by Ambassador
Books Ltd., 370 Alliance Ave., Toronto 9, Ontario

PRINTED IN THE UNITED STATES OF AMERICA

ACKNOWLEDGMENTS

Tʜɪs volume makes no pretence to original research. I have relied on the accredited research of historians who lifted the technique of staging in historic theatres out of the debris of accumulated misconceptions.

In addition to many recognized authorities, I am particularly indebted to a number of volumes not yet sufficiently well known to students of stage setting in this country: P. Decharme's *Euripides and the Spirit of his Dramas;* L. B. Campbell's *Scenes and Machines on the English Stage* for many of my Renaissance and Elizabethan sources; W. J. Lawrence's early studies of the Shaksperian stage as well as his later ones; L. V. Gofflot's *Le Théâtre au Collège;* G. Bapst's *Essai sur l'histoire du théâtre;* and for the stage-craft of mystery and passion plays to Gustave Cohen's *Histoire de la mise en scène dans le théâtre religieux du moyen age* and his extraordinary documentation of *Le livre de conduite du régisseur et le compte des dépenses pour le mystère de la passion;* also Max Grube's *Geschichte der Meininger.* A complete list of works referred to is appended in a critical bibliography. For the convenience of the reader I have modernized the language of Elizabethan documents.

For permission to quote from volumes published by them I wish to thank The Chicago University Press, The Harvard University Press, Macmillan and Co., Dodd, Mead and Co., Houghton Mifflin and Co., Little, Brown, and Co., Longmans, Green, and Jonathan Cape and Harrison Smith; for permission to reproduce illustrated material, Joseph Gregor of the Bibliothek National of Vienna, The Duke of Devonshire, Levin and Munksgaard, and the Max Hesse Verlag; also Professor Cohen and the Publications de la Faculté des Lettres de Strasbourg for permission to translate from his work; M. Rondel of the Bibliothèque de l'Arsénal, Paris, for his kindness in placing many of the treasures of his collection at my disposal; Mr. H. A. Mattice of the New York Public Library and Mrs. Blanche Hays for assistance in many details of translation and verification; Miss Dorothy Teall for her aid in correcting proof; and Mr. Ulric Moore for allowing me to consult his unpublished translation of *Die Musik und die Inscenierung*. I have, however, used my own translation in quoting from Appia's works.

I am indebted to Louis Untermeyer for his help on several chapters. Above all I wish to express my gratitude to Philip Littell for his patient interest while reading this book in manuscript, for the encouragement he gave me, and for his many valuable suggestions and corrections.

2

In view of the fact that I am one of the six directors of the Theatre Guild, Inc., I must remind my readers that this book is wholly a personal expression of my convictions and cannot be construed as reflecting in any way the program, policy, or opinions of the Theatre Guild as a body or of any of its other members. The Guild functions as a group expression of six distinct personalities, who agree upon a working program but who are not expected to subscribe to any one doctrine of "theatre art" or any one theory of play production, playwrighting, or stage setting. None of the ideas expressed in the following pages have been submitted to my colleagues or discussed with them. I have stated no facts in regard to the Guild that are not matters of public record. The official history of the Guild was published in 1929 under the subtitle *The First Ten Years*. The responsibility for the opinions, statements, and criticisms contained in these pages is entirely my own.

L. S.

CONTENTS

CONTENTS

ILLUSTRATIONS

INTRODUCTION TO 1963 EDITION

Plus que ça change. . . .

When I wrote in 1932 that the theatre in New York seemed to be strangling in a clutter of side streets we call Broadway, the statement may have seemed unduly pessimistic. Now, in 1963, it seems almost prophetic. At the moment, the professional theatre is in a state of progressive disorganization and panic, fairly gasping for breath. As reported in the New York *Times* for April 14th, 1961, Robert Whitehead, President of the League of New York Theatres—the association of producers and theatre owners—confirmed the fact that their board of managers had met "to discuss the state of emergency and ways to overcome economic disaster." One producer is quoted as saying, "We lost the battle with Actors Equity last June and if we lose this one with the dramatists we may as well quit producing." Another member said, "Many producers have already started working up properties for next season but cannot get investors to put up the money. Last season a total of $2,000,000 was lost by investors. This season the total loss will be at least $3,000,000. If we lose 'the angels'—Broadway's sobriquet for investors—eventually there won't be a Broadway." The general feeling, Mr. Whitehead asserted (changing his metaphors) is that "Broadway is on fire and the dramatists must do something immediately. We need a better economic basis on which to produce plays—and this means quick modifications of royalty rates." According to the present contract, which has just expired, the minimum royalty received by dramatists is 5% of the first $5,000 of a play's gross box office receipts, 7½% of the next $2,000 and 10% thereafter. For musicals authors receive a straight royalty of 6%. "These minimums made sense twenty or so years ago when ticket prices were low and grosses ran in the area of $12,000 a week. Nowadays . . . grosses are in the area of $40,000 for plays and $70,000 for musicals. The proposed reduction called for is that dramatists take a 50% cut for the first 15 weeks of a play's run and for the first 30 weeks of a musical."

Although the playwrights have acceded to this demand, it is not surprising that they view the necessity for this plea with the skepticism of Voltaire. Why should they subsidize a producer's errors in judgment in staging plays that no veteran playreader would have recommended for production? With a few notable exceptions, producers do not invest in the plays they stage but gamble with investors money for a possible profit of a quarter of a million dollars—if the play is "a hit," profits that may run into several millions or more if the production is "a smash hit." "My Fair Lady" has, according to current estimates, earned approximately $7,500,000 to date, and its eventual profits, including all subsidiary rights such as royalties from recordings, stock company and touring company rights both here and abroad, are estimated at $10,000,000 to $12,000,000 before taxes. Even established playwrights are averse to "opening cold" in New York without a previous tour of two or three weeks in neighboring cities—Boston, New Haven, and Philadelphia—where the play can be "tried out" on successive audiences, revised or even largely rewritten at public rehearsals at the public's expense. Today the cost of a dramatic production, after a try-out tour, when it opens in New York is not less than $100,000; for a musical, $400,000 to $500,000. If a successful play's weekly gross is $40,000, the playwright's previous royalty would have been $730 per week. With the current deduction of 50% it will be $365 a week, or $5,455 for 15 weeks. However the cost of keeping a show running usually involves two or three star players at weekly salaries of $1000 or more and a varying percentage of the gross, as well a director of star caliber, who in addition to his fee of $5,000 may also receive at least 2% of the weekly gross until the investment is recovered, and thereafter 3% to 5% of the profits. One director commands 5% of the gross and 10% of the profits. A weekly savings of $365, unless the producer has reserve funds to invest or can subsidize the production by a sale of the movie rights, will not mean the difference between keeping a play running or being forced to close it. The same holds true of a musical, even if the weekly saving under the new contract is $2,100, for in addition to the same percentages of the weekly gross and of the profits incurred by a dramatic show it must pay the salaries of a choreographer, a group of dancers, and a minimum of 10 musicians and 18 stage hands.

The theatre in New York is indirectly subsidized by the Bureau of Internal Revenue which considers "entertainment" a tax deductable business expense for the thousands of business executives and buyers who stream into the city annually. With ticket prices ranging from $9.80 to $7.50 in the orchestra to $6.90 in the first balcony and $4.60 for the rear rows, where the sight lines are usually poor, it has become a luxury theatre for those in the upper income brackets. The average playgoer goes to the theatre once or perhaps twice a year to celebrate a birthday or an anniversary, or waits to see the movie version of a hit. The cost of theatre tickets, with production costs at their present levels, remains high due to the fact that most theatres have a capacity of not more than 1,200, some even less. The chances of success for a producer remain one in five. The stakes are higher. The few investors who have consistently made money over a period of years are those with large capital resources who can risk a quarter to half a million dollars and sustain their less-successful productions with some of the profits of a "smash hit." The most difficult seats to sell are those in a second balcony and many of these are shut off. One producer recently echoed

Bernard Shaw's dictum: "Nothing is exorbitant if you have a hit. If you haven't, it doesn't make any difference." The Ziegfeld Theatre, designed by Josef Urban and one of the few with adequate back stage space, is now a television studio. The owner of the Hudson Theatre recently announced his intention of demolishing the building and erecting a garage, that presumably being a more profitable form of investment.

No theatre has been built in New York City since the Ethel Barrymore opened in 1934. The League of New York Theatres a few years ago petitioned for a change in the building codes which would permit building over both the stage and auditorium, thus providing additional revenue for any given plot of ground. Due to the technical advances in fire-proof construction, the petition was granted and the codes were changed by the Fire and Building Departments. But no theatre has yet been built under this proviso. Banking institutions do not look with favor on combining two types of building construction which adds considerably to the investment cost. They are especially unenthusiastic when part houses a theatre unit that may remain empty for weeks or months at a time until it eventually houses a hit. They prefer a steady return on their investments of five or six per cent. The financial problems of the producer continues to grow more critical. He must furnish 30% of the weekly cost of $1,500 for stage hands, ushers, two box office attendants, and a pro-rata share of the salaries of mail clerks handling advance sales, and telephone bills. If the weekly gross falls below $17,000 a week, or $40,000 a week for musicals, he can be dispossessed by the theatre owner on a week's notice. The theatre owner is guaranteed $10,000 a week deposited in advance. Of the first $20,000 of the gross box-office receipts for one week, 30% goes to the theatre owner, 70% to the producer, above that, 25% and 75% respectively. The producer's share in turn must be split between the playwright who receives up to 10% of the gross, and the producer. Half of the producer's remaining share is in turn split between the producer and his investors. Their maximum profit in the case of a hit is $5 for every $1 invested. But under these terms it will take many months, if not a year, for "angels" who risk a few thousand dollars to recoup their investment. It is therefore not surprising that it is increasingly difficult to enlist their support.

In 1960, the total receipts of the tax of 10% on the price of theatre tickets was less than one hundreth of 1% of Federal revenues. The Secretary of Labor, while arbitrating the wage dispute between the Metropolitan Opera Association and its orchestra and corps de ballet, advocated a Federal subsidy to diminish its annual deficit of some $860,000. Opera, in his estimation, being an essential cultural asset. If Rossini, Meyerbeer, Verdi, and Puccini, as well as Wagner, are cultural assets, is not the dramatic theatre equally important?

The Cost of Waste

Despite their cries of alarm and distress no concerted effort has been made by either theatre owners or producers to reduce some of their most conspicuous forms of waste. One of these is in the lighting of a play—the border and spotlights and their control by dimmers that regulate their varying intensities, the whole light plot that accompanies the action of any play. The equipment used was already antiquated in the 1930s, consisting of a series of five or more dimmer boxes, each weighing at least 500 pounds. A play usually ends its run in a New York house Saturday midnight. Every spotlight and border and its connecting cables has to be dismantled with a crew of electricians working through the night at overtime pay, stowed into trucks, also at overtime rates, and carted to a storehouse. As soon as the theatre is cleared another crew works around the clock, and through the night, again at double pay, installing tons of almost identical equipment in time for a light rehearsal, then a final dress rehearsal of a play coming in from its road try out. The total cost of trucking, setting up and dismantling of lighting equipment for these out of town try-outs and a New York opening has been estimated by the most experienced business manager I know at from $15,000 to $20,000 for each production.

In 1939, as consultant to the architects of Wisconsin's University Theatre, I installed the first remote control electronic lighting system. The dimmer control board was the size of a small lectern. The controls, circular discs, were approximately four inches in diameter, instead of some 2½ feet as in the Broadway dimmer boxes. The compact rheostat controls were placed under the stage. Two changes could be pre-set. Dimming was proportional; though some lamps might move from nearly full to nearly out and others through a shorter cycle, each completed the circuit at the same time. Any circuit of lamps that had to be timed with a particular bit of action could be selected and controlled separately. A single operator ran this control board which is still functioning perfectly.

There is a further source of waste. A producer must pay for assembling the lighting equipment he requires about $3,000, and then pay a percentage of its valuation—$28,000 in the case of Achard's "A Shot in the Dark" as weekly rental, 10% for the first three weeks, $450 each for the next three, $250 a week for the balance of the run, which in the case of a long run might more than equal the value of the lighting equipment used. Electronic switch-boards with control panels also no larger in size than a lectern have been perfected and are capable of as many as ten pre-set changes. The basic equipment of spot and border-lights could be easily standardized and installed in all out-of-town and New York theatres. Equipment for special effects could be added again at a much lower weekly rental than the current rates, but at a figure that would be profitable to firms supplying the equipment and at the same time achieve a great saving in expense for both theatre owners and producers.

Recession and Revival

There are 30 theatres operating at present, 16 controlled by the Shubert interests, 14 by independent managements, as contrasted with 70 in 1932 when this book was originally published. The number of those available is actually reduced to 23 due to the fact that seven houses are occupied by successful musicals that have run a year or more and will continue through next season, or are booked, in case they close, for other musicals. Although a few theatres have been repainted or otherwise refurbished, many are in a state of disrepair. Actors Equity recently submitted a list of complaints—leaking skylights, lack of showers for ballet dancers and chorus, lack of inter-com phones from the stage doorman to the box-office, need for a protected office for the stage doorman, and actor's mail boxes.

The theatre is shrinking out of town as well. In the last decade, the number of theatres in Boston has declined from 6 to 3, in Philadelphia from 10 to 5, in Chicago from 10 to 3. Except for the new Center Theatre (of the Music Center of the Performing Arts) now being completed in Los Angeles, there is only one legitimate theatre there; in San Francisco there are 2; Cleveland, St. Louis, Cincinnati, Baltimore, and Kansas City only have one each. The remaining major cities of the United States have none. Companies touring elsewhere are forced to play in concert halls, civic auditoriums or gymnasiums. I know of one instance in which a company played in a showboat still moored on the bank of a branch of the Missouri River.

The only modern theatres, with ample back stage space, workshops, complete lighting equipment, and electronic control boards are those now being built or planned at universities and colleges from New England to the far South and from the East to the West Coast. The first theatre-in-the-round was inaugurated some twenty years ago at the University of Washington. A number of other theatres are experimental in form, as at Baylor in Waco, Texas, Frank Lloyd Wright's at Dallas. The Loeb Theatre, in Cambridge an adjunct to Harvard College in Cambridge, Massachusetts, is completely flexible. Its form can be altered by electrical boards controlling elevator stages and the level of the stage itself, so that it can alternately place the spectators on three sides of a forestage, seat an audience in an amphitheatre of the continental type, and expand or retract the proscenium from 30 to 50 feet.

Recently I lectured for a semester at the University of California in Los Angeles and found an intense interest in the theatre among both the graduate and undergraduate students, whether or not they were enrolled in the Department of Theatre Arts. I attended a performance of Camus's masterpiece "The Just" (which has not been revived in France since its original performance some twenty years ago) newly and excellently translated, effectively acted, particularly by the feminine lead, who was given an enthusiastic notice by the drama critic of the *Los Angeles Times*. In a seminar on scenic design I conducted, I found the level of artistic ability extremely high. Two projects, one for the twenty-four sets of Strindberg's "Road to Damascus" and another for a re-staging of Obey's "Noah" showed a degree of dramatic imagination and technical skill that equalled the work of any of the leading scenic designs now active on Broadway.

A new theatre building will be completed at U.C.L.A. in 1963 with two large stages and backstage workshops, complete lighting equipment and electronic control boards. In the final plans for the university campus a site has been allotted for a repertory company of professional actors. The Los Angeles Music Center for the Performing Arts, now being completed has three stages and three auditoriums, all with ample backstage space. The first, which seats 3,200, can not only profitably house operatic performances and ballet troupes but also the most elaborate orchestras that can be toured. A medium-sized theatre can house most Broadway productions. A third auditorium seating 325 is for more experimental productions and has a projecting stage and a horseshoe-type plan. The theatre built at Minneapolis, where Tyrone Guthrie will train and direct a repertory company, has 1,600 seats.

What is needed is some coordinating plan which will link these university and community theatres, already built or in the course of construction, in a program that can again bring drama to the country as a whole, a national plan that will reach communities whose only theatre at present is television.

The other grave problem confronting the professional theatre, in addition to its economic plight, is an artistic one: the majority of actors no longer have the opportunity to act in contact with a living audience and project the emotional or intellectual quality of a role. They wait, hoping for the one chance in perhaps a hundred that they may be cast in a play that will be a hit. Only a fraction are employed during any New York season. Those, who can, support themselves in the interim by migrating to Hollywood or they act in television where, in order to facilitate national distribution, the play is usually pre-recorded on tape with the sequence of scenes jumbled. Their knowledge of the theatre extends only to the day before yesterday: the current Broadway successes or those of a year or two ago revived in summer stock. Actors can develop their talent and mature as artists only if they continue to act in a variety of roles.

The theatre throughout Europe has been sustained by permanent repertory companies since the days of Molière and his "Illustrious Company." The Ford Foundation has made a welcome beginning in contributing to the establishment of repertory groups in New York, San Francisco, and several other cities. The most significant aspect of Lincoln Center is not the new opera house and other buildings, but the repertory company to be organized and directed by Elia Kazan, and its school for training young actors. As in the decade 1920–1930 it is not Broadway but the off-Broadway theatres that have given authors, players, and audiences the opportunity of seeing some of the masterpieces of modern drama with revivals of *Uncle Vanya, Ivanov, Ghosts, Hedda Gabler,* and *Misalliance*. And the leading New York critics have, almost without exception, given laudatory notices to hitherto unknown young actors who undertook leading roles.

For the American public have always been passionately enthusiastic theatre goers. From the beginning of the 18th Century a British repertory company played successfully and profitably in Philadelphia, despite Quaker disapproval, until the outbreak of the Revolution. From 1810 and for seventy-five years more as recorded in "The Living Stage" by Kenneth Macgowen and William Melnitz, the American stage "was crossing the Alleghanies with the pioneers, flowing down the Ohio and the Mississippi, spreading across the plains and over the Rockies. . . . They travelled by rafts and river boats and covered wagons before the railroads came. . . . The St. Charles Theatre in New Orleans opened in 1835 at a cost of $350,000. . . . Mormon amateurs—among them Brigham Young, who played a priest in *Pizzaro* while they were still in Nauvoo, Illinois—had a temporary theatre almost as soon as they reached Utah. . . . And in 1860 they built a large playhouse in Salt Lake City, which was booking road companies as late as 1928. . . . By 1885 America had more than 5,000 playhouses in at least 3,500 cities and somewhere between 50,000 and 70,000 players. . . . In 1855 the great French actress Rachel visited America. . . . During the next three decades at least five other continental players of distinction toured the United States. All but one—the actor-manager Fechter—appeared as co-stars with Booth. Adelaide Ristori and Tomaso Salvini matched their Italian, and Fanny Janauschek her German against Booth's English." In 1851 when Edwin Booth at the age of nineteen accompanied by his father, Junius Brutus Booth, crossed the Isthmus of Panama and sailed into San Francisco harbor, there were no less than three theatres—the Jenny Lind and the American and one where plays were given in French. A French journalist commenting on the American remarked that, "In many ways the luxury and good taste of this little theatre remind one of the Opera Comique"—this is a frontier town where vigilantes carried out summary justice and where "it is hardly ever safe to walk alone and even if you go with a friend you must be sure to carry a revolver." When the Jenny Lind Theatre burned down it was immediately rebuilt, "and is now a handsome building with a balcony, three galleries, a parterre, orchestra stalls, and a dress circle. . . . The house is sold out every evening." He concluded that the theatres "were the only civilized distraction in this new city."

It is therefore perhaps not a forlorn hope that now, before the end of the century, the American theatre will no longer be an upper class luxury confined to New York City, but reach into the grass roots, revive the audiences that once nourished it across the nation and again become a national institution.

Lee Simonson

FOREWORD

Nothing is foreordained except in retrospect. Any event, once it has occurred, can be made to appear inevitable by a competent historian. This volume is to be read neither as a history nor as a prophecy of the theatre's destiny. It is written as one craftsman's analysis of his problem.

Such knowledge of stage-craft as I have acquired is presented not as an absolute insight into one art of the theatre but as a record of my own apprenticeship. After having studied abroad I started out to be a painter of easel-pictures and then turned to the theatre as a place where whatever graphic talent I possessed could be put to use. I adopted scenic design as my profession at the age of thirty-one, because I happened to become one of a group of friends who, in 1919, founded the Theatre Guild with the purpose of producing plays that dramatized ideas. Having designed most of my settings as part of such attempts to project ideas in the theatre, I have come to believe that a scene-designer must reconcile himself to the fact that the aesthetic values of his stage settings are relative and no more important than the production of which they are a part. He cannot cling to the apron strings of any one aesthetic dogma nor take refuge in the comforting arms of an absolute style. He must submit with directors, actors, and playwrights to the test of rehearsal and experiment. He has, as a rule, been trained to believe that by stamping an inanimate material such as paint or clay with a perfect pattern he can transmute it into a work of art. But in dealing with the animate material of the theatre he must learn that *caveat pictor*—let the painter beware—is the legend written over any stage door.

The art of designing stage settings is the art not of making pictures but of relating them to living presences. A scenic drawing is no more than the record of an intention, without value except as it is realized in a theatre. Whatever beauty a stage setting achieves is a by-product of the process of sustaining a play and in turn being sustained by it. The standard of value in the theatre is the event, the play as performed. Drawings for stage settings are working drawings valuable only for the work that they eventually do, not for their glamour as an illuminated calendar of far-off, and possibly divine, events towards which creation in the theatre is expected to move.

But partisans of the new stage-craft persist in envisaging such an event and glorify the modern scene-designer as a combination of Perseus and Parsifal. He is to exorcise a wicked enchanter, battening on the miasma of an industrial era, who has cast over the theatre a stultifying spell called Realism. The Designer will then rescue the Drama, now chained like a captive princess to a rock where she cowers before the monster Imitation, who will be slain by the sword of a new and perfectly tempered Style. The liberating Designer and the liberated Drama will then live happily ever after as coequal consorts, supported by the plaudits of an admiring populace who will go to every performance as to a religious rite and be eager to see none but mystic and symbolic plays for which only symbolic or abstract settings will be appropriate. Another golden age of the theatre will ensue. Has not Sheldon Cheney assured us, "For the first time in centuries the theatre is being imagined with at once an old unity and a new splendor . . . of all the arts it is the one best able to compass the vast truths, the ritualistic splendors, the precise perfections, the human-divine intimacy, of the age that is being born."

Unfortunately I cannot foresee the features of this new divinity with whom we are to be so humanly intimate. Nor can I anticipate the ritual with which a new godhead will be worshipped in a theatre-temple. However vast the truths that may be uttered in the age now being born, they will first be made articulate in the theatre by its plays, not by the stages on which these plays are acted. If, as has happened before, vaster truths are expressed in novels, poems, and scientific speculations, the scene-designer will be obliged to cut his pattern to the cloth that a playwright brings him.

I single out Mr. Cheney's book because it is typical of how the most fervent partisans of a supposedly new theatre art, made possible by innovations in scenic design, allot to the designer a rôle that he does not and cannot play in the life of the theatre. Consider such statements as the following: "Robert Edmond Jones, Norman-Bel Geddes, Claude Bragdon, these are men of long experience of staging who have clear vision of a different theatre in a different society—they are prophets as well as practitioners. To some of us it seems likely that their names are to live on in theatre histories longer than those of any recent American playwrights. They are more truly reshaping theatre practice. . . . And throughout the country little theatre groups produce unrelated miracles of lighting and staging—while awaiting the fine plays they so much need."

The ego of a scene-designer reading this passage may very well glow with pride and cry, Yes; his mind should know better and answer, No. For the implications of Mr. Cheney's eulogy are untenable. Modern stage settings are not so many lighthouses by which American playwrights can chart their course. There are other stars to guide them. Is Eugene O'Neill's development to be accounted for by the settings that Cleon Throckmorton designed for *The Emperor Jones* and *The Hairy Ape,* those made by Robert Edmond Jones for *The Fountain* and *Desire under the Elms,* and by me for *Marco Millions* and *Dynamo?* What had any of these to do with the genesis of *Strange*

Interlude, and what had Jo Mielziner's settings for that radically new form of play-construction to do with the creation of O'Neill's masterpiece to date, *Mourning Becomes Electra?* What essential connection has our work as practitioners with the vision of a different theatre in a different society? These settings for O'Neill's plays were each typically modern and each conspicuously successful. Will they live in theatre histories longer than the name of any American playwright, including O'Neill's? Did our scenic innovations more truly reshape theatre practice than did O'Neill's revival of the soliloquy in *Strange Interlude* and the trilogy form in *Mourning Becomes Electra?*

John Barrymore developed from an actor of farce into a tragedian whose performance as Hamlet was acclaimed as the greatest that this generation had seen. Was this because he acted in Jones's unit setting and had previously acted in Jones's settings for *The Living Corpse* and *The Jest?* Was his performance in *Justice* a negligible step in his development because Jones did not design the settings for it? Was it the privilege of being able to act in my settings that enabled Alfred Lunt and Lynn Fontanne to develop into two of the most accomplished actors of our day? Was it only my settings for *Liliom* and not the acting of Joseph Schildkraut, Eva Le Gallienne, and Dudley Digges that helped to make the production memorable? Granted that the value of their performances was enhanced by my designs, and the meaning of the play as well, how directly did that affect their subsequent careers as actors or Molnar's as a playwright?

I do not underestimate the importance of either antique or modern stage settings. The stage picture has been an indispensable part of play-production in every theatre from that of Greece to our own. There is no period in the theatre's history which failed to develop a technique of stage setting far more elaborate and also far more popular than is generally realized. I shall attempt to show why stage settings today are more integrally a part of theatrical performances than they have ever been, why the designer plays a more important rôle in the modern theatre than he has in any previous one. But his present importance cannot be explained in a strain of high prophecy. The value of scenic design in a living and experimenting theatre cannot be made clear by assuming that a critic of stage-craft is midwife to a new state of society and needs only to combine literary training with a gift for second sight. I place a sufficiently high value upon my own work and that of my confrères whose aims and methods are fundamentally related to my own. I do not deny that our settings gave life to *Liliom* and a hundred other productions; upon more than one occasion they were better than a particular script or a particular performance. But the fact in itself is not significant. It is far easier to design a beautiful setting than to direct a play or to act a rôle superbly. Paint and canvas, wood and electric light, are inanimate. Once given a particular form or a given intensity they remain fixed; nor can they answer back. The technical and artistic problems involved in setting a stage effectively, despite all the complications of unifying divergent detail, are nevertheless simpler than the problems incurred in attempting to fill a stage with the breath of life. Designers of stage settings will not transmute their craft into an art nor add a cubit to its stature by maintaining the pretence that scenic design can by itself develop the expressiveness of acting or anticipate the trend of playwrighting. The theatre of the future is not a wild animal in the wilderness of tomorrow which we can steal upon and capture while we hypnotize it with a flare of light. It is not a bird already on our doorstep that can be caught and caged because the scene-designer has put salt on its tail.

This book will attempt to deflate some of the pretensions lent to the scene-designer by his mentors and well-wishers. The effort has led me not to the theatre's mythical future, but to its past, immensely falsified by so many apologists of the "new art of the theatre" in their determination to make the present a door-mat on which the designer can wipe his muddy pilgrim's feet before crossing the threshold of an imminent golden age. I have always been sceptical of the existence of golden ages, whether past or future. Before this book was planned, I had tried to visualize the actual practice of stage-craft in Greek, mediaeval, and Renaissance theatres, the theatre of Shakespeare and the theatre of Molière, seen at first hand through the eyes of contemporary documents. The scenic methods employed by the hallowed past I found to be quite as pragmatic as our own. Their supposed gold proved to be an alloy mixed with the same baser metals of ornament, pictorial spectacle, realism and the literal imitation of nature, that are supposed to be the characteristic impurities of our own epoch. I have collected the evidence from the many available but scattered sources that have not, I think, been correlated before, in order to demonstrate that the doctrine of a lost art of the theatre, once nobler and purer than our own, is no less a romantic myth than the doctrine of the noble savage.

Nothing, as Santayana once reminded us, is further from a healthy people than the corrupt desire to be primitive. Greek theatres possessed at least one device for indicating changes of scene that Joseph Urban used successfully in a Ziegfeld Follies. I found it equally valuable in staging *As You Like It* and *Peer Gynt*. Ibsen's trolls, Wagner's Rhinemaidens or Walkyries wafted on wires, the staff that bloomed miraculously, the magic fire encircling Brünnhilde, the antics of a dragon, or the descents of gods and goddesses through trap-doors belching smoke, present more difficulties to the technical directors of our opera-houses than they ever did to the stage-managers of mediaeval mysteries, who pulled off twenty such effects in the course of a day. By the end of the seventeenth century, the theatres of the Italian Renaissance managed apparitions, conflagrations, and shipwrecks as easily as Drury Lane did in its heyday thirty years ago. Modern mechanics have added almost nothing to the technique of scene-shifting perfected in Italy during the seventeenth century, when as many as twenty-three changes of scene in the course of a single play were not uncommon. Our more elaborately equipped theatres do little more than enlarge the trap-doors of the Renaissance and propel them hydraulically or electrically. The one reputed innovation in scene-shifting, the revolving stage, was invented by the Japanese and in use in their "popular theatre" by 1760. A Munich technician, Lautenschläger, installed an adaptation of it on his own stage in 1898, where it became a typical modern improvement to be copied in all new municipal and royal theatres throughout Germany.

The present technique of building scenery by stretching canvas over wooden frames, the technique of painting it with water-colour mixed with size, is not materially different from what it was when Sabbattini published his handbook, *The Art of Making Theatrical Scenes and Machines,* in 1638. If Marguerite must pluck a daisy or Juliet smell a rose, the flowers are made of much the same materials and by much the same method used by the Master of the Revels under Henry VIII. Our one new instrument is electric light and our ability to control its most subtle fluctuations. But the note-books of one Renaissance impresario indicate that he succeeded in dimming his candles at the climax of a tragedy in what has come to be the modern method of modulating the intensity of light to fit the mood of a scene. Modern settings, as a rule, reproduce the accepted pictorial conventions of today, merely enlarging them for theatrical use, in much the same way that the pictorial conventions of mediaeval France, Renaissance Italy, and classical Greece were once translated to the stage.

Whatever the designer's future, he will do well, I think, to look at his past long enough to realize that he is not a prodigy whom the ages have conspired to produce. The presence of the artist-painter or the artist-technician in the theatre is not a uniquely modern phenomenon. The more important designers for the theatre of today will add their

9

names to a roster that already includes Sophocles, Leonardo, Brunelleschi, Peruzzi, Raphael, Clouet, Boucher, and Piranesi as well as Vuillard, Derain, Dufy, and Picasso. My purpose is not to belittle either my own efforts or those of my confrères by pedantically proving, once again, that there is nothing new under the sun. My effort, on the contrary, is to free our work from attempting a specious originality. Precisely because beautiful stage-pictures are no new thing in the theatre, all that can make modern settings important is our ability to relate them to the needs of our own day. I shall attempt to show what these needs are and how, in meeting them, the designer becomes a necessary workman in our theatre as one interpreter of a script.

As an interpreter he remains bound to a theme given him. He is not an independent creator like the painter of easel-pictures. The designer's subject is assigned. If present predictions as to his grandiose future are realized, we may see playwrights become his secretaries, turning out scenarios to fit his aesthetic preoccupations. Master scene-designers may by that time be sufficiently exalted as artists to hire a theatre in which to display their stage settings, just as painters today hire a gallery in order to display themes that incite them to create works of art—apples, anemones, or Arizona. Possibly the dramatic reviews of the future will read somewhat as follows:

Possessors of the new supersize television screen spent a stimulating evening yesterday in witnessing the most recent work of Owen Caig, whose growing mastery of the atmospheric values of mountain vistas has already won him his eminence as one of the foremost exponents of modern drama. His crystalline evocation of three-dimensional space recalls some of Leonardo da Vinci's scenic backgrounds in the "Mona Lisa" and the "Virgin with Saint John." The play, ranging as it did from the Apennines to the Andes, afforded admirable scope for Mr. Caig's dramatic climaxes. Such actors as were necessary to provide the compositional balance for these superb theatrical compositions remained appropriately in the background, never obtruded themselves, and in no way interfered with the meaning of the play.

Or possibly:

The success of the mass drama Eons *and* Ions *at the Civic Arena continues unabated. After the concluding liturgy, 842 persons in the audience announced their conversion and were immeditely ordained in the new faith in the presence of the chorus and the entire cast.*

For the present, however, the scene-designer remains what he has always been: one member of a group of interpreters. As such he must, usually in four weeks' time, construct a home or a palace, costume princes or paupers, transport any corner of the five continents or any one of a number of Arcadias to the theatre, provide any object that the actors must touch or handle, whether a throne or a kitchen chair, a dead sea-gull or the Sphinx, and out of paint, glue, canvas, gauze, wood, and papier mâché create a world real enough to house the conflicts of human beings. What is this reality of a theatrical performance? To what extent can a designer help to create it? Precisely what can he add to the value in performance of a contemporary play or to the revival of a classic? What is his rôle in the modern theatre, and how indispensable is his contribution? How does it differ from his past contribution in the so-called great ages of the theatre? Is his task to recover a supposedly lost purity of style or is he maintaining a tradition aesthetically as sound as any that has ever before existed? How are pictures turned into scenery? How much does the designer for the stage borrow from pictures in frames, known as art? What new values does he create in the process?

The way a scene-designer works is determined very largely by his convictions as to where he belongs and why he is needed on the modern stage. Before contemporary stage settings can be judged, the designer's relation to the theatre of today needs to be critically analyzed. In attempting to do this I have tried to preserve a necessary scepticism of my instrument. That I fail to see the theatre existing under an unclouded heaven of yesterday or tomorrow is, I think, due to a remark made to me by George Santayana twenty-five years ago while I was taking his course on Plato. I had written my semi-annual thesis on some aspect of Socrates' teaching, and, feeling the need of a climax, concluded in words to this effect: "How marvellous to think of these epoch-making thoughts evolved by a few friends, in simple raiment, conversing in a little courtyard, under a blue sky." The paper was returned with a single comment. In the margin opposite the words, "blue sky," Santayana had pencilled an afterthought, "Perhaps it was raining." Perhaps it was.

L. S.

Pelfryshire Road,
Port Henry, New York.
1931.

PART ONE

SCENERY IN THE THEATRE OF IDEAS

CHAPTER I

THE STAGE AS A WORLD

I. NEW PICTURES FOR OLD

Toward the close of the sixteenth century the theatre, which had heretofore set its stage in amphitheatres, cathedrals, market-places, and courtyards, crowded itself indoors, its stage constricted between an ornate frame—the proscenium—and a blank wall. This space became shallower with every succeeding generation as the concentration of population into cities raised the cost of building-sites. At the beginning of the nineteenth century the world pictured in the theatre had become a realm of paint and canvas as flat and shallow as the stage it occupied. In 1890, Antoine exclaimed, "We are still using ridiculous back-drops which have no atmosphere or depth, on which we do not hesitate to paint furniture or even a staircase within three metres of the footlights." Any interior seemed an enlarged doll's house. Every exterior had an air of having been cut out of cardboard, set up as a plaything by some titanic child. The canvas tree-trunks of a forest faced each other, in parallel rows; above them hung parallel layers of serrated canvas foliage, like flounces cut from a giantess's petticoat and hung out to dry on an invisible clothes-line. The stones of huts and castles were obviously painted, including the shadows cast by an overhanging cornice or a neighbouring tree. An unrelenting blare of light underlined each brush-stroke. Its fierce impartiality illuminated with equal brilliance the heroine at the footlights and the back-drop where hills and sky were united in a single plane with the precision of a magnified steel-engraving.

At the beginning of the twentieth century a certain number of modern painters entered the theatre, first in Germany and Russia, then in Austria, France, and England, and finally in the United States. With the aid of the electrician they created behind the proscenium frame some of the beauty with which modern painting, since Delacroix, had invested reality within the picture-frame. During the last twenty-five years pictorial beauty in the theatre has become a new tradition and the technique of achieving it part of the technique of play-producing itself. The designer, by one method or another, has made the sky as infinite and enfolding as Perugino's. The stage is illuminated by a light that can simulate the cycle of day and achieves the illusion of *plein air* which the Impressionists evoked with pigment: the iridescence of dawn, the blare of noon, or the transfiguration of dusk celebrated by Whistler, "when the evening mist clothes the riverside with poetry, as with a veil . . . and the warehouses are palaces in the night, and the whole city hangs in the heavens." The trees that arch above the trysts of lovers, whether Pelléas and Mélisande or Liliom and Julie, possess the feathery grace of Corot's foliage or cast the magic gloom of an ancient wood. Hovels and palaces have the apparent solidity which delights our eye as architectural forms themselves do by the balance of structural surfaces and the play of light upon them. We can today look through the frame of a stage at plastic pictures that occasionally hold us spellbound.

2. ANOTHER FINE ART

Although its materials are intrinsically tawdry and its forms fugitive, the designing of stage settings in the United States has within the last ten years been added to the roster of the fine arts, a place accorded scenic design in Europe a decade earlier. In 1900 the American scene-designer was, as a rule, a scene-painter, an anonymous craftsman turning out stock patterns or stereotyped back-drops by the square yard and delivering them to the stage-door without much preoccupation as to their effect in the theatre. Today he adopts the pretensions and accepts the responsibilities of any other artist. Not only is his work applauded by audiences at the rise of the curtain but also he is held to account by director and actors for his share in the interpretation of a script. His rôle is accepted as a definite part of any performance. If he is successful his scrap-book bulges with clippings and notices like any leading actor's. He is invited to attend banquets as a guest of honour and to lecture on his art at colleges, women's clubs, municipal art societies, and museums. He contributed to an imposing international exhibition at Amsterdam in 1922. Three museums, the Musée des Arts Décoratifs in Paris, the Victoria and Albert in London, and that of the National Library of Vienna, have set aside space to hang his sketches. He finds himself writing for the fourteenth edition of the Encyclopaedia Britannica as an authority on scenic design, stage equipment, and theatre building. Within the next decade he will probably be considered eligible for an honorary degree by one of the numerous universities that have made courses in stage-craft part of their curricula.

In explaining the meaning of his art, the scene-designer has followed the painter of easel-pictures on the fashionable pilgrimage from the plain of imitation to the summit of abstraction, and en route has evolved as many theories of aesthetic method: Selective Realism, Stylized Realism, Presentation as opposed to Representation, Neo-Realism, Formalism, Expressionism, Constructivism, the new Theatricalism. He has defined "the relief stage," "the formal stage," "the plastic stage," "the sculptured stage," the "emphasized void" or "space stage." Scenic design has come to be considered a typically modern "movement" and its trend is as incessantly debated as that of every other form of contemporary art. Criticism of stage settings is no longer confined to newspaper reviews of the morning after. It overflows into magazines, pamphlets, monographs, *de luxe* portfolios, and elaborately illustrated histories. Indeed, discussion of the function of scenery in the theatre has come to be a separate field of criticism. It has already produced a sizable reference library, where rival schools of doctrine battle and ranking historians keep abreast of the latest developments by issuing a new compendium every few years.

3. THE THEATRE'S THEOLOGIANS

Unfortunately many of these historians have become the theologians of the modern theatre. Dogma, disconsolate and discredited in the fields of ethics, politics, and the natural sciences, has come to roost like a prophetic bird among the temples of the arts. Practitioners of the fine arts begin to feel isolated and irrelevant in a machine age. Secretly terrified by the ruthless laboratory of modern experience, they are comforted by dogmatic finalities and oracular certainties. The development of modern painting is punctuated by treatises and manifestoes from Courbet's to the French Cubists' and the Italian Futurists', each asserting that the truly modern art has at last been discovered and defining its immutable laws. In the theatre as elsewhere the myth of a godhead persists even among iconoclasts, and belief in creation by the will of a father clings to innovators. Adolphe Appia and Gordon Craig were hailed as prophets who could save the theatre from encircling doom. For the modern theatre has been continuously envisaged on the brink of damnation or on the verge of an apotheosis, as the titles of its successive gospels testify: *Towards a New Theatre, The Creation of a Living Art, The Theatre Unchained, The Theatre of Tomorrow.* Every discussion that pretends to be fundamental ends with an indication of the perfect and final stage setting, a substitute for the pigtail that Moroccan Berbers still cultivate and hide under their turbans, so that at death Allah can conveniently yank them into Paradise.

We have been assured that the theatre has been regenerated because its new backgrounds emphasized and aureoled the actor, then that every form of tangible background must be destroyed in order to give proper emphasis to the actor picked out by a spot-light from the void. The theatre was to be redeemed by making stage settings of nothing but light, pulsing like music and controlled by keyboards as flexible as a piano's. More recently we have been told that the modern stage must be as bare as the walls of a factory and scenery nothing more than the outline of its construction, as rigid as the steel skeletons of skyscrapers, derricks, or railway trestles. Over these, actors are to mount into eternal life as the gods once ascended a rainbow into Valhalla. Or the theatre is to be saved by ignoring the proscenium frame and becoming an arena or a circus; the final renascence will result from the actor's mingling freely with his audience.

A sense of sin and a hunger for salvation pervade all such theorizing. Original sin has been successively paint and the scene-painter, the actor and the spoken word, realism of any sort, decoration in any form. And the prototype of salvation has been discovered in every golden or gilded past; the baroque ball-room of the Hofburg Palace in Vienna hung with tapestries and lighted with crystal chandeliers, the platforms of Elizabethan inn-yards, the naves of cathedrals, the ritual dances of Asia and Africa, and the amphitheatres of Greece.

Since 1890 the independent or free theatres of Brahm in Berlin, Antoine in Paris, and Grein in London, the Moscow Art Theatre and the "art theatres" of Lugné-Poë, Rouché, and Copeau in France, Reinhardt in Germany and Austria, Tairov and Meyerhold in Moscow, the brothers Čapek in Prague, the Abbey Theatre in Dublin, Granville-Barker's short-lived repertory theatre in England, and in New York the Washington Square Players, the Provincetown Theatre, the Neighborhood Playhouse, and the Theatre Guild, have carried on the business of theatrical experiment and achieved international repute.

But none has satisfied the votaries of the New Stagecraft. To each they cried, "Not yet, not yet!" and waited for the portals of the indubitably New Theatre to open. The tedium of their vigil has been relieved by a master of improvisation, Gordon Craig. American criticism still echoes his messianic preludes. Each of them, like a musical theme stated but not developed, announced a new theory of salvation. But at the appointed moment there was always a hitch in the ceremony. The doors of the new theatre-temple did not open. Lest the audience become restless the music continued, using new stops and achieving more sonorous climaxes with soaring diapasons. The original devotees who came to witness a dedication remained to enjoy an organ recital.

4. SIN AND SALVATION

For slightly more than twenty-five years the effort to define the original sin of theatrical art and the attempt to establish an orthodox method for the theatre's salvation have persisted, with Gordon Craig officiating as master of ceremonies. In 1905 he proclaimed realism the original sin and in 1911 banished the actor, with his distracting "tremors of the flesh," as a lure of the devil. A supermarionette was announced as the redeemer. The playwright was banished at the same time as an unnecessary interloper in sacred precincts. Drama was to become a succession of mystic revelations mimed by mechanical puppets who were to have the dignity and grace of a new race of gods. And Craig solemnly predicted that when this new art of the theatre had been perfected it would be so divine that a new religion would be founded upon it.

No one, not even Craig himself, succeeded in articulating the supermarionette. Actors continued to gesticulate and to use their vocal cords. A new generation of players found no difficulty in holding audiences spellbound in all the theatrical capitals of Europe and were acclaimed as artists by the best critical minds of their generation. New schools of playwrighting were founded on new moralities, such as Fabian socialism, but no one attempted to found a new religion on a novel technique of staging plays. Craig, however, having adopted prophecy as his profession, like most professional prophets continued to prophesy. He looked at the Catholic Church and found the archetype of true drama to be the ritual of the Mass. Here nothing deceived the eye, nothing was counterfeit pasteboard and tinsel. Here were marble and jewels, silks and brocades, veritable silver and gold. Let the theatre become a church and emulate the splendour of the Holy Roman faith. But the theatre shed its glamour on settings where splendour continued to fall on marble halls made of painted canvas. Craig then escaped into the open air, declaring that the theatre had died when it came indoors. Drama, like architecture, needed the sun on it to live. The first-rate was not Shakespeare but Aeschylus. In the process the actor was rediscovered; in the open-air theatres of the Greeks, drama had been triumphant because there had been no division between performers and spectators. "Actors did not come on like white mice in a silent room . . . they came on forward and straight for the spectators —into the very centre of them, surging, leaping, gliding." Dramatists, however, failed to leap at the opportunity so eloquently presented to them. They persisted in writing for the experimental theatres of Moscow, Berlin, London, Paris, and New York, which showed not the slightest disposition to emigrate to the Riviera or southern California. A few American communities generously built open-air theatres or endowed open-air performances by way of changing the trend of modern drama. But its direction was not visibly affected. The most pretentious of these pageants was given in a New York stadium at night. Joseph Urban summarized the temper of an electrical age when, after an all-night light-rehearsal, he saw the first glints of dawn in the sky and exclaimed, "There comes that damned sun again and spoils us everything!"

The drama refused to come out into the sunlight. Craig finally followed it indoors and announced his culminating invention: scenic backgrounds deliberately artificial, blank screens, which, by a system of mechanics never disclosed, could be manipulated in endless permutations and be made to seem the interior or exterior of any mud hut or temple, Harrod's department-store or the halls of Versailles. At the same time these screens remained abstract and were painted entirely by light. As a public speaker once remarked, like Caesar's wife they could be all things to all men. But they were above suspicion of any traffic with realism. Craig finally renounced the sun and gave his allegiance to the electric lamp, not for its own sake but for the sake of the actor. Stage scenery had been overemphasized because actors had lost their power to act. What they needed was not the privilege of leaping or diving headlong into the audience but the certainty of being properly emphasized by a spot-light against a chameleon screen. They would then recover their lost authority and the theatre would be finally and indubitably saved.

It is amazing that the theatre, being offered the choice of so many panaceas, did not attain a new state of grace. It could achieve beatitude by banishing the actor and abolishing the playwright. It could also revive the all but lost art of acting. The new stage-craft alone possessed the patent elixir. The theatre, like a rickety child, could cure itself by dancing in the sun. But it could also heal itself with an electric substitute for sunlight. The new theatre might compete with established churches and might emulate the Roman Church by imitating its ritualistic trappings. It might also emulate the Greek theatre, the theatre of Shakespeare, and the *commedia dell' arte*.

Never have such widely heralded and accepted theories of theatre art borne less relation to its immediate life, to the ferment of social and intellectual forces from which stimulation for its actual experiments was distilled. But American critics seemed hypnotized by Craig's shibboleths. Realism was assailed and the magic of symbolism invoked at a time when the American theatre was beginning to be revitalized because American playwrights were becoming realistic enough to reappraise their environment. The American theatre came of age and became increasingly cynical and sceptical in settings that called for the paraphernalia of water-front saloons, tenement-house bedrooms, or the overstuffed parlours of suburbia. The modernity of American plays began to be important because the attempt was made to see American character with the remorseless eye that had once produced Gavarni's and Daumier's lithographs. In the process, like paper stencils eaten by etcher's acid, an entire gallery of stereotypes disintegrated—including a variety of nature's noblemen, deep-dyed villains, loving mothers, wise fathers, and virgins stiff and starched with purity, freshly laundered by God. But a picture of artistic virtue no less pure and stencils as sentimental of noble and wicked theatrical art were all that critics of modern stage-craft succeeded in offering to workers in the theatre, who, eager to voice their faith and express their enthusiasm, accepted a ready-made formula.

Apocalyptic fervours burned in the bosoms of leading American scene-designers. In 1919, in the catalogue to one of the few collective exhibitions of American scenic designs ever held, Norman-Bel Geddes declared, "In the middle of the fourth century the theatre went to sleep. . . . Ten years ago it rubbed its eyes." In that sleep Shakespeare and Molière among others had no doubt merely snored. Joseph Urban asserted, "In our future life the stage must have the same influence that the Christian church has had in the past." Herman Rosse, echoing Craig, invoked "a new type of churchlike theatre, with reflective [reflecting] domes, beautiful materials, beautiful people," and prophesied that "this developing of the background at the expense of the actor will remake the dynamic play. Imagine beyond the proscenium a void in which planes and bodies will develop themselves in limitless graduation of color and shape in one great rhythm with the co-ordinating music." Robert Edmond Jones alone was realistic enough to declare: "To create an impression of livingness in the presence of spectators, to recall life to them—that is the necessary thing. There are numberless manners of working in the theatre and there is no real quarrel with any of them. Realism, simplification, stylization, are fashions in the theatre all of which can carry energy in the hands of artists." But a few years later he recanted and wrote: "Let us drop in on a performance of Ibsen's *Hedda Gabler* . . . The play begins . . . Here is no solemn public ritual, no spoken opera, but a kind of betrayal. We are all eavesdroppers, peering through a keyhole, and minding other people's business." These words paraphrased the dominant doctrine of the day then being voiced by Kenneth Macgowan: The proscenium was nothing more than an enlarged peep-hole, the current theatre a peep-show. "Realism, in any but a very extraordinary sense, is a cramp upon art." "We have had Ibsen and Strindberg, and lesser men absorbed with lesser lives. I can only believe that the crushing oppression of nineteenth century industrialism held them all bowed. . . . I can only affirm that the new stagecraft, had it come earlier, would have aided in their release, and that it is to play a great part in the release of our future playwrights." The yoke of oppression that industrialism clamped on the theatre was the rigid picture frame of the stage opening. "It is not too difficult to see in the proscenium arch the reason for the barrenness of the realistic theatre. Directors and actors who have felt this have tried to find a playhouse that lies nearer to the masculine vigor of Aeschylus and Shakespeare." Sheldon Cheney was forced to admit, "Much as we may enjoy Ibsen and Shaw, they did go far toward destroying that theatre in which Euripides and Shakespeare and Sheridan were possible—or Scaramuccia or Grimaldi." Apostles of the new stage-craft were the first to see, as dramatic critics, that theatre architecture had stunted such dramatic genius as Shaw, Schnitzler, Becque, Gorki, or Chekhov possessed.

5. PILGRIM'S PROGRESS

At the beginning of the nineteenth century a visit, during a grand tour of Europe, to the half-excavated site of some pagan temple, was obligatory for any critic who believed that the future of plastic art depended upon reviving its past. Similarly, at the beginning of the twentieth century, interpreters of the new stage-craft undertook pilgrimages to Europe to discover the possible site of the new playhouse that would restore to the theatre the combined vigour of Aeschylus, Sophocles, Shakespeare, Sheridan, and Scaramouche. Macgowan's *Continental Stagecraft* is typical of these quests in that, like all accredited accounts of modern scenic design, it begins as history and ends in the strain of high prophecy. Its description of Continental experiments in non-realistic productions is the record of a pilgrimage, for Macgowan travelled as a pilgrim, believing that deliverance was at hand and that every time a play began the redeemer of the theatre might stand forth. Was he Jacques Copeau in the Théâtre du Vieux Colombier, who staged Shakespeare, Mérimée, and Vildrac on an austerely bare stage at the end of an open hall? Was deliverance to come from Berlin, where two directors, Leopold Jessner and Jürgen Fehling, kept their stages equally bare and used a single staircase or platform as a pedestal for their players? "They both throw overboard every shred of actuality that stands in the way of inner emotional truth." Actors are put forward "as actors on an abstract stage, and you think of them only as living, intimate presences." Reinhardt's attempt to create a "Theatre of the Five Thousand" by remodelling an old circus so that his actors could swarm from the stage into the audience, was already an acknowledged failure. But it was significant as a portent of "the way a player can come forward to the edge of a forestage and stand there alone, a brave figure in a great dim space. This is something you cannot feel in the chummy confines of a picture frame." So far Macgowan, like most American critics, verified Craig's doctrines. The theatre was to be saved by making scenery sufficiently abstract and by concentrating enough light on an isolated actor. But when Macgowan reached Vienna I received a postcard: "We have found it at last. . . . It is Copeau gone to heaven."

Heaven at the moment was the Redoutensaal in the old Hofburg Palace. Here, set at the end of Maria Theresa's eighteenth century ball-room, was a stage consisting of nothing more than a platform placed under the balcony at one entrance to the hall, lighted by the same crystal chandeliers that illuminated the hall itself and its grey panelled walls margined with gold and hung with Gobelin tapestries. But this stage was significant because the actor was again "backed up by space," final proof that the theatre's essential need was for a "defined and permanent artificiality that shall give the actor scope." This splendid room "does not obtrude . . . with . . . its mirrors and its tapestries. . . . Always . . . the living actor, driving his message directly at the spectator, dominates them all."

Such was the culmination of what the new theatre of ten years ago had to give. But eighteenth century panelling, gilded mouldings, tapestries and crystal chandeliers, although an ideal background for the modern theatre, were not its ultimate one. Macgowan, like other prophets before him, was finally driven to a height and the theatre of tomorrow was vouchsafed to him in a vision.

The height is a well-known hill—the Hill of Montmartre. And the dream comes to him in a circus, the Cirque Médrano, already immortal in Degas's pastels and Lautrec's lithographs. While the clowns gambol he sees, in a sudden apocalypse, that the playhouse of the future is a circus—not a colossal arena like Reinhardt's, but a circus like this one, an intimate circus with a single ring. He sees *Hamlet* performed there. The neurotic prince is in the central ring. The ghost appears above the topmost ring of seats. The audience divides them. "Marcellus . . . [is] pointing to the figure of the dead man where it moves above the last row of spectators. No mixing of actors and audience, but what a thrill to see the ghost across a gulf of turned and straining faces, what a horror to see him over your own shoulder!" It is the theatre where actor and audience are ideally united and the final form of scenery is revealed. "There is the actor in the center with the audience around him; there is the actor on the rim drawing the audience out and across to him. . . . And there is the sense of all this which the audience has as it looks down, Olympian, from its banks of seats." "The Médrano supplies a living background, the background of the audience itself."

This is journey's end—1922. Since its conclusion Copeau's theatre, like Reinhardt's arena, has been abandoned. Reinhardt's Festspielhaus at Salzburg as originally planned has not yet been begun. Clowns, bareback riders, acrobats, and trained dogs continue to perform in the Cirque Médrano and the Cirque d'Hiver. But in Sheldon Cheney's recent (1929) volume, *The Theatre: Three Thousand Years of Drama, Acting and Stagecraft,* the evolution of stage-craft is still conceived to be a pilgrim's progress through the ages. It must shed its trappings of ornament and decoration like another Mr. Worldly Wiseman in order to find grace and to be redeemed. Realism is again portrayed as the Slough of Despond into which the theatre tumbled during the nineteenth century and from which it is slowly ascending as to a city of heavenly light. The trumpet shall sound, the veils of theatrical illusion be rent. The arch of the proscenium will fall. The Theatre of the Future will arise, a place of platforms, plinths, and terraces, backed by naked screens or bare walls. Presumably a new race of dramatic poets will breed such theatres, or when enough have been built, they will breed a new race of dramatic poets comparable to Shakespeare and Sophocles. The mask will again dignify the pudgy, elastic, and alas, all too realistic human countenance. The actor parading before blank pylons or circling in circus rings will become a dominant and majestic figure, aureoled by the mystery of his calling. And drama will regain its lost paradise of poetic ritual.

6. HOLIDAY

The unmistakable brilliance of such recent visions of a new theatre is due to the fact that like search-lights prodding the night, their focus is only large enough to isolate a single object. In the enveloping darkness lies the structure of society of which the theatre is a part. The relation of the modern theatre to its audience is today not fundamentally different from what it was when tragedy and comedy were, supposedly, born on an Attic hillside. The form of any theatre is determined not by the kind of dramatic literature it expects to house, for that can never be foreseen, but by the holiday habits of its people. And these are determined in turn by an entire nexus of social, political, religious, and economic habits, customs, conventions, and taboos that have no immediate relation to the theatre whatsoever. We in the Western world have always gone to the theatre as part of a holiday—a week, a day, an afternoon or an evening off; from our cubicles in apartment-houses and hotels to the blinking electric lights of Broadway; across the Thames and over the fields to The Globe or The Curtain of a fine afternoon; after the dank winters of the Norman and Flemish plains to the cathedral town to see priests in sacerdotal raiment, burghers in brocades and furs, great ladies in jewelled hennins on the balcony; or, "when the hounds of spring are on winter's traces," the sea open again, the first foreign ships in the harbour and strangers and ambassadors arrived, up the side of the Acropolis in singing pro-

cession. We can stand at any theatre door as Faust did at the city's gate
and see a populace, released, escaping,

> *Out of the musty cells of humble homes,*
> *Out of the bonds of trade and handicraft,*
> *Out of the crushing straitness of the streets,*

and exclaim with him,

> *Here is the people's heaven!*

We go not only to see a show but to be part of the show ourselves,
to show off, in our best clothes, our finery, our swallowtails, our jewels
if we have any. We go to feel our contact with the great world under
a single roof, within the circle of a single arena or the boundaries of
a single public square; to see the guardians of the state and the priests
in the first row near the altar, the gentry sitting at the edge of the
stage, a king or a duke in his royal box, the millionaires at the opera
in their golden horseshoe. In the words of Emily Dickinson:

> *The show is not the show,*
> *But they that go.*

A play can be rehearsed to a handful of spectators, but what theatre
has ever aimed to perform its plays except to crowds? We go to the
theatre to be part of the crowd, to experience an electric extension of
our personality, to laugh with a thousand throats, to roar approval
with a thousand voices, to clap with two thousand hands. We become
part of a mass that has power, one that is, for an hour or two, king
or tyrant, passing irrevocable judgment, conferring favour and success,
decreeing failure and oblivion. The elemental satisfaction in theatre-
going for every playgoer from pit to gallery, from the first ring of an
amphitheatre to its topmost retaining wall, is this orgiastic release of
emotion and the sense of power its expression gives him in contact

with a crowd of his fellows. Set him alone in an empty house and you throttle his capacity for emotion and more than half destroy the satisfaction he can feel only when elbow to elbow and knee to knee with a mob.

Few laymen can appreciate how decisively a full house affects the reaction of audiences, how inhibited they are in a half-empty theatre. I have watched plays given at final dress-rehearsals to invited spectators, two or three hundred scattered over an auditorium, as friends of the management predisposed to show their appreciation. They laugh fitfully, applaud half-heartedly. The same situations played in an identical manner a day later on opening night, before an audience of a thousand or more crowded in without a vacant seat, evoke a din of laughter and applause often lasting a full half-minute. The first hand-clap, the first guffaw, instantly ignites five hundred others as a spurt of flame will set off an explosion. The explosive force of an audience's emotion, like that of powder in a cartridge, depends very largely on how tight the audience is packed. This necessary compactness can be, and has been, achieved in theatres of any shape, indoors and out of doors: arenas, marketplaces, cockpits, and royal opera-houses.

Always there is ornament, splendour, magnificence, appropriate to a holiday that can lift us out of the groove of our daily routine, pomp that is inseparable from pageantry, gilt and glitter that evokes gaiety, if not on the stage then in the auditorium, if not in the setting back of the actors then in the costumes of the actors themselves. The supposedly austere and simple ritual of Greek tragedy required the state to draft its richest citizens as choregi, in order to mount the annual dramatic festival. "The dresses of the chorus . . . were often . . . magnificent," says Haigh. "The comic poet . . . mentions the case of a choregus who ruined himself by dressing his chorus in gold. Demosthenes supplied his chorus of men with golden crowns." The defendant in one of the speeches of Lysias tells us that a tragic chorus cost him thirty minae, a sum which this authority on the Greek theatre estimates to be the equivalent of $2,500; Haigh adds: "Nicias is said to have owed a great deal of his power to the splendour of his choruses, upon which he spent more money than any of his contemporaries or predecessors." "It is easy therefore to see that there was not much exaggeration in the complaint of Demosthenes that the Athenians spent more upon their festivals than they ever spent upon a naval expedition." A second-rate classical tragedy, like many a second-rate modern play, could be turned into a success by lavish investiture. No doubt comments of the morning after on an Athenian prize-winner were often summarized in our terms: the play was poor but the sets and costumes saved the performance.

The marketplace stage of a mediaeval mystery-play may seem crude and primitive in retrospect. But the total outlay for a mystery performed at Mons in 1501 totalled 2,281 Flemish pounds, the equivalent of 5,018 gold francs today or about $1,000. For the *Mystère des Trois Doms* at Romans (1509) the total cost of the performance was 22,120 gold francs or roughly $4,500. The scenery and machinery cost no less than the equivalent of 8,342 gold francs; construction of the stage itself cost 8,221 francs, making a total of approximately $3,500. The author's royalties amounted to 3,247 francs; musicians' salaries, 1,146 francs. The receipts, including paid admissions and the sale of all the material that could be salvaged, were about $1,900, leaving a deficit that the town defrayed. A mystery at Valenciennes, possibly because it enjoyed the benefit of a long run, twenty-five days, showed a profit of nearly $1,000, although the expenses of production were roughly $3,300. Such outlays are extraordinary if one remembers that these cities were no more than large towns. The *Mystery of the Acts of the Apostles* at Bourges (1536) achieved an orgy of extravagance. The expenses are estimated to have run into millions of francs—"A number of the most important merchants ruined themselves. It is easy to believe this, considering the extraordinary debauch of satin, damask, velvet and silk of every kind, and recalling the rubies, pearls, topazes, diamonds and sapphires that glittered in the women's headdresses and on the men's oriental turbans. The Queen Dampdeomopolys wore a coat of gold cloth 'bordered with precious stones valued at 2,000 écus,' that is, a minimum value of 10,000 francs."

The cost of mounting many other mysteries might have been as ruinous but for the fact that the important personages were dressed in the costumes of the time, so that much accoutrement such as Nero's in this same performance could be borrowed for the occasion: "Nero was clad in a lined cloak, all blue striped with golden bars after the antique style, and slit with open seams so that the lining of crimson satin appeared, adorned also with another design of ornaments and knots of gold thread; it was lined at the collar with crimson velvet, made with inverted points . . . and prodigally scattered with large pearls. At these points hung large strings of other pearls. . . . His golden crown of three tiers was decorated with all sorts of precious stones. . . . He supported one of his feet on a stool covered with silver cloth and ornamented with a large number of precious stones. . . . In his hand he carried a beautifully gilded battleaxe . . . his tribunal and he were carried by eight captive kings who were within and of whom nothing was seen save their golden-crowned heads."

For the mystery of *Julius Caesar* performed at Amboise in 1500 the arsenal of the château supplied complete outfits of contemporary armour for Caesar's legionaries. A bourgeois named Lechevallier who played the rôle of Pilate at Rouen in 1503 ordered a resplendent throne from a local painter. The painter's bill for an equivalent of 1,000 gold francs (or $200) was disputed by his patron and the record of the ensuing lawsuit survives as a testimony to the continual effort to achieve spectacle and splendour in mounting plays that were not confined within a gilded proscenium arch.

The spectator at The Swan may have found little to delight his eye on the stage, although the pillars that supported its roof were painted to imitate marble. But in The Fortune he could gape at the elaborate splendour of costuming, of which Alleyn's cloak was typical—"velvet embroidered in silver and gold, lined with black and gold striped satin," which cost £20 10s—more than Shakespeare received for several of his comedies. "It is scarcely an exaggeration to say," writes one scholar, ". . . that the value of the costumes housed in an old Elizabethan theatre was equivalent to the value of the theatre itself." When the dormitories of the most fashionable girls' boarding-school of Louis XIV's reign were reconstructed to make a stage on which Racine's *Esther* was given its first performance, the king lent the "diamonds" and pearls used in the court ballets to ornament the costumes, and the cost of the costumes themselves totalled 14,000 livres, the equivalent at that time of as many dollars. For this and *Athalie,* which followed at the same school, the cost of one minor item used to refurbish the costumes—remounting 2,054 "diamonds" and purchasing certain others—was 1,223 livres. A certain M. Kraft, in a monumental folio on stage carpentry published in 1822, laments the destruction of "that magnificent decoration of *Perseus and Andromeda* . . . which represents a very grand palace of which the columns, grounds, the arches and the ceilings were entirely covered with small crystals of divers colors, cut with sparkling facets and set and joined against one another . . . as precious jewels are set in gold. It was destroyed by the burning of the opera house in 1780. The molten metal which proceeded from it streamed around the stage and terminated by running into the cellars as into a reservoir."

The play is always a show. Even in those classic periods which, owing to the simplifications of our text-books, we think of as formal and restrained, drama contrived to be a spectacle. The holiday exuberance of a show in the theatre in every epoch verges on the spectacular.

The reputed triumph of realism did not prevent either Berlin or New York from flocking to the mediaeval pageantry of Reinhardt's staging of *The Miracle*. The sophisticated subscribers of the Theatre Guild may resign themselves, once the curtain is up, to looking into a Hungarian hovel. But once the curtain is down they delight in the curtain's grandiose velvet expanse stamped with a Renaissance pattern and the polychrome ornament copied from the Davanzati Palace on the beamed ceiling over their heads.

No holiday public of a generation that produces dramatic masterpieces is awed by them in the theatre. In Athens, where the production of plays was part of a religious rite and nominally a sacred event begun by ritual at the altar, the holiday crowds never listened with that passive reverence that we associate with church-going. Greek audiences interrupted their tragedies continually with vociferous demonstrations of approbation or disapproval, and hurled olives, figs, or any other convenient missiles into the arena.

"If our modern playgoer in ancient Athens were an American," says Flickinger, "and so accustomed to staid conduct in a theatrical audience, he would be surprised at the turmoil of an Athenian performance. A Frenchman, familiar with the riots which greeted Victor Hugo's *Hernani* or Bernstein's *Après Moi,* would be better prepared for the situation. But in any case he would soon discover that a prize was to be awarded both in tragedy and comedy, and that each poet had his friends, partisans, and claque. The comic poets at least made no attempt to conceal the fact that there was a prize and that they were 'out' for it. . . . The total effect of these arrangements was to render the judges extremely sensitive to the public's expression of opinion, which was manifested by whistling, cat-calls, applause, knocking the heels against the seats, etc." The theatre at Athens held between 17,000 and 20,000 people and the uproar must have been very like a football crowd in a college stadium yelling for a touch-down after a first down near the goal-posts. On more than one occasion Athenian audiences stopped a performance. Aeschylus was nearly killed because a passage in one of his tragedies was supposed to have revealed part of the sacred mysteries; he saved himself by taking refuge at the altar. An impious reference to Aphrodite in Euripides' *Danaë* caused a riot. The play was allowed to continue only after the author appeared in the arena and explained away the impious allusion. The actor Aeschines was once hissed off the stage and narrowly escaped being stoned to death. Demosthenes repeats one of the popular jokes of the day: a musician, upon borrowing a supply of stone from a friend to build himself a house, promises to repay him with the stones collected in the theatre after the next public performance. "On the other hand, encores were not unknown, if particular passages took the fancy of the audience. Socrates is said to have encored the first three lines of the *Orestes* of Euripides."

A festival honouring the god of wine, the annual tragic contest of the Greeks sacred to Dionysus, was a time of universal license. Among the stock comic figures of later Roman comedy were the bastard children born during a dramatic festival. The mediaeval crowds so speedily took matters into their own hands that the Church eventually repudiated the worldly display of the mysteries. Henry IV of France "found it necessary to prohibit persons quite explicitly from throwing stones, powders or other missiles upon the stage." After several performances at Trinity College in 1578-79 we find a record:

It. for thyrtye foote of new glasse after the playes in the hall windowes. XV s[hillings].

It. for new leading of thirtye foote in the great hall windowes. V. s[hillings].

Aristotle complained of the ignorance of Athenian audiences. Plato records his distrust of them in the *Laws*. Shakespeare expressed his

35

contempt for the taste of the groundlings as persons "who for the most part are capable of nothing but inexplicable dumb-shows and noise." We may write eloquently today of a theatre of tomorrow that is to be a solemn and hushed cathedral. But which of us, as a theatre-goer, does not treasure memories of those moments of bedlam, and an audience seemingly gone mad with delight, when an actor "stopped the show" or the climax of a scene "brought down the house"?

7. THE PLAYWRIGHT'S EYE

A theatre then is a holiday centre to hold a vociferous crowd, eager not only to laugh and weep, but to applaud, stamp, hiss, cheer, and riot. It has always been built for that purpose with rule-of-thumb expediency. Custom decrees that the entire population of a city must gather twice a year for a dramatic festival; the slope of a hill is hollowed to receive banks of seats centuries before architects developed the use of the vault and arch that could make such a structure self-supporting. When the aisles of churches grow too small for the elaboration of a mystery-play, the marketplace is commandeered and the audience stands. Bear-pits and inn-yards are converted to house plays, stages are erected in the assembly-rooms of colleges or in the banqueting-halls of palaces; tennis-courts are roofed over. When the Renaissance architect sets out deliberately to construct a theatre to fit the play and attempts to bring the classic playhouse indoors, he bases his plans upon inaccurate information in the manuscript of a Roman architect, Vitruvius, and then finds himself violating the classic tradition by hanging balconies from the theatre walls so that the crowds of high-born and low-born can ogle one another. As a result the royal theatre with its tiers of balconies and boxes is perfected in the eighteenth century. So little progress has been made by modern architects in modifying that plan because they can devise no more efficient way to cram into one building the crowds needed to pay for a production and to give it life. At the same time they keep the stratification of rich, well-to-do, and poor that a capitalistic society demands just as a monarchy exacts a visible demarcation between the aristocrat and the commoner.

Because the play-house has always been to a greater or less degree a makeshift, the dramatist has always ignored any of its physical limitations that set bounds to his fancy or his imagination. Is the theatre's background a single immovable palace-front? He will nevertheless set his action in one play before the Temple of Apollo at Delphi and then at the Areopagus in Athens; in another, before Ajax's tent and then on a lonely stretch of seashore. The gods must descend even if it be with the aid of an obvious crane from the palace roof. Is the stage a platform in a sunlit marketplace? The playwright will notwithstanding call for angels to circle about God's head, the heavens to darken, or the Holy Ghost to "descend as a flame." On a stage with nothing but the most rudimentary means of indicating a change of place Shakespeare demanded continual changes of scene, leaping from palace to heath and back again, or put a girdle round the earth in forty minutes. He did upon one occasion send on a chorus to apologize for the strain upon the spectators' imagination, but it never occurred to him to confine his own imagination or to limit the structure of his stories to the structure of his stage. On a stage ideally suited to observing the unity of time and place, as a dramatist he rightly refused to observe either. Although the stages of the Italian and French court theatres were originally planned for revivals of Greek and Roman tragedies, they were very soon given over to such scripts as *Le Nozze degli Dei* and *La Finta Pazza,* with incessant shifting of scenery. The descent of the gods in glory—*la gloire*—became the traditional finale at the Paris Opéra, where "a whole Olympus descended from the empyreal regions and reascended through the waves of movable clouds, the whole distributed over eight platforms fifty feet in length by five in breadth, at fixed and

various heights, and supporting together more than sixty individuals."
When such glories were abandoned, M. Kraft is somewhat consoled
by a device he has seen at Le Théâtre de la Gaité for the *Bouton de
la Rose:* "The devil constructs suddenly an openwork spiral staircase in
a cage insulated [isolated] at an elevation of 18 feet in order that a
tyrant whom he favors may conveniently reach a virtuous princess
who has taken refuge upon the summit of a very steep rock; but
through the intervention of a fairy, the protectress of innocence, the
staircase returns to earth in proportion as the persecutor climbs up its
steps; so that panting with rage, the latter finds himself still on the
ground at the very moment when he thought he had effected his
criminal enterprise."

Such mechanical ingenuity is the forerunner of other devices whereby
innocence eluded villainy—forest fires, railroad wrecks, bursting dams,
and buzzing saw-mill wheels—in melodramas that delighted our
grandfathers. And no sooner are we convinced that we have outgrown
such picture-book pleasures and decreed that the playwright of the
modern theatre shall develop symbolic unity and simplicity, than
Georg Kaiser calls for the nightmare rapidity of the twelve scenes of
From Morn to Midnight, in one of which a snow-covered tree magically changes to the outline of a skeleton before our eyes; and Eugene
O'Neill in the first act of *Marco Millions* passes in review the architectural façades of five separate civilizations during thirty minutes of
playing time.

The scene-designer is no Perseus trailing clouds of glory and coloured lights who will liberate the playwright from a devouring monster. Thoughts are free. The playwright's imagination is never confined to the frame of any stage. He sees with his mind's eye. He will,
for the sake of having his play performed, accept any compromise or
any degree of illusion, however inadequate, that a particular type of
playhouse can give him. But when he writes "sky," it is the actual

heaven he sees and not a back-drop or a plaster cyclorama. The stars glitter; he does not waste a minute wondering whether they are to be miniature electric bulbs, silver spangles, or to be projected by a lantern-slide, whether, in fact, they can be reproduced at all. When he writes "forest" he treads an actual wood where love-letters can be nailed to the bark of trees and he can sit on stumps, gather flowers and leaves, hear birds sing, or lose his way. He is never impeded or inspired by the thought of how any of this can be achieved with paint, canvas, or papier mâché, screens, or cloth draped in folds. He will, when he needs them, call for a three-story power-house, a galleon, a Sphinx, a fog at sea, an avalanche on a mountain-top, without ever stopping to consider how they can be simulated, built, or moved on and off any stage.

A play occurs first of all when it is written. It is enacted in the mind of the playwright before it is acted in front of an audience. Before it is performed in the theatre it has already taken place. Dr. Tesman's drawing-room is Dr. Tesman's drawing-room, whether the mouldings of its doors and windows are subsequently imitated on the stage with painted canvas or with solid wood. The palace of the Troll King is a rock cavern; the trolls are terrifying green hobgoblins with misshapen bodies. Only later are they actors, painted and padded. For Shakespeare, Juliet leaned over the balustrade of a palace transfigured by the moon-light of an Italian night, although he knew as he wrote that the scene of his lovers' tryst would become a wooden balcony sometime during the afternoon. And Juliet was a woman despite the fact that she would have to be impersonated by a boy, probably one Robert Goffe. A creative playwright will no more alter the visual background of his play to suit the scene-painter and the scene-carpenter than Euripides would have modified the lines spoken by Electra or Iphigenia because these also had to be uttered by the tongues of men.

The dramatist of imagination does not write for any particular theatre. The theatre approximates his world as best it can. The playwright everywhere and at all times gives his imagination free rein; pictures and spectacles have always been an inherent part of his imaginings. Throughout the entire history of the theatre, the constant job of the stage technician, like that of the actor, has been to keep at the heels of dramatic poets for whose imagination everything is possible, sooner or later catch up with them, and make the playwright's world on the stage as real to an audience as it is to the playwright. Stagecraft at best is nothing more than the tail to the poet's kite. Designer and mechanic hold the string so that the kite can soar.

It is ludicrous to speak of freeing the playwright's imagination, which is inherently free, by constructing one type of theatre building or canonizing one method of designing scenery. Any and every new device that proposes to re-create stage design—painted perspective, the revolving stage, screens, a plaster sky, or solid forms unified by the chiaroscuro of projected light—invariably attempts to vindicate itself by visualizing anew the inherent splendours of a poet's imagination: the battlements of Elsinore, the witches' heath, the rock where Brünnhilde sleeps, or the palace doors before which Cassandra prophesies.

We may reconstruct our playhouses to achieve any number of necessary improvements in sight-lines, scene-shifting, seating, and acoustics. But the belief that architecture can breed poetry is on a par with the suburban habit of purchasing ready-made bird-houses from manufacturers of garden furniture in order to entice orioles or thrushes to brighten the front lawn. They usually nest elsewhere. The one thing our experimental playhouses cannot do is to breed plays to fit them. Appia's simplified platform-stage at Hellerau has possibly evoked the ultimate beauty of modern stage-craft, but no dramatic literature. Not even the prolific German playwrights could keep open Reinhardt's Grosses Schauspielhaus, with its arena seating five thousand and its open stage that made it easy to send crowds of actors surging into the aisles to mingle with the audience. That opportunity produced not a single script of any theatrical power. The "Theatre of the Five Thou-sand" was abandoned as a playhouse almost as soon as it had been pro-claimed the theatre of the future. The one production most effective in this architectural frame was *Danton's Death,* written in 1835 by an obscure medical student who had not the slightest notion of how his succession of thirty-two separate scenes could be fitted into a theatre, but who wrote of the French Revolution as though he were in its midst. Playwrighting is not based on architecture. Its direction is not determined by the development of stage-craft, a trick or two of car-pentry, an approximation of the more elementary constructions of modern engineering, or the illusions of which electric lamps rather than candles or gas-jets are capable.

In so far as the playwright is an artist he not only portrays deeds but also penetrates to the nexus of motive and emotion that breeds them and gives them meaning. He expresses a fresh sense of the springs of human character and the values of human experience. He learns this outside the theatre, not within it. The dull and lifeless epochs of playwrighting are invariably those when dramatists see life too neatly in terms of the theatre and repeat some one method of fit-ting the pattern of life into the frame of a particular stage. The theatre comes to life at intervals when a dramatist such as Euripides, Shake-speare, Molière, Ibsen, Shaw, or O'Neill sees life in the theatre in terms of what he believes to be the truth of life about him. We have accepted, as the best description of the playwright's vision, the asser-tion: All the world's a stage. But to the playwright, as he writes, any stage is all the world.

CHAPTER II

REALISM AND REALITY

I. MIND'S EYE

DRAMATIC geniuses who revolutionize the methods of writing plays rarely make a single innovation in the method of staging them. A performance is at best an inadequate approximation of an event that has already taken place in the limitless realm of the imagination. Like the most uninspired journeyman, the dramatist of genius wants to get his play put on, and in order to have it acted will accept any convention that the theatre of his day imposes. He accepts men and boys to play his women. He accepts sunlit balconies for nocturnal lovers' trysts, or a painted back-cloth for a heaven tingling with stars. Corner him in a theatre during a rehearsal and you will, as a rule, find him abysmally ignorant of how the backgrounds of his story can be realized, unaware of the fact that the tempests, floods, avalanches, fogs, rainbows, enmeshed with the action of his play, may be so inadequately approximated by the mechanics of the stage for which he has written as to become ridiculous. In regard to scenic methods he remains an opportunist, and rightly so. Old-fashioned scenery will often satisfy a modern playwright as well as a modernistic substitute. The test he expects either to meet is the fundamental one: Will the audience believe it during a production as they believe in the actors and the play if the play succeeds? His answer to all questions of scenic method is usually the equivalent of Manet's dictum as to the right method of painting: *"Si ça y est, ça y est. Si ça n'y est pas, faut recommencer. Tout le reste est de la blague*"—"If you get it, fine. If you don't, try again. Everything else is humbug."

The audience is equally empirical. It sees not only with its eye, but like the playwright, with its mind's eye as well. Almost any scenic convention can succeed in making the world of the play real provided it gets itself accepted quickly enough after the play begins. Like the playwright, the audience transcends or ignores the physical shape of any particular playhouse. It is stirred, its emotions are aroused, primarily because the play touches ideas, faiths, fears, or beliefs it already recognizes and follows, even when these are attacked or discredited. It is manifest nonsense to say that the Greek theatre moved its auditors because it thrust the actors into the midst of the audience. The majority of Greek audiences were further from the protagonist of a tragedy than present-day base-ball fans in the bleachers are from the diamond, or the crowds in a college stadium from football players. A spectator at a football game in the last row of the Harvard stadium is ninety-one feet from the side-lines. A spectator in the last row in the theatre at Athens was two hundred and twenty-seven feet from the front of the orchestra where a tragedy was performed. The worst seats at a Harvard football game correspond to being down front at a performance of Aeschylus. Athenians ninety-one feet from a tragedy were in the twenty-eighth row of seats. There were forty-two tiers of seats behind them. Nevertheless the play at Athens was no more remote from its audience than a football game is from ours. For the Greek theatre succeeded in doing what every vital and popular theatre does: it did not thrust the players into the midst of the spectators; it thrust the theme of the play into the minds of its audience.

A great play lives in its day, as third-rate ones do, by its ability to touch the passions, prejudices, ideals, ambitions, hopes, and memories of its generation. The actor's dominance depends not upon any physical relation to his spectators but upon his power to stir popular imagina-

43

tion. The Japanese actor of the "popular theatre" aroused the emotions of his hearers because he impersonated familiar gods or heroes, not because he entered the stage on a wooden trestle, "the flowery way," from the midst of his audience. We have reproduced the device and found no better use for it than to parade chorus girls at a musical comedy. The Japanese drama of *The Forty-seven Ronin* revived such vivid memories of an aristocratic feud that the descendants of the rival clans fell to duelling in the theatre. The authorities, faced with the necessity of preventing further bloodshed, very wisely suppressed the play instead of remodelling the playhouse. I have seen great clowns such as Grock or the Fratellinis convulse an audience with their antics as easily from the "peep-hole stages" of two Paris vaudeville theatres as from the tan-bark rings of the Cirque Médrano or the Cirque d'Hiver. The cadences that reverberated through Greek masks, and now seem so purely poetic, originally blazed with jingoistic pride, imperialist ambitions, specific codes of honour, with local memories of victory, disaster, and exile that time has erased as it has washed away the terra-cotta, blue, and gold once blazoned on the Parthenon, leaving instead its core of honey-coloured stone.

It was not because the Athenians were seated about the actors in a semi-circle that they fined Phrynichus for referring to a military defeat or brought charges of impiety against Euripides for a single speech in *Hippolytus* that seemed to deny the sanctity of an oath that the gods had witnessed. It was not a purely spatial relation measured on an arc or a radius that related actor and audience so directly that after the first verse of *Melanippe the Philosopher*—

> *Zeus—whoso Zeus is: this I know not, save*
> *By hearsay—*

the audience rose in a riot of protest. The miracle of Sister Beatrice did not become either more miraculous or more credible because Rein-

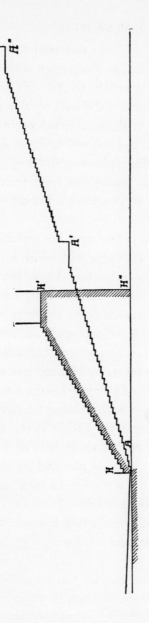

COMPARISON OF THE AESCHYLEAN AUDITORIUM AT ATHENS—A, A′, A″

(RE-DRAWN FROM FLICKINGER)

AND THE HARVARD STADIUM—H, H′, H″

hardt's supernumeraries brushed our ears with their shields as they came trooping down the aisles. The groundlings whose demonstrations annoyed Shakespeare were seated in the pit—our present orchestra. But London audiences boo a play today with equal heartiness from the gallery. Play a melodrama in the local grand opera-house or in the largest theatre to be found, and you will hear the applause greeting such lines as "Better death than dishonour" or "Rags are royal raiment when worn for virtue's sake" come first from spectators who most easily identify themselves with so noble a sentiment even though they are crowded under the roof.

The reality of a theatrical performance has no inherent connection with its realism, the degree of fidelity with which it reproduces or reflects the facts, as we say, of actual life. A play becomes real to the degree that any audience succeeds in identifying itself with the lives and deeds portrayed. Events on a stage are real to us because we accept them as true although they occur, supposedly, in Heaven or Hell. A dramatic story becomes unreal the moment it fails to convince us that it is a true account of human nature and human motives, even when it takes place in a reproduction of a tenement-house kitchen. No amount of imitation of nature, such as water running through faucets into the kitchen sink or gas whistling in the kitchen stove, can make the play an imitation of life if we find it to be false to what we conceive "real life" to be. Once we accept the play and say to ourselves, "This is the way things happen—this is real—this is true," our conviction can be reinforced by naturalistic detail. But it cannot be created or destroyed because faucets, with great artistic restraint, fail to run water, and a stove, aware of the laws of art, does not get hot enough to fry a pan of bacon and eggs.

If we are inclined to believe that the Garden of Eden was an actual place, the most literal imitation of a tree in papier mâché hung with artificial leaves will not destroy our conviction that we are beholding the Tree of Knowledge. But we cannot be transported to Heaven and believe that we are communing with saints and angels solely because the stage setting is a sufficiently abstract arrangement of fathomless blue and rays of light. Stage settings cannot create reality. They can at best either reproduce or symbolize the kind of reality in which we are inclined to believe. The reality of a theatrical production is established by a tacit fiat on the part of an audience: we will to believe. Our will can be served equally well by literal imitation or by conventional symbols. Up to a certain point our belief that the stage is a world is evoked by the imitation of ourselves in the person of the living actor, and by the imitation of things that are real to us because we come in contact with their counterparts daily. But no imitation can be complete enough to deceive us. We are always watching a play. Beyond a certain point we agree to deceive ourselves. Water runs from the kitchen faucet. But we know, if we stop to observe the stage carefully, that the wall at the back is not plaster but painted canvas. We also know, although actors climb the stairway seen through a door, that the room is not part of a building with a story above and another below. We know that the sunlight streaming through the window is not the rays of the sun, that the actress leaning over the sink is not the cobbler's wife. Nevertheless the stage is a kitchen in a tenement-house, the actress is the cobbler's wife and a denizen of the slums. We are to witness the Crucifixion; a stage at Oberammergau is Calvary and Anton Lang, wood-carver, who yesterday sold us souvenirs, is Christ. We behold a god; Pallas Athene herself descends from Olympus even as we see the crane and hear the pulleys creak.

2. MAKE-BELIEVE

An element of make-believe is inseparable from the theatre. We cannot accept the first words of any play without saying to ourselves, in effect, "Let's pretend." The basis of scenic design seems rooted in a paradox because the reality of any performance on any stage is itself a paradox. A performance in the theatre is obviously make-believe, a mimicking of life. Yet the lives it portrays often seem to us more real than our own. During every minute that we watch actors performing we know that they are dressed up as we dressed up when children, "pretending," as we used to say then, playing at being kings, queens, gods, heroes, or persons like ourselves. We acknowledge this when we interrupt them to applaud them for acting—that is, pretending—so well. But the interruption does not snap the spell. The human beings portrayed can become more real to us than a wife, friend, mistress, or child seated at our side. The emotions aroused by an obvious imitation of love or death can be more violent than any we have felt during our own love-affairs or our personal bereavements. Dramatic criticism, from Aristotle's *Poetics* to Hamlet's speech to the players and down to the discussions of our own day, revolves about this central problem of why and how life as portrayed in a play can become more real than life itself. "What's she to him or he to Hecuba?" is a doubt that may profitably assail the playgoer on his way out of the theatre, but if it occurs to him during the performance, the production fails. For audience, playwright, and actors are engaged in a tacit conspiracy every time a play begins, united in saying, "Let's pretend; let's make believe." Once that resolve is taken and the interest of an audience is sufficiently aroused, the audience does believe in the reality of what it sees and hears. Everything on the stage, by the magic that a successful drama communicates, becomes what it pretends to be. The theatre is so fundamentally based upon a convention that no amount of imitative detail in setting a stage can destroy its art or make it wholly an imitation of life. At the same time the theatre, in its effect, is so complete an imitation of life that no degree of convention can destroy its reality as a picture of existence.

No play, however realistic in intention, can ever be wholly so in the

48

theatre. There remains always, even where the aim is photographic accuracy, an element of transparent illusion. A dramatic critic may hail a masterpiece of naturalism, but he knows, like the most illiterate theatre-goer, that the aged characters are not as old as they seem, that the sick and suffering have no actual malady, that murder and death are obvious pretence. Probably the only drastically realistic performance that ever occurred in the theatre took place at Tournai in 1549 at a Jesuit production entitled *The Triumph of Mardocheus, the History of Esther, and the Death of Holofernes,* given in honour of the triumphal entry of Philip of Spain. The organizers selected a criminal already condemned to death to play the rôle of Holofernes, erected their stage at a cemetery, and the criminal, no doubt flattered by the honour of being selected for a leading rôle and ignorant of the play's conclusion, docilely allowed himself to be beheaded. On the other hand, however rigid the conventions of any stage, it must contain innumerable facsimiles of the natural world. No other art has as its means of expression so complete a piece of nature as the living body of the actor. Actors handled rapiers, lighted candles, or kindled altar-fires—and the candles and altar-fires actually burned in the theatres of Molière and Aeschylus—just as they switch on electric lights in the theatre of today, shoot pistols, sit on chairs, and lean on tables that are facsimiles of those outside the theatre's walls.

Whether or not they continue to do so and smoke cigarettes as they converse while seated on garden or drawing-room furniture, will depend not on how many higher or lower categories of scenic art we can invent but on what playwrights make actors do that interests audiences. So long as audiences find comedies, like Bernard Shaw's, staged in clergymen's studies, artists' studios, Salvation Army barracks, and physicians' consulting-rooms, as provocative as they once found Molière's comedies staged in the drawing-room of a marquis or a misanthrope, the designer will be forced to imitate, to a greater or less

49

degree, rooms such as we habitually inhabit. These will seem real although built of canvas and not of lath and plaster. Whenever a playwright can interest an audience by dramatizing Caesar's adventure in Egypt or Don Juan's escapades in Spain, the stage will have to contain as part of its setting a portable Sphinx or a statue of the Commander that an audience will accept as real although neither is made of stone. Neither would be more real to an audience if made of stone. As one philosopher has remarked, origins have nothing to do with values. The aesthetic value of any form on the stage depends not upon its source but upon its use, not on its intrinsic nature or material but on what it expresses as used in the course of the play. Significant form is a phrase currently used to describe the plastic qualities of modern painting. In the realm of scene-designing any form can become significant. Whatever beauty is achieved results from an object's expressiveness and its effect as used. For a given purpose, a kitchen chair from the nearest hardware-store, clothes from a rag-picker's bag, fire that burns, or water that runs may be as indubitably expressive, and so art, as geometric shapes, electric illusions, or symbolic uniforms. It is of no importance how many kinds of art, by definition, happen to be mixed in staging a single play. Let the scenic designer, like any other artist, aim for a binding unity of style. But let him also realize at the same time that he cannot begin to serve his apprenticeship in the theatre until he avoids the folly of becoming an aesthetic prude.

The purpose of a playwright, who is also a creative artist, is to convince an audience of the truth of what it sees and hears, whether or not his story is embodied by familiar types from around the corner, historic personages of 300 B.C., or legendary figures of two thousand years hence. For he knows that until a performance achieves this immediate reality, no audience can identify itself sufficiently with the human beings on the stage to be able to share their emotions or to be interested in their experiences. The audience wants to believe in the reality of what it sees performed just as ardently as the playwright wants it to. An old adage reminds us that "seeing is believing." But what we see in the theatre depends on our habits of seeing elsewhere.

The particular degree of imitation, the number of things on a stage that reproduce the forms and textures of our daily experience, or the kind of conventions and symbols employed in any scene, are in themselves of no importance. What matters in the theatre is the moment when all the elements of a stage setting cohere and become a world that the audience accepts as the world of the play. How and when that moment occurs will depend not on some special aesthetic quality that pictures can acquire once they are transferred to a theatre but upon the kind of pictures that outside the theatre are accepted as revealing the nature of the world we live in.

3. SEEING AND BELIEVING

Walter Lippmann, in analyzing the creation of stereotypes that make public opinion, says: "For the most part we do not first see, and then define, we define first and then see. In the great blooming, buzzing confusion of the outer world we pick out what our culture has already defined for us, and we tend to perceive that which has been picked out in the form stereotyped for us by our culture." And he goes on to demonstrate how largely our conclusions about the world we live in are based not on a fresh perception of experience, but on the stereotyped pictures of the world already in our heads.

The process is particularly patent in the theatre. Where a public accepts the allegories and symbols of Catholicism to chart the universe, any evocation of these symbols on a stage, whether crude or elaborate, literal or abstract, will establish a real Heaven and a real earth in the open square of a market town. Where gods, heroes, and demigods are accepted as the guardians of civic life, they can be brought to life in the theatre by forms that reproduce their symbolic attire and gestures already depicted on monuments and temples. When, as during the Renaissance, certain kinds of painting, sculpture, and engraving come to be accepted as a revelation of nature, their counterparts create the world of nature in front of a curtain or behind it. Bernhard Berenson has pointed out, "What with the almost numberless shapes assumed by an object, what with our insensitiveness and inattention, things would scarcely have for us features and outlines so clear but for the stereotyped shapes that art has lent them." Goethe, who directed a theatre and made sketches for a number of his productions, wrote, "The appreciation of Poussin grows more widespread, and it is precisely this painter who offers the designer the most splendid models for the treatment of landscape and architecture." His stage-directions for *Pandora* read: "The scene is to be conceived in the grandiose style of Poussin."

The effectiveness of any picture of the world in the theatre depends very largely on how nearly it evokes the pictures we bring to the theatre already in our heads. And these in turn depend on the racial and cultural backgrounds of an audience, its folk-ways, its habits of visualization, the tests of truth it applies in daily life. The public that delighted in the theatrical realism of the nineteenth century did not consist, in the main, of connoisseurs of the graphic arts. It was a public that had begun to accept photography as the test of truth, believed that the camera could not lie, worshipped the accuracy and precision of its industrial machines, and relied increasingly on the mechanical reproduction of photographs and the reporting of its daily press for its sense of what the world was like. "Get the facts" seemed to be the answer to every problem. Fact-finding became a cult. Increasing numbers of people believed that the patient observations of chemists and physicists, microscopically and mathematically accurate, would reveal the secret of life. The same public tended to demand—and still does today—stage backgrounds complete and authentic, based upon accurate observation, before it could accept them as places where people were assumed to be living and dying. At the same time in an era of mechanistic invention and "speeding up" its eye began to accept the brevities and simplifications of certain forms of modern graphic art: the finality of an impression or a sketch, the value of abbreviation. Our daily habits of apperception reflect these stereotypes. On the stage a setting that is the equivalent of a sketch can be a real place. The more fantastic simplifications of modern scenery are accepted to the degree that we have accepted graphs, diagrams, caricatures, and cartoons as methods of communicating ideas. The conflicting tendencies of current scenic design, which prompt designers to make a column solid, and so real, rather than paint it, but at the same time make them build only a fragment of it in order to evoke an entire cathedral, reflect our fluctuating standards whereby alternately the fact and the impression, the case-history and the head-line, the complete report and its abbreviation, become the tests of the truth or the value of any experience whatsoever.

4. PICTURE PATTERNS FOR THE UNIVERSE

But as Lippmann has also made plain, "the stereotyped shapes lent to the world come not merely from art, in the sense of painting and sculpture and literature, but from our moral codes and our social philosophies and our political agitations as well." Practitioners of the plastic arts are, as a rule, unaware that their choice of a style or a method is often predetermined by the theories of dead philosophers and is based on an unconscious acceptance of religious, political, or metaphysical doctrines that modern artists are prone to declare have no relation whatever to the forms of aesthetic expression. Many recent experiments in painting derive from the literary ideas of a previous generation and these in turn are rooted in previously accepted moral or metaphysical concepts. Art forms give belated emphasis to the truth as philosophers define it in their incessant preoccupation with the nature of reality in the physical world, the springs of human behaviour, and the goals of human experience.

Modern painters' readiness to believe that it is as important to look at a cat as at a king, their predilection for selecting as subjects humble or common people, the compassion with which Millet, Daumier, and Steinlen invested peasants, mountebanks, shop-girls, and washerwomen, stem from the French social theorists of the late eighteenth century and doctrines that assumed the inherent nobility of the common man, his fundamental importance as the corner-stone of society. These ideas, accepted as gospel by the early nineteenth century, became an almost universal belief that some form of democracy based on universal suffrage was the ideal social state. The consequent tendency of political philosophers to dramatize the development of society as a conflict of masses or classes, the emphasis placed upon environment by the development of such sciences as biology with its doctrine of evolution, and the popularization of such pseudo-sciences as eugenics and sociology, were reflected not only in plays but also in stage settings. An individual came to be conceived as part of a class, as typical of a group, as expressing himself through his environment no less than by his person. Hence the room in which he lived, the furniture on which he sat, the number of books on his shelves, the pictures on his walls—witness the stage-directions of Bernard Shaw—became, at times, as significant as his words. To paint furniture or a staircase on a back-drop seemed ludicrously inadequate. The trend of nineteenth century painting, influenced by the progress of the science of optics, emphasized this in turn by training us to see the human figure not as an isolated form bounded by a hard and arbitrary outline but enmeshed in atmosphere —*plein air*—in ambient light that tied a person to his visible surroundings. The present methods of electric lighting on our stages, our deliberate efforts to avoid light that is bland and uniform, such as Poussin and Ingres shed upon their classic landscapes and allegories, are a legacy of Impressionist painting, which translated into pictorial terms a fresh picture of nature originally established by the natural sciences.

The place of nature in the art of the nineteenth century was also determined by the concepts of eighteenth century philosophers. The cult of landscape-painting was stimulated by Rousseau's romantic doctrine of a return to nature, the liberation to be achieved in purifying our souls and cleansing our minds by the healing contact of hills, streams, and trees. The ensuing nature-worship enabled a painted landscape to be considered sufficiently important to occupy a canvas by itself. Until then it had been a subordinate background to figure-painting; the meaning of nature had to be separately personified by dryads, nereids, nymphs, and satyrs. The rendering of landscape forms in Bruegel's *Spring, Summer, Autumn,* and *Winter* places them among the masterpieces of landscape-painting, but they are peopled by crowds practising the occupations appropriate to the four seasons. In the landscapes of Bruegel's Dutch successors, Ostade, Ruisdael, Hobbema, and Cuyp, the human figure grows progressively less important; nevertheless no vista is complete without its spectators. They do not disappear entirely until the beginning of the nineteenth century, when a new concept of nature had established itself.

This fresh sense of nature had become so popularized by the last quarter of the nineteenth century that it finally influenced the representation of nature on the stage. Nature could not be adequately expressed by the flat blue of the sky poured on to a back-drop or by a painted rock no thicker than a piece of heavy cardboard. A painted landscape on the stage, or a painted ship upon a painted ocean, began to seem as unreal as a painted staircase. The meaning and the importance of forests and fields could no longer be expressed by two dimensions. A third dimension was required. The illusion of the depth of celestial space given by an illuminated plaster dome superseded the sky-drop; plastic trees supplanted foliage borders and regimental wood-wings. Reinhardt began one revolution in 1905 when he sent the lovers and the sprites of *Midsummer Night's Dream* scurrying among the solid trunks of three huge birch-trees. Another revolution was announced when forests began to be made of towering columnar draperies, reinforced with shadows so as to suggest the girth of giant trees dappled with sunlight that seemed to trickle through unseen foliage.

Neither device is, objectively considered, more real than the traditional borders and wings. Painted groves can give an illusion of depth and distance that, for a previous generation, was miraculous to the point of seeming a counterpart of nature itself. Such prospects and perspectives may be well enough painted to qualify pictorially as works of art. To the present generation they are artificial and ugly because they do not convey the particular kind of reality that we ascribe to nature today. For our sense of the fundamental character of the world about us shifts as metaphysical or scientific assumptions become accepted stereotypes through which, like lenses, we view our environment. Graphic methods seem important to the degree that they are able to invest a portrayal of the external world with qualities that we have come to believe are fundamental.

The importance ascribed today to rendering the third dimension in painting is primarily an outgrowth of the formulation of laws of perspective in Italy during the late Renaissance, particularly Leonardo da Vinci's discussions in his note-books of methods for evoking the depth and distance of receding planes within a single picture-plane. But the exaggerated emphasis placed by recent aesthetic doctrines upon the desirability of picturing the third dimension is also due to the picture of the cosmos originally drawn for us by physicists and astronomers, in particular to the mass of Newton's universe, first calculated in 1666. "His feat in calculating the mass and specific gravity of the sun, as well as of all the planets that had satellites, was pronounced by Adam Smith to be 'above the reach of human reason and experience.' " For the two ensuing centuries many minds that no longer felt the controlling hand of God derived a feeling of immense security from the mathematical certainty of the laws of motion and the spectacle of such vast agglomerations of matter held together by the impersonal force of gravity. That feeling is now so actively shared by even the average newspaper reader after a lapse of two hundred and sixty-five years that in January, 1931, the New York *Times* considered worthy of its first page the news that the earth had been weighed once again by Dr. Heyl on his new cosmic scales at the United States Bureau of Standards in Washington, and calculated to be six thousand million million million tons. But even more significant is the *Times's* comment: "The scientific interest in the earth does not lie so much in its weight as in its gravitational pull. This is a constant. Until 1923 this constant of gravitation was considered to be 6.53. . . . Dr. Heyl's new figures make this 6.58. Small as the difference is it will help military engineers to calculate the range of projectiles and astronomers to predict the motions of planets." Our concrete picture of the world we live in is so directly affected by abstract concepts of space, time, and mass in motion that the variation of five one-hundredths in the force of gravitation becomes front-page news. We have been so sedulously schooled to expect from such mathematical calculations an almost miraculously extended control over our environment that today popular imagination, like Shelley's dome of many-coloured glass, stains the white radiance of Eddington's or Einstein's most abstruse theorems.

We have also been schooled to believe that the weight of the most minute particle of star-dust determines the character of every object on the star itself. The nineteenth century, engaged in exploiting the explosive force of steam and oil and in testing the tensile strength of iron and steel, felt that the core of the universe had been discovered when

the traditional elements of the Greeks—earth, air, fire, and water—
were disintegrated into ninety-two indivisible metals and gases, and
their atomic weights were calculated. The invisible atom assumed by
Democritus became real because it could be weighed. Twenty-five
years ago, as a college sophomore I was taught that extension in space
—weight and mass—were the primary qualities of any object and part
of the object itself; its sound, taste, and colour were secondary, because part of our individual sensory impressions of it. Common sense
accepted the distinction as fundamental, for no one confused the shapes
of dice and billiard balls or tried to put square pegs into round holes.
But we might argue endlessly as to how blue the sky was that let fall
Bryant's fringed gentian, how red Robert Burns's red, red rose could
be. When psychology attempted to become a modern science by measuring and analyzing our mental processes, it established for a time the
primacy of our sense of touch and made all other senses extensions and
verifications of it. Common sense again vindicated this conclusion, for
as infants we had accepted the world outside ourselves as real as soon
as we barked our shins upon it. Who has not marvelled at the feat of
a blind deaf-mute who by touch alone experienced a world that corresponded to our own and so achieved intercourse with her fellows?

The weight of matter, whether of an invisible atom or of the farthest
visible star, was the touchstone of reality for the nineteenth century.
The concept sank deeply into popular consciousness and affected all
modes of thought. The practical man who had no time for abstract
theorizing and wanted results (by God!) accepted blindly the most
abstract assumptions of physicists, which he could no more follow than
could the equally practical burgher of the Middle Ages decipher the
exegeses of mediaeval theologians, although their dogmas ultimately
became his own. Scientific axioms have replaced prayers as a means
for cushioning the blows of destiny. Modern wisdom has been munifi-
cently subsidized by ignorance, research laboratories have been en-

dowed, as chapels once were, in order to insure the intercession of seers and saints. The ability to conceive the nature of space and the motions of bodies within it has from Newton and Kant to Millikan and Einstein been accepted as the mark of the transcendent power of human intelligence. Shortly after Einstein's theory of relativity had been announced, one read in the New York *World* head-lines:—

4000 IN STAMPEDE AT EINSTEIN MOVIE.

ONLY 1400 SEATS FOR THEM IN

MUSEUM AUDITORIUM.

STRUGGLE ENLISTS POLICE—

and on the front page of the New York *Times:*

4500 BATTLE IN MUSEUM TO SEE EINSTEIN FILM.

POLICE QUELL STAMPEDE AFTER 8 GUARDS FAIL.

When Einstein visited New York the crowds who knew that they could not understand a line of anything he had ever written gaped at him so persistently that he had to be barricaded aboard ship to protect him from sightseers. They were not essentially different from the crowds that once followed some monk reputed to have worked miracles.

5. UNIVERSAL PATTERNS IN STAGE PICTURES

The plastic arts could not fail to reflect such incessant preoccupation with the nature of space and our experience of it. For the field of speculation in any given epoch is not laid out in parallel lanes, but arranges itself on a plan that resembles the radiating boulevards of Paris, which converge to the same *rond-point,* where a statue commemorates an epoch-making victory. In cutting across from one avenue of thought to another we look down a vista to the same monument. Space was the transcendent concept of pure reason, the arena where our imprisoned senses were liberated. The entire structure of the universe was determined by the periodic rhythms of star-masses in motion and the characteristic weights of the most minute particles of matter that composed them. It is therefore not surprising to find that the standards of aesthetic beauty have been successively "tactile values," "space composition," "significant (three-dimensional) form," and "architectural idea." Bernhard Berenson in 1896 (under the influence of James's *Principles of Psychology*) changed the trend of art criticism by revaluating the Florentine painters of the Renaissance on the basis of their tactile values, stating: "To realise form we must give tactile values to retinal sensations . . . the artist who gives us these values more rapidly than the object itself gives them, gives us the pleasures consequent upon a more vivid realisation of the object, and the further pleasures that come from the sense of greater psychical capacity . . . the chief business of the figure painter, as an artist, is to stimulate the tactile imagination. . . . I do not mean to imply that we get no pleasure from a picture except the tactile satisfaction. What I do wish to say is that *unless* it satisfies our tactile imagination, a picture will not exert the fascination of an ever-heightened reality." In analyzing the Central Italian painters of the Renaissance, Perugino and Raphael are placed on a pinnacle as masters of space composition. "Space-composition . . . is not an arrangement to be judged as extending only laterally, or up and down on a flat surface, but extending inwards in depth as well . . . space-composition differs even more widely from ordinary composition in its effect. The latter, reduced to its elements, plays only on our feeling for pattern. . . . Space-composition is much more potent. Producing as it does immediate effects . . . on the vaso-motor system, with every change of space we suffer on the instant a change in our circulation and our breathing—a change which we become aware of as a feeling of heightened or lowered vitality. The direct effect, then, of space-composition is not only almost as powerful as that of music, but is brought about in much the same way."

Three years after Berenson published *The Florentine Painters* Adolphe Appia revolutionized all theories of stage-craft then current when he published *Die Musik und die Inscenierung* (*Music and Stage-setting*), stated: "When stage pictures take on spatial forms dictated by the rhythms of music they are not arbitrary but have the quality of being inevitable," and declared space-compositions of solid forms against open vistas to be the only type of stage-setting in accord with Wagner's music.

Theories of aesthetics as applied to painting have followed the direction originally set by Berenson; theories of the aesthetics of stage setting still continue to apply their counterpart in the ideas of Appia. In 1914 Clive Bell made "significant form" the test of aesthetic value and, paraphrasing Berenson, defined it by saying: "A sense of three-dimensional space is essential to the full appreciation of most architectural forms. Pictures which would be insignificant if we saw them as flat patterns are profoundly moving because, in fact, we see them as related planes." In 1915 in *Modern Painting,* Willard Huntington Wright expressed the prevailing point of view by declaring: "We demand a greater stimulus than an art of two dimensions can give; our minds instinctively extend themselves into space." "After Michelangelo there was no longer any new inspiration for sculpture. After Cézanne there was no longer any excuse for it. He has made us see that painting can present a more solid vision than that of any stone image." The latest doctrine, evolved by R. H. Wilenski in *The Modern Movement in Art* (1927), says: "What then is this idea of art which the artists of the modern movement consciously serve? Stated briefly it is the idea of architecture as typical art."

Stage design has also taken architecture as its model and grown increasingly plastic. The third dimension is no longer simulated with painted perspective but is reproduced by carpentry; pilasters, columns, cornices, friezes, and entablatures solidly built in full relief replace the elaborately painted façades of a century ago with their carefully painted, cast shadows. These new backgrounds, because of their tactile values, are supposed to give spectators the "fascination of ever-heightened reality." Working drawings to scale, accurate to one twenty-fourth of an inch, for the stage carpenter, like an architect's blue prints for his builder, are today as necessary a part of the technique of executing a scenic design as colour sketches are for the scene-painter. Indeed the stage-carpenter has become as important as the scene-painter, who often has only to apply a uniform tone, breaking it into layers of spattered pigment in order to avoid monotony. The aid of modern engineering has been enlisted so that, as at the State Theatre and Opera House in Dresden, palace porticos or triple banks of terraces, instead of being painted on a back-drop, could be built and supported on a stage floor that was the platform of a huge hydraulic elevator, be sent to the cellar, filled with new constructions equally solid, and lifted again to the stage level. Smaller forms were mounted and moved on platforms electrically propelled over railroad tracks.

But stage scenery is now more fundamentally plastic than it could become by imitating the details of architecture. The symbolic forms of one new "movement," Expressionism, are almost always sculpturesque. The scene-painter, like the painter of easel-pictures, holds flat pattern in contempt and finds stage pictures, in the words of Clive Bell, "profoundly moving because we see them as related planes." The newest tendency in stage design, Constructivism, takes "the idea of architecture as typical art" for its model and reproduces architectural structure in generic form without a scrap of surface ornament. To its practitioners there seems to be an inherent virtue in performing a play on two, three, and sometimes four levels, so that actors continuously ascending and descending causeways, stairways, and ramps at times achieve a parody in miniature of mountain-climbing. Appia's later drawings show stone terraces and pylons that recall the primitive architectural forms of the Aztecs and the Mayas. Gordon Craig's most visionary projects for Shakespeare's tragedies are none the less surprisingly solid, abounding in towering turrets and castle walls five stories high. One scheme for *Macbeth* requires it to be played on a stairway winding about an enormous column, another that it be played near the summit of a rock. "I see a lofty and steep rock, and I see the moist cloud which envelops the head of this rock."

The more recent impulse not only to make scenic structures abstract but also to believe that stage settings become more significant when less particularized, the mystic meanings ascribed to abstraction in all forms of art, have been stimulated by new conceptions of the structure of the universe, originating in the more recent speculations of physics and chemistry. The accepted picture of nature is no longer composed of Newton's masses. Having shattered the crystal spheres, they have in turn been disintegrated by concepts of matter so fluid as to be almost nebulous. The indestructible atom is now pictured as filled with molecular solar systems held together by electric cohesion, seething and exploding about a nucleus. To popular imagination nature is no longer a purifying haven to which we can return. The universe conceived in the dizzying distances of light-years and interstellar spaces seems increasingly vast and featureless. Millikan in 1930 spoke of the continuous building of matter in the depths of interstellar space by "cosmic rays," for which he found "excellent experimental evidence," and added, "Indeed has not modern physics thrown the purely mechanistic view of the universe root and branch out of its house?" Therefore an increasing number of designers and critics become convinced that the moments in the theatre capable of inspiring awe, mystery, and terror can acquire new beauty by being set in the impenetrable or vaguely defined areas of an "emphasized void" or "space stage" and are elated when an actor is "backed by space," or "stabbed by a great white light" that picks him out of the engulfing darkness.

On a stage fifty feet deep, a meadow on a back-drop, framed by painted trees, extends to an illusory horizon, apparently a mile away. The eye of one generation, carried through space, is exhilarated, and prompts that generation to cry, "Beautiful!" and to applaud reality in the theatre. A solid tree-trunk is placed twenty-five feet from a curved plaster wall, or a column of canvas is hung and knocked into folds; the eye of another generation, tricked by the play of light and shadow, sees a vast forest. By the same means a shelving platform of wood and canvas appears to be a solid stone building, a lofty cliff, or a moun-tain-top. A new reality in the theatre is applauded and proclaimed beautiful. The same stage is shrouded in darkness, and to the eye of the next generation, again tricked by the play of shafts of light thrown across it, a space fifty feet deep and seventy-five feet high seems illimi-table. In the dim religious light the audience applauds, cries, "Beauti-ful!" once again, and decides that the theatre has at last achieved its apotheosis.

We bring to the theatre a preconceived pattern of the universe. The frame through which we see any play that pretends to express the realities of existence or to interpret the meaning of life is not the proscenium frame of a theatre but the frame of our own minds. What-ever beauty we see in stage backgrounds depends upon the degree to which they suggest or approximate what, in any particular epoch, we believe the nature of reality to be. The dramatic conflict of any play, as we see it performed, is part of a larger scenario wherein we have already dramatized the forces of society and assigned to nature a definite rôle in shaping the destiny of man. The greatest plays, which we return to as classics and masterpieces, are also expressions of the social and cosmic outlook of their times. The theatre that we eventually prize is the theatre of ideas. Its scene is our picture of the universe, compounded in every age of fact and fancy, of the tangible and the intangible, of things felt to be real because they can be touched, seen, and heard, and of symbols of things felt to be no less real despite the fact that they can only be deduced, dreamed, or divined. Such pictures have been created by dominant religions. But the theatre, even in epochs when religious faith flourished, did not create a picture of a universe. It reflected a picture already created. Modern designers must abandon their ridiculous pretence that by manipulating coloured lights and blank screens they can evolve a new religion or a substitute for one. They may succeed in illustrating whatever picture of the universe a modern religion evokes, if such a religion is ever evolved. That evocation in the theatre may require personifying microbes and electrons instead of demons and furies, reproducing radio antennae and high-tension coils instead of a wooden cross and a crown of thorns, suggesting the immanence of invisible energy instead of an omnipresent deity, imitating electric-spark gaps, echoing the whine of high-tension current rather than the flash and rumble of Jove's thunderbolts. If the theatre of tomorrow becomes the arena of a religious faith, any one of its settings will necessarily be a fragmentary evocation of a cosmos and be made of the same mixture of material and immaterial elements, of symbol and fact, of suggestion and representation, that have always been necessary components of stage scenery. The most literal reproductions in any stage setting are made real, just as its symbols are made significant, by the same act of faith that makes an imitation of human activity an expression of the meaning of existence. The reality of a theatrical performance is itself an illusion, its illusion the equivalent of reality.

The standards that determine the designing of stage scenery are therefore relative, not absolute. The goal of stage-craft is no final perfection of form or purity of style. The business of the stage-designer is not to create a work of art that can be judged as having a life of its own as a more or less beautiful picture, but to bring to life the world pictured by a play. The reality of a theatrical performance is not created either by the realism or the formalism of its script or by its scenic backgrounds. It is established by a tacit conspiracy between a playwright, his actors, and his audience. The designer can discover his rôle in the theatre upon condition that he is willing to connive at an ancient and eternal practice, part exercise of imagination, part imitation of fact, whereby miming and mimicry while a play is enacted become what we believe the truth of life to be and the sham of paint, glue, wood, and canvas conveys what we conceive to be the reality of a world where we adventure as human beings.

CHAPTER III

PLAYERS IN THE PULPIT

I. A CENTURY OF FAIRY-TALES

Recent attempts to save the theatre by assailing realism are so far removed from the actuality of theatrical production in our age—or in any other—that they can rescue themselves only by staging an apocalypse in a conveniently remote future. The tendency to discuss art in terms of its "movements" and to catalogue literary history as a succession of "schools" is a class-room habit abetted by university professors in order to simplify the difficulties of instructing immature minds. An illusion of order is created, as in some of the deliberate distortions of perspective drawing, by establishing an arbitrary horizon and a fictitious vanishing point.

It is of course convenient to summarize the nineteenth century as an age of realism, and point to Ibsen's *Hedda Gabler*, Becque's *Les Corbeaux*, Strindberg's *Miss Julia*, Hauptmann's *The Weavers*, Chekhov's *The Cherry Orchard*, and Gorki's *The Lower Depths*. It is easy to forget that it was also the age of Wagner's *Niebelungen Ring*, Maeterlinck's *Pelléas and Mélisande* and *The Death of Tintagiles*, Andreiev's allegories of *King Hunger* and the *Life of Man*, Rostand's romantic tragedies, *Cyrano de Bergerac* and *L'Aiglon*, D'Annunzio's romantic legends, *Paolo and Francesca* and *The Daughter of Jorio*, which were either the literary sensations of their day or its popular successes, as were Synge's *Well of the Saints* and *Riders to the Sea*, and also the Celtic revival in which Yeats evoked *The Land of Heart's De-*

sire and sent Cathleen ni Houlihan and other legendary figures wandering in the Celtic twilight. Dunsany set marching the stranger *Gods of the Mountain* and portrayed more than one *Golden Doom*. The song that marks the death of the child in Yeats's *The Land of Heart's Desire*,

> *The wind blows out of the gates of the day,*
> *The wind blows over the lonely of heart,*
> *And the lonely of heart is withered away*
> *While the faeries dance in a place apart,*

might serve as appropriately as any dictum of Ibsen or Becque to tag the dramatic writing of the nineteenth century, which continued into the twentieth with a succession of fairy-tales, assuaging the lonely of heart and transporting them to the land of their heart's desire. The vogue of Maeterlinck's *The Blue Bird* and Barrie's *Peter Pan* was world-wide. Hauptmann's fairy-tales, *The Sunken Bell* and *Hannele Enters Heaven,* eclipsed the reputation that a series of naturalistic peasant tragedies had begun. In Scandinavia Strindberg's most popular play is his fairy-tale fantasy *The Dream Play*. Ibsen's reputation rests as securely on his fairy-tale *Peer Gynt* as upon *The Pillars of Society* or *A Doll's House*. His later plays, however realistic in idiom, contain such allegorical figures as a mysterious Rat-Wife, wraiths of white horses that presage death, harps that sound in the air as an architect falls to his death from a roof-tree, and a mystic "marriage feast" consummated in an avalanche on the "Peak of Promise." The stage of the nineteenth century abounds not only in starving peasants, tramps, slum-dwellers, prostitutes, bawdy-house keepers, and town councillors that have the photographic quality of facsimile, of being taken "straight from life," but it is peopled as well by such figures as a nobleman who improvises a ballade in a duel and makes puns in battle, princesses who drop rings into bottomless wells or beat against doors that do not open, princes in exile, lovers in enchanted woods, children who go to Heaven, or go to live with the fairies, or go to live at the bottom of the sea, and a peasant boy who defies hobgoblins and becomes Emperor of Morocco. The tendency is so irrepressible that it continues into the twentieth century. The fairy-tale form becomes a vehicle for projecting ideas that deal with immortality, modern warfare, revolution, and the doom of machine industry. Bernard Shaw crowns his career with a fairy-tale homily, *Back to Methuselah.* Werfel begins his career with a Faustian fairy-tale, *Mirror Man,* and continues it with a fairy-tale allegory, *Goat Song.* The brothers Čapek startle Prague with a fairy-tale melodrama of mechanical men, the Robots, and follow it with a fairy-tale satire of the World War, in which slackers are seen as butterflies, conscripts parade as ants, and war profiteers appear as dung-beetles.

The dramas of the late nineteenth century and of the first decades of the twentieth that can with any certainty be classed as literature are peopled not only with our contemporaries but with gods, saints, prophets, visions and apparitions, fairies, demons and trolls and monsters such as the Boyg or the invisible Beast of *Goat Song.* They have forced modern stage-craft to resort to the tricks of parlour magic and sleight-of-hand in visualizing a prophetess who suddenly expands to gigantic size, anvils split by a sword, mountain caverns that crash, Walkyries galloping through the clouds, dragons breathing smoke, and the snake of the Garden of Eden speaking with a human voice.

For the purpose of a particular piece of propaganda it is easy to write of the depressing dominance of realism in the last century and ignore the fact that its dominance was fiercely resented by both the populace and its police, its vogue established with the greatest difficulty by embattled minorities. Performances of Hauptmann's *The Weavers* and *Before Sunrise* were originally forbidden by the German police in several cities. *Ghosts* was banned by the British censor, *Mrs. Warren's*

Profession was closed by the police of New York City on its opening night in 1905. In 1890 the Parisian censor refused to allow a
performance at the Porte Saint-Martin Theatre, for the general public, of *The Prostitute Eliza,* which Antoine had given to subscribers in
his own theatre. The interdiction was the theme of a lengthy debate
in the Chamber of Deputies, Léon Bourgeois, Minister of Fine Arts
and Public Instruction, defending the government, and Millerand,
future President of France, then deputy for the Seine, making a fiery
plea for the Théâtre Libre. Many of the milestones of the realistic and
naturalistic drama were set in the comparative seclusion of small theatres that evaded police interference by becoming private stock-com-
panies or clubs, as the British censor is evaded by London stage societies
today.

The theatre of the nineteenth century at the same time that it fought
for the right to tell unpleasant sociological and biological truths
afforded innumerable evasions of such truths for any one eager to
forget the tedium, the sordidness, and the brutalities of a machine age.
It nourished the romantic aspirations of dying gallantly in love, in
battle, or at a banquet, and enabled a theatre-goer to live under the sea
with a sunken bell, to consort with the fairies, or to enter Heaven.
Examine the rôles in which popular clamour forced the greatest actors
and actresses of the supposedly realistic, naturalistic nineteenth century
to appear hundreds of times, and you discover that they are predominantly sentimental or romantic: Sarah Bernhardt as L'Aiglon or Marguerite Gautier, Coquelin as Cyrano, Maude Adams as Peter Pan or
as Lady Babbie in *The Little Minister,* Mansfield as Beau Brummell
or the Baron Chevrial of *A Parisian Romance,* Henry Irving as Ma-
thias in *The Bells,* Jefferson as Rip Van Winkle. The greatest popular
successes of the American theatre had the same fairy-tale unreality:
Ben Hur, The Count of Monte Cristo, and also *The Old Homestead*
and *Uncle Tom's Cabin,* which cannot be classified as realistic ac-

counts of American life on Northern farms or Southern plantations.

In this respect the nineteenth century is not different from any other. The bulk of its dramatic output has very little connection with its literary novelties, or with the qualities of its occasional masterpieces that in retrospect we thread together as so many pearls wherewith to deck the throat of Thalia. If the reader doubts this, let him try to plough through the texts of plays by the most important of Shakespeare's contemporaries that were also popular when Shakespeare's were first performed: *Old Fortunatus, Satiromastix, Alphonsus, Friar Bacon and Friar Bungay, The Golden Age, The Blind Beggar of Alexandria, If It Be Not Good the Devil Is in It, The Massacre at Paris, David and Bethsabe;* or those that were performed in the Theatre of Molière by Molière's own company: *Scévole, Artaxerce, La Mort de Sénèque, Pylade et Oreste, Zénobie, Eurymédon* (or *The Illustrious Pirate*), *Le Martyr de Saint Genest* (or *The Illustrious Comedian*).

In the main the theatre of the last century provided what the bulk of any theatre-going populace in any century demands: a flight from the frustrations of daily life. Even our so-called intellectuals do not always go to the theatre to discover the springs of behaviour hidden from themselves in their own lives. More than half the time, with the vast majority of audiences, they go to a play to magnify their egos in the person of a living protagonist—women to find the completely happy love-affair or to sin with impunity in an unhappy one; men to be the irresistible lover, the great adventurer, the conquering hero, in one guise or another. This vicarious process of transference provides the easiest satisfaction to be found in theatre-going: we escape from our own lives and for a few hours are able to believe in a simplified picture of life where we find our beloved transparently pure, beautiful, and faithful unto death, perform great deeds, and so evade a world where we rarely find our true mate, seldom achieve any of our ambitions, and never face rivals so obviously wicked that they can be speed-ily brought to justice and conveniently swept out of our way.

We may identify ourselves, in the realistic theatre, with lives and deeds that reflect our childish wishes and its immature day-dreams. A play written in the most realistic idiom may nevertheless be a flight from any of the recognized realities of life. A picture of existence es-sentially false can be created by imitating colloquial speech quite as easily as by rhymed couplets, iambic pentameters, or dithyrambic choruses. The triumph of realism as a literary experiment in the nine-teenth century neither inhibited its playwrights nor depressed its audi-ences. Nor did it leave them by way of reaction eager for poetic speech, symbolic dance-dramas, or visionary pantomimes. After the literary theatres of the advance-guard had created a vogue for realism the pop-ular theatres appropriated its tricks for their own purposes. The fact that a heroine at the kitchen sink remarks, "Gawd, ain't I fed up! This place is lousy. I wanna be rich," does not prevent the play from being the thousand and first retelling of the tale of Cinderella. A hero is often no more than a substitute for Dick Whittington, even though he cries, "What the hell! I'm gonna make good."

What an audience most often demands is not enlargement or clarifi-cation of its experiences but their simplification. The romantic or melodramatic love-story is one of many simpler, gayer, fairy-tale pic-tures of life as it cannot be lived, which the theatre perennially sup-plies. These in turn produce false sentiment, bombast, or hokum (as we call it today), so that the term "theatrical" applied to anything out-side the theatre is usually synonymous with a degree of empty exag-geration and sham. The vaguer and more inarticulate our sense of the inadequacy of our lives, the cruder will be the play that satisfies us. The crudest melodrama is in essence a kind of poetry that simplifies "the sorry scheme of things entire" and then attempts to "re-mould it nearer to the heart's desire": vice is punished, virtue rewarded, and the curtain invariably falls upon "poetic justice" dispensed by a forgiving father, a lover returned in the nick of time, or the discovery of a missing will. Because coal-heavers and washerwomen need such reassurance they patronized *Bertha the Sewing-Machine Girl* rather than *The Lower Depths*. But well-fed intellectuals who applaud Gorki's portrayal of human dregs are not immune upon other occasions to a craving to see some picture of life in the theatre that is more satisfying than their own immediate experience has been. The process of simplifying and prettifying life continues through a rising scale of sophistication and penetrates to the play of "high society" and the more cynical comedy of manners. It is rarely that the most sophisticated play does not provide a large number of its sophisticated auditors with scenes where they can happily identify themselves with brilliant conversation that they cannot call forth at their own dinner-parties, or where, as the "smart" host and hostess, they meet the titled or distinguished guests whom they do not encounter on week-end visits in the suburbs. We feed our vanity in the theatre even when we throw our egos a scrap of wisdom.

No one of us is entirely primitive or completely sophisticated; we are emotionally stratified so that we find satisfaction in many plays at more than one level. We can appreciate the philosophic nihilism of Andreiev's *He Who Gets Slapped* and at the same time enjoy the Cinderella story impersonated once again by the love of the equestrienne Consuela for the bareback rider Benzano. We may also be lured by the proverbial glamour of the circus, reviving boyhood memories of the days when, following the circus-parade, we dreamed of running away and becoming a lion-tamer or a bareback rider ourselves. During the New York run of Andreiev's play hardened intellectuals could be seen sniffling shamefacedly or weeping openly at Consuela's death, although it is medically no more soundly motivated and dramatically no less preposterous than the death of Little Eva.

73

The vicarious satisfaction to be found in theatre-going is more often emotional than it is intellectual. To most of us our feelings are more immediate than our ideas. Our quickest memories are of moments of intense emotion rather than of moments when the goal of our desires was more clearly realized or the purpose of our existence more intelligibly comprehended. We are all, to a greater or less degree, haunted by a sense of the inadequacy of our lives. That sense is, however, due in the main not to a conviction that we failed to understand the meaning of love, death, success or failure at the crises of our individual careers, but to our recollection that at moments which shaped or shattered us as human beings we were almost ludicrously inarticulate. Emotions filled us that were of vast import. We acted upon them but we could not express them in words. What sounded from our seething plexus most often resembled the whine of a pricked balloon. The climaxes of our lives, as we look back at them, sound like anticlimaxes. We were the true lover; we felt the force that moves the sun and stars. When the lady yielded we may have begun a happy marriage or a successful love-affair. But to an eavesdropper we would, in all likelihood, have seemed a stammering, comic bumpkin. At a bier we resented the presence of a hired orator, clergyman, priest, or rabbi, who filled a dead mouth with the rotund phrases of ritual that failed to express a vanished personality. But we know that we shall probably die ignobly without an appropriate word on our lips, blubbering or frothing feebly in a sick-bed. Hence the undying popularity of death scenes in the theatre when, in the person of hero or heroine, we expire eloquently in bed or nobly on a field of battle, vindicate our ego to the last breath, and pronounce our own valedictory in the process. Hence also the perennial popularity of love scenes, where love is elaborately articulate under moonlit balconies fringed with roses or honeysuckle, and speaks to the accompaniment of nightingales and off-stage music.

74

Even when we are comforted by a sense of having lived successfully we are disquieted by the memory of having acted a leading part badly. Our lives, as Browning put it, hang patchy and scrappy. But their ineffectiveness is not irremediable. In the theatre we always have another chance. In the actor's person we vindicate ourselves. We retrieve not only what we have said badly but also what we have not dared to say. Our emotional release is therefore punctuated not only with tears but with laughter, as when through the mouth of Bluntschli we call a woman's bluff. I shall not easily forget the roar of satisfaction that rose from an audience, predominantly masculine, in the Hudson Theatre one September evening in 1905, when Tanner, reversing the usual technique of courtship, told Ann that she was the pursuer, he the pursued, the marked-down and the hunted. We can identify ourselves as well with emotions that we have no conscious desire to experience, provided an actor can make their expression sufficiently intense, thus giving us a pleasurable expansion of our personality. We no longer fabricate myths wherein a hero saves us single-handed from catastrophe; we worship instead the magnetic "power of personality," to the point of patronizing quacks who pretend to be able to cultivate it in any one, and we believe it can open all doors, triumph over any obstacle. Much of our primitive tendency to create heroes and worship them is diverted to the theatre; it centres there less on the type of hero impersonated by the actor than upon the leading actors themselves. They become idols, "matinée idols," and embody every one's private dream of dominating his or her particular world as the leading lady and the leading man dominate not only the other characters in the play but also the audience.

2. THE HUMAN CORNER-STONE

Our readiest means of identification in the theatre is with the player rather than with the content of the play. Prophets of the new stage-craft may aver that in the near future manipulations of stage scenery will replace both author and actor. But the actor has already more than once successfully dispensed with both script and set. A limited but highly effective theatre can be made by the actor alone. Yvette Guilbert is the archetype of the great actor entirely divorced from the play. She succeeded in turning songs and ballads into miniature dramas. Ruth Draper's monologues, without recourse to grease-paint and with nothing more to aid her than a chair or a shawl, project the quintessence of both comedy and tragedy. Such vaudeville teams as Clayton and Durante repeat the success of the *commedia dell' arte* that improvised its dialogue and festooned its antics about a rigid set of stage-directions. Playwrighting in another Puritan upheaval might be suppressed by edict and every playhouse demolished. The actor as impersonator could still continue to provide, single-handed, much of the satisfaction that the current theatre gives.

Every gifted actor is aware of this. The "born actor" usually sees a play as nothing more than a vehicle providing opportunities for emotional display. A play to him is primarily a rôle, a succession of big scenes that he can "put over" the footlights. A script is no more than a sketch to be filled in, a scaffolding that serves as a spring-board. A great actor is often able to give to scenes, superficial as characterization, values in performance that can move us profoundly. The actor establishes his importance most easily at the expense of the playwright and very readily becomes an accomplice to the process of degrading his material. He has done this in every epoch. Shakespeare, well aware of the practice, warns his clowns through the mouth of Hamlet "to speak no more than is set down for them" and berates them as villainous for improvising gags that keep the audience laughing while some "necessary question" of the play is being considered. But once dead and immortal, he could not prevent his scripts from being garbled, chopped, and revised in the versions of Cibber and others for the better part of two centuries to make an actor's holiday for Garrick, Kean, Wilkes, or Booth. In the English-speaking world that projects memorials to the "greatest dramatist of all time" it is still a rare occasion when any one of his plays can be seen in performance integrally as he wrote it. We still go less often to hear Shakespeare in the theatre than to hear a performance of Macbeth or Hamlet; we wait for the famous soliloquies as we do for well-known arias at the opera.

This impulse to subordinate the play to the performer is an ancient one. As early as the fourth century B.C. in Greece it became necessary to pass a law to prevent actors from tampering with the texts of classic tragedies in their desire "to introduce what they considered improvements." Lycurgus enacted "that a public copy should be made of the works of Aeschylus, Sophocles, and Euripides, and deposited in the state archives; and that the actors, in their performances, should not be allowed to deviate from the text of the copy." We are less inclined to legislate against the practice than to acquiesce in it. Bernard Shaw is probably the only living dramatist whose contract, echoing the marriage service, reads that the manager must not "allow the performers to do anything that would have the effect of misrepresenting the author's meaning either for better or worse."

Critics often find that an actor's performance more than compensates for an inadequate production or a poor play. Julius Bab, a German critic of reputation, remarks: "When Adalbert Adamowsky appeared on the stage, Shakespeare was there. The supers might racket, every kind of scenic blunder be allowed by the management—suddenly Shakespeare was there." Similar confessions can be culled at random from American critics. Heywood Broun, writing of a play he acknowledged to be trivial, said: "The actress filled the stage with a great gust of passionate tenderness. She threw open a window and said, See my heart and soul. We did." Robert Benchley, reviewing Bernstein's *Mélo,* remarks: "Of course, without Edna Best I don't know just what *Mélo* would have been like. Miss Best . . . gives a performance which takes your heart out, tears it into small pieces, and puts it back all wrong. Her casual, one-handed playing as she stands by the piano in an exquisite scene . . . her agonized realization that she is about to be caught in attempted murder . . . and the pitiful grace with which she executes her little somersaults which end in the river, these and many other moments of artistry on Miss Best's part help immeasurably to make memorable the two acts of *Mélo* in which she appears." John Mason Brown admits: "To almost every one Miss Cornell seems to be the foremost of our younger actresses. . . . Nor is it anything but natural that hers should be referred to, not merely as the most promising among those talents that are now in their full prime, but that she should also be singled out as the actress who comes nearest to being blessed with the qualities of which greatness is made." Nevertheless on the next page Mr. Brown must also admit that Katharine Cornell has achieved this eminence by appearing in "such a trashy bit of clap-trap as *Dishonored Lady*," and that after *The Letter* and *The Green Hat* "it has begun to seem as if she had a preference for the adventuresses, the murderesses and the constant nymphomaniacs who have strayed through these piffling scripts."

Miss Cornell of course did nothing more than continue the great and grand tradition of Bernhardt and Duse, Mansfield, Irving, and Joseph Jefferson, who sustained their greatness upon such dramatic trash as *La Sorcière, Fédora, A Parisian Romance, The Lyons Mail,* and *Rip Van Winkle,* and found them quite as satisfactory as *Ghosts, Hamlet, Phèdre, The Rivals,* or *The Devil's Disciple.* The commercial theatre today is very largely a survival of the dominant non-realistic theatre of the nineteenth century that inflated the art of acting, avoided plays that dramatized significant themes, exploited instead stereotyped notions of vice and virtue readily accepted by audiences, established the cult of the "star actor" who could give these stereotypes factitious

life, and left a record of an extraordinary number of great performances in an extraordinary number of unimportant plays.

The only challenge to this easy exploitation of an audience's emotions was made by the realistic theatre of the nineteenth century, which
defied the current codes of honour and duty and the accepted conceptions of sin and salvation. It stressed the importance of relevant theme
and subordinated the actor as a vehicle for emotional display to the
ideas he expressed or embodied. It became and still is the dominant
theatre of today not because of the final importance of a realistic technique of playwrighting or stage setting but because its ideas nourished
the aspirations of men and women seeking to understand their place
as individuals in a new social and economic order. As usually happens
with artistic experiments, the superficial novelties of realism were
seized upon by both its detractors and its apologists—the imitation of
colloquial conversation, the literal reproduction of a local bar-room,
butcher's shop, or bawdy-house. Realism as a method is not important
because it utilizes current idiom or reproduces our habitual surroundings. Every form of art has done this incidentally, even when the total
effect of its style can be catalogued as decorative and formal. A record
of modes and manners down to the niceties of dressmaking and the
details of household furniture can be compiled from Persian and Indian miniatures, the scrolls of Chinese painting in the Sung and Ming
dynasties, Japanese colour-prints, Egyptian bas-reliefs. Editor's foot-
notes to Euripides as well as to Aristophanes, to Shakespeare no less
than to Molière, remind us how directly they allude to current events
—the advent of a comet, a military victory, the success of a rival company, the particular discussions then raging in drawing-rooms or the
marketplace. Many classic lines when first uttered had the impact of
newspaper head-lines. Few classics are without critical comment on
the life of their day. The more deliberate attempts to achieve classic
nobility and grandeur in all of Voltaire's and Dryden's tragedies, and

in many of Corneille's and Racine's, result in resounding emptiness. Dramas planned to have universal meaning rarely have any that survives the generation for which they were written. Plays written to celebrate a local legend or a parochial event often acquire a universal meaning as succeeding generations rediscover themselves in their protagonists. The royal road well ballasted with the rock of ages as a rule leads the playwright to horizons already obvious. A dominating point of view in the theatre that embraces the world is more often reached by a local trail that begins half hidden in a thicket, unmarked by any signpost.

Reliance upon realism as a technique is largely based upon this perception. The playwrights of the nineteenth century who had no convictions as to the rôle of the individual in modern society embraced the obvious artifices of traditional poetry. The realistic playwrights, who had ideas as to the scope of human effort in the world today, were convinced that the road to Heaven or Hell began in the back parlour or back of the kitchen stove and they succeeded in restoring to the stage the force of tragic poetry. The nearest approach to the emotions of Oedipus, Electra, Iphigenia, and Antigone is to be found not in the tirades of Sardou's tragedy-queens nor in the burnished words of Yeats's shadowy gods, but in the madness of Strindberg's Father, the agonies of Mrs. Alving and Nina Leeds, the ecstatic faith of Hilda Wangel, or the prophecies of the Lady Mayoress, wife of a coal-dealer, at the wedding-breakfast of a bishop's daughter. The photographic details of realism were often part of a deliberate effort to make us recognize contemporary Lears and Medeas. Such arch-realists as Hauptmann, Strindberg, Ibsen, and Shaw were poets in wolf's clothing and very naturally gravitated to constructing fables and allegories that nevertheless retained the rhythm of everyday speech. Poetry on the stage resides in the effective enunciation of wisdom no less than in verbal cadence. The happy ending that we seek continually in the theatre is a reconciliation to our fate as human beings. We do not enjoy tragedy because we weep; we weep because the idea of fate embodied by Hamlet or by Hecuba seems binding on us. We revel in comedy not because we laugh; we laugh because for a moment we are made wiser than the fools who parade their folly before us.

It has been said that there are only thirty-six dramatic plots: the story of any play must be a variation of one or another. It might be said that all plays which are not a flight from the realities of human experience deal with the tragic and comic variants of a dual theme: the nature of good and evil, the meaning of wisdom and folly. The mechanics of action, the habitual gestures of living—eating, drinking, making love, or committing murder—are monotonously alike from one age to another. The movements of the human body have no lure of novelty except in an acrobat. If the theatre depended entirely upon gesture, pantomime, and facial display, acting would be no more than a kind of dance. Human activity is turned into drama by the different goals that beckon, the different gods who preside. In any period when the theatre has vitality, action is presented as affording a clue to the discovery of our place in nature and in society, our relation to a deity or to our own conscience.

Distinctions between "inner actuality rather than outer" in the theatre are the sheerest casuistry. The inner actuality of a play, that is, its truth, is not inherent only in the form of the play itself or in the way it is staged, but is engendered by contact with the aspirations of an audience. In the nineties a group of socialist wage-earners—printers, plumbers, carpenters, and seamstresses—founded the Volksbühne (People's Theatre) of Berlin by subsidizing performances of Anzengruber, Zola, Strindberg, Hauptmann, and Ibsen, as part of their struggle for economic and political liberation. A variety of realistic and naturalistic plays immediately seemed immensely important. The Silesian dialect of Hauptmann's peasant weavers became prophetic, not because their words were consciously socialist propaganda, but because the disinterested observations of an artist, like the testimony of a sinner, confirmed the need for a particular form of salvation and fortified a belief that the inner actuality of modern life was what Marxian doctrine conceived it to be. Because a section of the German working-class needed such confirmation for their belief in a specific doctrine of working-class revolution, naturalistic playwrighting acquired the traditional function which dramatic poetry possessed when Greek playwrights attempted to reconcile men to the fate meted out by Olympus. Tested by other aspirations and other needs, the same cycle of plays can become nothing more than vivid reporting of local murders, suicides, and riots.

Most of the time we go to the play as a means of escape from ourselves. But for part of the time we go to the theatre to discover whatever wisdom can be gleaned from the spectacle of human suffering. We bring to a play a deep-seated hunger for healing wisdom. The most fundamental satisfaction that we can find in the theatre springs from the same source as our craving for the solace of theatrical stereotypes: a sense of the inadequacy of our individual lives. We are impelled to transcend our particular limitations and to share experiences more profound than any we have been able to live through, which, as soon as they are impersonated before our eyes, can have the immediacy and validity of our own. Our more lasting dissatisfaction with ourselves is assuaged not only by a recognition that we are, for the most part, emotionally inarticulate, but by a realization that our loves and hates, our joys as well as our sorrows, have been superficial if not trivial. The identification with the actor that becomes a flight from reality is superseded by an identification with the beliefs and ideas which he expresses or implies, so that we dominate some typical experience not merely by sharing it but also by understanding it as never before. Our emotional satisfaction as spectators is then found not in a display of emotion but in the emotions that arise in us as we gain a fresh insight into ourselves.

3. THE BREACH

Before we can attain even that momentary insight we may have to spend a bad quarter of an hour renouncing every cherished belief, every hope that habitually sustains us. We are, sooner or later, driven to seek tormenting self-realization in the theatre, and yet resistance to that form of painful experience is universal. It was palliated on the Greek stage by removing the hero to a mythical past or making him historically remote. If we are to hear sad stories in the theatre we prefer that they be of the death of bygone kings. High-school pupils are invariably urged to attend a revival of *Oedipus.* But a play such as *Vatermord,* dealing with a contemporary parricide in which a boy of high-school age murders his father, caused a riot of protest in Berlin at its first performance a few years ago. When faced with Oswald's dementia, audiences that had accepted the madness of Orestes called for the police. Nothing dignifies depravity so speedily as the distance of a remote past, or lends the same enchantment to the bleakest tragedy. Any degree of sin on the stage, any depth of human suffering, is readily acceptable until it concerns persons too recognizably like ourselves. The more nearly the stage represents our familiar surroundings, the more fiercely we resent any figure on it that destroys our illusions or our "ideals" and arouses terror of a fate that may possibly be our own.

The creative playwright in the past has often had to overcome the resistance of his audience. But he has never had to challenge his auditors as persistently and as deliberately as he must today. The mandate to the playwright in the past has been from priests and lawgivers, prescribing certain subject-matter and the recognition of an accepted code of conduct. But the audience of our theatre today is no longer a homogeneous body of freemen assembling twice a year to revere a legendary past. Neither are we, as playgoers, a body of peasants and burghers united by a dominant and undisputed religious faith which we can celebrate by re-enacting the creation of the world and the death of a Saviour. No city-state, church militant, or feudal court can give prestige and glamour to a single code of honour or to a divinely ordained structure of society to which even groundlings can adhere. Neither playwright nor scene-designer can achieve a formula of beauty, because life can no longer be seen as a fixed or codified pattern of behaviour. The designer can achieve no symbols that have universal meaning, because the playwright can find no symbols for human values that are capable of being universally accepted. Society is no longer in agreement as to the meaning of life or the nature of human destiny. The actor no longer dominates the stage, because man is no longer seen as the measure of all things and the centre of his universe. There can be no single picture of the world inside the theatre because there is none outside its walls.

To say that the actor will be freed by performing in a circus-ring or under a chandelier or against blackness in a solitary spot-light expresses nothing more than our desire for an ideal unity between the player and his audience that existed to a greater degree in the past and has become increasingly difficult to achieve in the present. Our incessant theorizing about the art of the theatre, our attempt to decree a single scenic or literary form for modern drama, are nothing more than a roundabout recognition of the one thing that sunders our modern theatre from every other: the breach, growing daily more inevitable, between the imagination of the playwright and the mind of his audience.

The modern theatre's theologians revert to the naïve expedients that have always characterized American evangelists. It is always easier to go to Heaven than to face the bewildering alternatives of contemporary life. To determine the final and ultimate art of the theatre is but another way of distributing ascension-robes of a uniform pattern. To revive the Greek mask or the classic amphitheatre indicates nothing more than our temporary uncertainty as to where the goal of our own drama lies. We revert to the prestige of a golden past as any adolescent reverts to some transparent substitute for home and mother when he is momentarily baffled by the problem of finding his place in the world about him.

If the modern mind is the child of the Renaissance, classical antiquity is its wet-nurse. The inner insecurity of the American pioneer has expressed itself before by periodic classic revivals: the agricultural pioneer in the Doric columns of his dwellings, the Ionic capitals and fretwork of his churches and meeting-houses; the industrial pioneer in the Corinthian ornament and the Roman colonnades which disguised his banks and railway stations. Our theatrical pioneers repeat the same tendency. The occasional Greek theatres they have built will, fifty years hence, be as picturesque but as irrelevant as farmhouses of the classic revival of 1800 are today in the fields of New England or on the estuaries of Maryland. We stage plays today in theatres constructed upon classic models. It is no more and no less ludicrous than buying a ticket for Trenton at the New York ticket-office of the Pennsylvania Station, which is copied from the Baths of Caracalla.

Reverting to any classic past is, however, becoming daily more difficult, because we are dominated not by one past but by every past that the world has ever known. The playwright and his audience are alike the victims of the eclecticism of modern culture, which has become the wise man's burden. For more than three centuries every form of knowledge has been cultivated in universities and for a century has been disseminated by all the agencies of popular education. The more modern we become, the more irretrievably we are influenced by the remotest reaches of antiquity. Anthropologists and archaeologists continue to unearth the past, in order to feed our minds, as relentlessly as industrial engineers explore the six continents and the seven seas for new materials with which to house and feed our bodies. Faced with this towering accumulation of knowledge, we have as a public decreed that no part of it can be irrelevant. We have endowed without stint three storehouses which serve as our modern temples—the university, the public library, and the art museum. But because we can learn so much more than we are able to assimilate, the purpose of education is patterned on electrical engineering: we wire our minds so that they can be illuminated at the turn of a switch. We consider ourselves liberated because knowledge of truth and beauty is no longer limited to the pedestrian progress of pilgrims, apprentices, and disciples. Our minds become the counterpart of the automobile; we can take the wheel and turn them anywhere, using as a convenient road-map any of the increasingly popular outlines of history, art, science, and philosophy.

That portion of the public known as cultured and educated, excited by Woolley's latest excavations at Ur, Carter's discovery of the spoils of Tutankhamen's tomb, or the reconstruction of Maya ruins at Chichen-Itzá, but knowing no more of them than can be gleaned from the Sunday supplement of the New York *Times* or from the *Illustrated London News,* is lured to the theatre in order to learn more of the past than it has succeeded in retaining from college and high-school text-books. We find our cultured audiences witnessing Shaw's *Saint Joan* and *Caesar and Cleopatra,* O'Neill's *Marco Millions* and *The Fountain* (Ponce de León), Sherwood's Hannibal on the *Road to Rome,* Werfel's *Maximilian and Juarez,* Masefield's *Pompey the Great,* Drinkwater's *Abraham Lincoln.* Within one season the play-readers of the Theatre Guild received scripts that staged John Brown's raid on Harpers Ferry, the life of Charles Lamb, three plays depicting the life of Rasputin, two recounting the life of Nicholas II of Russia from his ascension to the revolution of 1917, another retelling the Dreyfus case where Zola and Anatole France appear, and a chronicle of the outbreak of the World War in 1914 in which Von Bethmann-Hollweg, Jaurès, Von Berchtold, and Lord Grey are used to reanimate the exchange of diplomatic notes in unread White, Yellow, and Blue Books.

The same public looks to the playwright rather than to the clergyman or the college professor to explain the nature of constitutional monarchies, the permanence of marriage, the possibility of immortality, the problems of race prejudice among Jews and gentiles, Negroes and whites. The sensations and scandals of our daily press are promptly re-edited for the theatre in topical plays that present an execution in the electric chair or prison riots in order to inveigh against the death-penalty, re-enact murders in order to ridicule the gullibility of our courts and daily press, or lampoon our police for their alliance with the political bosses who run the bootlegging gangs and direct the rackets of our underworld. The problem play from which we once recoiled has become a current form of popular entertainment. An increasing proportion of the successes of every New York season point a moral, and there seems to be no limit to our eagerness to hear the sexual impulses of the gin-drinking younger generation discussed, deplored, defended, or reproved on the stage.

The essential eclecticism of our culture forces us to be as cosmopolitan in the theatre as we are elsewhere. Play-producing is as international as trade. Every capital imports foreign successes as regularly as it imports Paris models for its gowns, London patterns for its overcoats, or bananas, dates, and alligator pears to vary its diet. Budapest felt impelled to translate and produce *Broadway* and *Burlesque,* although their subject-matter was so local that it could hardly be understood. New York, London, and Berlin reverse the process every season. Our commercial theatre reflects the eclecticism of our daily habits. Our art theatres reflect the eclecticism of our education and revive not only

Aristophanes but the Japanese *Bushido,* the mediaeval *Everyman,* or the East Indian *Little Clay Cart,* which appeal to audiences educated to believe in the necessity of appreciating the masterpieces of every other civilization as well as those of their own. At times our art theatres seem to have become the substitute for world cruises. We press the playwright into the service of helping us travel everywhere in past, present, and future time, see everything, know everything, understand everything. He is encouraged to consider every age his quarry, every manner his prerogative, every myth a challenge to reinterpretation, every major incident of history a tale to be told again.

As a result, every force that arouses our intellectual curiosity and impels us to satisfy it in the theatre, or that stimulates our desire to extend the realm of our experience, widens the breach between the creative playwright and his audience. For precisely to the degree that he is creative and has an original mind, he is led to challenge accepted codes of morals, sexual taboos, and vested religious creeds. Such challenges are the exception rather than the rule in the Greek trilogies, the mediaeval mysteries and moralities, or the English and Continental drama from Shakespeare through the eighteenth century. But the single characteristic common to almost every play of the nineteenth century that we now classify as modern is the tendency to attack the sacrosanct traditions of its generation, its stereotyped notions of heroism, patriotism, honour, love, and duty—in general, its accepted concepts of right and wrong. How little this tendency has to do with realism or the shape of the proscenium arch is proved by the fact that it persists in such poetic fantasies as *Lazarus Laughed* and *Paul Among the Jews.* O'Neill revives Lazarus in order to proclaim a conception of immortality that has no connection with Christian doctrine; Werfel retells the tale of the fall of the Temple and contradicts every gentile tradition as to what we can learn by harking to the preaching of Paul, every Jewish tradition as to the lessons that could be gathered at the feet of Gamaliel. Shaw seemed to have modernized the chronicle-play in *Caesar and Cleopatra* because the greatest Roman conqueror talked as colloquially as a modern prime minister being interviewed, and Cleopatra was as pert as any débutante. In reality the play was modern because Shaw, in retelling an exploit of Julius Caesar, succeeded in expressing a modern scepticism as to the value of conquests and the traditional methods of imperialism, making Caesar a great man according to our conception and not Rome's of what a wise conqueror and statesman should be. *Arms and the Man* seems modern still because it holds up to ridicule a gullible major who took the heroics of war at their face value. Although he charged gallantly into the jaws of death in the best Tennysonian manner, he is worsted, to our delight, by a cynical and sceptical mercenary who sees through the technique of modern warfare, bolts at the first sign of defeat, and carries chocolates instead of cartridges. Our stage heroes are rarely heroes in the accepted sense. They are as often as not devil's disciples. Many of our villains are patterned on uncompromising idealists like Werle, who insists on telling the whole truth and driving a child to suicide, or Mrs. Alving, so faithful to her marriage vows that she condemns her son to syphilitic insanity.

As a public we return to the playhouse to be taught and if possible to be converted. At heart we long for the wisdom that our thin and sporadic education has not given us, the nourishment that our heterogeneous culture fails to provide. We had hoped to germinate the seeds of knowledge in the hothouses of universities and then disseminate the fruit through the gardens of popular education as a nurseryman starts plants under glass, pricks them out, and hardens them off to be grown everywhere. The seeds proved to be serpents' eggs. We are ravaged today by a hydra that worships every past, sets up a hundred conflicting tests of human experience, and prophesies every conceivable future. We exist in a state of "unrest" described by our novelists; we lack the guidance of any acknowledged authority, a fact continually deplored by parents, professors, and preachers. We live in the absence of accepted standards of conduct, a condition persistently analyzed by our moralists and summarized by such phrases as "deep dissolution," "the loss of certainty," "the break-down of authority," in Walter Lippmann's plea for a new and more modern religion. The same public that buys fourteen printings of his *Preface to Morals* turns in increasing numbers to the theatre not only to evade life but also to face its problems and to understand them with a greater clarity than the traditional emotions of pity and terror can give. Our audiences are more and more composed of people for whom, although they may not always admit it to themselves, the excitement of drama has come to be the revelation of the meaning of good and evil in the world today, the scope of human destiny that is not revealed to them elsewhere. Because we can no longer accept truth revealed by a priest or a king from the seats of the mighty we go, more often than ever before, to hear it in the seats of a theatre spoken from the mouth of a mime.

4. THE BRIDGE

The modern theatre stages not one world but a hundred, no one of which is the accepted world of its audience. The art of the theatre has therefore become primarily the problem of interpreting ideas new and alien to a majority of cultured, educated, and generally enlightened spectators. The actor has not lost his individual importance because he has been buried under scenic decoration or shoved into a peep-hole. He cannot add a cubit to his stature by stepping out in front of the proscenium. The actor has ceased to dominate the modern theatre because he has been dominated by its dramatic material. The implications of modern plays demand more for their successful interpretation than histrionic ability, even of the highest order, can supply. Single-handed the actor cannot project wholly by his own person a world that so often differs from the world accepted by his auditors. Mansfield, after impersonating Dick Dudgeon, confessed in a letter to Shaw that he was beaten by the problem of Marchbanks in rehearsal. And although offered *Caesar and Cleopatra* he refused to attempt the part of Caesar. There was of course nothing in the rôle itself that exceeded Mansfield's technical ability as an actor. He was bewildered by the play and its ideas, which he could not conceive clearly enough to impersonate successfully.

Like Mansfield, the actor has been beaten and bewildered by the material of modern drama. For that reason the epoch of the actor-manager, the star, the soloist in the theatre, has passed. The dominant mime was superseded in every country in Europe by the dominant director: Antoine, Reinhardt, Jessner, Fehling, Granville-Barker, Copeau, Stanislavsky, Tairov, Meyerhold. The actor today is dependent on the director and dominated by him. The modern play is not only acted—it is produced. The way it is acted is determined by the mind of a director for whom the scenic designer, whether painter or architect, is almost as essential as the actor himself in interpreting dramatic material and arousing the emotions of an audience. Stage scenery has not acquired new importance because novel ways of building, painting, and lighting a setting have been discovered. Settings have acquired a new value because they can aid in bridging the gap between the mind of a playwright and that of his audience. The revival of scenic design as an important factor in the art of the theatre coincides exactly with the emergence of the director as a commanding and necessary figure on the modern stage.

It is these directors who realized the need of changing the rôle of scenery from that of a static and perfunctory background to that of a dynamic element in projecting a play. The record of their productions is the history of modern scenery in all its phases. But to compare pictures of this half-century of renovated stage settings and discuss them in pictorial terms, as though they were pictures in frames, is to miss the essential quality that made them a new art. For it is only as a factor in impinging the imagination of a playwright upon a particular audience under particular social and political conditions that modern stage settings, even as a craft, have any new meaning. It is only as part of an event that they contribute new life to the theatre.

To Stanislavsky and Dantchenko the method of meticulous realism had all the authority of law and all the finality of a true art of the theatre. In staging *The Blue Bird* they proved themselves masters of fantastic decoration and every trick of illusion; at one moment two players turned into golden bubbles that danced in darkness. But realism became their method primarily because Chekhov was the only important playwright that the Moscow Art Theatre discovered. The success of that troupe was based very largely upon Chekhov's career as a playwright, so much so that a sea-gull became the emblem of the Art Theatre. Stanislavsky felt very rightly that in Chekhov he had found a profound intuition into Russian character and the typical dreams and dilemmas that confronted the Russian soul. But to Russian audiences Chekhov's insight was at first neither plausible nor convincing. At the outset they refused to accept these helpless intellectuals as either significant or typical, just as they could not accept their elliptical and casual colloquies, that seemingly led nowhere, as having any dramatic force whatsoever. The whole effort of the Moscow Art Theatre was to evolve a method of acting that made these ineffective gentlefolk the accepted symbols of their time, until every play said in effect: "This is you, this is really Russia. We are nothing more than this. At our best we do nothing more than this." And the plausible solidity and equally plausible detail of realistic background, of costume and make-up, were only part of the effort of two producers to make Chekhov's characters and his themes a part of the recognizable and unmistakable texture of Russian life.

After the revolution of 1917, when these politically impotent intellectuals were wiped out as a class and replaced by a militant and dominant proletariat, the realism of Stanislavsky immediately seemed "classic" and old-fashioned. The Moscow Art Theatre today is the First Academic Theatre. A non-realistic formula of stage setting, of constructivist skeletons, in which the industrial and mechanical structure of the world is symbolized, seems a significant form and the final type of scenery to a populace eager to graft the dictatorship of the factory worker on a nation of peasants dominated by statesmen who conceive a political Utopia in terms of industrial efficiency. Precisely because this is the vision to which the imagination of present-day Russia responds, constructivism has become appropriate even for reviving French operettas of the Second Empire such as *Giroflé-Girofla,* in which singers swing from trapezes and chorus-men turn handsprings on trestles like acrobats. *Lysistrata* is made hilarious by grotesque mobs that chase each other over and under a skeleton Acropolis. *Carmen* is rewritten so that it can be sung by a people's chorus.

Outside of Russia, where collectivism is not a dominant creed, constructivism has been imported and accepted as an art form. Nevertheless, despite constant critical acclaim, it has failed to become an appropriate setting for accepted masterpieces. And the playwrights who hail it as a great liberation and write scenes that can be interpreted only on trestles, chutes, and elevator-shafts, invariably write empty and pretentious allegories. Where collectivism is not a faith outside the theatre, constructivism within it very quickly degenerates into an occasional stunt.

Reinhardt's career at first glance seems the inevitable triumph of one form of theatre art over another. In reality, it is a record of a director's triumphs over successive types of audiences. When Hauptmann's *The Weavers, Rose Bernd,* and *Fuhrmann Henschel* were a revelation to Germans of their national character, Reinhardt very rightly exploited every naturalistic device to give them added force and plausibility. When Tolstoi's peasants seemed the creations of an equally important vision, the peasant yard in *The Power of Darkness* was complete to the last shed and the stage floor was littered with straw. The appetite of a rigorously educated German bourgeoisie for the classics was sustained with period backgrounds of convincing completeness for Schiller and Goethe. Shakespeare's poetry, dulled in translation, was heightened with the all too solid pictures of which the revolving stage was capable, rotated with such precision that the entire text could nevertheless be given in three hours.

When the growing prestige of democratic consciousness asserted itself in opposition to the waning prestige of Kaiserdom, the tragedy of *Oedipus* was performed with a chorus enlarged to a mob in whose gestures the horror of his fate could be magnified. After the collapse of the monarchy *Danton's Death* was expanded into a circus-arena, "The Theatre of the Five Thousand," and the sans-culottes howled and swirled among the audience. When the economic consequences of the peace wiped out the German bourgeoisie as an effective audience and made a repertory of the classics financially precarious, Reinhardt rediscovered the theatrical methods and manners of the eighteenth century. His productions became festivals, his audiences cosmopolitans on summer pilgrimages to Old World shrines and these, in turn, his "ideal stages," where the glamour of baroque palaces and churches could, as backgrounds, add a romantic glamour to the play.

The aesthetic methods of the stage-designer, like those of his director, are determined by factors not in themselves aesthetic. Design in the theatre today is nothing more than a kind of visual eloquence, integrally part of the act of interpreting a theme. Whether it illuminates the present or revives a fresh sense of the past, it will be vital only where it is a necessary factor in the struggle to impregnate spectators with a dramatist's idea. The style of modern stage setting, therefore, cannot be deduced from any formal concepts of pure beauty nor be evolved by avoiding any specific ugliness. Its beauty will be only the vividness with which it reflects dramatic ideas that a producer can bring to life, its finality, as form, no greater than the insight or the imagination of which audiences of today are capable.

CHAPTER IV

THE RÔLE OF THE SCENE-DESIGNER

I. THE DESIGNER AS INTERMEDIARY

IF DESIGNERS had docilely accepted Gordon Craig's dogmas and turned scenery for all poetic plays into uniform screenery, their settings could never have had any relation to a living theatre. Modern scenery has been associated with "art theatres" because these have been born not of an interest in art, in its formal sense, but of an interest in ideas, and a wide-spread conviction that the theatre is, at this moment, suited to reinterpreting life and reconceiving the world. It is typical that theatrical designing rose to the rank of a separate profession, in this country, in "art theatres" like the Washington Square Players, the Provincetown Theatre, and the Theatre Guild—theatres that were dedicated not to providing visually beautiful spectacles, but to propagating what seemed to be important ideas in terms of dramatic stories. The importance of design in setting a stage was made plain just as often in stage pictures of drab fo'c'sles and peasant kitchens as in vistas of kings' palaces or visions of the Garden of Eden. The incentive to design has been primarily the necessity of making the world of the play as real to an audience as it was to the playwright. The scene-designer has been enlisted as part of the job of "putting the play over," of creating the backgrounds that made seeing believing. And he has been most necessary in theatres where the theme of the play, the picture of life it conveyed, was neither accepted nor obvious. Plays that arouse none of this conflict with the audience are not often mounted with beauty. Themes that are universally accepted are rarely staged with any distinction of style because they have no need to be. For an audience of editors of the Variorum Edition and the old lady to whom Shakespeare is so full of familiar quotations, any set of dull and puffy costumes and drab flats from the nearest storehouse are enough to dress any of the tragedies or the comedies. Molière has been staged for generations with solid dulness at the Comédie Française, where he was a universally accepted classic. The backgrounds of *Don Juan* in Russia, where the world of Molière was an alien one, needed the brush of Golovin and the hand of Meyerhold and "hundreds of wax candles in three chandeliers . . . little negroes flitting on the stage here to pick up a lace handkerchief from the hands of Don Juan or there to push the chairs before the tired actors . . . handing the actors lanterns when the stage is submerged in semi-darkness." "These," writes Meyerhold, "are not tricks created for the diversion of the snobs; all this is . . . the main object of the play: to show the gilded Versailles realm."

For *Peer Gynt,* back-drops no better than enlarged postcards of Norwegian fiords did well enough for years in Norway, where Peer Gynt was a national hero, his story part of a national folk-lore. The hills and valleys of his adventures first had the lure of a legend in Berlin and New York, where he was the mouthpiece of an exotic legend. If *Liliom,* as I have been frequently told, was more beautifully staged at its New York première than in Budapest, the reason was simply that to his native audience the amusement park where he flourished as a barker was as familiar as Coney Island is to us. It was, in fact, so fresh in their memory that the meanest suggestion of it in the theatre was sufficient. Here it had to be designed, in order to make it live vividly as part of Liliom's life. And the impulse to invest the squalor of his world with beauty was based upon the fact that, to the Theatre Guild, the play was something more than the story of a thief, full of amusing bits of first-hand observation, twisted into a highly sentimental ending. Liliom was less recognizable as a fact than as a symbol. The play seemed worth doing not as a picture of a foreign underworld, but as an expression, through the mouth of a thief, of a romantic faith in human compassion eloquent enough to make it poignant allegory. For that reason it became essential to give beauty even to the tumble-down shack where this tough lived and the dusty corner of a city park where he fell in love with a servant-girl under the light of a lamp-post.

Shakespeare was first restaged in every variety of style of which the modern art theatre of its day in Germany was capable, beginning with the Duke of Saxe-Meiningen's company, long before audiences in England or America felt the necessity for anything but the back-drops of their grandfathers. It was not until the spell cast by the word-magic of *Midsummer Night's Dream* began to lose some of its potency that Granville-Barker and Wilkinson created a more magical and iridescent forest. When Hamlet's agony over his mother's incest, no longer a sin to us, begins to make his tragedy seem remote, we become supremely modern, announce *Hamlet* in modern clothes, and put him in a dinner-jacket in order to make him one of us. It is only because so much of the fun in *The Taming of the Shrew* begins to be heavy and meaningless that we send Petruchio and Katharine rattling from Verona to Padua in a Ford.

Stage design is part and parcel of the total effort of interpreting script, an integral factor in overcoming the resistance of an audience to dramatic ideas that transcend its stereotyped expectations. But design is as necessary for staging the accepted masterpieces of the past as for plays that are assumed to be masterpieces of the present. The presentation of significant ideas where the theme of a play is based on contemporary material, because of the idea's relevance, involves a definite struggle with an audience's preconceptions and taboos. The presentation of the significant ideas of the past becomes a struggle to over-come their seeming irrelevance because the audience is inclined to be not antagonistic but indifferent. Ancient kings, queens, heroes, and demigods can no longer be seen invested with the power or the divinity once attributed to them. Present-day labourers or harlots often obscure the dramatic value of a scene because the author gives them an inherent dignity or virtue entirely at variance with popular prejudice. In accepting a current masterpiece in the theatre we must accept a new creed as we listen to the play being acted. In order to accept an ancient masterpiece we must recover a creed while its story is being played. To establish the relevance of Hedda is as difficult as to establish the relevance of Hecuba. Wedekind's Marquis of Keith in a dress-suit may be a stranger figure than Macbeth in armour.

The meaning of a classic can rarely be recovered or revived; it must nearly always be re-created. The supposedly universal ideas commonly ascribed to classics originally clarified a certain range of human experience under a particular aspect of eternity that can never again have exactly the same significance. For a Greek mother the fate of an unburied son killed in battle, doomed to a restless life in death as a perpetually wandering spirit, held the same terror that a mother today would feel for the fate of a son who had contracted leprosy and was doomed to the exile of death in life at Molokai. Unless a performance of *The Suppliants* can re-create that state of terror, its lamentations will affect us less than the wails of widows at a mine-pit after an explosion. Let the same play be performed shortly after or during a great modern war, when miles of our own dead lie unburied in shell craters, and we can share the force of an ancient sorrow. The spiral of history does not create many such parallels. In most instances a stage setting must help to revive a conception of life that was part of the original background of a play existing in the mind of its original audience. It must contrive to imbue the present stage background with the emotional quality of those associations with which this lost audience invested the event enacted. The total stage picture, the choice and arrangement of its details, are of aesthetic importance because they determine to a great extent the kind of emotion a performance will release. When witches were believed to exist and the sight of any old crone mumbling to herself in a twilit field was enough to send any man on a wide detour for fear of having the evil eye put upon him, three old women hunched over a black kettle, provided their noses were sufficiently beaked and their hair unkempt enough, could evoke the weird sisters of *Macbeth*. Today they must be given an added dimension of terror if we are to shudder at the sight of them and accept their power to inspire murder. The palace doors behind Clytemnestra or Jocasta must have the quality of majesty and the scale of doom that these queens can no longer convey wholly by their presence.

Shylock tends to be a victim rather than a villain for a society that subscribes to the liberation of oppressed races and is avowedly humanitarian. Hamlet seems the greatest tragic figure because inhibition is felt to be the source of so much tragic frustration in contemporary life. A bourgeois father of today may transfer to Lear his dread of old age and his fear that his property will be insufficient to retain the loyalty of his children—property being still the bulwark of his authority. In so far as the absolute authority of the father no longer seems just or desirable, Lear tends to become a pathetic rather than a tragic figure. Reinhardt attempted to overcome this by making him a barbaric king, his exactions those to be expected from a tribal leader who was also a high-priest, whose whims could be received with awe by a primitive clan. To a majority of Elizabethans, Macbeth and Richard III personified upper-class privilege vested in the dominant nobility of the day, who could attain wealth and power by murdering with impunity. Envy of this effective way of rising in the world, denied to commoners, was appeased by the spectacle of aristocratic villains so corroded by ill-gotten gains that they were brought to dust before they could enjoy any of the fruits of power. Because political murder is no longer an upper-class privilege, Macbeth and Richard become more and more mechanical villains and a production of either play calls forth the greatest imaginative efforts of a designer such as Robert Edmond Jones, Emil Pirchan, or Gordon Craig in order to lend it the scope of tragedy. Murder for profit has, however, recently become a lower-class privilege, a certain road to millions for poor men courageous enough to run the occasional risk of being shot on sight, uneducated "wise guys" who "make good" even though they can be classed as mentally deficient in other respects. The average man's thirst for power is at present slaked in melodramas, on the stage or on the screen, that glorify successful gangsters patterned on our greatest beer-baron, Scarface Al Capone. Dime novels once glorified Jesse James's defiance of authority in the glamorous Far West and so appeased a generation unable to make millions by buying up railroad franchises or timber reserves from Western State legislatures. The interpretative power of scenery is not yet needed in order to make the gangster's relevance plain. It may be called upon by a later generation if our more plutocratic criminals are then put forward as archaic heroes, inarticulate precursors of a revolt against the entrenched hypocrisy of American legislation and the class distinctions of our present reign of Law and Order.

A director's genius depends upon his ability to understand the forces of contemporary life and to determine the emphasis of a production that in turn outlines its central idea. He relates the actor at every moment to the particular kind of reality that is being created and to the preconceptions of his audience. This reality is illustrated by the scene-designer. He can accomplish this by the design of a drama's background because outside the theatre the pictorial quality of a background affects one's emotional reactions to whatever happens in front of it, a fact acknowledged by the amount of effort that we habitually devote to creating appropriate backgrounds for every variety of human activity that occurs in parks, gardens, public monuments, and homes. In the theatre as well as outside of it the designer tries to give to the background of action some kind of design relevant to the experiences that it is supposed to shelter. Very largely for this reason, the practice of architecture very often proves an excellent training-school for scene-designers and conversely scenic design often provides an excellent preparation for the practice of architecture. Thus Claude Bragdon after completing the railroad terminal at Rochester can step into the theatre and almost at once become a scenic designer of authority, as Joseph Urban did when he stopped designing Viennese villas. And Urban, like Norman-Bel Geddes, after an apprenticeship of ten years or more in the theatre, finds himself equipped to solve architectural problems imposed by modern ways of living. However, although stage settings, as structures housing human activity, perform many of the functions of architecture, they are also pictorial in immediate effect. And as pictures modern stage settings are able to provide the kind of aesthetic satisfaction that painting no longer affords.

The applause that often greets a stage setting at the rise of the curtain measures the appetite of a public for pictorial interpretations of human experience which modern easel-pictures do not provide. Since the middle of the last century, after Géricault dramatized the survivors of the wrecked frigate *Medusa* perishing on a raft and Delacroix completed *The Massacre at Scio,* drama has been eschewed by painters of the first rank. The doctrine was established that painting was to interpret nothing but itself, and the literary subject was exorcised as a temptation of the devil. In consequence galleries of modern art are filled with episodic masterpieces: jockeys pirouetting at the starting-post of Longchamps and not horsemen winning a battle, canoeists lunching at an inn on the Marne instead of guests feasting at Cana, elderly women climbing out of tin tubs rather than Susanna at her bath or Venus rising from the sea. Peasant wenches, wading or washing in a stream, replace nymphs and nereids. Milliners trimming hats are substitutes for Flora and the Graces ushering in spring. Instead of portraits of saints and saviours we contemplate the portraits of barmaids, nurse-girls, and village letter-carriers. Modern painting has been acclaimed as great and imperishable without ever touching the same popular imagination that has been stirred by contemporary poets, novelists, and scientists, for the reason that so many masterpieces of graphic delineation intensify no experiences more important than those of a man about town or the distractions of a week-end in the country. The villages of modern landscape-painting are, as a rule, deserted villages. An occasional picnicker plies his punt in a bend of the Seine, but no one embarks for Cythera.

Dramatists of genius, however, continue to exploit themes that painters of genius have abandoned. They set themselves to interpret the meaning of fate and the rewards and punishments of human behaviour by reviving ancient myths to point new morals, retelling the doom of princes, the doctrines of prophets, and the deeds of saviours. Painters of easel-pictures were once willing to illustrate such themes; their imagery fixed the types of gods and heroes, their pictorial compositions dramatized the crucial vicissitudes of the human race. Today it is in the theatre that we can most easily enter the Garden of Eden, interrogate the Sphinx, sit at the feet of Gamaliel, or with Marco Polo set sail for Cathay. We witness a Day of Judgment as machine-made men destroy the fabric of machine production and with it the human race; we listen to an invisible Pan piping the goat-song of revolution and tremble at an apocalypse as his shadow leaps across the sky and swallows the stars. When the stage-designer helps to stage the mob movements of *Danton's Death*, *Goat Song*, or *The Weavers* he faces problems of pictorial composition once solved by Tintoretto and Goya. The necessity of costuming the trolls of *Peer Gynt* brings him face to face with the necessity of devising appropriate masks of evil analogous to those evolved by Van der Weyden and hundreds of his contemporaries when they painted altar-pieces such as the triptych at Beaune, where graves open and Hell sucks in the damned. In setting important modern plays the scene-designer is forced to interpret significant themes and recovers the painter's historic rôle of image-maker. His imagery, like that of the fine arts in the past, achieves beauty not by appealing to a supposedly separate aesthetic sense but as part of the process of illustrating the meaning of life.

The conventions of modern painting often achieve a relevance in the theatre that is not apparent in the field of their origin. A human body made of metal tubes or pipe-joints, a face articulated like a machine, have no obvious importance in establishing a likeness of Mr. X. But they acquire an immediate and obvious value as the costume of an actor playing the part of a mechanized factory-hand in a play projecting our fear that machine production may destroy the soul of man. The angular clash of opposing planes may not make the fact of a guitar reposing on a table more important, but they can intensify the tragic conflicts of Macbeth or Electra at war with their environment as well as with themselves. The picture of a street in Paris, Düsseldorf, or Canton, Ohio, so distorted that windows are awry and houses lean from the perpendicular, may, in a picture-frame, be an irrelevant nightmare. But the same distortion acquires new meaning as the background of a play where the frenzy of a modern city drives the hero to the point of madness and a megalopolis of sky-scrapers is felt to be on the brink of destruction. The fresh values that so many novelties of modern art acquire on the stage is due to the fact that they can effectively illustrate or symbolize ideas that revaluate or reinterpret the forces felt to underlie existence today.

2. EXPERIMENT IN PRODUCTION

My conviction that the designing of stage settings is integrally a part of and so subordinate to the values of a play as interpreted and acted, has not been arrived at entirely by a process of dispassionate analysis. Most of my designing, having been done for the Theatre Guild, has necessarily been a part of an effort to project ideas not already obvious to New York theatre-goers. Some of these ideas have proved less significant than they seemed at first. But at the time no other management competed for scripts that seemed morbid, precious, oversubtle, or obscure—as a whole undramatic and unactable. Shaw himself, when he learned of our determination to produce *Back to Methuselah,* considered a contract unnecessary, remarking, "It isn't likely that any other lunatics will want to produce it." Both *John Ferguson* and *Jane Clegg,* by St. John Ervine, were rescued by Lawrence Langner from the comparative obscurity of a shelf of miscellaneous drama at Brentano's. *Liliom,* one of Molnar's first plays, was regarded as a fledgling failure and had been all but forgotten despite the success of other plays such as *The Wolf* and *The Devil. The Guardsman* had been attempted by another management and abandoned as preposterous. Not even the endowed Burgtheater considered *Goat Song* an acting play, although Werfel's reputation as a poet was already established in Vienna. I do not of course pretend that we were always Daniels come to judgment. We selected many scripts that when acted turned out to be superficial and unimportant. But in the main the scripts we chose were free from the stereotypes that could be expected to win easy recognition from New York audiences.

Our first ten years were animated by the nightly adventure of convincing an audience by the time the curtain fell of the importance of some theme that seemed remote or irrelevant when the curtain rose. Ibsen had proved to enlightened theatre-goers that any wife had the right to run away from a fatuous husband. Would they grant the same right to Jane Clegg, a forty-year-old domestic drudge, whose home had never been a doll's house and who could not dance her way into the heart of the next man by performing the tarantella? Or would they dismiss her as an elderly fool who had better make the best of it? It is notoriously difficult for American democracy to grant the same freedom to working-men and their wives that it accords to a bourgeoisie and to millionaires. "Find God and be cleansed of your sins" is a doctrine entirely acceptable to American church-goers provided the sinner does not object to going to jail as part of the process. But how would they react to a play where the act of finding God was enough? After struggling with the powers of darkness, a peasant is cleansed of sin at the moment that the child he murdered is supposedly in the cellar under his feet. A wife-beater is an object of contempt to all right-minded Americans who subscribe to the Anglo-Saxon code of conduct befitting an officer and a gentleman. Could they accept the truth of a parable in which a wife-beater is absolved after he returns from Heaven to beat his posthumous child? During our first seasons at the Garrick Theatre such reflections were not literary exercises in experimenting with progress from the particular to the universal. We had at times less than a thousand dollars in the bank. To outrage our audiences without convincing them meant the closing of our theatre and the end of our experiment.

The same excitement of challenging audiences continues today. Could we make them accept Nina Leeds, who deliberately connives at the abortion of her legitimate child, breeds a bastard, and takes a lover not as indulgence in sin but as her inherent right? What purgation could prosperous New Yorkers, bobbing like happy picnickers on the tides of post-war prosperity, feel when faced with the *tragos* of revolution in *Goat Song* or the dreams and dirges of a battling proletariat in *Man and the Masses?*

Having designed settings as part of such experiments that at times succeeded and at times failed, I conclude that a scene-designer must reconcile himself to the fact that a stage setting is no more important than the production of which it is a part. It fails or succeeds to the degree that a total cohesion of lights, forms, gestures, and voices succeeds in illuminating the script as performed. We continually forget that no play, even when written by a master dramatist, will play itself. The words themselves, the most minute stage-directions, furnish no more than a clue as to how it is to be acted. To have a script read by a dozen voices rather than by one does not make a performance. To turn dramatic dialogue into drama that can be accepted even by the most uncritical audience as an imitation of life or an interpretation of it requires an immense effort of co-ordinating the intonations of speech, the pantomime of facial expression, subtle variations of gesture and movement, and, by incessant repetition, fixing their emphasis, rhythm, and interplay. In the language of Broadway, a play must "get across the footlights." And even where footlights are obsolete, there is always an invisible line, marking the frontier of any stage, that separates the pretensions of the players from the expectations of their audience. Every performance is a battle with spectators which must be won again every night. Stage settings, realistic or symbolic, abstract or imitative, are nothing more than the ramparts of a battle-field where a victory over an audience has been won or lost.

No one method of setting a stage can be repeated everywhere as an aesthetic formula. The most radically different ways of staging may, in different environments, be equally good theatre art. Pitoëv mounted *Liliom* in Paris in a deliberately fantastic manner, the park, the shack, and the street fair, as well as Heaven. *He Who Gets Slapped* was staged almost diagrammatically with a single poster and the outline of a tent indicated by a red ribbon. If one wanted to compare these settings with the more realistic ones made for the Theatre Guild, one would have to ask not whether formalism as a picture is superior to realism, but against which background Liliom became a more significant figure, *He* more articulate? I have seen Richard III storm up and down the blood-red stairway provided for him by Jessner and Pirchan at the Berlin State Theatre. But his malignity was as successfully dramatized by Arthur Hopkins and Robert Edmond Jones in New York, where a reproduction of the gate at the Bloody Tower backed every scene like a fanged jowl that alternately menaced and devoured. The single background of the prison that was the background of every character's fears and ambitions became as effective a symbol as a single stairway. To compare settings as pictures is to forget that their pictorial qualities exist only as part of interpreting a play to a public. There are as many ways of setting a play as there are effective ways of acting it.

Any setting that I have designed might have been done equally well, if not better, in an entirely different manner. Had I been faced successively with the necessity of expressing Copeau's, Reinhardt's, and Jessner's ideas of how the meaning of the plays mounted by the Theatre Guild could be projected, the backgrounds I designed for them would have been different from those I evolved in expressing the convictions of Emmanuel Reicher, Feodor Komisarshevsky, Herbert Biberman, Jacob Ben-Ami, and Philip Moeller. The realism of *Liliom* is not inevitable, nor the formalism of *The Tidings Brought to Mary,* nor the isolated vignettes of *The Failures,* the roofless house and church of *Goat Song,* the unit frame that held *Faust, Marco Millions,* and *Volpone.* The justification of these settings was the total impact, the value and the meaning of each play as performed. Now that the performance is past, they will presently seem old-fashioned, if they do not seem so already, like the side-burns and the hoop-skirts of our great-grandparents—what inappropriate raiment for a grand passion!

3. PROP TO PLAYWRIGHTING

Directors are often criticized for depending too much on the scenic background of a play in order to illustrate its meaning. No doubt this happens occasionally, although playwrights often do not realize the full implications of what they have written. But the increasing emphasis placed upon stage scenery is due not only to the director's reliance upon it, but to the fact that playwrights themselves use it more and more as a prop to playwrighting and depend on the details of stage setting to do the work that they formerly had to do entirely with words. The careful specifications of the details of Roebuck Ramsden's or the Reverend James Morell's studies, such as portraits of Cobden, Spencer, and Huxley, or a conspicuous "autotype of the chief figure in Titian's Virgin of the Assumption," let an audience know at a glance, in conjunction with all other details of furnishing, the education, approximate income, habits, and social class of a leading character and prepare his entrance much less clumsily than by marking time while an audience listens to a maid and a butler discussing the master and telling each other what they already know: "What a lot of books the Master has—" (business of dusting) "a learned man for sure," and, "How he worships the blessed saints" or "honours the grand old men of England." Molière's leading characters usually establish their position by their costumes, their manners, elaborate verbal explanations of themselves or equally elaborate verbal descriptions of them by the other characters in the play. But in these days when costumes are standardized and there is so little that can distinguish a duke in a one-button cut-away from an undertaker in a one-button cut-away, or a successful sculptor in a blue double-breasted suit from a successful travelling salesman in a blue double-breasted suit, every object on the stage serves not only the immediate purpose of being used by the actors, handled or sat upon, but also the ultimate purpose of characterizing a social milieu that underlines everything that the actors do.

As an example read the stage-directions of an unpublished manuscript:

A living room in W——'s home within easy commuting distance of New York. [This cannot be specifically expressed, but the author plainly invites the designer to make the room unmistakably suburban.] *The room is comfortable, much lived in. All the evidences of a cultured family, a grand piano open with music on it, books everywhere, flowers, etc.*

W—— is a patient idealist of the Carl Schurz period and the room if given the proper atmosphere underscores the restlessness and incipient revolt of his two children, long before he makes his appearance toward the end of the act.

In *Meteor*, where S. N. Behrman tells the story of the rise of a penniless young college student to the dazzling position of "a captain of industry" and multimillionaire, Act I takes place in the study of the professor who encourages his confidences. But when Act II begins he is already the Napoleon of Finance that he bragged of becoming. The fact is announced by the stage setting at the rise of the curtain:

Act II: Three years have elapsed. The scene is in a living room of a house off Fifth Avenue in New York, a nobly proportioned room with great dull yellow curtained windows in the rear. A carved ceiling, a chastely square marble fireplace. Old Florentine pieces—a richly mellow rather sombre room that could only have been achieved by a person of opulence and exquisite taste.

There is no more awkward problem for a playwright than to make convincing any such sudden metamorphosis, particularly one that takes place off stage between the acts. And there is no doubt that the setting called for saves a good many pages of equally awkward exposition, and by presenting tangible evidences of a meteoric change says as convincingly as the words of any character or chorus, "Lo—look what has happened—what a change is here!"

Settings have become more than backgrounds for action. They are often so much part of a play that the meaning of dialogue depends on them. In *Hotel Universe* Philip Barry attempts to create a mood of mystic insight into life and death, and to express transcendent intuitions of their nature. But he does not attempt to do so by words alone. The particular shape of the terrace is almost as important as the words spoken on it; in fact it prompts them, and recurs as a symbolic *leit-motif*. The stage directions carefully specify its shape:

> *Over and beyond the wall nothing is visible: sea meets sky without a line to mark the meeting. There the angle of the terrace is like a wedge into space.*

A director or designer who, for pictorial reasons, preferred a terrace with curved walls, a railing parallel to the footlights, or an illusion of a deep-blue expanse of the Mediterranean Sea, as I did when first planning the setting—by way of disguising the line that sea and sky make in meeting on a stage floor, at least to the balcony seats—would find, as I did, that nothing but the particular shape and the horizonless sea called for could be used, because the dialogue continues to refer to them.

Hope: *I tell you, you're all in a state.*
Pat: *I don't doubt that the people who used to come here were too.*
Lord knows it's on the edge of the world.

A few minutes later:

Ann: *. . . What are you doing there, Pat?*
Pat: *Me? Oh, just looking—*
Ann: *But I thought you didn't like views.*

Pat: *This isn't a view. For a view you've got to have a horizon. There's not a sign of one out there. The sea meets the sky without a line to mark the meeting. The dome begins under your feet. The arc's perfect.*

Shortly after this the complete picture of the terrace is made a symbol:

Lily: *It's fantastic, this terrace. It just hangs here. Some day it'll float off in space . . . like an island in time.*

After the announcement by

Stephen: *. . . Space is an endless sea, and time the waves that swell within it. . . . Now and again the waves are still and one may venture any way one wishes. . . . They seem to be still now. . . .*

the terrace does become this island in space; past and present are jumbled as one character after the other re-enacts a crucial scene of his or her youth. The effective movement of the actors depended, we found, and as Barry had intended, upon the triangular shape of the terrace railing, so that one or another of them could, at a given moment, stand there as on the prow of a ship, voyaging silently on an ocean of time between two worlds. The terrace plays its rôle to the end. A few moments before the curtain Lily repeats her refrain:

It's fantastic, this terrace. It just hangs here. Some day it will float off into space and anchor there, like an island in time.

By rights the terrace should not have appeared in the stage-directions, but at the head of the program:

CHARACTERS (IN THE ORDER OF THEIR APPEARANCE)
A Terrace, of triangular shape, that seems to hang in space.
Pat Farley
Tom Ames, etc.

Even such minor details as a fan-backed cane chair and a fig-tree
are indispensably tied up with the action. Artificial foliage is always
ugly. A high-backed garden chair takes up a great deal of the playing
space, already cut down by the triangular boundaries of the set. Why
not eliminate both, and instead of cluttering the setting, simplify it so
that its symbolic outline is austere and apparent? Again the dialogue
intervenes:

Alice: . . . *Last night I woke up and couldn't get back to sleep . . .
so I came out on the balcony. It was a funny light. Everything was
—I don't know—awfully pale. For instance that fig-tree didn't
seem to have any colour.*

If not a fig-tree, some other variety of tree must be used, for more
important than a single line—which might be cut—is the fact that
twelve pages before the final curtain, Stephen Field, presumably exhausted by his efforts to play Prospero to a set of sentimental and in-
tellectually shallow souls, dies of apoplexy on stage. The effect of the
final scenes depends very largely on the contrast of the presence of
death unsuspected by the departing guests and the daughter, who,
hand in hand with her lover Pat, says, "Thank you, Father," as a cock
crows. Pat says, "It must be dawn somewhere," and she replies, "But
of course, dear, always," unaware of the corpse within a few feet of
her on an open terrace. Unless this seems plausible to an audience, any
suspense to which the scene can build snaps. The shadow of a tree
and the high fan-back of the chair help to establish this plausibility.
If the playwright had not thought of them the director would have
had to invent their equivalent.

My point is not that such dependence on scenic details is to be deplored or that the play would necessarily have been better if it had
ignored them. I see no reason why Barry or any other playwright
should not have his characters affected by the sight of a terrace rather

than by such dusty stage properties as the first evening star, a rose, or a daisy. If metaphors are part of dramatic love-making, they can be made as effectively poetic, and possibly more so, by apostrophizing a terrace that seems to hang in space as by alluding to a star that also seems to hang there. My point is, on the contrary, that the designer cannot be expected to put less emphasis upon a play's scenic background than the author has already placed on it.

Hotel Universe is a typical, not an exceptional, instance. A director, instead of playing the first two acts of *The Lonely Way* successively in Professor Wegrath's suburban garden and his living-room, may simplify his setting by having them played in a room that overlooks a garden. But unless he wishes to change the script he cannot eliminate a pear-tree *en espalier,* which Schnitzler thought important enough to mention specifically in the lines of the opening scene. In Romain Rolland's *The Game of Love and Death,* the eighteenth century salon cannot be reduced to an abstract design symbolic of the aristocratic intellectuals who find refuge in it. A painting must be hung, so that when the mob of sans-culottes breaks in, it can prompt the line, "Spare that fragile work of art." The fire-place must be built so that the same mob can stuff it with straw and attempt to smoke out a Jacobin supposed to be hidden there. But the play is a romantic homily, full of rhetoric that aspires to poetic significance, and not a "transcript from life." *Berkeley Square* is a dream play about a room quite as much as about its hero—a Georgian room in an old London mansion that hypnotizes its American tenant into re-living the love-affair of one of his ancestors. A portrait, presumably by Reynolds, but painted so as to be startling in its resemblance to the leading actor, must be conspicuously hung, for it supplies the first clue. And the details of the room itself, from its period furniture to its panel mouldings, as well as its general atmosphere of a bygone century, are dramatically indispensable in building the situations that lead to a flight into the past. *Street Scene* is meaningless without the complete reproduction of the façade of a typical tenement-house. The rôle of scenery is occasionally pushed to such absurd lengths as in *Recapture,* given a few seasons ago, where an old-fashioned open *ascenseur* in a small French hotel cued most of the action by sticking between floors and brought about the dénouement by snapping a cable, falling, and killing its dummy occupant.

One cannot point to dependence on scenic detail as the mark of realistic playwrighting. *Berkeley Square* and *Hotel Universe* are dream plays, the former praised for having achieved metaphysical subtlety in romantic terms, the latter commended for having attempted it. Nor can one point the usual moral and say that only plays dramatically feeble are dependent on scenery and invariably fail for that reason. If *The Game of Love and Death* and *Recapture* were financial failures, *Berkeley Square* and *Street Scene* were hailed by the press as little short of masterpieces and ran through two seasons. Such a traditionally decorative and picturesque background as the Sphinx can be made a purely decorative silhouette in *Peer Gynt* but not in *Caesar and Cleopatra.* Its paws must be modelled to hold Cleopatra, be large enough to half hide her during Caesar's soliloquy and not distract the audience's attention. But once he finishes, Cleopatra must be obvious enough in a shaft of moonlight to attract Caesar's eye instantly. A shaft of light is often as tangible an aid to playwrighting as the less ambient elements of a scene. To take only one instance out of a possible hundred: In *Fata Morgana* a mondaine friend of a country family arrives unexpectedly and finds the house empty except for the son studying under the dining-room lamp. The act ends by her deliberate seduction of the boy. "Turn out the lamp," she says. He obeys. As it goes out she is covered by a shaft of moonlight that strikes her from a near-by window. And that conventional transfiguration is conceived to be the final touch of romantic excitement which entices the youngster. Deliver the setting of *Le Misanthrope* for a performance of *Le Malade Imaginaire* and the play could still go on. But deliver the wrong set of scenery for a production of a modern playwright and the curtain could not go up. Let an electrician miss his cue, so that a lamp or a candle does not go out on the instant, and the curtain may as well come down.

This situation is not, as is often maintained, the result of a world conspiracy of modern scene-designers to enslave dramatists, but the consequence of the methods that modern dramatists adopt in order to dramatize their experiences. Occasionally a designer, too timid to look modern playwrighting in the eye and face the consequences, affects an attitude of humility, asserts that scenery is purely a background, to be forgotten five minutes after the curtain is up. But playwrights today, bored with such self-effacement, are continually asking the setting to speak up and lend a helping hand. *Marco Millions* is of course a scene-designer's holiday and nowhere more so than in its opening scenes before a mosque, a Buddhist temple, and the Great Wall of China. In each of these O'Neill calls for the figures of a ruler, a priest, a soldier, in a semi-circle consisting of a mother nursing a baby, two children playing, a young couple in loving embrace, a middle-aged couple, an old couple, and a coffin. Three times these figures are repeated in different costumes. In order to make the production financially feasible, the Guild, with O'Neill's consent, omitted them, with the exception of the one or two in each lot who had lines to speak. But as a result each scene was made dramatically feeble. For this recurring circle of figures placed Marco not in a particular temple of the Far East or at one gate in China, but in the presence of the patient pattern of Eastern civilization. His trivial conversation was given point by being addressed to a circle of human beings most of whom were too wise, too indifferent, and too contemptuous of his inanities to open their mouths. By the time this had been repeated three times, the ironic climax that O'Neill had in mind was achieved. These mute figures were no more than scenery, conceived as statues and supposed to have some of the monumental quality of Oriental sculpture. But with O'Neill's complete picture the sequence of scenes had dramatic force. Without it they seemed pointless and the play did not begin as drama until the second act.

Sounds and off-stage effects can be as integrally related to drama. The Hairy Ape must be lighted by the glow of his particular hell in a steamer's stokehold, and the rhythmic crunch of coal is as essential an accompaniment to his diatribes as the chant of any chorus. Shortly before *Dynamo* went into rehearsal, the following memorandum was received from O'Neill:

The stage effects in Part One and Part Three (the thunder and lightning in Part One, and the sound of the water flowing over the near-by dam and the hum of the generator in Part Two):

I cannot stress too emphatically the importance of starting early in rehearsals to get these effects exactly right. It must be realized that these are not incidental noises but significant dramatic overtones that are an integral part of that composition in the theatre which is the whole play. If they are dismissed until the last dress rehearsals (the usual procedure in my experience), then the result must inevitably be an old melodrama thunderstorm, and a generator sounding obviously like a vacuum cleaner; not only will the true values of these effects be lost but they will make the play look foolish.

I may seem to be a bug on the subject of sound in the theatre—but I have reason. J—— once said that the difference between my plays and other contemporary work was that I always wrote primarily by ear for the ear, that most of my plays, even down to the rhythm of the dialogue, had the definite structural quality of a musical composition. This hits the nail on the head. It is not that I consciously strive after this but that, willy nilly, my stuff takes that form. (Whether this is a transgression or not is a matter of opinion. Certainly I believe it to be a great virtue, although it is the principal reason why I have been blamed for useless repetitions, which to me were significant recur-rences of theme.) But the point here is that I have always used sound in plays as a structural part of them. Tried to use, I mean—for I've never got what the script called for (even in "Jones"), not because what I specified couldn't be done but because I was never able to over-come the slip-shod, old-fashioned disregard of our modern theatre for what ought to be one of its superior opportunities (contrasted with the medium of the novel, for example) in expressing the essential rhythm of our lives today. This sounds complicated but to illustrate: This is a machine age which one would like to express as a background for lives in plays in overtones of characteristic, impelling and governing mechanical sound and rhythm—but how can one, unless a correspond-ing mechanical perfection in the theatre is a reliable string of the in-strument (the theatre as a whole) on which one composes? The only answer is, it cannot be done. Looking back on my plays in which sig-nificant mechanical sound and not music is called for (nearly all of the best ones) I can say that none of them has ever really been thor-oughly done in the modern theatre *although they were written for it. Some day I hope they will be—and people are due to be surprised by the added dramatic value—*modern *values—they will take on.*

After which dissertation (which has little or nothing to do with "In-terlude" or "Marco" but a hell of a lot to do with "Dynamo"), I would suggest that some special person with the right mechanical flair be sicced on this aspect of "Dynamo" to get perfect results. It can't be done in two or three days. What is needed is lightning that will sud-denly light up people's faces in different parts of the set, keep them in the general picture—not literal lightning, but a reproduction of the dramatic effect of lightning on people's faces. And thunder with a menacing, brooding quality as if some Electrical God were on the hills impelling all these people, effecting their thoughts and actions. The queer noise of a generator, which is unlike any other mechanical noise (it is described in the script), its merging with, and contrast with, the peaceful, soft Nature sound of the falls, also needs some doing. The startling, strained, unnatural effect of the human voice raised to try and dominate the generator's hum (in the scenes in the generator room), is also important and part of my conception. All this can be done—and easily—if the person on this job will get a little expert information from the General Electric and go out to the plant at Stevenson, Conn., I visited, and look around and listen in. My scenic scheme is a concentration of the features of this plant.

Thus such impersonal things as sounds can have the importance of dramatis personae and, no longer the traditional thunder-clap or blinding flash, also have a carefully plotted and sustained rôle to play. Is it an exaggeration to say that the details of setting a stage have become an integral part of the technique of playwrighting itself?

4. TRAGICAL-COMICAL-HISTORICAL-PASTORAL

One reason so little progress has been made (or can be made) in simplifying the mounting of contemporary plays is because contemporary playwrights in their work have achieved so little consecutive unity of style. Eugene O'Neill is typical of a period in which dramatists have as many literary methods as subjects and change in swift succession from the idiom of sailors, stokers, and tramps to the idiom of traditional poetry—and even mingle them in one and the same play. A play that calls for masks abounds in colloquial speech. In *Marco* the Orientals indulge in rhetorical phrasing associated with lofty minds. But Marco, his father, and his uncle, presumably thirteenth century Venetians, talk like small-town shopkeepers fresh from any one of our Main Streets. "The scheme for the sets," O'Neill added to his memoranda on *Dynamo*, "seems to me to embody all that is sound theatre in Constructivism while giving an obvious, natural reason for being." Nevertheless

119

he advised the designer to visit the particular power-house he had seen and consult the experts of the General Electric Company. I did, and found that O'Neill had so definitely related the death of his hero to the top of an already old-fashioned dynamo, had so concretely imagined it taking place on this machine, that there was no alternative to copying it for the stage on a slightly smaller scale. Had I visited a more recent installation of motor generators, mounted not horizontally but vertically, there would have been no end of trouble in staging the climax of the last act as O'Neill had written it.

Franz Werfel, another visionary, is in exactly the same case. Like almost every other modern dramatic poet, he will not continue one literary method long enough to remain in any one scenic scheme that reformers dream about. The backgrounds for his fantasy *Mirror Man* are decorative and pictorial. The episodes of *Juarez and Maximilian* require realistic vignettes. The stage-directions for *Goat Song*—allegory as relevant as any that the modern theatre has achieved—are astonishingly realistic in detail. When I met Werfel in Vienna and showed him photographs of the Guild's production he seemed astounded, as well as pleased, at the amount of simplification that Ben-Ami and I had been able to achieve.

Attempt to catalogue the literary genre of our most imaginative dramatists and you end with a catalogue paralleling Polonius' tragical-comical-historical-pastoral, that extends to scene individable or poem unlimited. Nothing else is to be expected, as I have already pointed out, in an eclectic period of transition such as ours, where no single mould has been imposed by any one tradition or authority upon any form of expression. American playwrights are possibly disinclined to summarize life today symbolically because they are still exploring it. They are, at present, as realists debunking the American scene, substituting observation at first hand for inherited theatrical clichés and sentimentalities, and getting audiences to accept their increasingly cynical and sceptical findings as to what we are like. As a nation we are getting on to ourselves in the theatre and its greatest progress in this direction has been made in such popular successes as *What Price Glory?* which debunked the war, *The Silver Cord,* which debunked the great American cult of home and mother, *Holiday,* which attempted to debunk the American millionaire, *The Front Page,* which debunked the press, *Chicago,* which debunked our criminal courts, and *Once in a Lifetime,* which debunked the movies. Our attempts at poetry are most successful when they are most colloquial, even parochial. *The Green Pastures,* acclaimed by the New York press as the American *Divine Comedy,* projects an interpretation of the Bible seen through the minds of illiterate Southern Negroes. God sits at a roll-top desk and smokes a five-cent cigar; Heaven is a Sunday-school picnic where ice-cream and fried fish are handed out. But its poetic power was acclaimed by critics who all but wept with ecstasy. The devout declared it the most deeply religious play ever brought forth in the modern theatre.

The instinct of our ablest playwrights to renew their strength, like Antaeus, by touching earth and returning to nature on every possible occasion is probably a sound one, for they do not, as yet, soar very successfully in the realm of dogma and idea. The feebler portions of *Hotel Universe* are dictated by Barry's desire to effect a mystic reconciliation of life and death. The words of a father-seer are little more than lovely verbalisms, thoughts that attempt to flower but wilt because they have no roots. The vital portions of the play are those where Barry, with his usual adroitness, interprets an enfeebled smart set by reproducing their small talk. On the printed page Elmer Rice's *The Adding Machine* is no doubt superior to his *Street Scene,* but in the theatre the deliberate allegory of the former, with its scene in Heaven, is far less convincing as a picture of the pathetic fate of mediocrity than is the journalistic account of murder in a side-street. The average man, symbolized by Mr. Zero, is less convincing even as a type than is the cumulative picture of the kind of mediocrity produced by our large cities which Rice dramatizes in a succession of individual portraits of tenants in a cheap flat-house. In performance the explicit symbolism of *Dynamo* at its moments of apostrophe proved to be pathological. But its implicit meaning was alive in the personalities of a small-town bigot and a small-town sceptic, the one a preacher and the other an electrical engineer. The formal soliloquies that break the dialogue of *Strange Interlude* and revive a poetic convention treat it at times with the most thorough-going informality and realism. Some of these secret thoughts are genuinely poetic in rhythm, but many are expressed in a style not greatly different from the conversation that they interpret and interrupt.

The most persistent efforts to reduce settings to a bare minimum, to formalize them almost out of existence, to make the group movements of actors the only pictorial element of a performance, have been made by the scene-designers themselves. But they have failed to establish a successful tradition in this country because playwrights would not join the movement. Norman-Bel Geddes once showed that a few convertible screens were sufficient for a revival of *The School for Scandal,* but the demand for completely carpentered box interiors continues from the same managers who bleat annually at the ruinous cost of building and painting the sets that they must have complete to the last door-knob. In a production of a play of many scenes laid in Morocco, Geddes created a single setting of rectangular rock forms which surprisingly gave the illusion of medersas, courtyards, streets, casbas, and even the dunes of the desert, on an open stage and without a scene-shift. But the setting was not recognized as a signpost pointing the way along which stage setting should proceed. No important piece of stage design has ever failed to win instant recognition from the New York press; the present position of scenic design as a recognized profession in this country is very largely due to dramatic critics, who hailed the début of Jones and subsequently made the reputations of Urban, Geddes, Mielziner, and myself. Nevertheless our critics, like our playwrights, prefer the concrete road of realism to any other avenue of development. When Mielziner, much against his will, had to reproduce the façade of a particular flat-house in the West Sixties for *Street Scene,* he was astounded to receive the most enthusiastic press of his career up to that date. The next burst of well-deserved enthusiasm was reserved for *The Affairs of Anatol,* but particularly for one setting where paper snow fell in front of a back-drop of a street winking with evening lights, a picture as appropriately old-fashioned as a coloured supplement to a Christmas *Illustriertes Monatsheft* in Anatol's own day. When Jones unified the castle of Elsinore there were snickers about burying Ophelia in the front parlour. The only time that I can remember his having a uniformly unfavourable press was when he attempted to set *Macbeth* in purely symbolic forms. When Komisarshevsky and I eliminated even a suggestion of a forest, a kitchen, or a road-side in *The Tidings Brought to Mary* and made all the scenic changes by a play of light on a platform containing nothing more than a single block, which served in turn as an altar, a bench, a table, and a bier, the production was praised but there was no outspoken recognition that stage setting had found the clue to its proper development. When I both directed and designed *Massemensch* and, basing my production on Jürgen Fehling's in Berlin, reduced the stage picture almost entirely to the mass movements of thirty actors, I was criticized by Alexander Woollcott for having sacrificed dramatic to pictorial values. I have received more praise for the towering scale of a battle-ship in *Roar China* than for a condensation of a cemetery or for a skeletonized room in the French Foreign Office in *Miracle at Verdun.* The value of suggestion has been recognized in scenes that were fragments of actual places, as in *Goat Song* or *The Failures,* where ceilings and side walls were deliberately omitted but, if carried to completion, would have made realistic box interiors. On the whole both public and press have preferred the decorative elaboration of *Marco Millions, Volpone,* and *Elizabeth the Queen.*

When Robert Littell as dramatic critic of the New York *World* complained in his Sunday column of the "materialistic millstone that hangs around the theatre's neck in the shape of . . . expensive realism," I replied in an open letter which contained the following:

Let me go on record as offering a standing challenge to Sidney Howard, Elmer Rice, Eugene O'Neill, Philip Barry, S. N. Behrman, Paul Green, or any other American playwright who dares to accept it. Namely: Let one of them write a play in which lines and business are so independent of scenery that it can be played on a bare stage, with no more furniture than three chairs, one couch, and one table, and with no more dependence on doors and windows than a comedy by Molière. An open air scene will be allotted two potted plants of any description, or leaf shadows cast by a stereopticon. I'll gladly offer my services free to light the show. But I am making a safe offer. It won't be taken up. If it is, what you will see will be, not a new school of stage setting, but a new school of playwrighting.

To date the offer has not been accepted except by a few aspirants who have yet to prove that they can write a play. Faced with a grandiose but bare palace of art where their plays are free to soar and tower, our acknowledged playwrights murmur polite thanks, excuse themselves, and slip around the corner to a speak-easy, climb aboard a lugger, start on a tour to historic Rome or France, visit their country cousins, or spend another week-end on Long Island. Possibly their instinct as to what their material is and the way it must be handled is sounder than any theory of how they might write plays in order to improve the art of scenic design. Shaw once complained that the last thing to be found in the theatre was the ideas encountered everywhere else. But even he could not inject into a play ideas that had not permeated society long enough to create recognizable mouthpieces. Socialism had to be pruned into vigour by the Fabians, with Shaw's aid as a stump speaker, and then watered down with sentimentality, Nietzsche's dogmas be given time to create romantic Nietzscheanism, before either Morell or Tanner could go on talking. Shaw's emancipated mothers, daughters, and philanderers were not wholly invented but at least partially observed in Soho, Chelsea, and Mayfair. Shaw of course got the jump on his fellow playwrights by putting these and similar doctrinaires on the stage before their ideas had become truisms. But as a result many of their discoveries are already so commonplace that Shaw's plays, when revived, are often dismissed as being dated. They will not have a secure place in repertory until the passage of time takes from them the air of novelty with which Shaw himself ushered them on to the stage.

The modern playwright seems no more likely to invent a *Weltanschauung* for society than a religion for it. In the main he summarizes and does not anticipate. His satire rebounds best from a society that is fixed rather than fluid; he dreams and moralizes most freely in a historic past rather than in an ambiguous future. There is of course every reason to reconstruct our cramped and cluttered playhouses so that they can be ready to meet, with the speed and precision of modern machines, the constantly changing demands of modern plays. But I cannot believe that any one technique of stage setting or any one method of reconstructing the stage itself will free the actor, the dramatist, or the designer. Could we be picked up bodily by some friendly genie and deposited in any ideal theatre of tomorrow, the theatrical values of its plays, their impact in performance, the significance of their ideas, and the forms necessary to emphasize or illustrate them would have to be established before an audience by the same process of experiment in production that exists in the theatre of today. No single method will solve the theatrical problems of tomorrow until the theatre can reflect a single picture of the world outlined by a universally recognized religion and play to audiences that adhere to an accepted moral code by which all behaviour can be satisfactorily judged. Whenever and wherever societies emerge that succeed in achieving a unified view of man's existence, in society and in nature, we shall have periods of theatrical art that reflect it and therefore appear in retrospect classic in their purity, simplicity, and unity. The theatre of the day after tomorrow will probably hark back to them as we do to the Greeks, a prey to the immortal superstition that by handling some fragment of the past, we can be healed or be given new powers like true believers who touch in a reliquary the shin-bone of a saint or a fragment of the true cross.

I doubt that the mechanized forces of industrial democracy will be able to create a state of society so unified that its theatrical art can become uniform. I am not inclined to believe in a theatre of the future where playwrights will provide the gospels, actors be ordained priests, and scene-designers supply a composite substitute for organ, choir, incense, stained glass, and chasuble. I believe, on the contrary, that if the etched intentions of Gordon Craig, the sepia water-colours of Robert Edmond Jones, where figures in vermilion and silver challenge the Calvinistic gloom of rooms and battlements, or the drawings of Norman-Bel Geddes, in which Dante's dream ascends again from Hell to Heaven, survive as records of our stage, they may seem pallid and meagre compared to the prodigious invention and the lavish pictorial beauty of the seventeenth and eighteenth century stages, already catalogued in the archives of the Bibliothèque Nationale or the Albertina. The librarian of 2032 will probably compare our sketches patiently in order to discover some common aim that could establish them as evidence of a revolution in theatrical art. He will probably smile if he finds this footnote telling him that the revolution was really in our minds and that an age which abandoned its churches and paraded its scepticism did believe that the theatre was a place where the meaning of the past and present, as well as the promise of the future, could be made plain. Nor will he perhaps suspect that even as pictures, the beauty of our stage settings moved us because they were primarily part of adventurous moments of new-found wisdom, of insight, and, occasionally, of ecstasy.

PART TWO

MYTHS OF LOST PURITY

CHAPTER I

GREEK REALISM—FIFTH CENTURY B.C.

I. FALSE PASTS

As WE struggle to maturity, sooner or later we are all haunted by the memory of some lost Eden: the heaven supposed to lie round us in our infancy, the little grey home in the west, the old oaken bucket that hung in the well, the noble savage, the wisdom of our forefathers, the glory that was Greece—a golden age of one sort or another to which we long to return, where the fruits of knowledge are not sparse and bitter, but gleam on the original stem in a remote but radiant earthly paradise. We cannot return there, so we are told, because we have lost the garden's key: an original purity, welded out of the pristine ores of sobriety in private morals and simplicity in aesthetic taste. But the invaluable key is never found, because at heart we do not want to find it; we prefer the solace of a dream to the simple labour of examining it in the light of our accumulated knowledge.

We habitually ignore the findings of anthropologists and romantic poets, distrust the noble instincts of savages except in well-policed protectorates, and exterminate primitive peoples in sufficient numbers to make such protectorates possible. We build a bloated replica of the old homestead instead of returning to it, install plenty of bathrooms, and are careful to avoid typhoid by connecting the running water with the town sewer and the county reservoir. The sight of a typical fragment of Greek glory, such as a statue of the Periclean period, in its original coat of pigment, or of the Parthenon under a covering of gesso as

131

brightly painted, would set most classicists' teeth on edge. Many of their "ideal" Greek philosophers and poets were homosexuals who, could they be reincarnated, would be jailed by the police before academies of letters were able to elect them to membership. If a society for the protection of civil liberties succeeded in getting them out on bail, and by way of cheering them up allowed them to give a performance of any work of their greatest comic poet, they would be promptly returned to jail by the nearest magistrate for offending public decency and corrupting the morals of the young. Their only chance of acquittal would lie in the plea that, Greek no longer being a required study in schools and colleges, no one in the audience could have understood a word of what was said. But they would be immediately reindicted for the display of huge phallic bladders dangled in front of each actor, and be sent to the nearest reformatory. These creators of classic glories might be more comfortably confined in an asylum for the nervously diseased, provided they had been able to retain the services of an eminent psychiatrist who could convince a court that their classic sexual exhibitionism was not deliberate but congenital and predetermined. In any event, they would be incarcerated while the leading newspapers sent forth editorial hosannas in praise of the vigilant Lord Chamberlain or the intrepid district attorney who had, once again, defended the perilous frontier separating civilized art from barbaric licence. Nevertheless the American and Anglican myth of the purity of classical antiquity persists. We continue to think of its leaders, whether poets, philosophers, or statesmen, as pallid replicas of the plaster casts in our museums, and envisage the rest of the population with the complexion of schoolgirls or Boy Scouts, feasting decorously or parading with garlands, as in the paintings of the late Royal Academician Sir Laurence Alma-Tadema.

We cling to an analogous myth in regard to the Puritan forefathers. Unimpeached documents demonstrate that their leaders passed a succession of sumptuary laws in a futile effort to prevent their fellow parishioners from indulging in lechery, drunkenness, and the extravagant display of "wicked finery," such as brocades, powdered wigs, silver lace, and silk stockings. Attempts to limit intoxicants to one half a pint of wine per person proved as abortive as our present attempt to limit the alcoholic content of beverages to one half of 1 per cent. And debauching Indians with rum remained a popular pastime. Demivirgins abounded, although the term had not yet been minted. The God-fearing parents of respectable households encouraged courtship and saved firewood by bundling a daughter into the same bed as her swain, virginity being protected by the petticoat that the young lady retained under her night-gown and the fact that her wooer kept on his shirt and his breeches. The best families resented the sermons that thundered against the practice and the popular ballads that jeered at it. These broadsides, once the rural pedlar's stock in trade, would not be printed today; no publisher could afford to subject himself to criminal prosecution under any one of our numerous obscenity laws or the federal statute against sending indecent matter through the mails. In a single Massachusetts court, from 1680 to 1682, approximately one third of the convictions were for fornication. A century later the records of a church in Groton attest that approximately one third of both its male and its female communicants confessed to fornication before marriage. But Professor Henry Lawrence's erudite and entertaining volume, *The Not Quite Puritans,* in which such facts as well as a hundred similar ones are amiably recorded, will not dispel the accepted picture of our purer past. What text-book repeating such findings could be accepted as the basis of instruction in schools and colleges? Our emotional need to consider ourselves the heirs of an innocent childhood or of a righteous father will continue to fabricate false pasts enshrined as authentic memories.

The purity of theatrical art in the past has, for the same reason, become a recurrent myth. Stage-craft, so we are told, is debased today, become tawdry, ostentatious, literal, and overelaborate. It was once simple and pure; the imagination of the audience supplied what the designer today needlessly furnishes. There are four such prevalent myths:

1. The myth of an austere and bare Greek stage without any attempt to create scenic illusion—the prototype of all pure and noble theatrical art to which our theatre must somehow return. It created the only true tragic drama, a higher reality, above the mêlée of mundane affairs. These were properly reserved for the lower art of comedy.

2. The myth of the spiritual simplicity of the mediaeval stage—bare platforms in an open square, also without scenic illusion or any interest in creating it.

3. The myth of a bare, therefore vigorous and masculine, Elizabethan stage, typified by Shakespeare's playhouse, where signs—"This is the Forest of Arden"—replaced sets.

4. The myth of a similarly bare and vigorous Theatre of Molière, final proof that all that is needed to mount a play is three boards and a passion.

One or another of such assertions is used today, like a court fool's bladder on a stick, to rap the head of the designer when he is felt to grow too self-important. A certain number of critics inflate these doctrines perennially with pious breath. They remain none the less empty wind.

2. THE EVENT ILLUSTRATED

Imagination, in any art, when it is freshest and freest tends to be specific and concrete. Abstractions are the refuge of jaded artisans or those for whom image-making has been forbidden. The only backgrounds of action that past theatres did not portray were such as could not be visualized on account of the physical structure of the playhouse or technical limitations due to the construction of the stage. If the entire background could not be reproduced, a portion of it was, often with an exactness that seems to us now naïve or ludicrous. The imagination of the audience was relied upon not at the outset, but in the last extremity.

Aristotle credits Sophocles with the invention of scene-painting, an innovation ascribed to Aeschylus as well. However meagre Greek scene-painting may seem in comparison to our own, it is evident that a completely bare stage for tragedy did not satisfy the tragic dramatists themselves. If they had not felt the need for a background of some sort, they would not have invented it. The impulse to visualize and particularize the background of action was as persistent in the Greek theatre as it subsequently proved to be in every other. Its scenic background was devised for the same reason that every other form of scenery has been subsequently fabricated, as a result of the playwright's need of it in helping to build his dramatic situations and as an aid in contributing to his dramatic effects. The unbacked stage—the circular *orchestra*—of the original Greek theatre, overlooking native hills or harbour, definitely hampered playwrighting, once dramatic technique got beyond its archaic phase of antiphonal responses between chorus and protagonist. As soon as dramatic action was conceived with sufficient realism to make possible the trilogies that we know, the physical limitations of a completely open stage became apparent.

As no more than three speaking actors were allotted to a play, speedy doubling of rôles and a quick change from one character to another became indispensable before the story of a tragedy could deal with more than three people. Without continual doubling none of the traditional legends could be retold as drama or effectively acted. On a completely open stage such substitutions were delayed; the suspense of many situations was let down before an actor could reappear; others were dissipated because it took too much time to bring an actor on or get him off. He remained in sight of the audience too long before he entered into a dramatic situation or after he was no longer part of it. Dramatic plausibility was often vitiated when gods as well as mortals, enemies as well as friends, seemed always to come from the same direction; and the same procedure deflated the dramatic tension of recognition scenes between long-lost parent and child, sister and brother, so essential a part of tragic pathos to the Greek mind. Seeming strangers could hardly fail to give the impression of having already met if they entered the stage as though they had come by a single route. The general pattern of movement on the completely open stage was undoubtedly pure enough to have satisfied many modern aesthetes; but Greek playwrights, like all practising dramatists since their time, were realistic enough to be concerned less with the purity of their art than with the possibility of making their story-telling convincing to an average audience. The permanent scenic façade, with its three doors, more than doubled the number of entrances to the stage and gave the dramatic poet immensely greater freedom in elaborating his plot and in creating dramatic tension by the opportunities provided for speedy change of rôles, the added number of characters that he could utilize, and the effective timing of their entrances and confrontations.

This permanent façade was very definitely scenery to a Greek audience when it was first set up at the back of an empty circular *orchestra*. At the outset of wood, "its construction was flimsy enough for it to be capable of being easily rebuilt or remodeled to meet the scenic requirements of each drama . . . it was not until long after the introduction of a scenic background that the plays were uniformly laid before a palace or temple." The doctrine of a necessary unity of place was therefore not forced upon the Greek playwright. He invented it, as he had scenery, when he felt the need of it, to help him in the telling of his story. Having established a permanent setting as a visual background for action, he saw in it a possible aid to the literary unification of his script. But like many another liberating innovation the permanent set very soon became an incubus. By the time the archaic theatres had been remodelled and the scenic façade built of stone—in Athens it was one hundred and fifty-two feet wide—the Greek playwright, rather than invariably fit his plays to it, welcomed every means of defeating its rigidity.

An audience was not expected to know whether the permanent stone setting was a palace or a temple. If a temple, a statue of the presiding deity identified it. For tragedies such as Sophocles' *Oedipus at Colonus,* which takes place in a grove, painted panels could be set between the columns of the single façade of the stage house; "in some theatres the proscenium columns were shaped so as to hold such panels more firmly in place." Another limitation of the immovable stone façade was the inability it imposed on playwrights of showing an interior scene. But a common desire to picture their tragic climaxes realistically enabled them to circumvent the difficulty and at the same time to nullify a religious taboo that forbade portraying the act of murder itself. The device used was a wagon-stage—the *eccyclema*—rolled out through the palace doors an instant after the murder had occurred, upon it the bloody tableau of catastrophe. Its use was common enough to be referred to in the burlesque of Euripides in *The Acharnians:*

Good Citizen: *Ho! slave, slave! . . . call your master.*

Slave: *Impossible!*

Good Citizen: *So much the worse. But I will not go. Come, let us knock at the door. Euripides, my . . . darling Euripides. . . .*

Euripides: *I have no time to waste.*

Good Citizen: *Very well, have yourself wheeled out here.*

Euripides: *Impossible.*

Good Citizen: *Nevertheless . . .*

Euripides: *Well,—let them roll me out . . .*

(*Bosschère edition.*)

The difficulty of indicating a change of scene was met by another device, the *periaktoi*—upright three-sided prisms, set flush with the palace or temple wall on either side of the stage, mounted on wooden pegs, the three sides painted to indicate different localities as they were turned to the audience during the course of the play. This mechanism is so practical that it has been periodically revived. When the stage-decorators of the Renaissance attempted to devise ways and means of shifting stage settings they found their first models in the Greek theatre. In 1596 *periaktoi* were utilized in a performance of *Arimène* at Nantes. Inigo Jones used them in 1605 at Oxford before he had discovered any other means of shifting scenery. The stage

was but a false wall fair painted and adorned with stately pillars, which pillars would turn about, by reason whereof, with the help of other painted cloths, their stage did vary three times in the acting of one Tragedy.

However incomplete to our eyes any of these devices may be, they were all in the direction of as much imitation and literal reproduction as could be obtained, and demonstrate that the Greeks, far from accepting the inflexibility of their stage, were sensitive to many of its limitations and offset them whenever possible by use of both scenery and machinery.

When mechanical expedients could not be resorted to the Greek dramatist did not hesitate to insert speeches that have no other purpose than to make more plausible his continual scenes in the open air, his instinct in this connection being as definitely realistic as the motivation of exits and entrances by contemporary playwrights. We find tragic heroes and heroines stopping to explain their presence out of doors before a palace portico as they would today if all plays had to be acted on the porches of country-houses. Flickinger points out that in Euripides' *Alcestis* Apollo explains his presence as an escape from

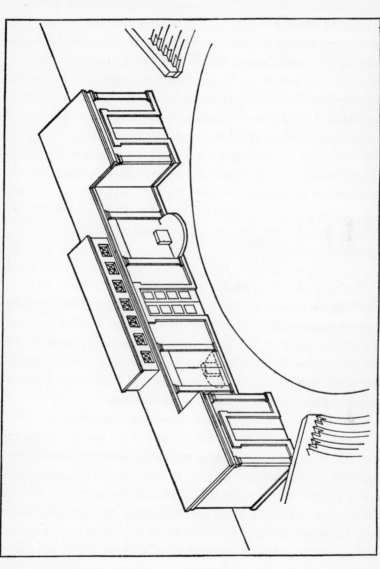

THE ATHENIAN THEATRE ABOUT 460 (RE-DRAWN FROM FLICKINGER), SHOWING AN
EARLY FORM OF ECCYCLEMA OR WAGON STAGE

being polluted by being near the corpse within the palace of Admetus, and Alcestis, although dying, explains that she has come forth to look upon the sun for the last time. In the *Medea* the nurse explains that the sorrows within have grown so unbearable that she must proclaim them to the sky, and in the *Cyclops* Polyphemus explains that he has left his cave to visit his brothers. In Sophocles' *Oedipus the King* Oedipus explains that he is so concerned with the afflictions of his subjects that he cannot endure the thought of making enquiries through a servant and has come forth to learn the situation in person. The effect is much the same as if Ibsen had been asked to stage the *Enemy of the People* on the veranda of Dr. Stockmann's house. In that case the doctor might have prefaced the opening act with the remark that the scandal in regard to the town water-supply had reached such alarming proportions that he could no longer remain in his study, but must interview each passer-by and argue with him if necessary. If Dumas had been forced to put the dying Marguerite Gautier on a terrace in front of her villa, she would undoubtedly have opened her death scene by an explanation similar to that of Alcestis, namely, that her bedroom having become stifling, she could breathe her last more easily in the open air. Where the conventions of a theatre cease to be taken for granted and playwrights become conscious of them to the point of inventing reasons for their use, it is because these conventions have already begun to seem clumsy, unnecessary, and even absurd.

The crane that made the descent of a god at the end of a tragedy a literal fact, a blatantly bare piece of machinery on a palace roof, seems to us to destroy illusion rather than to create it. But the point to be stressed is again the fact that the Greek audience so wanted the descent of a deity actually displayed before their eyes that they could ignore ropes and pulleys in full sunlight. In this they showed a typical Occidental temper, which always tends to elaborate its symbols until they reproduce experience rather than accept symbolic equivalents for it as Oriental audiences do from one century to another. If the Athenians had been as eager for a purely formal art of the theatre as their modern apologists maintain, they would not have hoisted their deities through the air, or demanded a tableau of murder trundled into sight. The words of a messenger describing the catastrophe or an emblem of divinity, such as the horse-hair plume in the Chinese theatre, would have been sufficient. Because the original instinct of the Greek theatre was toward realism rather than away from it, new machines were added in the Hellenistic period: the *hemicyclon,* a semicircle of canvas to give a view of a distant city—the prototype of the panoramas and cycloramas of today—and the revolving *stropein* used to show heroes in heaven or battles at sea, ultimately elaborated into the mimic sea-fights of flooded Roman amphitheatres.

The machine for hoisting gods was capable of producing intensely spectacular effects, as at the end of Euripides' *Medea:* "While attendants are still battering at the door," read the stage-directions of Gilbert Murray's translation, "Medea is seen on the roof, standing on a chariot of winged dragons, in which are the children's bodies." This is no mere supposition of a scholiast, for the poet himself calls for the chariot and Medea's words point to it:

> *What make ye at my gates? Why batter ye*
> *With brazen bars, seeking my dead and me*
> *Who slew them? . . .*
> > *Out of this firmament*
> *My fathers' father, the high Sun, hath sent*
> *This, that shall save me from mine enemies' rage.*

"She rises on the chariot and is slowly borne away" as Jason curses her. The dramatic termination of the play as written depends on this picturesque use of dramatic machinery. Certainly the picture must have been striking, the defiant, barbaric sorceress reining dragons instead of steeds against the sky and disappearing as she hurls her last cries of hate at the lover who had abandoned her and who lies grovelling on the ground below. The elaborate apotheoses of the eighteenth century stage in France, *les gloires,* when not one but a dozen gods and god-desses descended for the final curtain, found their model in such classic Greek spectacle. The Athenians on more than one occasion must have got an eyeful in their theatre and no doubt, like all audiences since, enjoyed it.

3. THE MASK AND THE FACE

The mask that hid the features of the Greek actor remains in many ways an anomaly in Greek art. More than any other people of antiq-uity the Greek people saw even their gods as replicas of athletic men and women and embodied them on pedestals and pediments complete to the last toe-nail, the least ringlet of Apollo's or Athene's hair. Why did this same people hide their own faces when they dramatized human history? Their statues define the muscular ripple of an ath-lete's torso, reproduce the precise folds of a statesman's tunic, the greaves of a soldier's armour. They have left a gallery of indubitable portrait records. Nowhere except in the theatre did they give the slightest indication of sharing our modern conviction that an imitation of nature is an aesthetic sin to be avoided in the interests of producing monumental art. Why did they conceal in the theatre their features, which they revealed elsewhere, without altering their human propor-tions, on public monuments and temples?

In attempting to explain this seeming mystery, the performance of a Greek tragedy is made a stylist's holiday by theorists who see that, in utilizing masks, the Greeks anticipated the genius of Picasso and shared the aesthetic insight of Congo Negroes. The mystery is promptly dissipated when we remember three obvious facts connected with a performance in a Greek theatre: 1. The number of speaking actors allotted to any play remained limited to three. 2. The play was given in an open bowl, for a unique performance, before seventeen thousand spectators at Athens and in other cities before even greater numbers, more than half of whom were seated more than a hundred feet from the circular *orchestra* where a play was performed, farther than the college graduates today, assigned seats in the last row of the Harvard stadium, are from a football game. 3. Greek spectators were not supplied with field-glasses or acousticons. The mask was therefore retained in Greek drama primarily for technical, not for aesthetic, reasons. It became an indispensable adjunct to playwrighting by enabling actors to double and sometimes triple their rôles and so enormously enlarged a playwright's ability to build dramatic situations. The technique of substitution was pushed to the point of requiring actors to make "lightning changes," often in the space of six verses. Like the numerals pinned on the sweater of tackle or quarterback, the mask enlarged the actor's scale and enabled spectators on the farthest perch to identify a leading character and follow the play before them. But the principal advantage of the mask was an acoustic one; it acted as a sounding-board and carried dialogue to the farthest reaches of vast civic arenas.

These acoustic properties are no longer a matter of supposition; they have been verified by laboratory experiment. In Neuburger's *Technical Arts and Sciences of the Ancients* one finds:

Following a suggestion by Castex, replicas of such masks were made for special acoustic experiments in which both actors and singers . . . basses, sopranos and others participated. A number of spectators were also engaged in order that the action of these masks should be thoroughly tested in every direction. The very first experiments . . . revealed that to the hearers the intensity of the human voice appeared strikingly increased. Words spoken in a low voice without a mask were found to be unintelligible to the audience, but when a mask was applied the words were easily understood in all parts without the speaker increasing his efforts. Further, the voice became more distinct. The result was considerably more marked in the case of tones of a higher pitch. The tone was neither blurred nor did it acquire a nasal quality through the mask. The peculiar formation of its mouth caused the tone to be conveyed . . . not only toward the front but toward the sides of the auditorium. The actor at once felt in his voice . . . increased carrying power. He found the simple face-masks to be acoustically superior to the animal masks which covered the whole head. . . . The result of these experiments all point to the conclusion that the actors of antiquity were well aware of the advantages gained by the use of the mask.

It is also important to remember that Greek acting was undoubtedly far less like what we consider acting to be than like the delivery of operatic recitative or arias. The prime requisite for an actor was a vocal organ that, with the aid of a mask, had enough volume, the proper pitch, and sufficient resonance to carry in the open air. "Whenever an actor is mentioned by an ancient author, he is referred to in language which at the present day would seem more appropriate to . . . an operatic singer. It is always the excellence of the voice which is emphasized, little regard being paid to other accomplishments. And it is not so much the quality as the strength of the voice that is commended. The highest merit, on the Greek stage, was to have a voice that could fill the whole theatre." Sophocles abandoned acting in his own plays because his voice was too weak.

Successful actors were rare in the Greek theatre for the same reason that great opera-singers are rare in ours: phenomenal voices do not occur very often in any one generation. When they did occur in ancient Greece they commanded salaries almost as spectacular for their day as those now given to leading tenors and sopranos. Vocal virtuosity, being a phenomenal exception, aroused the same intense popular interest as that of our Melbas, De Reszkés, and Carusos. Aristotle, disgruntled, complained that actors had become more important than authors—the tragic poets—and explained the fact on the ground that most of the audience, too ignorant to be familiar with the legends on which the trilogies were based, judged the merit of the play by an actor's voice. An actor's public performance was in fact judged by a huge gallery of "fans" who either cheered him or pelted him with the figs and olives they were munching, just as the gallery gods in provincial Italy, self-appointed guardians of the traditions of *bel canto,* still bombard a singer with bravos or oranges.

The noblest tragedy was not immune to such interruptions. "If the Athenians were dissatisfied with an actor or a play, they had no hesitation about revealing the fact, but promptly put a stop to the performance by means of hisses and groans. . . . They were able to do so with greater readiness, as several plays were always performed in succession, and they could call for the next play, without bringing the entertainment to a close. . . . There is an instance of such an occurrence in the story of the comic poet Hermon, whose play should naturally have come on late in the day; but, as all the previous performers were promptly hissed off the stage . . . he was called upon much sooner than he expected and in consequence was not ready to appear."

In addition to their public appearances, the annual contests of actors for a substantial money prize—the winners of the Olympic games had to be content with the amateur's guerdon of an olive sprig—attracted as excited a gallery as any of our recitals do, probably a more interested audience than ever attends the annual prize-giving at the Conservatoire of the Comédie Française. Alexander's statement, after one of his favourite actors had been defeated in a competition at Tyre, that rather than have it happen he would have preferred to lose part of his kingdom, is an exaggerated reflection of the hero-worship accorded acting throughout the Greek world for the previous century. Acting was so popular that, like horse-racing in England at present, it became fashionable for a king to patronize it.

But neither the mask nor the costume of the Greek actor concealed his personality or made him an anonymous mouthpiece. Depending primarily on the prodigality of his voice, he could nevertheless display the capacity for impersonation which distinguishes a Mary Garden or a Chaliapin from the singer who can do no more than punctuate a rôle with a few set gestures and the routine of traditional pantomime. By the third century B.C., casting to type, supposedly the bane of our Broadway stages, was in practice. One actor specialized in acting messengers, another in female parts. As there was a separate annual prize for both comic and tragic actors, this tended to make them specialize as well in either comic or tragic rôles. "No performer in both tragic and comic rôles is indubitably known until 106 B.C., when Praxiteles performed at Delphi as a comedian and nine years later as a tragedian." A typical example of casting to type is the case of Appollogenes: "At Argos he impersonated Heracles and Alexander, at Delphi, Heracles and Antaeus, at Dodona, Achilles, etc., in addition to winning a victory in boxing at Alexandria. Evidently this actor was a pugilist for whom rôles and plays were carefully chosen which would display his physique and strength to the best advantage." Or, in Broadway terms, the gentleman was a "star" and plays were chosen for him as "vehicles." Theodorus also "pulled star stuff," by insisting on having the first entrance in any play in which he performed. As this could not be done without rewriting tragedies that might be opened by a minor character, there was evidently sound reason for the law passed by Lycurgus placing the official texts of plays on record and fining actors for any deviation from them. The law was observed, for there is a record of Alexander's having paid a fine of ten talents for another of his favourite actors who was penalized for having interpolated one line in a comedy.

Nothing, however, prevented the personality of the Greek actor from dominating the Greek theatre of the fourth century B.C. as effectively as actors dominated the European theatre in the nineteenth century A.D. "In Athens the fourth century"—the heir of Aeschylus, Sophocles, and Euripides—"was the period when acting was brought to the greatest perfection. . . . The effect upon dramatic writing was most pernicious. The poets began to write their plays with a view to exhibiting the capacities of the actors. Scenes which had no connection with the plot were introduced for the sole purpose of enabling an actor to make a display of his talents. Sophocles is said by one of the old grammarians to have been guilty of the same sort of practice. . . . The charge might be brought with more plausibility against the monodies of Euripides, which are often feeble from a literary point of view, but would enable an actor with a fine voice to make a great impression." The actors' guild, the Actors' Equity of its day, called the Artists of Dionysus, finally became powerful enough to secure perpetual exemption from military service and exemption from arrest except for debt for all its members—an extraordinary privilege in view of the fact that all other able-bodied citizens were liable to military duty until sixty years of age.

However constrained the gait and gestures of a Greek actor may seem when we reconstruct them, freighted as they were with voluminous robes and weighted sandals some six inches thick, there were schools of realistic as opposed to more formal methods of delivery. The *Poetics* records the name of one actor who called his new-school rival an ape. Possibly the ape replied that his old-school rival was a pompous windbag. "The actors of the fourth century were censured by many critics for having degraded the art of acting . . . and for having introduced a style which was unworthy of the dignity of the tragic stage." On the other hand the dignity of the old stage evidently led to results that we find so stilted and boring in Shakespearean actors of our old school. The "booming and bellowing" of their Greek proto-types are mentioned and also the fact that two players, popular on tour in the country districts of Attica, were nicknamed "the ranters." Aristotle records the name of one actor as memorable because he invariably spoke in a natural voice. Obviously the realists celebrated their triumphs in the Greek theatre as they do in ours. The necessary touch of nature was possibly as much admired and desired by Pericleans as by Elizabethans.

The mask itself was far more realistic than its partisans who propose to revive it as an instrument of salvation for the modern stage would lead us to suppose. It was not an abstract face but a very concrete one, minutely particularizing a human type. Pollux lists no less than thirty masks for comedy, differentiated as to age, complexion, facial expression, colour of hair, carried to such details as "hanging eyebrows," "oldest" and "not quite so old," "a 'fair' man of a pleasant complexion," "a 'fairer' man, rather paler and displaying a countenance which betokens distress or sickness." Among the tragic masks there are six old men of varying degrees of whiteness, baldness, greyness; eight types of younger men varying from the godlike countenance to a squalid character with livid cheeks; three servants and eleven women, from the grey-haired crone to the young child. The comic mask of an old domestic servant has "two molar teeth only in each jaw." The types of women portrayed range from hags to young girls, including virgins, false virgins, and prostitutes, each distinguished by precise differences of complexion and head-dress. How much more distinctly could actresses today with wigs and grease-paint characterize a similar set ranging from flappers to society matrons? "The first glimpse of approaching actors enabled an ancient audience to identify the red-headed barbarian slave, the pale lovelorn youth, the boastful soldier, the voracious parasite, the scolding wife, the flatterer, the 'French' cook, the maiden betrayed or in distress, the stern father, the designing courtesan, etc., much more easily than a playbill of the modern type would have done."

The Greeks themselves, unlike their modern apologists, were sufficiently uninhibited by the formal plan of their playhouse to do portrait masks when the occasion demanded. In Aristophanes' comedy *The Clouds*, which lampooned Socrates, the philosopher stood erect during the performance so that the public could compare his features with the player's mask and marvel at the likeness. Aristophanes had to smear his face with wine lees and act Cleon in *The Knights;* no one would risk persecution by appearing in a mask of the tyrant. Choruses, whenever necessary, were carefully characterized. "Euripides' *Phoenician Maids* is laid in Thebes; but dress, accent, and the habit of oriental prostration mark the women in the chorus as non-Hellenic." According to Greek tradition the Furies in Aeschylus' *Eumenides* with their "black garments, bloody faces, and snaky locks produced so frightful an impression that boys fainted and women miscarried."

Far from exploiting the formalism of the mask, Greek playwrights often were aware of the dramatic limitations imposed by its rigidity. The subtleties of facial expression—so large a part of acting to our eyes—could not have carried far enough in a Greek theatre to be generally seen. Nevertheless the instinct of the Greek playwright was so far from holding verisimilitude in contempt that he occasionally inserted lines to explain the set facial expression of a mask unable to change with the emotions of a scene. Sophocles' Electra, mourning for Orestes, whom she believes to be dead, is suddenly faced with him. In order to make her grief-stricken expression plausible to the audience, Orestes asks her to "continue her lamentations and not allow their mother to read her secret in her radiant face," and she replies that her "old hatred of her mother is too ingrained to allow her countenance to be seen wreathed in smiles, but that her tears will be tears of joy."

4. RAGS AND CRUTCHES

The greatest period of Greek playwrighting, which began with Aeschylus, culminated in the tragedies of Euripides. It is precisely his realism that was assailed as a dangerous novelty. As Gilbert Murray says: "The disciple of the sophists did not leave these romances where he found them. He liked to think them out in terms of real life." Aristotle, while admitting that Euripides is the most tragic of all the poets, criticizes him for failing to idealize his characters, for depicting men "as they are" and not, like Sophocles, "men as they ought to be," and censures him as well for his "motiveless degradation of character"; or, as a modern pedant would put it, for needless preoccupation with morbid psychology. Aristophanes' *The Acharnians* caricatures Euripides in person, and makes his rags and tatters typical of a number of tragedies that have survived only in fragments. Witness part of the colloquy between Euripides, perched on the roof of his house composing a tragedy, and the Good Citizen.

Good Citizen: *You perch aloft to compose tragedies. . . . I am not astonished at your introducing cripples on the stage. And why dress in these miserable tragic rags? I do not wonder that your heroes are beggars. But, Euripides, on my knees I beseech you, give me the tatters of some old piece; for I have to treat the Chorus to a long speech, and if I do it ill, it is all over with me.*

Euripides: *What rags do you prefer? Those in which I rigged out Aeneus on the stage, that unhappy, miserable old man?*

Good Citizen: *No, I want those of some hero still more unfortunate.*

Euripides: *Of Phoenix, the blind man?*

Good Citizen: *No . . . you have another hero more unfortunate than him.*

Euripides: *. . . Do you mean those of the beggar Philoctetes?*

Good Citizen: *No, of another far more the mendicant.*

150

Euripides: *Is it the filthy dress of the lame fellow, Bellerophon?* . . .
  Ah! I know, it is Telephus, the Mysian.
Good Citizen: *Yes, Telephus. Give me his rags, I beg of you.*
Euripides: *Slave! Give him Telephus' tatters; they are on top of the*
  rags of Thyestes and mixed with those of Ino.

(*Bosschère edition.*)

Finally, after the Good Citizen has in addition wheedled from him a
beggar's hat, a basket, and an earthen pot, Euripides exclaims:

Miserable man! You are robbing me of an entire tragedy.

If some Drama League pundit today were capable of writing burlesque and, alarmed at the lack of interest shown by O'Neill or Gorki
in the True Ideal of the Drama, wanted to belittle their interest in low
life and their insistence upon "unpleasant and depressing facts which
have no place in the theatre," he could, by laying the scene in a municipal lodging-house and filling it with crippled beggars and drunken
longshoremen, easily write the skit in Aristophanes' terms. However,
in the case of Telephus, the innovation took, and whenever the beggar
king appeared thereafter he continued to wear rags, even in the plays
of Sophocles.

In *The Frogs* Aristophanes returns to the same charge, staging a
satirical debate before Dionysus, patron god of the dramatic festival.
Aeschylus berates Euripides for being a "crutch-and-cripple playwright." Euripides indicts the older playwright's heroics as "a torrent
of pure bombast" and defends his own realism:

I put things on the stage that came from daily life and business,
Where men could catch me if I tripped; could listen without dizziness
To things they knew, and judge my art. . . .

Their squabble runs on through nearly half the play and repeats all
the stock arguments, both as to style and as to subject-matter, that have

been used ever since when classicists and realists come to blows, including the typical rags.

Aeschylus

When heroes give range to their hearts, is it strange if the speech of them over us towers?

Nay, the garb of them too must be gorgeous to view, and majestical, nothing like ours.

All this I saw, and established as law, till you came and spoilt it.

Euripides

How so?

Aeschylus

You wrapped them in rags from old beggarmen's bags to express their heroical woe. . . .

(*Murray's translation.*)

The Frogs was produced twenty-one years after *The Acharnians*. Obviously poking fun at Euripides was always good for a laugh, for in *The Woman's Festival,* seven years previous to *The Frogs,* he is again lampooned for his realistic treatment of feminine psychology. Popular jokes are not made on esoteric subjects and an audience of twenty thousand would not, by the most successful comic author of his day, be expected to laugh at a quarrel about definitions confined to two literary cliques. The realism of the new school of tragedy must have been as much a matter of common knowledge and as obvious as our own distinction between high-brow and low-brow, before it could be made a sure-fire joke in the theatre.

5. THE POET AS JOURNALIST-HISTORIAN

The picture of contemporary affairs so evident to us in Greek comedy was less direct, but to Greek audiences none the less apparent, in more than one tragedy, even in such purely local matters as lawsuits, Athenians being apparently as eager to do jury duty as we are to evade it. Flickinger reminds some of us: "Inasmuch as from the time of Pericles citizens . . . received a slight stipend for serving upon juries, which ranged from 201 to 2,500 in membership and sometimes reached an aggregate of 6,000, there was scarcely an Athenian but was personally acquainted with courtroom procedure and not a few practically supported themselves in this way. Moreover, this situation was intensified by the fact that the fifth century witnessed the rise of formal oratory at Athens and its exploitation by numerous rhetorical and sophistic teachers. It is hardly possible that all these influences should have allowed contemporaneous drama to escape unscathed. Their first effect is seen in the actual introduction of a courtroom scene, as in Aeschylus' *Eumenides,* in which Orestes is put on trial before the Council of the Areopagus for having murdered his mother. Athena is the presiding judge, Apollo the attorney for the defense, and the chorus of Furies conducts the prosecution. . . . Euripides' *Trojan Women* . . . degenerates into a quasi-trial in which Menelaus presides as judge, Hecabe, ex-queen of Troy, represents the prosecution, and Helen pleads her own cause. . . . Finally, since in the law courts the addresses of the contending parties were equalized by means of the 'water-clock' (the clepsydra), it is not surprising that the speeches of sharply contrasted characters in tragedy are occasionally made of exactly the same length." Zimmern, in *The Greek Commonwealth,* in the same connection, remarks, "Aeschylus wrote his *Trilogy* to show us what a great advance of the human spirit the first city criminal court embodied; but we are so used to State justice that we prefer the murder to the trial—the *Agamemnon* to the *Eumenides*—and think his lesson an anti-climax."

Aeschylus inserted in *The Persians* a eulogy of Athens—"For all Greece submissive, when this city falls, will fall—" that could not fail to arouse patriotic cheers. The play itself, as one translator notes, "has the interest of being a contemporary record of the great sea-fight at

Salamis by an eye-witness." The inscription on Aeschylus' tomb celebrated his career as a soldier and contained not one word in regard
to his victories as a playwright. Athenians believed that Sophocles was
appointed one of the ten generals in command of the expedition
against Samos immediately after the *Antigone* was performed "on
account of the excellent political wisdom shown in certain passages."

Legendary history was often made contemporary history by the
deliberate choice of some part of the tale of Troy and Pelops' line that
paralleled current events. Euripides' *Andromache* was played shortly
after a moment during the Peloponnesian Wars when Sparta had
just broken the Peace of Nicias by refusing to surrender certain stipulated towns in the territory of one of Athens' allies. The resentment at
Athens was naturally intense and the traditional hatred of her great
military rival welcomed an outlet such as this play afforded in invective nominally addressed to Menelaus and his house, but in reality to
the Spartan militarists of the year 445 B.C.

> *If spear-renown*
> *And battle-fame be ta'en from Sparta's sons,*
> *In all else are ye meanest of mankind.*

Or:

> *O ye in all folk's eyes most loathed of men,*
> *Dwellers in Sparta, senates of treachery,*
> *Princes of lies, weavers of webs of guile,*
> *Thoughts crooked, wholesome never, devious all—*
> *A crime is your supremacy in Greece!*
> *What vileness lives not with you?—Swarming murders?*
> *Covetousness?—O ye convict of saying*
> *This with your tongue, while still your hearts mean that!*
> *Now ruin seize ye!*
>
> (*Way's translation.*)

The murders in this case referred to a particular violation of the sacred right of asylum which corresponded to the Hague conventions of our day concerning the Red Cross flag and the protection of non-belligerents. "Some helots had taken refuge as suppliants in the sanctuary of Poseidon at Cape Taenarum; the Lacedaemonians treacherously induced them to come out, took them off and killed them." Substitute the word Prussia for Sparta and imagine Euripides' invective as part of a performance given in any Allied capital just after the invasion of Belgium, Von Bethmann-Hollweg's reference to a treaty as a scrap of paper, the shelling of Rheims Cathedral, or a submarine attack on a hospital ship, and one can get some idea of the effect of poetry in the Athenian theatre at the time it was spoken.

The Suppliants contains another glorification of Athens, addressed to Theseus, one of her mythical rulers, but at the time the play was written vividly expressive of the ambition which animated the city to engage in a military struggle in order to dominate the entire Greek world.

> *Thou hast seen men scorn thy City, call her wild*
> *Of counsel, mad: thou hast seen the fire of morn*
> *Flash from her eyes, in answer to their scorn.*
> *Come toil on toil; 'tis this that makes her grand:*
> *Peril on peril!*

And the same speech makes a withering reference to the timid neutrality of cities that were then hesitating to become Athens' military allies, a passage as contemptuous in tone as any that interlarded the editorials of our pro-war press in 1916.

> *And common states, that stand*
> *In caution, twilight cities, dimly wise—*
> *Ye know them, for no light is in their eyes.*
> (*Murray's translation.*)

In the same play, Athene's speech to Theseus—

> *Let yon Adrastus swear. . . .*
> *Be this the oath—that never Argive men*
> *Shall bear against this land array of war;*
> *If others come, their spear shall bar the way.*
> *If ye break oath, and come against our town,*
> *Call down on Argos miserable ruin—*
>
> (*Way's translation.*)

refers to a then recent offensive and defensive alliance with Argos, a temporary but brilliant diplomatic victory over Sparta scored by Alcibiades. The essential terms of the treaty—a copy of which on a stone inscription was unearthed at Athens in 1876—including the provision never to invade Attica and to attack any army that did, are precisely those mentioned by Pallas Athene. Moreover, the hatred of Thebes voiced by these suppliants for refusing to allow the burial of their dead recalls an exactly parallel incident, fresh in the memory of every Athenian who heard the play: four years previously when the Thebans were victorious after the battle of Delium they refused the same privilege to the defeated Athenian troops.

We fail to realize how much Greek poetry was a kind of exalted journalism and deliberate propaganda timed, like the orations of statesmen, to provide criticism of history in the making. The *Erectheus* contains what is probably the most eloquent recruiting speech ever penned, when Praxithea declares:

> *One name the whole state hath, but many dwell*
> *Therein: dare I give ruin to these,*
> *I who for all can yield my one to death?*
> *If in mine halls I had, in daughter's stead,*
> *Male seed, and flame of war enwrapped this town,*
> *Should I for dread of death forbear to send them*

Forth to the strife of spears? Nay, be my sons
Such as shall fight, and win renown with men,
Not be vain outward shows our walls within.
When mothers' tears escort their sons to war,
Oft they unman them on the verge of fight.
Out upon women, who, in glory's stead,
Choose for their sons life, counsel craven fear.
My child—mine according to the flesh—
I give for my land's ransom. . . .
Countrymen, use ye this fruit of my womb:
Be saved, be victors! . . .
My country, O that all who people thee
Might love thee even as I!

(Way's translation.)

In the theatre this exhortation had an instant and much wider application than the willingness of a legendary Attic queen to sacrifice her daughter at the bidding of an oracle in order to propitiate the gods and repel the invasion of a Thracian king. Our fancy picture of the Athenians has become so sentimentalized that we rarely remember that, however much less Prussian than the Spartans they may have been, military service was compulsory in Athens and war almost continuous during the period when her greatest tragedies were written. Praxithea's appeal was as a matter of fact recognized as a model homily on patriotic duty. The orator Lycurgus quotes the words as an example of "a greatness of spirit and a nobility worthy indeed of Athens."

Euripides missed few opportunities to refer to the events of the day. In 415 the Sicilian expedition left Athens. The chorus of the *Daughters of Troy,* performed in the same year, declare that they have heard of "the rare excellence of the land of Aetna, consecrated to Hephaestus, of Sicily mother of mountains, opposite the Phoenician shore." Two years later in the epilogue of *Electra* the demigod Pollux, who appears as the *deus ex machina,* declares that he is about to fly as far as the Sicilian sea in order to save the vessels there. Nothing could be more extraneous to the moment when Orestes has just been pardoned by him than his words:

> But hark, the far Sicilian sea
>> Calls and a noise of men and ships
>> That labour sunken to the lips
> In bitter billows; forth go we,
> Through the long leagues of fiery blue
>> With saving. . . .

(*Murray's translation.*)

A few months before *Hippolytus* was acted, Pericles had died of the plague. At the conclusion of the play the chorus chanted:

> On the city hath lighted a stroke without warning,
>> On all hearts desolation.
> Rain down, O ye fast-falling tears of our mourning!
> When the mighty are fallen, their burial-oblation
>> Is the wail of a nation.

(*Way's translation.*)

The militant patriotism of the passages cited was not simulated in order to play to the gallery. It was experienced, for Euripides, like every other Athenian citizen, was not released from military duty until the age of sixty. "He had had forty years of it, steady work for the most part; fighting against Boeotians, Spartans, Corinthians, against Thracian barbarians." As a poet he identified himself with the cause of a victorious Athens until, known as the "tyrant city," she became the victim of her own militarism, like every other nation which has since waged war to end war. Euripides' growing disillusion can be traced in tragedies that were prompted by the changed political conditions about him.

Pericles had warned the Athenians: "Do not imagine that you are fighting about a simple issue, the subjection or independence of certain cities. You have an Empire to lose, and a danger to face from those who hate you for your empire. To resign it now would be impossible—if at this crisis some timid and inactive spirits are hankering after righteousness even at that price!" Substitute for "timid and inactive" the word "pacifists," for "hankering after righteousness" the phrase "peace without victory," or "peace at any price," and how near in temper and in logic Pericles comes to the arguments made in defence of the British Empire from 1914 to 1918! It was not long before Athens and her allies, like England, were fighting with their backs to the wall, and in panic clung to "strong men," tyrants and demagogues, Lloyd Georges, who might save the day—Alcibiades, Creon, and his parody, Hyperbolus. "All Greece—we have the emphatic and disinterested testimony of Thucydides for the statement—was gradually corrupted and embittered by the long war." This state of mind is reflected in Euripides' *Ion*, where that hero, when asked why he prefers to remain in Delphi rather than go to Athens, "the glorious earth-born state," and claim his birthright, replies:

> *Then, if I press to Athens' highest ranks,*
> *And seek a name, of dullards shall I win*
> *Hatred; for jealousy ever dogs success.*
> *Good men, whose wisdom well could helm the state,*
> *Who yet hang back, who never speak in public,*
> *To them shall I be laughing-stock and fool,*
> *Who, in a town censorious, go not softly.*
> *And statesmen who have made their mark, mid whom*
> *I seek repute, will hedge me in, and check*
> *By the assembly's votes. 'Tis ever so;*
> *They which sway nations, and have won repute,*
> *To young ambitions are the bitterest foes.*

159

And he adds that in Delphi,

> *no villain jostleth me*
> *Out of the path: it galls the very soul*
> *To yield the pass, and vail to baser men.*

(*Way's translation.*)

Plainly the Athens that is referred to is not the primitive city-kingdom ruled by Erectheus, but a contemporary Athens of the same intriguing and jealous demagogues whom Aristophanes pilloried in *The Knights* and *The Peace*. The passage may refer as well to the persecution that Euripides had himself suffered at the hands of a censorious town, when he had been called before the committee in charge of the annual Dionysiac contest, for which tragic trilogies were written, and later been arraigned by a certain Hygiaenon, on charges of impiety. The passage voices the cry always raised in a corrupt state that the best men are afraid to speak out and too disillusioned to come forward.

The play as a whole is a passionate indictment of Apollo and his Delphic oracle. It seems surprising that it caused less protest than slighter expressions of impiety in other plays had aroused, until we are reminded that at the time "an attack on the god of Delphi was not particularly objectionable in Athens. For that god, by the mouth of his official prophets, at the beginning of the war, had assured the Spartans that if they fought well they would conquer and that He, the God, would be fighting for them."

In 416 occurred a flagrant violation of neutrality with Athens playing the rôle of Prussian despot. Melos, one of the common states that stood "in caution . . . dimly wise," a small island of agriculturists, refused to become a military ally. Athens besieged the place, overwhelmed it with numbers, deliberately killed every able-bodied male citizen, enslaved every woman and child, and sent five hundred Athenians as colonists to rehabilitate the ruins. This bit of unnecessary military brutality profoundly shocked sensitive Athenians' minds, already alienated by the excesses of the war party. Thucydides devotes no less than twenty-six chapters to his account of the occurrence. The following spring, Euripides produced *The Trojan Women,* which strips the greatest conquest of legendary Greek history of any patch of glory and shows the bloody futility and the horror of victory in terms of the death and slavery of Trojan women and children. Can there be any doubt that they were also the women and children of Melos whom Athenians had just seen in the streets as prisoners of war on the way to the slave market? Was it not Melos as well as Troy where "groves are empty and the sanctuaries run red with blood"? And when Poseidon concludes:

> *How are ye blind,*
> *Ye treaders down of cities, ye that cast*
> *Temples to desolation, and lay waste*
> *Tombs, the untrodden sanctuaries where lie*
> *The ancient dead; yourselves so soon to die!—*
>
> (*Murray's translation.*)

his words evoked not only pity and terror for an ancient holocaust but for its repetition against a defenceless population, a deed in which the soldier-citizens in the audience had either connived or actually taken part. The words were prophetic. Many of those addressed were about to die only a few years later on the ill-fated Sicilian expedition where the Athenian empire met its military doom.

6. THE POET AS A CRITIC OF SOCIETY

A critic of militarism when victory perches on the banners of a returning army may be forgiven or forgotten, silenced in the uproar of jubilation. But a pacifist who indicts an army when disaster lowers and desperate expedients are being resorted to is promptly pilloried for destroying fighting morale. And when disaster has arrived his words are remembered and he with them as an enemy of the state. Euripides' disaffection contributed to his growing personal unpopularity and was one of the many reasons for which, as an ancient historian says, "The Athenians had a grudge against him," an unpopularity that finally led him to end his life in voluntary exile. Aeschylus had embraced the same alternative as a result of the unpopularity of his political and religious opinions. A year after *The Persians* he wrote a trilogy of which *The Seven Against Thebes* survives, which was definitely anti-imperialist in idea, "directed against the policy of aiming at the supremacy of Athens by attacking other Greek states, and, in brief, maintained the policy of Aristeides as against Themistocles." Three years later he was, like Euripides, charged with impiety, on the ground that he had been realistic enough to reproduce certain rites of the sacred mysteries on the stage. Although acquitted, he left Athens the same year, remained at foreign courts for the next ten years of his life, and returned to Athens only two years before his death. But his last trilogy was construed as a reactionary protest, "religious, social and political, which culminated in the assertion of the divine authority of the Court of Areopagos" then under attack. Popular feeling was so aroused against him that he again left Athens, to die two years later in Sicily. Such was the supposedly impersonal and abstract art of Greek tragedy!

But there were many more reasons for Euripides' becoming *persona non grata* in Athens. His sceptical and unorthodox mind criticized the entire range of Greek habits of thought and Greek moral conventions, and brought him official reprimands and continual attacks from literary critics. How antagonistic his point of view was to Athenian officialdom is evinced by the fact that of his eighty-eight tragedies only twelve were awarded prizes. His specific criticisms of accepted codes made his plays as much problem plays when they were first acted as Ibsen's were when they were first printed. He seized upon a subject such as *Melanippe the Philosopher* in order to expound his ideas about the origin of matter, for Anaxagoras had startled every one with his doctrine that the sun was a burning rock, and Euripides disagreed with him. Elsewhere he expresses his contempt for the early astrologers

> *whose pestilent tongue flings random lies abroad.*

Nevertheless he is no believer in the accepted religion of his time. The opening lines of the *Melanippe*—

> *Zeus—whoso Zeus is: this I know not, save*
> *By hearsay—*

started a riot in the theatre, and in response to public clamour he later substituted others. But he managed to slip the same idea into other plays. Heracles remarks, "Zeus—whoever Zeus may be," and Orestes declares:

> *We are the slaves of the gods, whoever the gods may be,*

and again:

> *Whoe'er thou be, O past our finding out,*
> *Zeus, be thou a Nature's law, or mind of man,*
> *To thee I pray.*

For Zeus, substitute the word God, or Christ, and then decide how far this is from a type of free thought that was revolutionary only yesterday.

Such ideas were also revolutionary in Athens of the fourth century, but Euripides was not unique in holding them. "Socrates," runs a fragment of verse from an unknown comedy, "piles the faggots for Euripides' fire," and Socrates was to drink the hemlock. Euripides was an intimate friend of Protagoras, who read to him from the same book that was publicly burned when the philosopher was prosecuted and condemned. During Euripides' lifetime, a century after Pythagoras,

163

the first astronomer to conceive of the earth and the planets as spheres, Anaxagoras, was imprisoned for his doctrine that the "sun was a red hot stone made of rock larger than the Peloponnesus," and was ultimately exiled. "The age in which Euripides lived is at one and the same time the age of the most daring criticism, of the boldest denials, and of the most active religious feeling," strikingly like our own in its intellectual conflicts between vested religious and political authority, and in its opponents, who used as their weapons the first purely scientific and mathematical concepts of the origin of matter and the nature of things. Euripides echoed that criticism as definitely in his tragedies as Shaw has in his comedies. One of his last plays, *The Bacchae,* is very largely a discussion pro and con of the values of Bacchic mysticism and its orgiastic rituals. He criticizes the mysteries of a new cult, the Orphic sect. In the *Alcestis* and the *Hippolytus* he lectures the gods for their love-affairs, which bred demigods and heroes —"Gods should not have the same passions as men"—and indicts them with such statements as "If deeds of shame gods do, no gods are they." In describing the sins and passions of men he is always ready with his *tu quoque,* and reminds Olympus that its own escapades have set a thoroughly bad example.

> *How were it just then that ye should enact*
> *For men laws, and yourselves work lawlessness? . . .*
>
> *For, following pleasure past all wisdom's bounds,*
> *Ye work unrighteousness. Unjust it were*
> *To call men vile, if we but imitate*
> *The sins of Gods:—they are vile which teach us this.*

If you happen to be a pious church-goer, put yourself in the place of equally pious Greek temple-goers who heard these words. Would they have been any less scandalized than you would be by analogous assertions that Jehovah was a bad-tempered tyrant and the Virgin was not different from any other woman who had had a love-affair and borne an illegitimate child? Euripides in fact reached the point of view which bred our own biblical criticism and our own atheism. He sees any deity as no more than the projection of our own desires—

All folly is to men their Aphrodite.

A good many years later Plutarch was frightened by the same point of view into asking: "Into what an abyss of impiety shall we fall if each deity is for us only a passion, a force, a virtue?"

Euripides is equally critical of such minor aspects of piety as consulting soothsayers and oracles, who could read the will of the gods in a flight of birds, and he refuses to consider an oath taken in the name of the gods necessarily binding, or the right of asylum sacred.

Sheer folly this
Even to dream that birds can help mankind. . . .

With sacrifice
To Gods, ask good, and let soothsayings be. . . .
Sound wit, with prudence, is the seer of seers.

When an unrighteous man takes sanctuary
At the altar, I would set at naught the law,
And, fearless of the Gods, to justice hale him.

Hippolytus replies to his nurse: "That is an oath my lips have sworn; no oath is on my soul." These are not moralizings *in vacuo.* Swearing by the gods was considered just as necessary as swearing on the Bible is now when we take the witness-stand. Consulting oracles was a recognized practice. Nicias, for a time the political boss of Athens, never made a move without consulting several and even had a soothsayer as part of his household to be ready for any emergency. Just before the

Sicilian expedition sailed, Athens was thrown into a panic because certain sacred images of Hermes placed at street corners were found to have been damaged by vandals. To deny the right of sanctuary was as startling as if an author today showed a thief at confessional and then praised the priest who denounced him to the police. Characters who uttered such challenges were not mythical but actual personages, as definitely rebels as Nora or John Tanner, arguing about the alternatives that their contemporaries had to face.

Aphorisms that are no more to us than wise saws were modern instances to Euripides' fellow citizens. Socrates is said to have left the theatre when Electra declared "the wisest course is to leave to chance all judgment about human virtue." The anecdote may be apocryphal, but such stories do not originate about a theatre in which the writing of tragedy is concerned with nothing more than retelling sad stories of the death of kings. Any number of respectable citizens may easily have been shocked enough to walk out of other performances. When Aeolus cries to his son:

Canst face mine eyes, fresh from thy deed of shame?

and the son replies:

What is shame, when the doer feels no shame?

were there no Athenian fathers who wondered what the younger generation was coming to, or how the official play jury could permit a script containing such an appalling example to come to public performance?

Euripides pushed the expression of his personal opinions to the point of becoming what conservatives today call a dangerous radical, primarily because he was a thorough-going and consistent democrat. We used to refer glibly to Athens as a democracy, which in our sense of the word it was not, being a small body of hereditary free citizens, landlords, soldiers, and bureaucrats who could no more have gone into trade without disgracing themselves than the son of an English country gentleman could before the twentieth century. Their trading was done for them by a small group of resident aliens, imported for the purpose; their income was earned for them by peasant serfs tilling their fields and slaves working their silver-mines. In 431 there were 40,000 adult male citizens in Attica and 55,000 male slaves—with their women and children counted, nearly 100,000. But Euripides on every possible occasion is outspoken in his sympathy for these underdogs. In one instance he suggests that the word "master" be reserved for addressing Zeus. *Alexander,* the concluding play of the trilogy opened by *The Trojan Women,* took a supposed slave for its hero. Aristophanes voices a general complaint when he says that in Euripides' plays servants speak with as much authority as their masters. Were there no protests from other patricians convinced that this was putting dangerous ideas into the heads of the lower classes, who should be taught to look up to their owners if the prosperity of Athens was to continue? Could they as good patriots have failed to hiss? But Euripides outraged them still further by introducing, into tragedies supposedly consecrated to royalty, peasants who were presented not as bumpkins, but as the first of nature's noblemen, the peers of the more aristocratic protagonists. He introduces a peasant in *Orestes,* whom he points to as a paragon, "a stainless man who led a blameless life." He invents a peasant husband for Electra. When Orestes is astounded to find her living with him in a cowherd's hut she defends him: "Yes, he who dwells here is poor but has a noble soul." Orestes, pondering upon his nobility, is converted, and concludes:

> *Lo, there is no sure test for manhood's worth. . . .*
> *I have seen ere now a noble father's son*
> *Proved nothing-worth, seen good sons of ill sires,*

> *Starved leanness in a rich man's very soul,*
> *And in a poor man's body a great heart. . . .*
> *For this man is not among Argives great,*
> *Nor by a noble house's name exalted,*
> *But one of the many—proved a king of men.*
>
> (*Way's translation.*)

Thus he anticipates by slightly more than two thousand years the political implications drawn from the same sentiments when every man was declared to be the equal of a king, and democracy was finally established by making it possible for even the poorest newsboy or *camelot* to become President of a republic.

7. THE CULT OF THE PSEUDO-GREEK

Evidently the trend of the Greek theatre was in the direction not of pure art and aesthetic generalization but of the most concrete identification with immediate experience that it could contrive. Limited to retelling the miseries of archaic rulers and their progeny, it nevertheless turned these legends into a reflection of contemporary life and a propagandist's vehicle for moulding public opinion. It developed scenery as a background necessary to dramatic action, established the first attempts at scene-shifting, and pushed the exactitude of costuming to the point of dressing a beggar in rags and defining the exact number of teeth to be seen in the jaws of a hag. Its actors were not quasi-priests intoning a liturgy but virtuosi admired for their ability to characterize human beings and capable of arousing mobs to a frenzy of enthusiasm or rage by voicing opinions as well as by miming emotions. The purpose of a Greek playwright was to describe and analyze the problems, moral and political, that were the problems of his day, not to limit himself to exercises in pure poetry and so become the prototype of the literary gentlemen whose treatment of lofty themes never offended either the dear Queen or the Archbishop of Canterbury. Innovations that brought an imitation of life into the theatre, then as now, outraged the guardians of propriety. In methods as well as in subject-matter, two of the three greatest Greek playwrights hurdled the established rules as to the proper scope of drama, and left dramatic critics, then as now, mending the fences of dogma behind them. Greek dramatists were not a separate race of men telling fairy-tales in a tragic Never-Never Land but fellow townsmen of the comic poet whose genius for journalistic lampooning, homilies on local foibles, and political satire is not approached again until Molière writes *Les Précieuses Ridicules* and Shaw begins his *Plays Pleasant and Unpleasant*. No better summary of Shaw's prefaces will in all probability ever be written than Aristophanes' praise of his own comedies—equally applicable to Euripides' tragedies—spoken by the chorus in *The Acharnians*:

As for you, never lose him who will always fight for the cause of justice in his comedies; he promises you that his precepts will lead you to happiness, though he uses neither flattery, nor intrigue, nor bribery, nor deceit; instead of loading you with praise, he will point you to the better way.

But these efforts were received, as they always are in a living theatre, as part of the process of being entertained by an exciting or amusing show. It is interesting to compare Sheldon Cheney's reconstruction of the mood of an Athenian audience, in a chapter entitled "The Noble Greeks," with the descriptions of it that occur in the records of classical authors. "At the end of this utterly moving, purging, terrible drama," says Mr. Cheney, "we spectators wake gradually to the world around us. There is something absurdly trivial about the things we do . . . we stand and stretch, and perhaps turn a little away from the sun—and titter because a man is sobbing near us. Our feelings are very close to the surface, and we have a tendency to lose sight of the audience around us in recurring fits of 'star-gazing.' . . . Twice more we are to suffer through the tragedies of Sophocles this day. Ah, but we shall welcome them. We await, content." Contrast this with what certain of the ancients saw, as summarized by Haigh: "There was the man of taste, who prided himself on his superior discernment, and used to hiss when every one else was applauding, and clap when every one else was silent. There was the person who made himself objectionable to his neighbours by whistling an accompaniment to tunes which happened to please him. There were 'the young men of the town,' who took a malign pleasure in hissing a play off the stage. There were the people who brought out their provisions during the less exciting parts of the entertainment. There was the somnolent individual who slept peacefully through tragedies and comedies, and was not even waked up by the noise of the audience going away." How like ourselves—our own *hoi polloi* at amateur night at a burlesque house, our own intellectuals at a "brilliant" opening at an art theatre, or our own "tired business men" dragged to a performance of *Parsifal!*

The contrast reminds me of that immortal caricature by Max Beerbohm in which Mrs. Humphry Ward as a child in pinafore and pigtails looks up reproachfully at Matthew Arnold and remarks, "Why, Uncle Matthew, oh, why, will not you be always wholly serious?" The Athenians, alas, were not wholly serious, but we can be when in Mr. Cheney's company. The instances I have cited are not my own suppositions but a compilation of the conclusions upon which such authoritative scholars as Haigh, Flickinger, Murray, and Decharme are in agreement. Their volumes on the Greek theatre are accepted works of reference, most of them available at public libraries for the last twenty years. None of their findings has been seriously disputed. But we shall probably continue to ignore them and invoke a Greek theatre where an audience did not roar and riot, playwrights achieved a species of pure poetry that they never desired to write, and stage setting presented a kind of blank formalism that was not attempted. And the next prophet of the new stage-craft who bids us emulate a Greek theatre that never existed will no doubt be listened to with respect. Possibly we shall always need such myths as the pure art of a fictitiously noble Greek or the personal virtue of a fictitiously pure Puritan. For when we fail to impose false standards of art or morals on the life around us, it is far more comforting, rather than admit that they are false, to transfer them to a past where we can pretend that they existed.

CHAPTER II

NATURALISM—1501

I. THE STAGE-MANAGER OF MONS

A PIECE of research by an English scholar usually bears some resemblance to a sportsman's holiday. Cover is beaten, furtive facts take to the open, and a satisfactory number are then brought down and bagged. A sporting code is observed: the subject is not exhausted, just as a country-side is not depleted of game. After the trophies are counted, the discussion has much of the ease and urbanity of conversation over the dinner-table between friends who share the same hobby. We follow a German *Forscher* as we might clamber after a mountain guide in the Bavarian Alps, wondering how a fellow so fat manages to keep ahead of us despite his beer-inflated waist and leave us winded in his wake. We are weighted down with concentrated samples of all previous knowledge of the subject, packed in the *Rucksack* that cuts at our shoulders, heavy with its excessive ration of condensed nourishment. We make ready for every danger, encumbered with hobnailed shoes, rope, and ice-axe. Thunder rumbles; in the humid atmosphere of a storm that never breaks we are hauled up the dizzying faces of deductions without a visible foothold and over frozen crevasses of error. Finally in a flash of lightning the peak is revealed; the clouds break; we gain a new point of view like a panorama from a mountain-top, and sit contemplating it, exhausted, drenched with intellectual perspiration. But with a French savant as a guide, we usually seem to have come no distance at all, to have been led through a gap in the trees to the edge of a plateau where a typically broad French valley rolls at our feet. We investigate it at leisure. The storm is always past; the country-side is glitteringly fresh, washed with rain, every detail of it cleaned and clear. A neglected château has been reconstructed. All previous efforts in the same field spread about it like the neatly tilled acres of tenant-farmers who originally owed it allegiance.

Any number of references to the pageantry of mysteries and passion-plays had been pried from contemporary records, but no complete description of the setting and the direction of an entire performance was known until in 1913 Professor Gustave Cohen, of the University of Strasbourg and the Sorbonne, discovered in the archives of Mons a unique document, the prompt-copy of a manuscript, *The Mystery of the Passion,* performed there in 1501, completely annotated by the stage-manager with detailed directions for the settings used and precise directions for acting the script, which required four mornings and four afternoons to perform. These notes, as analyzed and published by Professor Cohen, reveal an amazing elaboration of stage-construction, an extensive use of stage-machinery and stage-effects, and an equally amazing concern for achieving naturalistic reproduction of biblical episodes. The fresh sides of beef that Antoine in the 1890's hung in his setting for *The Butchers* were considered a daring innovation and startled even those Parisians who had grown accustomed to the realism of Courbet. But for this production in sixteenth century Flanders, birds and beasts for the Garden of Eden were snared in the fields, turf was cut, bushes were uprooted and hung with both real and artificial fruit and flowers. Live fishes were supplied as well. Christ entered Jerusalem on an ass hired for the occasion; Mary used the same ass for the flight into Egypt, while Joseph led a living ox. A lamb was slaughtered for Abraham's sacrifice; the altar-fire was laid and actually burned. The mouth of Hell shot forth flames with a tremendous expenditure of spirits of nitre and gunpowder. Articulated dragons crawled and belched forth smoke. The water for the Deluge was piped over a roof abutting on the marketplace and fell in a downpour. Christ and the saints were "assumpted" into Heaven on pulleys, like the classic *deus ex machina*. The huge wooden platform-stage was pierced with trap-doors for sudden and miraculous appearances and disappearances. The elaboration of this spectacle would today have taxed the resources of any large country town, used the live stock of a small farm, depleted most of the stock in hand of a local lumber-yard, hardware store, and dry-goods emporium, including all the Fourth of July rockets, firecrackers, and pin-wheels, and kept all the available blacksmiths and carpenters busy for a month in getting the production ready.

There can be no doubt that these effects were not only planned but achieved, for the annotated script as found was accompanied by a complete expense account for every item, giving the names of the journeymen hired, the wages, the amount of material used, and the time consumed. The entries make valuable reading for any one inclined to believe that the spirituality of a performance of a mystery-play in an open-air theatre depended upon non-representative stage setting or avoided any of the literal imitations of nature for which the late Beerbohm Tree and David Belasco have so often been criticized. This typical production of a religious spectacle is full of the artistic sins supposedly not bred until the blight of realism attacked the stage four hundred years later.

2. LIVE STOCK AND FIREWORKS

Typical entries and expenditures are the following (the monetary units are 1 livre = 2.22 gold francs, 20 sols = 1 livre, 12 derniers = 1 sol):

To Jehan d'Ath, called le Cuppre, for 3 baskets of earth for the Hourt [platform-stage] *at 2s. apiece : 6s.*

To Jehan Du Quesne for 18 wagonloads of grass, also his horse and cart at 18d. apiece or : 27s.

To Jehan Foucquart, called Docque Docque, for feeding certain birds of every variety, to be used for the Creation : 6s.

To Ghendart, sergeant at Nimy, for live rabbits for the Creation of the beasts and birds : 5s.

For two live lambs . . . for the aforesaid Creation and also for the sacrifice of Abel and Abraham : 32s.

To Brouillon and his companion for various kinds of birds delivered by him this day for the aforesaid Creation and also for the Ark of Noah, 12s.

For live fishes for the aforesaid Creation : 16s.

To Jehan de la Desoubz and Collart Randoul for having brought various trees for the Earthly Paradise : 7s.

For apples old and new and also cherries to put on the trees of the Earthly Paradise : 5s.

Evidently dried apples appeared on the Tree of Knowledge after the Fall. But exotic fruits were imitated as well:

To Ogier Counin, for three days employed by him at the inn of M. le Maistre to make the apple tree of oranges and fig leaves at 8s. a day : 24s.

The effects of Hell's mouth involved flame-throwers, gunpowder, and machines for making thunder:

To Master Jehan du Fayt for 6 days employed by him for making powder for hell, at 8s. per day : 32s.

For 10 instruments for throwing flame in Hell and 2 large iron pipes : 24s.

Item for 4 pivots of iron, each having four iron bands and 4 rings to turn two handles, 16 staples to attach them to two large copper tubs for making thunder in Hell, weighing 24 pounds, at 2s. per pound : 48s.

To Pierart Viscave, tinker, for the installation of two big sheets of bronze for the aforesaid mystery, placed in Hell to make thunder, has been paid : 32s.

Certain of the damned were given an added aspect of terror by gnarled head-dresses made of the roots of trees:

To Master Jehan Machon, executioner, for 2 days employed by him in digging up several roots of trees for use in Hell : 24s.

Dragons and serpents, some of them breathing fire, were fabricated.

To Andrieu Ghislain, thresher, for having made the bodies of seven serpents of willow as agreed, paid : 4l.

To Andrieu Ghislain, for having made 2 serpents of willow—4 legs and 2 arms, including a basket : 36s.

To Jehan Des Quesnes, sabot maker, for 1 willow stump, for making the moulds for 2 heads, one of a devil and another of a dragon : 14s.

To Godefroy du Pont for five and one half days of his time employed by him for the fitting of serpents with pipes for throwing flames, at 8s. a day : 44s.

Lucifer was covered by a tent and held captive by three chains weighing a hundred and twenty pounds, paid for at the rate of 3 sols a pound. The entrance to Hell's mouth was through a gigantic "mask of a toad face." Its size may be gauged from the fact that a stone-mason and two assistants spent three days modelling it and used eighteen cartloads of clay. It was then covered with canvas and painted. The scenic effects of these infernal regions were so elaborate that seventeen stage hands were needed to work them:

> *To Master Jehan du Fayt and his assistants numbering 17 persons for having helped in Hell for nine days during the said Mystery at 6s. a day to each, 45l. 18s.*

Their routine was so intricate that they were supplied with special prompt-slips for timing "the tempests," "great tempests," "terrible noise," and the sound of cannon made by letting off fireworks in a box. (The sound of cannon is imitated off-stage today by shooting a revolver into a barrel.) One such stage-direction warns the chief mechanician:

> *Remind those who work the secrets of the thunder barrels to do what is assigned to them by following their instruction slips and let them not forget to stop when God says: Cease and let tranquillity reign.*

3. PLUMBING AND PULLEYS

Other crews of mechanics, probably counting as many men if not more, must have been needed to work the devices, called "secrets" in the script, which were elaborate machines. For the Pinnacle, at the top of the Temple in Jerusalem, where Satan carries Jesus to tempt him, twenty-six pounds of iron rings, an iron wheel, and handles to turn it as well as tenons and mortises for the moving platform, two locks, and forty-one pounds of rope were bought and paid for. These items are recorded as being used especially to raise and lower Jesus to the Pinnacle. The platform of Mount Tabor, which later became the

Mount of Olives, was seventeen feet long. During Christ's transfiguration clouds descended to mask it and one heard only his voice. Sixteen pounds of rope were needed to hoist into Paradise another platform holding Jesus and the angels. Painted clouds masked its edge. A wheel, for which the necessary carpentering and hardware are also specified, and to which the silhouettes of wooden angels were attached, circled above God's head, suggestive of the spheres of Dante's Paradise. At a certain moment these angels tremble as if about to fall. At another the veil of the Temple is rent, its stones fall, and "the dead arise and wander hither and thither without speaking." During the flight into Egypt, *"Joseph and Mary holding Jesus in her arms must pass before a temple and as soon as they pass, the idols fall to the ground."*

The final assumption of Jesus was also made actual with ropes and pulleys:

Here warn [the mechanics] *of the secret for lifting Jesus.*

Note that here Jesus must get on it, and if possible several angels also mount with him.

The stage held a small tank and water was hauled to fill it. One expense item records:

To Jehan Bracquet, boatman, for his salary for a small boat of wood to put in the water and for having gone to Jemapes [a near-by riverside town] *for water and brought it from the river to be used as the sea on the stage.*

This sea becomes the flood in which the Ark is held by a wooden cradle. The same carpenters who originally constructed it were the actors who built it on stage during the performance, putting its prepared pieces together with authentic precision. This same tank later becomes the Sea of Galilee. Eight Apostles get into boats and cross it. Previously, St. Peter and St. Andrew go through a pantomime of fishing.

At this point remind St. Andrew and St. Peter to go to the sea, enter and get out of the boats several times, act as though they wanted to fish and throw in and haul out their nets several times.

It is possible that the "live fishes" bought for the Creation were saved, placed beforehand in the submerged nets, and flapped when these were drawn ashore.

The most spectacular aquatic effect was the Deluge itself. The necessary expenditures for wine-barrels that served as temporary reservoirs on the roof of the Maison d'Allemaigne, overhanging the stage, are recorded, also a complicated system of pulleys, piping, and the "secret" that released the waters on cue by pulling a rope. The whole apparatus is elaborate enough to be referred to as an "engine." There can therefore be no doubt that when God called for the Deluge it was literally executed.

At this point give a signal to the deputies working the secret of the deluge to let the water come . . .

Down it came to the *"noise of thunder and tempest."* This was a favourite scenic effect in French and Flemish performances. During another mystery-play staged elsewhere, the downpour was so tremendous that not only the actors but also the spectators were drenched. But according to the record of an eyewitness they were so impressed by the technique displayed that they showed not the slightest resentment. In view of the careful specifications for hauling and piping water recorded in the expense-account at Mons, it appears certain that the hydro-mechanics and the stage-directions of other manuscripts were as literally reproduced, such as:

[The creation of the world] *should be seen as a sea with fish in it.*

[Water] *spurts forth in four streams in the manner of little fountains.*

Tubal drowns . . . here water covers the place where the mystery is played and one can have a number of men and women who pretend to drown but do not speak.

The platforms for divine ascents and descents at Mons are not exceptional; they are called for by other manuscripts. In the *Acts of the Apostles* a stage-direction reads: *"Here thunder must sound and a white cloud covers the apostles and brings them to the house where the Virgin is lying."* This was probably a trap in the balcony that served as Paradise, released on cue and let down to Mary's domicile placed beneath it. As today, wire was freely used in order to make the mechanics of the process less obvious. Another script, *The Resurrection,* carefully specifies that *"the ropes which carry the instrument on which Jesus stands should be hidden with canvas like clouds."* A burgher of Mons, could he be revived, would probably be neither shocked nor impressed by the sight of a solitary fountain playing in the garden at Belmont, Richard III entering on a white charger, Siegfried's dragon, or Peter Pan flying in and out of a window. He would not have been convinced of the marvels of modern progress in the theatre unless he had been resurrected when the Hippodrome tank and its Bathing Beauties were still in existence or when Bill Brady did his original flying leap from the Jersey water-front in *After Dark,* and emerged dripping wet.

4. PAINT AND ILLUMINATION

At Mons there was the same unconcern for the mixture of genres that has always characterized vigorous theatres. Side by side with naturalistic simulation, painted scenery was used as well. The salaries of five painters are recorded and there is a constant outlay for pigment of every kind, varnish, powdered silver, and gold-leaf. In addition to the painted clouds used during the Ascension and the Transfiguration, one back-drop of "canvas painted with golden stars" was sold after the performance as second-hand linen for 22 sols, as was also "a canvas on which are painted the sun and the moon." These may have been curtains drawn in front of God and his angels seated on the wooden balcony which served as the Heavenly Paradise. There are other back-drops painted to imitate damask, the blue stone of Écaussines (much used at the time and quarried in a neighbouring commune), also one on which columns were painted. The system of stage setting used was the simultaneous setting of mansions representing the House of Adam, the House of Abraham, the Temple, or the House of Joseph, the actors walking from one to the other. No less than sixty-seven such mansions are called for by the Mons manuscript. As the stage was no more than a hundred and twenty feet wide, many must have done double duty or been replaced between morning and afternoon sessions. But they were practical, for Jehan de Dours, cabinet-maker, was paid 48 sols for "making castles and turrets." The Pinnacle of the Temple had a turret with a door in it that was used. And the job of constructing and painting the settings needed for a passion-play was always a large order. There are records at Lyons of five hundred painters of importance in their day who, during the fourteenth to sixteenth centuries, from time to time painted stage scenery, most of it for open-air performances.

Lighting effects were attempted. One stage-direction calls for *"a great light and brilliance for the Nativity."* When Jesus is resurrected and rises from the tomb *"there must issue* [from it] *great radiance, smoke of incense and light."* Light was symbolized in one instance by make-up. *"Remember at this point to remind a painter to go to Paradise to paint Raphael's face red."* When Raphael takes his place at the tomb, he *"must have his face all red with the paint a painter will do for him."* A moving star worked by a "secret device" guides the Magi; atmosphere and mystery are suggested by gauze veils, a method still in use:

Note: There must be much light in Limbo and great brilliance and melody and the divinity, like a soul, covered with a tent of gauze must appear, with two angels.

After the final apotheosis:

Then a great sound of thunder is heard and the Holy Ghost descends in the form of tongues of fire.

The same pipes that made the dragons snort real fire could have been used to make the Holy Ghost a symbolic flame. At *The Mystery of Valenciennes* in 1547 the angels in heaven held gilded torches in their hands that resembled our Roman candles, for "from them issued crackling flames full of stars."

At Mons there is a characteristic mixture of the literal and the naïve in costuming. Peter and Andrew first appear as fishermen, later with the other disciples at the Last Supper in white robes. The distinction between the secular costume of the disciples and their symbolic one is carefully observed and the details of the latter are specified:

Note that all the Apostles must have white shoes on their feet, belts of white material on their robes; their mantles removed, and each a white staff in his hand like a pilgrim's staff.

Mary Magdalene at first appears in the most fashionable finery of the time. She makes an elaborate toilet, attendants bring her vials of rosewater, nard, a mirror, a sponge, and a comb. After her conversion the stage-directions call for her appearance in a simple dress and kerchief. When Jesus goes up into the mountain the stage-manager's annotations read:

Note that here Jesus must be dressed in a white robe, the whitest to be found, his face and hands burnished with gold and he must lift his hands . . .

God is costumed to suggest a high Church dignitary. He has a tiara, a purple robe bordered with marten's fur, and gloves. The Holy Ghost, sitting beside him in Paradise, also wears gloves like a bishop. How nude Adam and Eve were before the Fall is a matter of conjecture. But the stage-directions provide that after biting the apple "they each take a fig leaf from the fig tree" and add:

At this point remind God, who is underneath the hall of Paradise, to have two angels bring with them two fur robes which will be ready, to give to Adam and Eve when He returns to the Earthly Paradise [i.e. the Garden of Eden].

Christ's robe for the journey to Calvary, it is pointed out, must have an unsewn or ragged edge. Every practical difficulty is foreseen. The cross that Jesus carries is hollow so that it is not too heavy for an actor to lift. Changes of costume are very carefully provided for, and when there is not time for the change, the part is doubled by another actor.

Now Lucifer goes into the Earthly Paradise in the form of a serpent. Note that the personage of Lucifer does not move from hell until he is told to in what follows; but another person performs the serpent and goes to Eve, for the reason that Lucifer will not have time enough to be put into the body of a serpent.

In anticipating every important bit of action, every necessary costume change, and the preparation of properties and off-stage effects, this prompt-script of the year 1501 can still serve as a model for any stage-manager today.

183

5. FEINTS AND TRAPS

The mechanical tricks, known as feints, needed to ensure the successful running of a passion-play were a matter of such importance that the authorities of Mons incurred the expense of a messenger on horseback to the neighbouring town of Chauny, then famous for its acrobats and jugglers, to arrange for the services of the town's sergeant, Master Guillaume de le Chiere, and his mechanics. He is invited to Mons to settle the terms of the bargain and given an excellent dinner at a local inn, which being on the Grande Place must have been one of the best. Another messenger is despatched to Chauny to excuse the constable "before the Law" there for the time he has been kept away from his duties. Although the contract price finally agreed upon was exceeded—a not uncommon occurrence in present-day productions—the balance is paid without demur, the "secrets" delivered having been satisfactory. These included:

The secret of the Pinnacle, the false body of Saint John, the imitation sword of Herodias, the imitation sword with which Herod kills himself, the pulleys with which Judas hangs himself . . . two imitation pigeons of which one is red . . . two masks of the dead, the soft batons with which Jesus is beaten.

One of these "pigeons" was no doubt the dove which brought the olive leaf back to Noah, worked by a wire from the balcony of Heaven after a live dove had been released from the Ark, which, as the stage-directions state, *"does not return."* It was probably on the same balcony that the star of Bethlehem appeared, disappeared, and reappeared on cue. The fake swords were evidently like those still used on occasion today, weapons with collapsible or disappearing blades, so that they seem to enter a body and make the act of murder or suicide as realistic as possible. For the same reason a false body of John the Baptist was decapitated. The soft batons survive as the stuffed policeman's club of American vaudeville and English pantomimes, which thwacks resoundingly, springs back after each blow, and hurts no one. The pulleys from which Judas hung were of crucial importance because, so eager were audiences for the least details of the death-agony, the rôle was a notoriously dangerous one. There are several records of priests who very nearly strangled themselves while playing the part. At Metz, in 1437, a certain Jean de Missey died after he was cut down. It was a common practice to use fake bodies for scenes re-enacting the martyrdom of the saints, so that all the elaborate refinements of burning or mutilation might be practised on them. And these tortures were carried out to the last degree of realistic detail. The fifteenth century miniature of a performance of *The Mystery of Saint Appoline* would not have used a scene of martyrdom as its main subject if such scenes had not been both typical and popular. In another performance a "feint" consisted of making "a severed head jump thrice. And at each jump flowed a fountain [of blood]." In the mystery *The Acts of the Apostles,* after Judas hangs himself with the aid of two devils, *"his belly bursts and his entrails hang out."* The intestines of a slaughtered animal had been concealed in his robe and showed through the slit cloth.

Our own theatre's theologians inveigh against every form of realism in order that plays can "give the spirit a pervading presence in the theatre which it once had in the life . . . of the people of the Middle Ages." It is amusing to imagine them assisting at the actual performance of a theological drama. For the same mixture of realism and mechanism was in use wherever miracle or passion plays were given. A German manuscript repeats the injunction that the entrails of an animal must hang from Judas's robe when he stabs himself. *The Mystery of the Incarnation of the Nativity,* performed at Rouen in 1474, contains the stage-direction:

Whoever cannot procure the bodies of an artificial ass or ox may omit what follows. . . . But if they can be had, they must kneel before the infant and warm him with their breath.

"Be assured," adds Professor Cohen, "that they were procured, for otherwise the public, already spoiled by some ingenious inventor, would certainly have protested." He lists a veritable menagerie of mechanical animals used in various productions: David drives off a bear and a dog who attempt to devour one of the sheep he is guarding; a leopard stops in front of St. Andrew and sniffs him; lions kneel before St. Denis; a large camel, so well made that according to one chronicler it moved its head and stuck out its tongue, was used at Bourges. Another chronicler, writing the history of Valenciennes, terms such pieces of mechanical ingenuity "the new miracles." In a production given there, "little trees and the most beautiful flowers in season spring from the earth" during the creation of the world. Noah has hardly planted his vine when, by some mechanical trick, it bears grapes; but these are real, for a moment later he presses a handful and drinks their juice.

The other important "secrets" of the production at Mons were the trap-doors and openings concealed in the floor of the stage. They were in constant use in order to give the maximum verisimilitude to the movements of actors or at other moments to make them appear miraculous. After a particular scene the players, instead of making long crosses to a distant exit, disappeared promptly underneath the stage or appeared where they were needed. Only part of the company of actors and animals that entered the Ark are required for the scenes following the Deluge. The stage-directions read, *"All those who no longer speak this day go off by the secrets underneath the earth,"* i.e. the trap-doors underneath the stage. One of these is used for a burst of smoke and fireworks to accent the miracle of the healing of the daughter of the

Canaanite woman, the action being carefully placed near the trap-door in order to provide for the effect. The miracle of the fig-tree is literally achieved after Jesus' words, *"the leaves must fall."* When Jesus is resurrected the stage-manager notes that he must disappear through the trap-door used for the Deluge or the one used for the Crucifixion, put on the costume of a gardener, and reappear almost immediately to show himself to the Magdalene. He disappears through another trap-door, previously used in the prison scene of John the Baptist, confronts the three Marys, and disappears again through one of the trap-doors used for the Deluge. He shows himself to St. Peter and *"disappears suddenly."* Then again with the aid of a trap-door he enters the prison where Joseph of Arimathea is confined *"and leads Joseph out without breaking the walls of the prison."* The illusion of the miraculous is thus literally simulated.

The same tricks and hidden openings are used in other plays, for the production of Mons is not exceptional but typical of an already established technique of staging. In the fifteenth century mystery of *Le Roi Avenir,* the king persecutes the monks of Grammont, who have been successfully spreading the gospel throughout his dominions. He bakes several of them in an oven. An actual fire is lighted in the oven on stage and, in order to prove to the on-lookers that the fire is real, the stage-directions demand that

the baker will shove his bread in uncooked and will take it out completely baked.

After shoving in the monks in turn:

He stirs the fire in the oven and closes it and they descend inside the oven by a trap-door.

For an execution that follows the block is hollowed, the victim thrusts his head in it, a dummy head is substituted and cut off. As in all theatres that we consider primitive or archaic, nothing that can be imitated is left to the spectators' imagination.

6. MIMING AND MIMICRY

Perhaps the most amazing use of the trap-door is revealed by the direction in the Mons manuscript:

Note: Cain should kill Abel directly over the secret [passage] *where there will be the child who plays Abel's blood who cries for vengeance.*

The effectiveness of this bit of stage-management can be appreciated by any one who has ever struggled with the problem of an off-stage or a supernatural voice, the ghost's in *Hamlet,* for instance. If spoken by the actor it loses much of its mystery; if boomed in hollow tones from the wings it reveals its source. But here, in 1501, the problem is neatly solved by placing the voice directly under the prostrate body of Abel so that it seemed to come from the mouth of the corpse itself. How eerie and terrifying the sudden change of timbre must have sounded! It is typical of the desire for literal exactitude animating the entire production that the child was the son of the actor who played Abel. I can remember the difficulties encountered with the voice of God during rehearsals of the Prologue of *Faust* at the Guild Theatre. No single actor's was adequate. A chorus large enough to give an impressive volume of tone blurred the words so that they became unintelligible. But the stage-manager of Mons solved this problem as well. God speaks *"with three voices,"* that is, a tenor, a baritone, and a bass, chanting in unison. The effect must have been superb. Present-day stage-managers could do no better than to note it and use it at the first opportunity.

The trap-door under Abel's body was also used for another highly realistic effect, easily achieved by the use of a bellows concealed there. The smoke of the sacrificial fire Abel has lighted mounts at first in a straight column. A moment later the smoke must blow to one side. So exact is the concern for the slightest detail. The casting is similarly realistic in its desire for exactitude. For Mary as an infant one of the dummy children mentioned in the expense account may have been used, but:

When the melody sounds in Paradise, the new-born Mary must disappear and Mary aged 7 years appears.

A few scenes later:

Warn Mary aged 14 to be ready underneath the temple and [be ready to] *hide Mary aged 7.*

And again:

Here warn Elizabeth to show her stomach big with child. At this point Mary aged 7 is hidden and Mary aged 14 appears with her mother St. Anne.

The second child, seven years older, then enters. Could Antoine, Brahm, or Belasco have been more insistent upon visual plausibility? When *Queen Victoria* was performed a few years ago, the opening scene showed Victoria as a girl, receiving word of her accession, in her nightgown at the head of the stairs. The stage was kept dim enough for the same middle-aged actress to play this prologue and the scenes of the queen's maturity that immediately followed. But the stage-manager of Mons would not have consented to attempting anything so contrary to realistic exactness. For, after the forenoon of the second day's performance, he notes:

They all go to their houses in Nazareth. But after dinner Jesus aged 12 years will be hidden and Jesus aged 30 years will appear.

Mary's pregnancy is realistically pictured.

Here, remind Mary to raise her stomach to show that she is pregnant.

Probably she was to shove padding under her dress. For a page later the notation occurs:

Remind Mary to go towards Joseph and show her stomach big with child as has been said.

Do not let Joseph forget to appear pleased on beholding Mary big with child.

By way of making the raising of Lazarus more miraculous, the pantomime of the actors when the tomb is opened indicates that putrefaction has already set in:

Here remind [the actors] *to lift the stone and to hold their noses.*

Satan leaves Paradise not as a symbolic tempter, but as a crawling snake:

When the serpent leaves the Earthly Paradise he goes into Hell crawling on his belly.

Salome dances a local dance to the accompaniment of a tabor:

Then the tabor ceases but the young girl continues to dance.

The tribunal for the judgment of Pilate is carefully set in two levels so that his final verdict may be delivered more impressively from the higher one:

Note here that Pilate goes to his tribunal . . . and there is another throne higher up, and superbly ornamented, and a second throne where Pilate sits to conduct the trial of Jesus and interrogate him and he does not sit in the higher throne until he pronounces sentence and orders Jesus to be crucified.

The most minute details of the Crucifixion and the Descent from the Cross are as carefully prescribed:

Note that Joseph must have a pincers in his belt and Nicodemus a hammer. . . . Remember to get ready four new ladders to be used in lowering Jesus, for the Carpenter and others can easily help without speaking. . . . Joseph extracts the nail from the right hand . . . they mount to the left side

to do the same. The nails were of course fake properties. The actor who remained on the cross, in order to avoid the racking fatigue that his posture entailed, had his arms supported by metal brackets, which are noted in the expense account and cost three sols. The three "false nails" cost twelve sols. Innumerable pictures of the Crucifixion painted during the early Renaissance must have been less imagined than observed. Such minutely detailed theatrical performances of the Passion provided living models.

The entire production at Mons, like those elsewhere, represents a complicated technical achievement. In addition to the intricacies of realistic staging there were the difficulties of preparing and acting a script of 34,574 lines. Three hundred and seventeen actors were used, many playing two and three rôles, in some cases a single rôle being played in turn by two or three different actors. Their rehearsals took forty-eight days.

The performance itself, and the torch-light procession that preceded it, with the actors in costume headed by the clergy and officials in their regalia, satisfied the same craving for spectacle that is fed today by Fourth of July fireworks, the circus, or movies such as *The Birth of a Nation* or *Genesis*. Nevertheless the performance of this passion-play, like its counterparts throughout Europe, was intensely religious in spirit. Precisely because these Flemish townspeople believed that Christ was their Redeemer and that by cleaving to him they could be saved from Hell and snatched to Heaven, the literal reproduction of his agony, even to the details of pinning him to a cross, reaffirmed a sacred truth. The immediacy of Hell, with its elaborate pyrotechnics of tangible flame and smoke, made damnation not ridiculous but more terrifying. Hell being already conceived as an actual place of eternal physical torments, the more literally its torments were depicted, the more the value of religious virtue was affirmed. The bliss of Heaven was not less spiritual because God wore a cloak bordered with fur or the angels sang accompanied by the church organist. Realism and reality—in this case the reality of a religious truth—as I have already pointed out, are not contradictory terms. The spiritual values of a passion-play, like those of any other play, were created by the mind of its audience. And the performance, despite any amount of naturalistic detail, provided as violent a purgation by pity and terror as a classic tragedy could have given its hearers.

For the things of the spirit are created by the spirit. It is typical of an age of flaccid religious faith like our own that we tend to think of spiritual experiences as necessarily incorporeal and formless, somewhat like our sensations on going under ether on an operating-table or coming out of gas in a dentist's chair. But the cravings of a soul, once we are convinced we have one, are as definite and as immediately experienced as the cravings of a stomach. The spirit, when it is free from doubt, is militant. The visions of mystics are often extraordinarily concrete. The features of the saints who appeared to Joan of Arc were no less distinct to her than the faces of her judges. The spirit that animates any religious faith does not wait for its material embodiment to be rubbed thin before its light can shine through. It accepts whatever raiment its age will let it borrow, confident of being able to transfigure it. It is because our attempts at a modern religion are so tentative and nebulous that we feel the only appropriate means of conveying them to be the murky emptiness of a "space stage" or the flutterings of electric lights that illuminate nothing tangible back of the actors. If we ever achieve a religious faith, its meaning will be clear and comprehensive enough for us also to outline its mysteries distinctly and to define its symbols to the last nail.

CHAPTER III

DECORATION IN THE THEATRE
OF MOLIÈRE

I. THE STAGE MAGNIFICENT

THE increased graphic skill that the Renaissance spread throughout Europe carried on and further elaborated the already elaborate spectacle of the religious theatre of which the production at Mons is typical. The simultaneous settings of the miracle-play were carried into the secular theatre of France and continuously employed there until Italian mechanics, imported by Mazarin and Louis XIV, introduced the technique of scene-shifting. The note-books of two other French stage-managers, Laurent and Mahelot, who supervised performances including a number of Molière's plays at the renovated but shabby Hôtel de Bourgogne, have been preserved. They attest the fact that the passion for visible spectacle continued unabated both on the part of playwrights and on that of their public. A number of working drawings attached to the script prove that such stage-directions as the following were realized:

At the center of the stage is a very magnificent temple, used in the fifth act, the most beautiful possible, ornamented with ivy, glittering gold, balustrades or columns, a picture of Diana in the middle of the altar, two candelabras with candles. At the side of the stage a round prison in a round tower; let the grating be large and low enough so that three prisoners can be seen. Next to the prison there must be a spa-

cious garden ornamented with balustrades, flowers and trellises. At the opposite side of the stage there must be a high mountain; on this mountain a tomb, a pillar, and an altar shaded by trees and rocks, where one can climb the aforesaid rock before the populace. At the side of the rock, a cave, a sea, and a small boat. Beneath the rock, conceal a prison large enough for two persons. There is also [needed] blood, a sponge, and a small skin for the trick of throat-cutting by the sacrificial priest, a garland of flowers and a wax torch.

The naturalistic sacrifices of Mons survive among all this ornament, including the "secret" for making blood flow. If the stage was any less wide than the one hundred and twenty feet of the Mons platform, one wonders what space was left for the actors to turn in. Nevertheless they do not protest, and the demand for simplicity is not heard from the other side of the footlights. Magnificence continues to be the order of the day. For *Hercules,* a tragedy by Rotrou (1634):

The theatre must be magnificent. At one side the temple of Jupiter, constructed in the antique manner, surrounded by arcades. One must be able to walk around the altar. . . . The base must be modelled in relief in the antique manner, showing Jupiter. . . . The temple must be hidden. At the opposite side of the stage a mountain that one can ascend before the populace and descend at the rear. The aforesaid mountain to be covered with full-grown trees, and beneath the mountain there must be a funeral chamber filled with crystal drops, the superb tomb of Hercules.

One is reminded that plastic solidity in stage setting is evidently not entirely a modern innovation. Laurent and Mahelot were practising technicians and their note-books are records not of intentions but of actual performances, records made to guide them or their assistants when a production was repeated. If the prodigious detail of such settings as these could not have been executed, it would not have been noted as part of their working memoranda.

The same ascents and descents of deities from the clouds, apparitions, and blazing stars that delighted the audience at Mons reappear to delight Frenchmen a century and a half later:

In the fifth act, thunder, and after it the heavens open. Hercules descends from Heaven to earth in a cloud; the globe must be ornamented with the twelve signs [of the Zodiac] and the twelve winds, blazing stars, the sun blazing like a live coal, and other ornaments according to the imagination of the painter.

For *Astrée and Celadon* (1630):

In the fourth act Love appears in the air; there must be lightning and thunder. Love reappears in the fifth act.

Again:

Above the temple let Night appear in her chariot worked on a pivot and drawn by two horses, and make the stage dark, and when day comes, let nightingales be heard.

For *The Labours of Ulysses* (1631), the general scheme of the setting is almost a synopsis of the celestial and infernal regions of a mediaeval mystery above and below a platform-stage:

In the middle of the stage there must be hidden hell and the torments of hell. Above hell the heaven of Apollo and above Apollo the heaven of Jupiter.

Laurent and Mahelot, like Jehan du Fayt and his assistants at Mons, are called upon to provide:

Lightning, wind, thunder, flames, and noise . . . also fireworks in the bow of Ulysses' ship.

2. PLEASURES AND PALACES

This plethora of scenic decoration had been preceded by more than a century of resplendent investiture of court pageants and ballets. As early as the fifteenth century, pantomimes and dance-interludes, where elaborate settings and costumes were introduced, became the fashion. For one, known as *The Banquet of the Pheasant's Vow,* a church was trundled in, "with a cross, windows made in elegant fashion, with a bell that rang and four singers"; then, "a boat filled with every kind of merchandise and sailors"; and finally, "a castle and at the top of its principal tower Mélusine in the form of a serpent and from two smaller towers there flowed, at will, two streams of orange water that fell into the moat."

For the marriage of the Duke of Burgundy and Margaret of York at Bruges in 1468, a stage was constructed at the end of the banqueting-hall and *The Labours of Hercules* was acted in pantomime for three successive evenings. The actors descended from the stage and mingled freely with the audience in the most approved modern manner. The snakes that the infant Hercules strangled in his cradle crawled through the audience on to the stage. A draw-curtain was used while the settings were changed. These included numerous landscapes and seascapes.

The Cardinal of Lyons in 1548 reproduced the scenic splendours of an Italian court masque at a performance of Bibbiena's *Calandra* for Catherine de' Medici, Queen of France. A room used for choir-rehearsal was transformed into a theatre, ornamented with columns and garlanded arches. A Lyons artist of Italian origin painted the back-drops, including a view of Florence on which the Campanile, the dome of the Baptistry, the Ducal Palace, and the Piazza della Signoria were recognized.

But the most famous of all such court entertainments and the most elaborate was the *Ballet de la Reine* entitled *Circé,* performed in 1581. Because the leading parts were sung it is usually cited as the first opera given in France. But it is important in the history of stage decoration as showing how early elaborate stage settings were perfected for a stage that as yet had no well-established theatres or a repertory of plays to fill them.

Two-thirds of the hall in the Petit Bourbon theatre was given up to the stage. The scene was a garden. In the foreground, according to the author's account in the printed play,

a bower 18 feet long and 12 feet wide, . . . built in perspective higher in back than in front, surrounded by oak trees set 2 feet apart, of which the trunks, branches, leaves, and acorns were gilded and made with such extraordinary artifice that they had niches for nymphs and dryads when these were required to show themselves.

Behind the bower was seen

. . . a grotto which gleamed and glittered as if an infinite number of diamonds had been applied to it and was otherwise embellished with trees and covered with flowers so well made that one would have thought them natural and growing.

Atmosphere and mystery were supplied, as at Mons, by a veil of gauze:

The wood was veiled by a curtain made with so much skill that instead of serving to hide and obscure it, it served on the contrary to illuminate more naturally everything that the woodland contained.

A gauze is still one of the stock devices of scenic design. It is stretched either in front of the stage or across part of the setting; when lighted from the rear it is almost invisible and gives an atmospheric remoteness, but without blurring, that can be obtained in no other way.

At the opposite side of the stage, an arch of wood eighteen feet long and twelve feet wide was covered with large painted clouds. The interior was gilded and special lamps gave it a blue tone. This golden arch held ten musicians, and

was so delicate and beautiful that it repeated sounds like Echo and expressed the Platonic harmony of the spheres.

The celestial machines of the Greek and mediaeval theatres are again in evidence, and the pyrotechnics of passion-plays. Above the centre of the stage, a large cloud full of illuminated stars hid the platform on which Jupiter and Mercury and the chariot of Athene descended. Numerous other machines were used, including an enormous fountain of Glaucus carrying a bevy of Tritons, naiads, and dolphins, drawn by mechanical sea-horses that seemed to drag it on and off stage. At one moment Circe's garden was aflame with Bengal fire.

3. JESUIT POMP

For approximately two hundred years, roughly from 1450 to 1650, the French secular stage, like an unrepentant Magdalene, is loaded down with ornament and finery. And the religious theatre under the patronage of the Jesuits throughout Europe, far from restraining this worldly ornamentation, followed its example and at times outdid its decorative excesses. In their French colleges amateur theatricals held as important a place as they now do in most American universities. In this they systematized a practice general among French colleges, of encouraging an appreciation of the classics by performing Latin plays. The regulations of the College of Guyenne at Bordeaux in 1533 required that a professor must be able "to both write and speak orations, harangues, dialogues, and comedies." It is amusing to imagine the consequences of applying a similar rule in American colleges in the year 1933. Buchanan, whose tragedies, according to Sir Philip Sidney, were divinely inspired, occupied a chair at this college. Montaigne studied there seven years and acquired so great a reputation as an amateur actor that he recalls it in one of his essays, and points out the educational value even for young princes of playing in tragedies that follow classic models. At the Jesuit Collège Louis le Grand at Paris, the University of Pont-à-Mousson, and the colleges at Lyons, Rouen, and Troyes, a theatrical production was usually a feature of the annual graduation exercises. The plays, tragedies or pastorals, were written by Jesuit instructors, who retold the lives of biblical martyrs and saints and edited the exploits of classic heroes so that a Christian moral could be appended, but did not object to incorporating a ballet and the maximum amount of scenic display in the process. There are records of three hundred and twenty-six such performances between 1579 and 1770. Every college had a theatre; its stage was equipped for elaborate productions, which continued until the revolution expropriated the church schools. As early as 1585, one of the Jesuit fathers at Pont-à-Mousson felt it incumbent upon him to issue a warning about the lavish use of scenery, which reads like the advice given to scene designers ever since. "As to stage decoration, while striving to please both the eye and the ear, one must be on one's guard against using too much of it. In this respect our young masters often have not enough reserve. They think that they have composed an excellent tragedy if there is a sumptuous display of luxury, if the stage is decorated, if there are embroidered costumes and exquisite music."

The advice was universally ignored. In 1618 some mortars were borrowed by the college from the armory of Pont-à-Mousson to fire salutes during the performances of *Alexander's Triumph over Darius*. In 1623 a spectator describes *The Conversion of St. Ignatius:*

The actors outdid themselves. The stage was remarkable for its painted scenery . . . and for the great curtain that rose and fell all of a

sudden. The actors [were] *magnificently attired . . . There were interludes between each act . . . where one saw Nereids, Tritons, satyrs.*

This performance was followed within a few days by another so spectacularly staged that

*the figure of the saint, amidst great applause, changed into a tower that
sent forth fireworks. At the end of the play the saint appeared upon a
near-by housetop and descended with the aid of a machine as though
he were coming down from heaven and set fire to a château filled with
fireworks.*

These displays of pyrotechnics, which began with the mediaeval Hell's
mouth, continued to coruscate in classic vistas. By the eighteenth century a single play included a forest imitated in perspective, a series of
elaborate palaces and gardens, and, as a spectacular finale, "a hundred
palaces, aflame, reduced to smoke and ashes." The accumulation of
scenic equipment required for such spectacles—including Olympus,
machines for its deities to descend and disappear into clouds, titans to
scale, costumes for as many as one hundred extras for one play, and
complete military equipment for numerous pitched battles—had,
shortly before the Revolution, grown to such proportions that a
French historian remarks of the Jesuit college at Paris that its theatrical
storehouses were not as large as those of the Opéra but certainly larger
than those of the Comédie Française.

The popularity of these graduating exercises was enormous, not
only with fond parents but with neighbouring nobles and gentry and
townsfolk of quality. On occasion tradespeople and town councillors
rioted in order to gain admittance. In 1656 at Valenciennes the influx
was so great that the floor gave way and one hundred and sixty persons were injured. Jesuit performances had drawn crowds for a century. At Pont-à-Mousson in 1595, owing to the influx of the gentry

admittance was refused to the shopkeepers, who became so enraged that they rioted and broke in the doors. The performance continued only after the Duke of Lorraine sent his men-at-arms to restore order. A few years later, in order to avoid a similar rumpus, when *Alexander's Triumph over Darius* with its popular cannonade was revived, a second performance was given for the town. The popularity of these college shows is as great sixty-five years later. The tragedy of *Rosamund* (1659) was held up by an altercation between the municipal authorities of Troyes and the college. The mayor found that the seats reserved for himself and his councillors were not good enough. No doubt they were too far to the side. The city council insisted on its rights and the play was finally performed at the price of being opened by a prelude in which amends were made by casting the mayor for a leading part. On another occasion when these same obstreperous syndics were not invited they broke into the hall and broke up the show.

The prestige enjoyed by Jesuit theatricals was nation-wide; on numerous occasions they had the added *réclame* of being attended by the reigning sovereign, Charles IX, Louis XIII, or Louis XIV with his entire court. Can one imagine the President of the United States, and the cabinet and the diplomatic corps by official command, journeying to Princeton, Harvard, or Yale to witness the production of a play by the senior class? As the result of such patronage amateur theatricals became even more the fashion than they are now in our little theatres and comedy clubs scattered from Maine to Texas and from Boston to California. Renting theatrical costumes to amateurs was an established business. A tragi-comedy by Colletet mentions the shop of a M. Bourgeois who rents costumes for tragedies. Amateur performances became widespread enough to be recognized as possible rivals and the source of a possible loss of revenue to established theatres. When Lully was made Superintendent of Royal Music, it became necessary to obtain his written permission before performing a play with music in one's own home. One such authorization, dated 1671, has survived. It states that a certain M. Lescogne has Lully's permission to have his pupils, who lodge with him, perform tragedies with music written by their tutor.

The most lasting effect of the Jesuit theatres was that they fixed the range of French theatrical taste, for their colleges all but monopolized higher education in the seventeenth century and for most of the eighteenth. Not only the gilded youth of the day, such as the Prince of Condé and innumerable other young nobles, matriculated under Jesuit guidance, but the intellectual élite as well. Fénelon, Descartes, Voltaire, Corneille, and Molière, as undergraduates saw or took part in these annual dramatic performances. It is therefore not surprising that the battle to establish the reign of the three unities on the French stage failed to simplify its scenery or establish the unit setting. Scudéry (in 1637), writing of *Le Cid,* complains that unity of place is obtained by such a straining of plausibility that the spectator is bewildered:

The stage is so badly laid out that the same place in turn represents almost without change the king's apartments, those of the crown prince, the house of Chimène, and a street. The spectator half the time does not know where the actors are.

Corneille equivocated and conceded:

I am willing to admit that everything which is made to take place in the same city would have unity of place. Not that I desire the stage to represent an entire city—that would be too vast an undertaking—but only two or three particular places enclosed within its walls.

But Voltaire attacked any such compromise and championed the mediaeval practice of the simultaneous setting still in use at the Hôtel de Bourgogne:

The abominable construction of our theatres from barbaric times to our own day makes it impossible to observe the law of the unity of place. Conspirators cannot plot against Caesar in his own chamber; no one discusses secret plans in a public square; the same setting cannot represent in turn the façade of a palace or a temple. It is imperative that the theatre make us see every specific place called for by the action of the play—here a temple, there a palace, a public square, the streets in back of it, in short everything necessary to show the eye what the ear must listen to.

The last two phrases summarize the goal that has determined the development of stage-craft from Athens to the present day. The mechanical ingenuity of every stage has been employed to make us see every specific place called for by the action of the play. Like every subsequent analyst of the designer's problem, Gluck, in his preface to *Alcestis*, paraphrases Voltaire's words:

The stage designer must be a man of impeccable taste and be quite certain with every change of scene what the poet is driving at. Then while keeping in mind everything else including the costumes, he must arrange everything so that the eye is prepared at the outset for what the ear will hear.

4. MOLIÈRE'S ACQUIESCENCE

Had Molière stopped the momentum of two centuries of popular and official encouragement given to every kind of scenic decoration and established the "masculine vigour" of a bare and simplified stage, he would have inaugurated a monumental reform. As a matter of fact he made no such attempt. The reforms that engaged his attention were those connected with the subtleties of acting as opposed to the declamation of Montfleury and the royal tragedians. His criticism was confined to ideas that pricked the pretensions not of scenery, but of bigots, doctors, astrologers, hypochondriacs, and literary snobs. He risked failure and disgrace more than once for his militancy. It was only the king's patronage which saved him from Church censorship during his lifetime and at the last the monarch's personal intercession that obtained for him a secret Church funeral and a plot of consecrated ground to rot in. No sham of any class of society escaped his cauterizing ridicule. But he accepted the prevalent sham of painted settings and the elaborate scenery and machinery then in vogue. The vogue had been begun by Richelieu, who in 1641 built the first modern theatre of his day in his own palace, discarded the simultaneous settings in use at the Hôtel de Bourgogne, and by way of rivalling *Le Cid*, played his own drama of *Mirame* in scenery painted in true perspective. This theatre, known later as the Palais Royal, was enlarged and remodelled in 1647 by Cardinal Mazarin at a reputed cost of half a million livres, or two and one-half million gold francs. For that purpose he imported the Italian mechanician Torelli, staged the spectacular scene changes of *The Marriage of Orpheus and Eurydice,* and followed it with *Andromeda,* by Corneille. "The Greeks and Romans are surpassed," exclaimed the *Mercure,* "and the miracles of the Egyptian priests are not to be compared to the marvels of Corneille's settings." Plays written to exploit the possibilities of theatrical machinery, *pièces à machines,* became the rage. The king encouraged Mazarin to eclipse his previous efforts in spectacular staging, and the latter, discarding Torelli, imported another Italian technician, Vigarani, who by 1662 completed a royal theatre so packed with stage machinery that it was known as the Hall of the Machines. This Salle des Machines was opened by an opera, *Ercole Amante.* Its "outstanding feature . . . was Carlo Vigarani's great machine, showing the apotheosis of Hercules and Beauty and their ascent to regions divine. This immense moving platform was 60 feet long by 40 broad, and to the astonishment of the vast audience, bore upwards in easy progression all the members of the royal household, or no fewer than a hundred souls." "The fifth scene, a finely conceived Inferno, long haunted the imagination of the Grand Monarch, and to get rid of the obsession His Majesty finally commanded Molière to compose *Psyché* for its further exploitation."

Molière complied with alacrity, accepting Quinault and Corneille as collaborators and leaving most of the rhymed text to them. The fact is called to the reader's attention in the foreword to the printed play, but he is also reminded:

M. de Molière outlined the scenario of the play and supervised its execution, but concerned himself less with its exact details than with the pomp and beauty of the play as a spectacle.

According to the theory that Molière, like classic authors, was interested only in the "type of drama where illusion is not so important as emotional intimacy, directness and clarity," it should follow that secretly disgusted with a sycophant's job, he promptly abandoned the play once the king's whim had been satisfied. Unfortunately for the theory, Molière did nothing of the sort but revived the spectacle in his own theatre. His first theatre, Le Petit Bourbon, had been unexpectedly demolished by the court architect. The king had given him the use of Mazarin's Palais Royal. Molière at the time showed his dependence on stage scenery by requesting that all of Torelli's machinery be left intact. On taking possession of the house, he found that Vigarani, in a fit of jealousy, in order to wipe out every vestige of his predecessor's glory had dismantled the stage. The great comedian should have taken this as an unmistakable sign from the heaven of the Muses pointing out the direction in which a purer art of stage-craft ought to develop. But he failed to interpret the omen and spent an entire month and nearly 2,000 livres (10,000 gold francs) in remodelling his stage so that *Psyché* could be performed there. In addition he spent more than twice that sum mounting the production itself, and further, incurred an extra expense of 300 francs per performance for dancers, singers, and machinists. *Psyché* was part of the repertory of a highly successful season, for Molière was not only an actor and an author, but a shrewd and successful theatrical manager. The French public, like every other in Europe at the time, was as eager to see the spectacle indoors as it had been to witness it in open-air miracle-plays. Molière's astuteness was vindicated. During his lifetime "there were 82 performances of *Psyché,* earning a total of 77,119 livres" (or over 350,000 francs). Shortly after his death his company were thrown out of the Palais Royal by Lully, who wanted it for the royal opera. They were careful to select another theatre well equipped with theatrical machinery and recouped their fortunes completely with *Circé,* by Thomas Corneille, another *pièce à machines,* which grossed 23,400 francs in its first nine performances and was revived the following season for a run of sixty-six more.

The production of *Psyché* at Molière's own theatre included all the scenic effects that had delighted the court. Robinet in a rhymed epistle on the occasion confirms the fact:

> *As at the Tuileries*
> *The same splendor we see,*
> *And every scene-change*
> *Of vistas that range*
> *From deserts to bowers,*
> *Seas to palace towers.*
> *Pictured equally well*
> *Are Heaven and Hell.*
> *Here again one decries*
> *The gods in the skies,*
> *As chariots careen*

> *On a divine machine.*
> *Here all is recorded*
> *That the courtiers applauded.*

After reading the stage-directions it seems surprising that the Palais Royal could have been got ready for them in a month's time. For the prologue:

> *The foreground of the scene represents a meadow, and at the rear, a grotto through which the sea can be seen in the distance.*

> *Venus descends from the heavens in a great machine. . . . The scene changes to a great city where one sees palaces at both sides, and houses showing the different orders of architecture.*

For the second interlude:

> *The scene changes into a magnificent courtyard, ornamented with columns of lapis encrusted with golden figures forming a sumptuous and resplendent palace.*

The fourth interlude is even more elaborate:

> *The scene represents the infernal regions. One sees a sea of fire; its waves are in continual motion. This horrible torrent of flame is bordered by ruins also in flames, and in the midst of this seething torrent, one sees the palace of Pluto through the jaws of a horrible face.*

This *gueule affreuse* is another version of the toad face of a mediaeval Hell that spat fire and smoke at Mons. The favourite effects of the mediaeval theatre survive on the stage of the father of modern comedy. He does not hesitate to use all this traditional paraphernalia once more for *Don Juan, or The Stone Guest,* when "an abyss opens in the earth and from it issue immense tongues of flame." The stage-managers of the Hôtel de Bourgogne note that for Act V "there must be black resin."

208

This was one of the stock ingredients from which the stage-managers of miracle-plays had concocted their hell-fires. Molière's use of hell-fire may have seemed somewhat old-fashioned even in its own day. For it was shortly outdone by another version of the story by one of Molière's own actors, entitled *The New Supper of the Stone Guest, or The Atheist Struck by Lightning.*

It might be supposed that any one with so quick a sense of the ridiculous as Molière would foresee the ludicrous anticlimaxes lurking in the use of so much scenic mechanism. La Fontaine later described them:

> *I never find, when the prompter signals, "Next,"*
> *Scenes change as fast as in the text.*
> *Counterweights stick; a god who intervenes*
> *Caught in mid air cries out on the machines.*
> *A tuft of trees juts from the ocean's swell,*
> *And half of Heaven remains in the midst of Hell.*

But Molière was not intimidated. During his retirement at Auteuil, when he wrote to please himself rather than the king, one of the three plays he completed was *Amphytrion,* in which gods out of the machine are set in motion once again. Laurent's notes specify:

> *For the prologue a machine for Mercury and a chariot for Night. In the third act Mercury returns and Jupiter on his chariot.*

Molière's acquiescence in the scenic fashions of his time was in fact so complete that he moved his most intimate comedies to court stages and back again to his own theatre, retaining all the ballets and interludes that had made them a court *divertissement. Le Bourgeois Gentilhomme* was regularly concluded with the bizarre ballet *à la Turque,* first seen at Chambord, *Le Malade Imaginaire* with another ballet that burlesqued a candidate for the degree of Doctor of Medicine being given his diploma. *Le Misanthrope* was interrupted by a scene-change

to a street for a dance interlude. At times Molière, who had not de-
spised new-fangled theatrical machinery, availed himself without a
qualm of the old-fashioned practice of the simultaneous setting. In
Le Médecin malgré Lui the original stage direction was:

> *The stage for this act should be a spot near the houses of Sganarelle
> and M. Robert, only a short distance away from the forest where
> Sganarelle collects his faggots.*

It was the later editors of his text and not the playwright who simplified the settings. Le Pautre's engravings for *Le Bourgeois Gentilhomme* are evidently based on a performance. The apron of a stage is
shown with the privileged spectators seated on it, and also an amount
of painted scenery back of the actors that would now be considered
almost grotesque as a background for satiric comedy: vistas of baroque
architecture, columns, tapestries, and draperies. The vigour of Molière's
comic spirit was seemingly no more disturbed by it than it was in *Les
Amants Magnifiques,* wedged between a prologue in which Louis himself appeared as Neptune and interludes where nymphs, satyrs, and
shepherds danced, or in *Georges Dandin,* performed in the gardens of
Versailles, where "his stage was an entire garden complete with satyrs,
busts, fountains, terraces, and a navigable waterway." The point of
Éraste's comments on fashionable bores in *Les Fâcheux* is not dulled
because it was begun by a prologue spoken by Madeleine Béjart, appearing from out an enormous oyster-shell that opened as a fountain
spurted its twenty jets at her feet. Far from apologizing for dallying
with ballet-interludes, Molière in his preface to the printed play apolo-
gizes for the lack of unity in the way dances and comic scenes are combined. He points out that a new form of entertainment, integrating
both, is worth serious study and hints that there are classic precedents
for making the attempt.

Molière's comedies need far less scenery than he himself was willing to play them in. Possibly for our own day the austere platform that Copeau installed at one end of his Théâtre du Vieux Colombier is a better stage for projecting the comic values of Molière's characters. But Molière himself felt no need of it. His motto, *"Je prends mon bien où je le trouve,"* held just as good for his settings as for his subject-matter. He took what he thought good wherever he found it, and his vigour as a playwright triumphed over his borrowings by suiting them to his own purposes.

Our interest in a simplified form of stage setting devoid of any ornamental excrescences is an entirely modern preoccupation of a machine-trimmed age. For an industrial era the creation of ornament on a large scale without the aid of multitudes of thriving handicraftsmen is an immense effort, its results so patently clumsy and irrelevant on the machined surfaces to which they must be applied that we are oppressed by the effort. We then make the mistake of ascribing a similar sense of oppression to eras when, handicraft being the only method of manufacture, ornament was so naturally produced that it left nothing untouched. Its ramifications were supported by the entire structure of society with no more strain than is put upon a trellis propping the mounting tendrils of a vine. Its fruits were within easy reach of every walk of life. Not even the supposedly dark Middle Ages were dark enough to prevent multitudes of craftsmen from filtering what light there was through windows stained with emblems and legends, weaving narratives in the tapestries that kept out a draught, chasing armour and cross-bows with arabesques, and engraving garlands even on the forceps that probed a wound. Until the funeral plumes of factory smoke rose upon every other horizon, there was light enough for craftsmen to wind bronze acanthus leaves about the barrels of cannon, inlay hunting stories in the butt of a gentleman's fowling-musket, write legends on the tiled stove that warmed his feet when he came home, stamp patterns on the waffle-irons that baked his cakes, or set a cherub on the lid that capped his ale. Had a contemporary of Molière penned a defence of simplified stage setting, he would have had to do so attired in an embroidered coat and vest, as he sat on a heavily carved chair and at an encrusted desk. If he paused long enough to look over the top of his quill his eye would have lighted on garlands hung over every door and window in the room. The simplifications of design that we project were undreamed of in any philosophy except our own.

Compare the engravings of two performances of Molière's plays at court, one a ballet, *La Princesse d'Élide,* the other *Le Malade Imaginaire*. The settings are both strikingly similar in style, although the former is an actual alley in the gardens of Versailles framed to represent a stage and the latter a painted setting. Argon is seated in an armchair in the midst of a formal vista, a diminutive figure, dwarfed by two lanes of ornamental flower-pots higher than the lackeys stationed near them and backed by three large arches through which further vistas of arches and bowers are seen. To our sensibilities all comedy would be lost in so vast a piece of stage-decoration. But in Molière's day it was not lost. Before conquering Paris, he had seen his first venture, The Illustrious Company, go bankrupt. He toured the provinces for twelve years, heading another group of players. The scenic equipment that they were able to haul in their wake was no doubt rudimentary. If Molière, as either actor or playwright, had had any interest in simplifying theatrical décors, this decade of his life would have formulated his ideas on the subject. There is no evidence that he ever had any. There is every evidence, on the contrary, that he accepted all the decoration, even in its most elaborate forms, that was already a tradition in the theatre of the capital when he returned to it.

In this connection the moral of another engraving that I reproduce is obvious. It is undated but the costumes of the passers-by fix it as of the second quarter of the seventeenth century. Here is the theatre reduced to its bare essentials: a company of strolling players that have set up their trestles in a public square; three boards and a passion. But even this company is backed by a piece of painted scenery. The demand for a picture behind the actor is irrepressible.

5. THE GILDED CAGE

One innovation that our stage-reformers advocate the Theatre of Molière already possessed, namely, the practice of mingling actors and audience. The audience enjoyed the contact but actors and authors found it an unmitigated nuisance. The practice began as the result of a sold-out house for the first performance of *Le Cid,* when the management did not dare to refuse admittance to late-comers, among them a number of persons of quality, and placed chairs for them on the stage apron, as is done at a sold-out concert hall today. Commenting on the consequences of this habit, John Palmer in his life of Molière says: "A precedent was established and within a few years no man of fashion would sit anywhere else. Tallemant de Réaux writes in 1657: 'A practice began to intrude about this time which was disastrously inconvenient to the play. The sides of the stage were wholly occupied by young people sitting upon cane chairs. They would not go into the pit . . . this spoiled everything and one inconsiderate spectator might throw the whole performance into disorder.' . . . The dramatic art of France was thus obliged to conform itself to a practice which reduced the stage to a small open space with a backcloth, in which actors could do little more than deliver their lines. Marmontel, writing in the *Mercure,* in 1759, insisted that the classic drama of France must be judged almost entirely in the light of this practice. . . . The stage, he pointed out, had become a 'parlour to which all the players must be brought.'"

Mantzius in his *History of Theatrical Art* comes to the same conclusion: "If the French classical tragedy developed into a series of conversations and long speeches, sublime, passionate, spirited, but never characterised by a distinct *milieu* and always taking place in some indefinite spot, if we seldom *see* an effective event and only hear the description of it, may not the blame of all this talk without action be laid, to a certain extent, on these spectators . . . who not only prevented the public from seeing, but the authors also from writing plays with vivid dramatic action and picturesque situations? Certainly the times were not romantic . . . but we may be allowed to suppose that, if the stage had been free, the imagination of the poet might have had a wider scope for its flight than it could have in the cage, of which the little barons and marquises now formed the gilt bars."

We should be allowed to suppose nothing of the sort. Shakespeare's stage was also caged by the gilded youth of its day, the gay young bloods and wits among the barons and the earls. But it did not prevent the development of romantic playwrighting with any amount of blood-curdling dramatic situations. There was room for any flight that the imagination decided upon. To argue with Palmer and Mantzius that the imagination of French playwrights in the seventeenth century was inhibited by ignoring the proscenium arch and therefore produced an empty classicism is as foolish as to argue with Craig, Macgowan, and Cheney that the imagination of nineteenth century playwrights was bullied by their respect for the proscenium arch into producing trivial, peep-show realism. French classicists produced rigid and rhetorical tragedies because they were animated by a false conception of classic dignity, which outside the theatre produced pseudoclassic symmetries in history, poetry, and architecture. Had there been no established theatre, the salon of a marquis would have served almost as well for the declamations of their heroes and heroines. In the last century another set of artistic assumptions turned the novel into a peepshow, where we were "peering through a keyhole and minding other people's business," as well as in the theatre, where it was assumed that we had knocked out the fourth wall.

Historians of the theatre tend to exaggerate the effect of physical conditions in the playhouse on the production of dramatic literature. There is, in their opinion, always some condition that prevents the uninterrupted production of dramatic masterpieces. The truth is that nothing prevents the creation of dramatic masterpieces except the extreme rarity at any time of geniuses capable of writing them. If the theatre had ever depended even for a single century on a steady output of dramatic literature it could never have existed continuously enough to have a history worth being recorded. Most of the contemporaries of Shakespeare and Molière, like the contemporaries of Ibsen and Shaw, under precisely the same physical conditions in the theatre produced drama that ranged from the second-rate to rubbish. Only a fraction of the Greek tragedies written have survived. But there is no record in all of classic literature that any other playwrights were considered the peers of Aeschylus, Sophocles, and Euripides by the ancient world. If the Greek theatre itself could not produce a dozen such, a revival of Greek methods of staging cannot be expected to do so. Does any one suppose that if we reconstructed an Elizabethan stage to the last mortise and tenon and baited it like a fox-trap with a "tyring-house," an inner stage, and "a heavens," we should find caught within it one fine morning another Shakespeare or a second Marlowe?

Molière, if we are to judge by Éraste's sentiments in *Les Fâcheux,* thoroughly resented the presence of the audience on his stage and preferred to keep a play within a frame where, in the French phrase, it could withdraw the better to project itself. Like other managers he also welcomed *pièces à machines,* in order to use them as a pretext for utilizing every inch of stage space and sweeping the marquises and the wits back into the pit. The court stages were more to his liking, for there no one approached nearer than the king, and he sat well behind the hedge of musicians immediately below the players. But the mingling of players and audience is no talisman, even when the audience is impressed by the fact and does not interrupt. There is no more magic in thrusting the auditorium upon the stage than there is in putting the stage in the auditorium or in keeping the two separate. There is only one condition essential for the production of plays, and it is one that cannot affect their literary quality: a society which encourages the habit of going to the theatre and, at the same time that it prevents too much interference with it by vested authority, whether Church or State, enables the playwright to earn his living or subsidizes him if he cannot. The development of scenic art is worth examining not because more or less of it, one kind or another, might have produced another Molière, Shakespeare, or Euripides, but because the history of stage setting demonstrates that some kind of scenic picture has always been inseparable from playwrighting, good or bad, in every epoch when the theatre has flourished.

CHAPTER IV

THE SCENIC REVIVAL
IN SHAKESPEARE'S ENGLAND

1. MORE FIREWORKS AND FLAMING DEVILS

Is the Elizabethan playhouse the only one whose simplicity, to use Shakespeare's simile, shines like a good deed in a naughty world? To seekers for a lost purity in stage setting it seems a comforting exception. Their picture of "Shakespeare's stage" is bolstered by a well-known document, the drawing of The Swan made by a visiting Dutchman. But any number of other documents demonstrate that the half-roofed-over platforms of converted inn-yards, like the platform-stages of the miracle-plays, were crammed with every scenic effect that they were capable of holding: gods descending on machines, apparitions through trap-doors, blazing stars, hell-fire, squibs, devils, and cannonades. The cannon boomed from the upper story of Shakespeare's Globe, and so realistically that a spark set fire to the thatched roof and burned down the theatre. The realism with which Marlowe's *Faustus* was performed in 1620 is described by John Melton in *The Astrologaster:*

Another will foretell of lightning and thunder that shall happen such a day, when there are no such inflammations seen, except men go to the Fortune in Golding-Lane to see the Tragedy of Doctor Faustus. There indeed a man may behold shaggy-haired devils run roaring over the stage with squibs in their mouths, while drummers make thunder

in the Tyring-house, and twelvepenny hirelings make artificial light-
ning in their Heavens.

These effects had evidently been in use for at least eleven years, for
Dekker in 1609 remarks that "wild-fire flew from one to another like
squibs when Doctor Faustus goes to the devil." Heywood's boast in
Prologue to the Stage, where he asserts—

> *To give content to this most curious Age,*
> *The gods themselves we have brought down to the stage,*
> *And figured them on planets; made even Hell*
> *Deliver up its furies—*

is amply confirmed by the stage-directions of plays performed in
such open-air theatres as The Globe, The Fortune, and The Rose:
"lightning and thunder . . . here the blazing star . . . with a sudden
thunderclap the sky is on fire and the blazing star appears." This was
a favourite stage-effect. It occurs in an interact dumb show of Peele's,
The Battle of Alcazar (1589). *"The sky is on fire and the blazing star*
appears" recurs in *The Life and Death of Captain Thomas Stukeley,*
and continues to be used into the seventeenth century. Elizabethans
were adept in the use of fireworks, which greeted Queen Elizabeth on
her visit to Warwick Castle in 1572 and in 1575 on her visit to Kenilworth. "A curious reference in *A Warning for Fair Women* shows that
the end-of-the-century street urchin, like the latterday American boy on
Independence Day," writes one authority, W. J. Lawrence, "took great
delight in letting off crackers. Not a great while passed, indeed, before
fireworks were made an almost annual feature of the Lord Mayor's
Show. London boasted an expert pyrotechnist in the person of Hum-
phrey Nichols, a genius who covered himself with glory by his fireworks display in the Show of 1613." A volume entitled *The Mysteries*
of Nature and of Art, reprinted in 1635, gives a technical drawing

showing how the blazing star was worked and includes as well descriptions of how to make golden rain, rockets on lines, and flying dragons. "Moreover," says Lawrence, "when covered with orsedue or some other shining substance, and sent on their sputtering way down an almost perpendicular wire to an accompaniment of stage thunder, squibs answered remarkably well for those awe-inspiring thunderbolts which were obliging enough . . . to kill off the villain of the piece. [Did the Holy Ghost at Mons descend as a flame by the same device?] . . . That he might gain patient hearing for his glowing imagery, abundant rhetoric, and deep philosophy, the dramatic poet had to make occasion for the introduction of ghosts, enthralling combats, descending gods and goddesses, nay, even fireworks. There were few serious plays in which one or other of these spectacles was not resorted to, and one can only marvel over the adroitness with which they were frequently made integrants of the whole."

Indeed most Elizabethan plays were filled with enough sissing and booming to make them excellent substitutes for Fourth of July celebrations. For Heywood's three plays *The Brazen Age, The Golden Age,* and *The Silver Age,* the stage-directions call successively for *"thunder and lightning . . . Jupiter descends in a cloud . . . Juno descends from the heavens . . . the river Arethusa riseth from the stage . . . Hercules sinks himself; flashes of fire; the devils appear at every corner of the stage with several fireworks. . . . Enter Hercules from a rock above . . . Jupiter above strikes him with a thunderbolt, his body sinks, and from the heavens descends a hand in a cloud, that from the place where Hercules was burnt, brings up a star, and fixes it in the firmament."* In another play: *"Pluto draws hell: the Fates put upon him a burning robe and present him with a mace and burning crown . . . Jupiter appears in his glory under a rainbow . . . Jupiter descends in his majesty, his thunderbolt burning . . . As he touches the bed it fires and all flies up. . . . Fireworks all over the house. . . . Enter*

Pluto with a club of fire, a burning crown, Proserpine, the Judges, the Fates, and a guard of Devils, all with burning weapons . . . there falls a shower of rain." In Greene's *Alphonsus*, a stage-direction demands: *"Let there be a brazen head set in the middle of the place behind the stage, out of which cast flames of fire."* Despite the mixture of Christian and pagan mythology, the stage-effects are almost identical with those used for the passion-play at Mons and there are almost enough of them to have occupied Master Jehan du Fayt and his seventeen mechanics who worked the pyrotechnics of Hell's mouth.

The throne on which a god was let down seems to have been almost as necessary a part of an Elizabethan stage-equipment as an elevator in present-day office buildings. Gods and goddesses descend with monotonous regularity. Such demands as: *"Let Venus be let down from the top of the stage . . . exit Venus, or if you can conveniently, let a chair come down from the top of the stage and draw her up,"* recur like a refrain. In *Old Fortunatus* the hero is given a magic hat, wishes himself in Cyprus, and exits. The bystanders in the play remark that he goes *"through the air"* and *"through the clouds."* E. K. Chambers in his exhaustive work on *The Elizabethan Stage* concludes that this was realistically done. "Many Elizabethan actors were half acrobats, and could no doubt fly upon a wire." "Sleight of hand," says Lawrence, "became a necessary histrionic accomplishment."

The frequency with which the *deus ex machina*, fireworks, and flaming devils appear in Elizabethan scripts proves how popular such effects were. They became so common that a playwright who wished to advertise the superior literary pretensions of his play could stamp his work as exceptional merely by calling attention in his prologue to the fact that he had disdained all the usual theatrical effects. A simplified production on an Elizabethan stage was in fact so uncommon that it could be bragged about as a sign of distinction. Ben Jonson prefaces *Every Man in His Humour* with the well-known reminder:

Nor creaking throne comes down, the boys to please;
Nor nimble squib is seen, to make afear'd
The gentlewoman; nor rolled bullet heard
To say it thunders, nor tempestuous drum
Rumbles to tell you when the storm doth come.

And Shirley in his prologue to *The Doubtful Heir* brags likewise:

No shows no dance—and what you most delight in,
Grave understanders—here's no target-fighting.
Upon the stage, all work for cutlers barred; . . .
No clown, no squibs, no devil in't. . . .

But even without squibs and devils there was ornament and elaboration. The inventory of Henslowe, who built several theatres and managed one of the most successful companies, known as The Admiral's Men, lists painted scenery: two cloths, one of the sun and the moon and one of "the city of Rome," and such properties as "1 bay tree, 1 tantelouse tree, 1 tree with golden apples and 2 moss banks." The flowery bank of *Midsummer Night's Dream* and the moonlit one of the *Merchant of Venice* were in all likelihood imitated with artificial verdure and not imagined by the audience while the actors sat on stools. Trap-doors were in common use, as at Mons, for magic apparitions.

The Magi with their rods beat the ground and from under the same riseth a brave arbour.

And in another play:

Here Bungay conjures and the tree appears with the dragon shooting fire.

In *The Triumph of Honour:*

Solemn music, a mist arises, the rocks remove.

A trap-door is obviously the "quaint device" through which the banquet in *The Tempest* "vanishes" and through which Reapers and Nymphs *"after their dance to a strange, confused and hollow noise . . . heavily vanish."*

2. BLOOD AND WATER

The Elizabethan stage not only flames but also steams: *"exhalations of lightning and sulphurous smoke," "troubled smoke and dark vapour," "this sudden fog,"* Night personified *"rises in mists," "a thick mist"* in which a transformation of nymphs takes place, *"a damp arises"* to hide Io from Jupiter. It would have been an easy matter for the Elizabethans, who were able to imitate thunder and lightning with fireworks, to send up through trap-doors vapours and fumes akin to the steam-curtain of the Wagnerian music-dramas. A "mist" of perfumes was regularly used whenever the air became foul in order to ventilate the halls where masques and indoor performances were given. There is no reason why something of the sort should not have been used through the trap-doors of the open-air stages. It could be made sufficiently dense for stage purposes, for in one of Jonson's masques "there appeared at the lower end of the hall a mist of delicate perfumes; out of which . . . did seem to break forth two ladies"; in another, "There ariseth a mist suddenly which darkening all the place, Clarion loseth himself." Is it plausible to suppose that the effect was Jonson's invention and remained his unique property? There is at least one bit of evidence that the open-air theatres copied the effect. In *The Prophetess,* performed at the Globe in 1622, the prophetess raises a foggy mist. That it was literally imitated is indicated by the lines of the Chorus, which explain that it enabled the Persians to escape their pursuers. In any case stage rain was often as wet as it had been on the miracle-play stages, although the sound of it was also imitated, as it still is today off-stage, by rattling starch or dried peas. The shipwrecked mariners of the *Tempest "enter wet."* In *The Two Angry Women of Abington,* one character remarks to another, "Look, the water drops from you as fast as hops." Showers of rose-water fell on Henry VII during a pageant at York and on Elizabeth during a banquet at Oxford. During a masque performed for the marriage of Lady Elizabeth in 1612 a visiting Venetian observed that a slight shower of rain was made to fall when Iris prayed to Flora. There is again no reason why the shower of rain in *The Brazen Age* could not have been literally achieved or a similar stage-direction in *If It Be Not Good the Devil Is in It, "rain, thunder, and lightning."* If the lightning was made actual with squibs running on wires, why not the rain, which could certainly fall with as much impunity on actors' pates as on the heads of royalty?

But if the evidence here is circumstantial, there is very direct evidence, which Lawrence cites, to show that the Elizabethan stage literally ran with gore. The stage properties for one triple assassination in *The Battle of Alcazar* are given, namely, "three vials of blood and a sheep's gather." "Since a 'gather' consists of the liver, heart, and lungs, we are presumably to infer that one of these organs was to be torn out of each of the unhappy trio." Mahelot's blood sponges, which did the trick for the sacrificial priest in the temple of Diana, reappear when Prince John (in *The Downfall of Robert Earl of Huntington*) smites a messenger and *"he bleeds."* The tradition comes from the English mediaeval stage, as in France it descended from the "secrets" of the passion-plays. The pageant of St. Thomas the Martyr as given at Canterbury required *"a leather bag for the blood."* The traditional method is accurately described in two stage-directions:

Bragadine shoots, Virgil puts his hand to his eye with a bloody sponge and the blood runs down.

Edwardo strikes him, and they . . . cuff and struggle upon the floor and are both bloody, occasioned by little sponges tied of purpose to the middle fingers in the palms of their hands.

223

In Marston, Webster, and Shakespeare blood is smeared on *"arms stripped to the elbow,"* on a bloody poignard, and even on a painting. Torture scenes were common. Hangings and executions are as literally executed as in the French and German miracle-plays. Henslowe's diary records:

Paid, for pulleys and workmanship to hang Absalom . . . xiiii pence.

The stage-direction of an anonymous play published in 1649—

He thrusts out his head, and they cut off a false head made of a bladder filled with blood . . .

continues a stage trick noted in the 1616 edition of Marlowe's *Faustus,* where the doctor enters with a false head which is presently cut off. Lawrence, whose studies of the Elizabethan stage have done so much to wipe out our elementary high-school notions of its inherent simplicity, concludes some twenty years of research by saying: "In the old, open-roofed theatre . . . Elizabethan predilection showed itself to be for high romance expressed in terms of uncompromising realism." "Make-believe was never expected of the frequenters of the old public theatres save where the circumstances rendered it obligatory."

When the eye could not be filled with literal blood and thunder it was satisfied with accurate and elaborate costuming. Henslowe, otherwise close-fisted, records such extravagant outlays that one exclaims with Lawrence, "When one reckons that, in the late 16th century, money had something like ten times its present purchasing power, one can only marvel over the disbursement of as much as £19 on a fine cloak or fifteen shillings for a pair of silk stockings." Henslowe very probably did not relish such expenditures, but was forced into them, like theatrical managers nowadays, by the competition of other theatres, so keen were the supposedly imaginative Elizabethans for every kind of stage spectacle. "The Red Bull Theatre was the lowest-class house of its time, yet when Webster's *The White Devil* was produced there *circa* 1611 the ambassadors in the play were arrayed in the elaborate jewelled collars of their various orders. This was apparently somewhat of an innovation, and it set a precedent that rival companies could not afford to ignore. Consequently . . . when the King's Men came to produce *Henry VIII* at the Globe the play was 'set forth with many extraordinary circumstances of pomp and majesty, even to the matting of the stage; the Knights of the Order with their Georges and garters, the Guards with their embroidered coats and the like.' " As in France, the taste for scenic elaboration was typical of amateur theatricals as well as of professional performances. In 1594 the professors of Trinity College petitioned the keeper of the Tower as follows:

Whereas we intend for the exercise of young gentlemen and scholars in our College to set forth certain comedies and one tragedy, there being in that tragedy sundry personages of greatest estate to be represented in ancient princely attire, which is nowhere to be had, but within the office of the Roades at the Tower: it is our humble request your most honorable Lordship would be pleased to grant your Lordship's warrant unto the chief officers there that upon sufficient security we might be furnished from thence with such meet necessaries as are required.

A desire for archaeological accuracy pushed to the point of using "genuine antiques" is obviously not a nineteenth century perversion of David Belasco or the Comédie Française.

3. KING'S AND QUEEN'S REVELS

A theatre that spends prodigious sums for embroidered cloaks and bejewelled ambassadors and indulges in displays of fireworks, acrobats disappearing on wires, gods appearing in mid-air with flaming weapons, magical apparitions of arbours and dragons appearing through the stage floor, and descents through trap-doors to the accompaniment of thunder and lightning, is a stage bent upon achieving all the stage spectacle possible, not one bent upon avoiding it. Within the limitations of their open structures the "public theatres," as the open-air playhouses were called, attempted by every means at their disposal to imitate the splendours of the court pageants, masques, and parades that were no less an established part of upper-class pleasures than the display of fashion at the royal enclosure at Ascot is now. No Elizabethan at all interested in the theatre was ignorant of how elaborate and ornate scenery could be. By Shakespeare's day England was already in possession of an intricate and complete technique for building and painting scenery, which was developed by the Office of the Revels under Henry VII and Henry VIII, continued through Elizabeth's reign, and culminated under James I, in the masques of Inigo Jones. L. B. Campbell's entertaining description of the Revels Office contains any amount of documentary evidence of elaborate stage-craft. One entry (1573) states:

The chief business of this office resteth specially in three points; in making of garments, in making of head-pieces and in painting.

The requirements for the Master of the Revels are those that would qualify him for holding the post of scenic director in any well-organized repertory theatre today.

The cunning of the office resteth in the skill of devise, in understanding of histories, in judgement of comedies, tragedies and shows, in sight of perspective and architecture, some smack of geometry and other things wherefore the best help is for the officers to make good choice of cunning artificers severally according to their best quality, and for one man to allow of another man's invention as it is worthy.

226

For a Christmas entertainment of Henry VIII, the Revels Office notes an outlay of 18 shillings 4½ pence for painting the walls of a castle solid enough to withstand a mimic siege and to hold "on the walls and towers" seven musicians attired in "satin . . . white and green." Any designer who has ever had to support seven actors well above the stage floor will recognize that this tower must have been a heavy affair. The Revels accounts mention in detail almost every phase of stage-craft subsequently used for two centuries. The will of one John Carow in 1574 lists a final payment to him for stage properties, including not only guns, daggers, bows, arrows, halberds, headpieces, and armour, but "counterfeit moss," holly, ivy, bays, flowers, as well as "Monsters, Mountains, Forests, Beasts, Serpents," dishes for devils' eyes, "heaven, hell, and the devil." There is also noted a payment for such effects as a burning rock, aqua vitae to make the rock burn, and "rose water to allay the smell thereof." In 1571 one John Izarde was paid 22 shillings for "his device in counterfeiting thunder and lightning in the play of Narcissus." John Ross (1574-75) was paid on various occasions for "long boards for the stere of a cloud," pulleys for clouds and curtains, and double pulleys "to hang the sun in the cloud." Later he is reimbursed for "a hoop and blue linen cloth to mend the cloud that was borrowed and cut to serve the rock in the play of the burning knight and for the hire thereof and the setting up the same where it was borrowed."

We read also of wages paid (1564) for "painters working . . . canvas to cover divers towns and houses" and for "painters working upon divers Cities and Towns and the Emperor's Palace," to linen-drapers "for canvas to cover the towns withal" and "other provisions," including "a rock or hill for the IX muses to sing upon with a vayne [veil] of sarsenet drawn up and down before them." Sarsenet was the sheerest silk obtainable. The entire repertory of scenic effects used at Mons is used again, including the silk veil "like the tent of gauze" that hid the

Holy Ghost and was revived to add glamour to the Hill of the Muses for the *Ballet de la Reine*.

The fact that the labour of covering towns and palaces is listed separately from the labour of painting them demonstrates that scenery in England during Shakespeare's prime was built of canvas and painted as it is nowadays after first being stretched on wooden frames, then called "spars." There is also a continual expenditure for cardboard and glue, used for the fretwork of battlements and other details of architectural outline, just as three-ply veneer board, usually three-eighths of an inch thick, is scroll-sawed for the same purpose today. As at Mons, holly-bushes were cut and transported to the stage, but flowers, boughs, and garlands were also made of silk. "Colours for light" are also mentioned, though whether these lighted the stage or the auditorium is not clear.

4. THE ELABORATE AMATEUR

The development of every kind of decorative elaboration in stage setting exactly parallels the history of the French theatre from 1500 on. In England, as across the Channel, stage scenery flourished like a rampant vine. One of the earliest dramatic interludes at a court banquet to Katharine of Aragon in 1501 contains floats that almost duplicate those of the banquet of the *Pheasant's Vow*. "A castle right cunningly devised, set upon certain wheels and drawn into the said great hall of four beasts with chains of gold." In it were "viii goodly and fresh ladies . . . four in English, and four in Spanish costume," and in the four turrets children "singing most sweetly." This was followed, as in the French banquet, by "a ship in like wise set upon wheels without any leaders in sight, in right goodly apparel, having her masts, top sails, her tackling and all other appurtenances necessary unto a seemly vessel, as though it had been sailing in the sea." As in the Jesuit colleges of France, amateur theatricals were the order of the day at English uni-

versities and even at the grammar-schools. As in France, the court attended. The boys of St. Paul's School in 1527 acted an anti-Lutheran
play before the king and the French ambassadors, in 1528 the *Phormio*
of Terence before Cardinal Wolsey and the foreign ambassadors and
again for Wolsey *Dido,* a Latin drama written for them by their head-
master. In these as in other university productions staging imitated the
staging of royal revels and plays performed at court. For a performance
by the boys of St. Paul's grammar school in 1527, there was

*the great chamber of the disguisings . . . a great fountain occupying
the centre of the picture, while at one side was a hawthorn tree of silk
and at the other side a similar mulberry tree. Eight fair ladies sat in
gorgeous apparel. . . . After the play four companies of maskers
danced. . . .*

"That the universities, like the grammar schools, early accepted the
acting of classical plays as a method of educational training is proved
beyond dispute by the statutes of several colleges." These statutes date
from 1545 to 1560 for Cambridge and Oxford. But they undoubtedly
gave official approval to an established undergraduate custom and did
not invent it. For in 1511 a certain Edmund Watson was given a degree at Oxford for composing a Latin comedy as well as a hundred
poems in praise of the university. At Trinity College in 1546 Dr. John
Dee staged a performance of Aristophanes' *Peace* with an imitation of
a classical machine, used for

*the performance of the Scarabaeus, his flying up to Jupiter's palace,
with a man and his basket of victuals on her back: whereat was great
wondering, and many vain reports spread abroad of the means how it
was effected.*

For Queen Elizabeth's visit to Cambridge in 1564, the first stage built in
the hall of King's College was taken down because it seemed too small

and a larger one constructed for the occasion. On the Queen's visit to Oxford in 1566, according to a contemporary record:

The hall was panelled with gilt and the roof inside was arched and frescoed; in its size and loftiness you would say that it was copied after the grandeur of an old Roman palace and in its magnificence that it imitated some model of antiquity. In the upper part of the hall a stage is built, large and lofty and many steps high. Along all the walls balconies and scaffoldings were constructed; these had many tiers of better seats from which noble men and women might look on. . . . On each side of the stage magnificent palaces and well-equipped houses are built up for the actors and the masked persons.

For the final play of the occasion, *Progne,* the trap-doors and flames of the miracle-plays are again brought into use.

First there is heard distinctly there a sort of subterranean noise, shut in and fearful. Hence from infernal regions Diomedes ascends. That was truly horrible then: he foams at the mouth, he has flaming head, feet, arms, which flame not with a fortuitous, but with innate deep-seated burning; he himself in truth is only too wretchedly terrified and distracted with the glowing brands of the furies.

There is no end to scenic effects. When the Palatine of Siradia visited Oxford in 1583, *Dido* was given. The banquet at which the queen presided was enlivened with

a goodly sight of hunters with full cry of a kennel of hounds, Mercury and Iris descending and ascending from and to a high place, the tempest wherein it hailed small confects, rained rose water and snowed an artificial kind of snow, all strange, marvellous, and abundant.

On another similar occasion snowballs made of sponges and covered with lamb's wool were used. The splendour of university theatricals became proverbial, a name to conjure with. The diary of Roger Ascham's voyage to Flanders in 1550 uses those of Cambridge as a standard of comparison:

the city of Antwerp as much exceeds all other cities, as the refectory of St. John's Hall, Cambridge, exceeds itself when furnished, at Christmas, with its theatrical apparatus for acting plays.

So much theatrical show gave rise to the same disquietude that we hear voiced now by anxious parents who feel that their children at modern schools should spend less time rehearsing plays and more time upon "serious studies." In 1625, Jonson in *The Staple of News* exclaimed:

Is't not a fine sight, to see all our children made interluders? Do we pay our money for this? We send them to learn their grammar and their Terence and they learn their playbooks.

His sentiments paraphrase the recent convictions of the president of Harvard, who begrudged house-room to Professor Baker's courses on play-production and finally allowed them to emigrate to Yale rather than have the well-known scholastic ardours of his undergraduates further contaminated by the presence of so much dramatic revelry. The theatrical amateur was in fact as irrepressible in Shakespeare's England as in Calvin Coolidge's United States. In 1572 a scandal broke out in which the Yeoman of the Revels was publicly accused of letting out the costumes and properties of the queen's own masques "to persons of all degrees, noble and mean, both in the city and in the country." The plaintiff was a certain Thomas Giles, who made a business of renting costumes for amateur performances and discovered that the royal yeomen had been undercutting his prices.

5. FAËRY LANDS AND PERILOUS SEAS

Scenic elaboration reached its climax in England during Shakespeare's lifetime. Two years after Elizabeth's death and a year after the second quarto of *Hamlet* was printed, Ben Jonson collaborated with the architect Inigo Jones in *The Masque of Blackness* for James I. For Jones's setting

was drawn a landscape consisting of small woods . . . which falling, an artificial sea was seen to shoot forth, as if it flowed to the land, raised with waves which seemed to move, and in some places the billows to break, as imitating that orderly disorder which is common in nature.

The Masquers were placed in a great concave shell, like mother-of-pearl, curiously made to move on those waters and rise with the billows . . . the scene behind seemed a vast sea . . . from the termination or horizon of which . . . was drawn by the lines of perspective, the whole work shooting downwards from the eye; which decorum made it more conspicuous, and caught the eye afar off with a wandering beauty: to which was added an obscure and cloudy Night-piece, that made the whole set off.

A wash drawing for a similar night-piece made by Inigo Jones thirty-three years later for Sir William Davenant's *Luminalia* is preserved in the Duke of Chatsworth's collection and reproduced in Volume XII of the publications of the Walpole Society. The drawing reveals a typically modern feeling for the loose use of water-colour and an equally modern feeling for the technique of suggestion.

In a masque of 1608 (the probable date of *Antony and Cleopatra*), when Vulcan cried, "Cleave the rock," the stage

parted in the midst, and discovered an illustrious concave, filled with an ample and glistering light, in which an artificial sphere was made of silver, eighteen foot in diameter, that turned perpetually.

A year later, for *The Masque of the Queens,*

the part of the scene which first presented itself was an ugly Hell;
which flaming beneath, smoked unto the top of the roof, (but) on the
sudden was heard a sound of loud music; . . . with which not only the
hags themselves, but the hell into which they ran, quite vanished, and
the whole face of the scene altered, scarce suffering the memory of such
a thing; but in place of it appeared a glorious building, figuring the
House of Fame, in the top of which was discovered the twelve Maskers,
sitting upon a throne triumphal, erected in form of a pyramid and cir-
cled with all store of light.

Even more resplendent was a scenic change in *Tethys' Festival* (1610),
that a scene-designer today, with all the aid that modern mechanics
could supply, would be hard put to it to duplicate:

First, at the opening of the heavens, appeared three circles of lights
and glasses, one within another, and came down in a straight motion
five foot, and then began to move circularly; which lights and motion
so occupied the eyes of the spectators, that the manner of altering the
scene was scarcely discerned; for in the moment the whole face of it
was changed, the port vanished and Tethys with her nymphs appeared
in their several caverns, gloriously adorned.

6. STAGE SCENERY IN THE STREETS

It is easy to fall into the habit of theorizing about Elizabethan staging
as though the court masques and the university productions took place
in hermetically sealed compartments. But is it not obvious that neither
the hundreds of undergraduates at Cambridge and Oxford nor the
thousand and one retainers who witnessed a continual succession of
court pageants, masques, ballets, pantomimes, and revels of every sort
—nearly two hundred and fifty are recorded between the year 1588

and Elizabeth's death in 1603—could not fail to spread news of such marvels by word of mouth? And even if every common person among the spectators had had his tongue cut out by royal edict after each and every performance, the meanest tapster, the lowest varlet, could have seen similar attempts at scenic effects in the streets, where they were used upon every possible occasion for triumphal processions and entries in state.

"What," asks Burton in his *Anatomy of Melancholy,* "so pleasant as to see some pageant as at coronations, wedding, and such like solemnities, to see an Ambassador or a Prince met, received, entertained with Masks, Shews, Fireworks . . . ?" Elizabethans agreed with him, man, woman, and child. When Elizabeth during her coronation festivities passed from the Tower to Westminster, scenery was used to line her progress in the shape of four allegorical arches, symbolizing "The Uniting of the Two Houses of Lancaster and York," "The Seat of Worthy Government," "The Eight Beatitudes," and "A Ruinous and a Flourishing Commonweal." The queen halted at each one to acknowledge equally allegorical tableaux, accompanied by songs and speeches. For the coronation procession of James I pageants were presented along the route: "The Garden of Eirene and Euporia," "The Globe of the World," "The Temple of Janus," and "The Rainbow, Sun, Moon, and Pleiades." When the King of Denmark visited London in 1606, another arch was erected in Fleet Street and on it "Neptune, . . . Concord, and the Genius of London and a summer bower with shepherds and shepherdesses." A year later the Guild of Merchant Tailors spent £1,000 on a pageant accompanying a dinner in his honour. Londoners lined the shore when Henry was created Prince of Wales and the barges of the Lord Mayor went up the Thames to meet him accompanied by Corinea on a whale and Amphion on a dolphin. There were other "water triumphs" on the Thames. In one, a castle was assaulted and exploded fireworks. To welcome Prince Henry in

1610 a display of fireworks concluded a mock fight between merchants and pirates, and Burbage and the actors of the King's Men rode out to meet him on "two great fishes" and recited speeches from their aquatic perch. For the wedding of the Princess Elizabeth (1613) a fight between Turkish and Venetian galleys took place on the river and "a firework representation of St. George delivering the Amazonian Queen Lucida from Mango the Necromancer."

In the intervals between royal weddings and coronations, Londoners had their Lord Mayor's show, which has survived as a show to this day. As early as 1540 displays of fireworks, the traditional devils in red, and wild men in green were part of the festivity. The various guilds of London tradesmen in turn undertook the scenery and costuming. For one, the Merchant Tailors supplied a ship, a lion, and a camel, a schoolmaster from their own school, and ten pupils dressed to represent Apollo and the Muses. For another the Drapers, according to the account of a visiting Dutchman, provided "a representation in the shape of a house with a pointed roof painted in blue and golden colours and ornamented with garlands, on which sat some young girls in fine apparel, one holding a book, another a pair of scales, and the third a sceptre." The Guild of Ironmongers preserved their designs for one Lord Mayor's show and made its scenery part of the permanent decoration of their Guild-hall. The scripts for the coronation pageant of James I and a number of Lord Mayor's shows were written by such popular playwrights as Jonson, Dekker, and Middleton.

The citizens of London, like the burghers of Mons, had their equivalent for our annual circus and the Fourth of July. If they never entered a playhouse they found the theatre in the streets or on the riverfront. If they had attended a Latin school or a university they had seen stages flanked with painted palaces, where it rained rose-water and snowed a wondrous kind of snow. Some of them no doubt treasured as a souvenir snowballs of lamb's wool thrown to them by some great personage at the concluding banquet. As apprentices they had seen classic gods and mythical beasts cavorting on the Thames. As young men they had bribed the queen's yeoman and borrowed costumes from the queen's own revels for their private theatricals. As established and middle-aged tradesmen they had supplied scenery for state occasions and allowed their children to act in it. Shakespeare's audiences were well aware of almost every visual delight that scenic decoration could give. It is preposterous to suppose that merely because they entered an open-air theatre of an afternoon they lost all their appetite for spectacle and relied entirely on their imagination as a substitute for scenic pictures. As a matter of fact they relied on their imagination as little as possible and patronized plays that decked out ambassadors in jewelled collars, made it worth while for managers to spend £20 on a single cloak, were in fact so used to every kind of pageantry that in order to satisfy them by every possible scenic trick, a stage bare of painted scenery provided magicians, dragons, devils, and gods hauled up and down from Heaven before their eyes. These machines and creaking chairs no doubt were fit to please only small boys; but the grown-up boys who always comprise a large part of every audience enjoyed the descent of Hercules or Pluto, as they did the fireworks that accompanied him. Certainly they were not an audience so naïve as to conceive of no alternative to a bare stage and a few makeshift properties. Without the knowledge of an alternative half the fun of Pyramus and Thisbe would have been lost. A genuinely naïve audience would have accepted the lantern as a moon, two fingers as a crack in the wall, and would not have laughed at them. The scene is a parody on the inadequacies of staging that were forced upon the open-air theatres and the hilarity of the scene very largely depends on the fact that every one is aware of how ridiculous such makeshifts were. Shakespeare was himself well aware that the imagination of his audiences, unlike the quality of mercy, could very easily be strained. If presentation rather than representation had been popular with them, the Chorus would not have apologized quite so elaborately in *Henry V*:

> *Where—O for pity—we shall much disgrace,*
> *With four or five most vile and ragged foils*
> *Right ill disposed in brawl ridiculous*
> *The name of Agincourt.*

Shakespeare was not only a poet but a shrewd man of the theatre as well. He was shrewd enough to introduce into *The Tempest* the effects of faërie magic that court masques had made popular. And in this prologue he is also doing his best to counteract the appeal of such rival playhouses as The Bull, where battles more spectacularly staged were popular enough to draw crowds who preferred to feast their eyes rather than to use their powers of imagination.

7. BRIEF INTERLUDE

"Shakespeare's stage" was in many ways not typical of his age, an interlude, not a consummation, a makeshift and a stop-gap, a temporary phase of the Elizabethan theatre, hastily created by speculative builders like Henslowe and eagerly accepted by actors who had been pariahs until a lucky shift in popular and official taste gave them the right to a permanent theatre in the reconstructed inn-yards where they had taken refuge as strolling players. The imagination of the Renaissance was everywhere a pictorial one, and Shakespeare's dramatic imagination, like that of almost all his contemporaries, is no exception. His mind is constantly supplying pictures for the background of action such as prompted the elaborate painted decorations that flourished everywhere but in his own theatre, which, nevertheless, did its best to ape them piecemeal. He was so fundamentally at war with the pictorial limitations of his own stage that every modern school of scenic reform attempts to demonstrate its worth by visualizing the scenic backgrounds implicit in his text, whether with the archaeological accuracy of the Duke of Saxe-Meiningen's company, Craig's topless towers, Reinhardt's plastic hedges and birch groves, or Jessner's stairways. An adequate record of all the successive phases of modern stage-craft could be made by reproducing only scenes from Shakespeare as staged from 1800 to the present day.

Almost as soon as scenery was introduced in presentations at court, English critics, like the French, complained because it could not be shifted to illustrate the play's text. From the first, as in France, the demand was articulate that the eye should first see everything that the ear was later to hear. The necessity of introducing verbal descriptions of the backgrounds of action, which we now consider so great a stimulus to the poet, did not seem adequate to his audience. An imaginative age found no incentive in signs or tag-lines stating, "This is a Forest," or, "Here is a Palace." No defence of such simplifications has survived. But there is periodic derision for the practice of expecting an audience to supply scenery out of their own fancy. In 1596, Sir Philip Sidney, anticipating Scudéry and Voltaire, complained with elaborate irony of performances

where you shall have Asia of the one side and Africa of the other, and so many other under-kingdoms, that the player, when he cometh in, must ever begin with telling where he is, or else, the tale will not be conceived. Now you shall have three ladies walk to gather flowers, and then we must believe the stage to be a garden. By and by, we hear news of shipwreck in the same place, and then we are to blame, if we accept it not for a rock. Upon the back of that, comes out a hideous monster, with fire and smoke, and then the miserable beholders, are to take it for a cave. While in the meantime two armies fly in, represented with four swords and bucklers, and then what hard heart will not receive it for a pitched field [of battle]?

Jonson, in the prologue to *Every Man out of his Humour,* in turn sneers at the practise of imagining a stage to be a dozen different places.

Mitis: *No? How comes it then, that in some one play we see so many seas, countries, and kingdoms, past over with such admirable dexterity?*

Corditis: *Oh, that but shows how well the Authors travail in their vocation, and outrun the apprehension of their auditory.*

If the jibe had not been good for a laugh Jonson would not have written it. And it could raise a laugh only because Elizabethan audiences objected to having their imagination grow short-winded in supplying pictures for a play as it trailed after the playwright. *The Knight of the Burning Pestle,* in which an inn is made to serve for a castle and a barber's shop for Barbaroso's cave and the court of Moldavia, is a parody on the scenic inadequacies of the open-air public theatres. If these shortcomings had not been generally felt the parody would have been pointless.

Every attempt to make the play fit the theatre by observing unity of place proved as abortive in England as it did in France. An age of romantic voyaging and sensational discovery could not confine itself in the theatre to a Procrustean classic mould. The audience as well as the playwright wanted all the vicarious satisfactions of discovering new worlds while seated in the pit. Elizabethan dramatists persisted in travelling in their vocation, and the demand for more scenery rather than less was persistent. "Not all the efforts of Ben Jonson could succeed in establishing an aesthetic standard or a liking for neo-classic principles."

We forget, among other things, that the "Shakespearian stages" of the public theatres were not alone in the field. They very soon had competitors in the private or indoor theatre, where performances were given at night, a higher scale of admission was charged, and a more uniformly upper-class audience attended. As a result the painted façades already familiar in court plays were imitated. So cautious a commentator as Chambers concludes that as early as 1600 the private theatres "revived the methods of staging with which their predecessors had been familiar during the hey-day of the Court drama under Lyly; that these methods held their own in the competition with the public theatres, and were handed on to the Queen's Revels; but that in course of time they were sometimes variegated by the introduction, for one reason or another, of some measure of scene-shifting in individual plays." In a play written for the Children of Paul, the author asks for

a shower of Rose-water and confits, as was acted at Christ Church in Oxford, in Dido and Aeneas.

Shortly before the civil wars plays were acted at court and then at a private playhouse or vice versa. Sir John Suckling's *Aglaura* was acted in 1637 originally at the private theatre of Blackfriars and then played at court. A letter from one spectator states that the "play cost three or four hundred pounds setting out; eight or ten suits of new clothes he gave the players; an unheard of prodigality." Habington's *Queen of Aragon* was first presented at court by amateurs and then repeated at Blackfriars by professional actors. The established popularity of stage scenery by the year 1636 is attested by the fact that when the Chancellor of Oxford was asked to send to Hampton Court the scenery and costumes of the *Royal Slave,* originally performed at Christ Church, he asked the queen to assure him that "neither the play, the clothes, nor stage, might come into the hands and use of the common players abroad, which was graciously granted." The settings were by Inigo Jones, and were seen between shutters that opened and closed laterally for scene-shifts somewhat like our present-day curtain.

Within the shuts were seen a curious Temple, and the Sun shining over it, delightful forests also, and other prospects. Within the great shuts . . . were seen villages and men visibly appearing in them, going up and down, here and there, about their business. . . . It was very well penned and acted, and the strangeness of the Persian habits gave great content.

If such painted prospects had not been capable of becoming a commercial asset for the common players of the popular theatres, the Chancellor would not have taken such pains to prevent his settings and costumes from falling into their hands.

Completely mobile scenery is commonly supposed to have been first used on the English stage in 1656, when Inigo Jones's pupil Webb staged *The Siege of Rhodes* for Sir William Davenant. But in 1638 a masque presented at another private playhouse, Salisbury Court, was acted behind a special proscenium arch and had five changes of scene made behind a drop-curtain lowered while they were set. The proscenium "was . . . adorned with brass figures of Angels and Devils. . . . Within the arch a continuing perspective of ruins which is drawn still before the other scenes while they are varied." Rival playwrights continued, like Jonson, to protest in their prologues that their plays, actually as mediocre as their rivals', were better dramatic art because they disdained to rely on elaborate stage settings. Says one:

> *Opinion, which the Author cannot court,*
> *(For the dear daintiness of it) has, of late,*
> *From the old way of Plays possessed a sort*
> *Only to run to those, that carry state*
> *In scene magnificent and language high;*
> *And Clothes worth all the rest, except the Action,*
> *And such are only good those Leaders cry;*

and another:

> *Gallants, I'll tell you what we do not mean*
> *To show you here, a glorious painted Scene,*
> *With various doors, to stand instead of wit,*
> *Or richer clothes with lace, for lines well writ.*

By 1638 a poet, by way of paying tribute to the memory of Ben Jonson, is already lamenting the good old plays that were never typical of the good old days:

> *Thy scene was free from monsters; no hard plot*
> *Called down a God t'untie th'unlikely knot:*
> *The stage was still a stage, two entrances*
> *Were not two parts o' the world, disjoined by seas.*
> *Thine were land-tragedies, no prince was found*
> *To swim a whole scene out, then o' the stage drowned;*
> *Pitched fields as Red Bull wars, still felt thy doom;*
> *Thou laid'st no sieges to the music room.*

But the cause, never won in Shakespeare's own lifetime, was already a lost cause. By the time that the sons of his groundlings, born in the year of his death, were middle-aged playgoers, the scene-shifts of *The Siege of Rhodes* were such a success that Davenant promptly planned a larger theatre for bigger and better spectacles. Two years later at the Cockpit in Drury Lane he mounted, as announced on the play-bill:

> *The Cruelty of the Spaniards in Peru, expressed by Instrumental and Vocal Music, and by the Art of Perspective in Scenes. . . . Notwithstanding the great expense necessary to scenes, and other ornaments of the entertainment, there is good provision of places made for a shilling.*

242

Our own theatre advertisements assure us that there are always plenty of good balcony seats for the Ziegfeld Follies at one dollar. The prologue to *Henry VIII* had promised its spectators:

> ... *if they be still and willing,*
> *I'll undertake may see away their shilling*
> *Richly in two short hours.*

Their immediate descendants were still seeing away their shilling at the Cockpit as they once had at the pitched battles at the Bull, and getting their money's worth, beginning with

a Harbour ... where two Ships are Moor'd, and Sea-Carpenters are erecting a Pinnace, whilst others are felling Trees to build a Fort. The narrowness of the entrance to the Harbour may be observed, with Rocks on either side, and out at Sea a Ship towing a Prize. And likewise, on the top of a high Tree, a Mariner making his Ken. This prospect is made through a Wood, differing from those of European Climates, by representing of Coco-Trees, Pines, and Palmitos. And on the Boughs of other Trees are seen Munkies, Apes, and Parrots.

In 1645 Evelyn noted in his diary:

This night ... we went to the opera, where comedies and other plays are represented in recitative music ... with variety of scenes painted and contrived with no less art of perspective, and machines for flying in the air, and other wonderful motions.

Davenant's production of *Macbeth* is described by Downes as

being dressed in all its Finery, as new Clothes, new Scenes, Machines, as flyings for the Witches; with all the Singing and Dancing in it.

Addison witnessed similar productions in 1711, for he writes in *The Spectator:*

243

*Among the several artifices which are put in practice by the poets to
fill the minds of an audience with terror, the first place is due to thunder and lightning, which are often made use of at the descending of a
god, or the rising of a ghost, at the vanishing of a devil, or at the death
of a tyrant. I have known a bell introduced into several tragedies with
good effect; and have seen the whole assembly in a very great alarm all
the while it has been ringing. But there is nothing which delights and
terrifies our English theatre so much as a ghost, especially when he appears in a bloody shirt. A spectre has very often saved a play.*

But in the same year Addison's *Spectator* complains:

*The tailor and the painter often contribute to the success of a
tragedy more than the poet. Scenes affect ordinary minds as much as
speeches; and our actors are very sensible that a well-dressed play has
sometimes brought them as full audiences as a well-written one. . . .
But however the show and outside of the tragedy may work upon the
vulgar, the more understanding part of the audience immediately see
through it, and despise it.*

8. THE NECESSARY ILLUSION

The complaint is as ancient as Aristotle's and Demosthenes'. We are
all as self-contradictory as Goethe, who at one moment declared: "A
good actor very quickly makes us forget miserably inappropriate settings, whereas the most beautifully decorated stage is the first thing
that makes us aware of the lack of capable players"; and then as a
director of the Weimar theatre wrote to a friend: "We now have an
outstanding scene painter; if we can only keep him for a short time
next spring not only for the new settings at the Lauchstadt theatre
but also for our own here at Weimar, we shall be saved. The present
settings for *Palmira* are so beautiful that I would gladly pay the price
of admission to see them again without the play." The more under-

standing are forever seeing through scenery and despising it in print, although they rarely resist its spell in the playhouse. But the vulgar, ordinary crowds, whose shillings make a living theatre possible, are persistent in their demands that their eyes be prepared for what their ears will hear. They cannot be denied and never have been. Simplified stages that refuse to illustrate the backgrounds of action have never survived the generation for which they were invented. The stage picture has not been hatched in candlelight or under electric bulbs. Unabashed by the sun, it planted itself in every open-air theatre and established itself there even before the theatre went indoors. Stage scenery in one form or another is today what it has always been, an essential strut of the theatre, an ineradicable element in performing plays.

The roof of every theatre, even of the open-air theatre, has been the periphery of whatever universe its audience believed itself to be inhabiting. From it Jupiter or Athene, Christ or the Holy Ghost, descended. Although occasionally a pulley jammed and a deity became ridiculous, dangling panic-stricken, the ropes and pulleys of theatrical machinery continued to link Heaven to the stage floor. The stage floor covered not the cellar, but the bowels of the earth. Through trap-doors emerged the messengers of evil. Machines might creak but they continued to be invented and used. Every generation that supported a successful theatre decreed that it be as magnificent as possible. By one means or another—paint and veils of gauze, gilt and varnish, fire and brimstone, crystal spheres and thunder-drum— the effort has continued, without interruption, to make even the barest stage a spectacular reflection of a spectacular universe. Because we can never again see the world through the eyes of Pericles' Athens, Shakespeare's England, Molière's France, or with the vision of the miracle-mongers of the Middle Ages, it is futile to attempt to revive their scenic illusions, whether austere or ornate. But we cannot avoid the necessity of creating our own. We shall do so by the same process that bred theirs: by discovering our equivalents for Heaven and Hell and thereby defining the frontiers of our own world.

PART THREE

THE ACTOR AND THE THIRD DIMENSION

CHAPTER I

RENAISSANCE BY-PRODUCT

I. ITALIAN PATTERNS AND TEXT-BOOKS

THE principal types of painted scenery, the technique of building, painting, and lighting it, and the various methods devised for shifting it, which began as experiments in the sixteenth century and before the middle of the eighteenth century had become a formula for theatrical production throughout Europe, were, like the types and techniques of the other plastic arts, largely formulated by Renaissance Italy. The first text-book on scenic design is contained in Sebastiano Serlio's treatise on architecture, published 1537-47 and translated from the Dutch into English in 1611. In that edition the art of stage setting occupies seven folio pages, with two diagrams and three engravings that became copy-book patterns for the better part of a century. These showed three types of theatrical scenes, one appropriate for tragedy—a street flanked by neo-classic palaces—and another suited for comedy—a square, bounded by the buildings typical of an Italian city of the period. A third, rustic scene shows thatched peasant cottages in a grove where nymphs and shepherds, satyrs and shepherdesses, could appropriately disport themselves. For comedy "there must not want a brothel, or bawdy house, and a great inn, and a church." The buildings in the foreground must be lower than those in the rear so as not to obstruct the vista. They are thoroughly architectural, with tiled roofs complete to chimney-pots and cornices, balconies and loggias, or "an open gallery through which you may see another house." "All that you make above the roof sticking out as Chimneys, Towers, Pyramids, Oblisces and other such like things or images you must make them all of thin boards, cut out round and well coloured." Windows are of glass or paper through which lights can be seen. "Houses in Tragedies must be made for great personages for the actions of love, strange adventures, and cruel murthers (as you read in ancient and modern tragedies) always happen in the houses of great Lords, Dukes, Princes, and Kings." Like every stage-carpenter since his time, Serlio makes his "scenes of laths covered with linen" and then adds projections such as mouldings and cornices in solid relief. "Sometime it is necessary to make some things rising or bossing out, which are to be made of wood, like the houses on the left whereof . . . the pillars . . . stand all upon one base with some stairs and are covered over with cloth, the cornices bearing out." At the rear the perspective is carried off by a painted back-drop. "In the buildings that stand far backward the painting work must supply the place [of] shadows without any bearing out." But the trees and verdure of the pastoral scene are plastic, for "in our days these were made in winter when there are but few trees, herbs, and flowers to be found, then you must make these things of silk, which will be more commendable than the natural things themselves."

But more extraordinary in their anticipation of modern technique are the directions for using coloured lights, red, amber, blue, and white—the stock colours of the gelatines still in use to colour electric lights. The colouring matter—salammoniac for blue, saffron for yellow, and red wine for ruby—was properly dissolved, put in glass bowls rather like the jars in apothecaries' windows a generation ago, and solidly fastened on wooden brackets so that the tramping of actors and dancers could not upset them. A lamp or torch in back of each one projected coloured light on to the stage through the apertures of houses and palaces. "White wine alone will show like from Fransisco Maria, Duke of Vrbin: wherein I saw so great liberalitie vsed by the Prince, and so good a conceit in the workeman, and so good Art and proportion in things therein represented, as euer I saw in all my life before. Oh good Lord, what magnificence was there to be seene, for the great number of Trees and Fruits, with sundry Herbes and Flowes, all made of fine Silke of diuers collers. The water courses being adorned with Frogs, Snailes, Tortules, Toads, Adders, Snakes, and other beasts: Knots of Corals, mother of Pearle, and other shels layd and thrust through betweene the stones, with so many seuerall and faire things, that if I should declare them all, I should not haue time inough.   I speake not of Satirs, Nimphes, Mer-maids, diuers monsters, and other strange beasts, made so cunningly, that they seemed in them as if they went and stirred, according to their manner.   And if I were not loathsom to be briefe, I would speake of the costly apparel of some Shepherds made of cloth of gold, and of Silke, cunningly mingled with Imbroidery: I would also speake of some Fishermen, which were no lesse richly apparelled then the others, hauing Nets and Angling-rods, all gilt: I should speake of some Countrey mayds and Nimphes carelessly apparelled without pride, but I leaue all these things to the discretion and consideration of the iudicious workeman, which shall make all such things as their pattrons serue them, which they must worke after their owne deuises, and neuer take care what it shall cost.

SERLIO'S PASTORAL SETTING

topaz or chrysolite: the conduit of common water being strained will be like a diamond." Even the modern use of a reflector behind an electric bulb is anticipated. "But if you need a great light to throw more than the rest, then set a torch behind, and behind the torch a bright basin; the brightness whereof will show like the beams of the sun." The section "On Artificial Lights of the Scenes" concludes with directions for making thunder and lightning. "Commonly all scenes are made at the end of a great hall, whereas usually there is a great chamber above it, wherein you must roll a great bullet or cannon or some other great ordnance and then counterfeit thunder." Lightning is sent down a wire on a squib covered with gilt or satin.

The facts that trees of silk, towers and turrets of wood and cardboard, and coloured lights were already in use for the English revels, and that lightning descended on a wire in the Londen public theatres before the English translation of Serlio appeared, indicate that his rules summarized a technique already perfected in Italy by a good many years of practice and that knowledge of it had spread by word of mouth. Serlio's engravings are not projections of ideal settings but summaries of scenes such as his contemporaries had witnessed. One, given nearly twenty-five years before his text-book was printed, as described by Castiglione, who superintended the production, was

laid in a very fine city, with streets, palaces, churches, and towers, all in relief, and looking as if they were real, the effect being completed by admirable paintings in scientific perspective. Among other objects, there was an octagon temple . . . covered with beautiful stucco reliefs, the windows were made to imitate alabaster, the architraves and cornices were of fine gold and ultramarine blue, with glass jewels here and there, looking exactly like real gems; there were roundels of marble containing figures, carved pillars, and much more that would take me too long to describe. The temple stood in the centre of the stage. At

*one end there was a triumphal arch about two yards from the wall,
marvellously executed. . . . On the top . . . stood . . . a most beautiful equestrian . . . figure in armour . . . To the right . . . were two
little altars with vases of burning flame that lasted to the end of the
comedy.*

The play was the popular *Calandra* by Cardinal Bibbiena. For another
performance of it, Baldassare Peruzzi, architect of the Farnese palace
and a painter of importance in his day, designed a setting described
by Vasari:

*It appears to me difficult even to imagine how this artist has found it
possible . . . to exhibit such a variety of objects as he has depicted, such
a number of streets, palaces, temples, loggie, and fanciful erections of all
kinds, with cornices and ornaments of every sort, so perfectly represented that they did not look like things feigned, but are as the living
reality: neither does the piazza, which is the site of all these edifices,
appear to be, as it is, a narrow space merely painted, but looks entirely
real and of noble extent. In the arrangement of the lights also, Baldassare showed equal ability, in those of the interior, which are designed
to enhance the effect of the views in perspective. . . .*

For a performance given in honour of Giuliano de' Medici's arrival
in Rome "a perspective view or scene which this master prepared for
a Theatre . . . was so beautiful that nothing better could possibly be
imagined." Serlio was Peruzzi's pupil. There can therefore be very little
doubt that his rules for designing stage scenery were based not only on
his master's theories but also on settings that had been executed.

The same holds true of the second Italian text-book to appear a
century later, *The Practice of Making Scenes and Machines in
Theatres,* by Nicola Sabbattini, printed in 1638. His devices for moving
suns and clouds and rocking waves and ships had already been ex-

ploited for Jonson's masques. His rudimentary schemes for scene-shifting included a revival of the Greek *periaktoi* that had already been used in France and at Oxford by Inigo Jones. Most of his methods were already old-fashioned by the time his book appeared, for Sabbattini is so uncertain of the speed of his various methods for changing his sets that he advises distracting the attention of the audience by having some one at the back of the auditorium pretend to start a brawl or cry that the scaffolding under the seats has started to give way; or, as this might start a panic, accomplishing the same result with an unexpected blast of trumpets or a fanfare of drums. But only nine years later Torelli was astonishing the French court with the newest Italian inventions of counterweighted sets which changed from Heaven to Hell or from the Seine to the Elysian Fields half a dozen times in the course of a single evening. Indeed a few years after Sabbattini's handbook appeared, similar metamorphoses were taking place in Cardinal Barberini's theatre, where some of the earliest operas were given. The auditorium was capable of holding three thousand spectators, who were captivated not only by the singing but by a succession of scenic spectacles described by contemporary letter-writers. "The flight of the angel through the clouds; the appearance of Religion in the air . . . works of engineering . . . rivalling nature . . . the appearance of Heaven and Inferno, marvellous . . . the illuminated depth of that portico, with the most distant view of the garden, incomparable." Another letter exclaims over "the pleasing illusion of the mechanisms and of the changing scenes imperceptibly made to appear, now to disappear, an immense rock, and a grotto to come to view, and a river from which was first seen to rise the Jordan and then the Naiads . . . Armida is carried in a chariot drawn by dragons, and vanishes in a flash of lightning; now the ordinary stage is changed to a battlefield, the forest into a pavilion, and the perspective . . . into the walls of besieged Jerusalem . . . from some abyss of Avernus come demons pleasingly horrible in company with furies, who dance together; later, seated in infernal chariots, they disappear through the air."

Chi Soffre Speri, given in 1639, mingled the same kind of mechanical spectacle with elaborate realism. Its first performance was a gala occasion, attended by John Milton, who recorded the fact in a letter to Luca Holstein, but considered it more important to recount his flattering reception by the cardinal than to describe the play. A less illustrious spectator left a record of the stage settings used, including "a marketplace where there even appeared a cart drawn by oxen, a sedan chair carried by mules, with a person inside, and besides, a person on horseback following, and everything real and living." This scene, an interlude picturing the fair at Farfa, was the sensation of the evening. As described by Romain Rolland it seems like an elaborate latter-day production of the last act of *Carmen:*

The din of hawkers' cries sounds, venders and their customers haggle, passers-by stop to chat, grand seigneurs appear in their carriages; a wagon drawn by bullocks goes by. A quack mounts his platform and terrifies mothers into buying his amulets with descriptions of infants' maladies. The crowd looks on, chatters, is amused. A few young people start a dance. One of them kicks a dog, and is set upon by its angry owner. Swords are drawn, a duel begins, blood flows. The sun sinks on the horizon.

The sunset that was one of the celebrated features of the performance indicates how much progress the Renaissance had made in manipulating stage lighting even to the point of being able to dim candles and oil-lamps in unison. Sabbattini diagrams one device, a series of perforated metal collars controlled by a wire from which they were hung and then dropped on cue over the rows of candles. But either that or an equivalent method must already have been known and used for the better part of a century. In the dialogues of a Jewish theatre-director, Leone de' Somi, on *The Means of Theatrical Representation,* dated 1550, Somi remarks (as translated by Allardyce Nicoll):

> *Once I had to produce . . . a tragedy. The stage was brightly illuminated through all that part of the action in which the episodes were happy: as soon as the first unhappy incident occurred—the unexpected death of a queen—while the chorus was in exclamation that the sun could suffer to see such misery, I contrived . . . that at that very instant most of the stage lights . . . were darkened or extinguished.*

Somi seems also to have initiated the modern practice of darkening the auditorium during a performance:

> *As you know, in nature, a man standing in shadow sees much better whatever is brightly lit at a distance, than does one who stands in an illuminated position . . . Hence I place the fewest possible lights in the auditorium, while at the same time I endeavour to illuminate the stage brightly; the very few lamps in the auditorium I place behind the spectators in order that these should not interfere with their view of the stage.*

2. PAINTER'S HOLIDAY

Elaborating the traditional machinery of miracle-play pageantry was a pastime that diverted the energies of some of the greatest geniuses of the Italian Renaissance. Scene-painting became a painter's holiday. One of the minor feats of Brunelleschi, who erected the dome of the Florence cathedral after the engineering problems involved had baffled his rival Ghiberti, was a "paradise" hung from one of the vaults of the Church of San Felice, a platform with a miniature dome above it which, according to Vasari, held twelve children "dressed to represent angels with gilded wings, and hair formed of gold threads."

sopra coperti, lasciandoui solo vno spiraglio per essalare il fumo, e
dalla parte di sotto aperti. Compito questo si aggiustarà ciascuno
sopra il suo lume essendosi aperti. & accomodati, come nella quì à
basso Figura si vede, in modo che in vn sol moto per canto della Scena si calino i fili co i cilindri sopra i lumi, e con quest'ordine si oscura-
ranno: E ritornando i fili à i suoi luoghi di nouo s'illuminarà la Scena, ma si deue hauere in consideratione di porre detti lumi in manie-
ra, che nel tramutar le Scene non diano impedimento alcuno, come
si disse nel Primo Libro al Cap 39.

Quando ne gl'Intermedij si haueranno ad oscurare le Scene, si
doura mettere poca quantita di Lumi fuori della Scena, e porli al-
quanto lontani dal principio di essa, perche essendo in gran copia, e
vicini al Palco, si come è douere, poco si discernerebbe l'oscurare
de gli altri, e cosi tale operatione riuscirebbe vana.

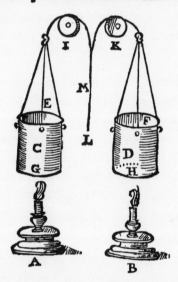

**Siano i due Lumi, che si hauranno ad oscurare A. B. & i Cilindri
C. D.**

A PAGE FROM SABBATTINI SHOWING HIS DEVICE FOR DIMMING
CANDLELIGHT

Above their heads hung "three chaplets . . . of lights . . . that could not be overturned, and . . . had the appearance of stars." This paradise, on the Feast of the Annunciation, was lowered by a windlass, the children carolled that Christ was risen and were then hoisted to the roof and disappeared behind trap-doors that closed horizontally beneath them. These added to the dramatic effect by rumbling like thunder and, once shut, made the floor of an angels' dressing-room. Leonardo da Vinci, in 1489, for the nuptials of the Duke of Milan devised a machine "representing the heavenly bodies with their movements on a colossal scale. Whenever a planet approached Isabella, the bride of the young duke, the divinity whose name it bore stepped forth and sang some verses written by the court poet Ballancioni." Bastiano da San Gallo in 1539 arranged an effect that Inigo Jones's crystal spheres later reflected:

Behind all the buildings of this scene Bastiano . . . constructed . . . a . . . lantern made of wood, with a Sun measuring a braccio in diameter, which was formed of a ball of crystal filled with distilled water; behind the ball were kindled torches, which caused it to shine in such sort that the ceiling, the decorations, and the stages were all illuminated by that splendour in a manner which made it appear to be the true and natural Sun.

San Gallo was also adept in "perspective views representing streets stretching far away into the distance," and for several productions collaborated with his neighbour Andrea del Sarto.

Raphael, who on Bramante's death became architect of St. Peter's, constructed a temporary wooden theatre for Pope Leo X in the Castle of Sant' Angelo and designed the settings for a performance of Ariosto's *I Suppositi.* A letter to the Duke of Ferrara relates that

once in the hall . . . and the crowd seated, which might easily have numbered two thousand persons, a drop was let down on which was

*painted Brother Mariano and a number of devils, frolicking with him.
. . . Music sounded, and the Pope, through his eye-glasses, admired the
setting, which was extremely beautiful and from the hand of Raphael
himself; in truth it was a beautiful view of streets and perspectives
which were greatly praised. His Holiness also admired the heavens,
which were marvellously done.*

The splendour of Italian court masques set the fashion for the rest
of Europe. Castiglione's letters describe the figures both living and
mechanical at a pageant for the Duke of Urbino that became traditional in court ballets as late as Louis XVI: Jason dancing in armour
with the Golden Fleece about his shoulders, "two bulls so lifelike that
several of the spectators took them for real animals, breathing fire
through their nostrils," Venus's chariot drawn by doves "that seemed
to be alive," the chariot of Neptune drawn by sea-horses, that of Juno
"ablaze with light . . . surrounded by numberless heads blowing the
winds of heaven. This car," in addition, "was drawn by two peacocks
so beautiful and lifelike that I could not believe my eyes, and yet I had
seen them before, and had myself given directions how they were to
be made." The imitation of nature even in allegorical fantasies continues to be the touchstone of art to Castiglione as it was to Vasari the
historian: "All of these were so well done, my dear Monsignore, that
I am quite sure no imitation ever came so near reality."

Serlio, in the midst of his technical directions, stops to exclaim over
the marvels of a masque designed by Jeronimo Genga for the same
court: "Oh, good Lord, what magnificence was there to be seen, for
the great number of trees, fruits, and the sundry herbs and flowers
all made of fine silk of divers colors. The water courses being adorned
with frogs, snails, tortoises, toads, adders, snakes and other beasts:
ropes of coral and mother-of-pearl and other shells laid and thrust between the stones. . . . I speak not of Satyrs, Nymphs, Mermaids and

259

divers monsters and other strange beasts made so cunningly that they went and stirred according to their manner. And if I were not desirous to be brief I would speak of the costly apparel of some Shepherds made of cloth of gold and of silk cunningly mingled with embroidery. I would also speak of some fishermen no less richly appareled than the others, having nets and angling rods all gilt. . . . But I leave all these things to the discretion and consideration of the judicious workman . . . which they must work after their own devices and never take care of what it will cost."

Mantegna's murals of *The Triumph of Caesar* formed the permanent background of the hall at the ducal palace in Mantua, where not only pageants but also revivals of Plautus and Terence were given. For one the stage was hung with a curtain, "The Triumphs of Plutarch," painted by Andrea himself. *The Story of Cupid and Psyche,* performed at Florence, contains the repertory of spectacular effects that later were used wherever masques were given:

In the hollow sky . . . which opened all of a sudden, there was seen to appear another sky contrived with great artifice, from which was seen issuing little by little a white and very naturally counterfeited cloud, upon which, with an effect of singular beauty, a gilded and jewelled car appeared, recognized as that of Venus because it was drawn by two snow-white swans. . . . She had in her company the three Graces . . . And all, as followers and handmaidens of Venus, were seen to sink gradually and with most beautiful grace toward the earth.

Later the stage floor swelled up into seven mounds that turned into seven abysses belching "a thick and continuous stream of smoke" and were finally transformed into a single "verdant mound all adorned with laurels and different flowers."

"The stage must be magnificent," was originally an injunction of the Italian Renaissance. Almost every department of the theatre as it exists today is an innovation of the Renaissance. It established the profession of theatrical director, for Leone de' Somi, as his dialogues prove, supervised not only the lighting of his performances but the costuming, casting, and rehearsals, in which he determined the tempo and inflexion of every scene. Sixteenth century Italy established scenic designing as a separate profession; it established as well the profession of technical director or machinist and supplied the text-books and the instructors for the rest of Europe. Artists and architects, particularly in France, many of them of importance in their day and some on the roster of immortals, continued the Renaissance tradition of designing for the theatre. Bérain, whose countless designs for furniture and metal-work very largely determined the style known as Louis XIV, made both the settings and the costumes for Lully's operas and with such success that he became known as "the father of the land of opera." Servandoni, the architect of Saint-Sulpice, was appointed scenic director of the Paris Opéra, and beginning in 1728 designed more than sixty settings, many of them enthusiastically reviewed by the *Mercure de France,* and invented a new form of theatrical entertainment known as "the silent play," successions of stage pictures accompanied by a musical score but without actors. The only human beings to be seen were painted on Servandoni's back-drops by François Boucher, who succeeded him at the Opéra, at a salary of 2,000 livres a year, and staged a succession of operas and ballets. One of his effects for the opera *Athys* made a sensation: a waterfall illuminated from the rear so that it seemed constantly in motion. Piranesi at the age of eighteen was painting stage settings at Rome at the same time that he was learning the technique of etching and engraving. He competed with a Florentine scene-painter, Galli, for a prize offered by a theatre in Florence for the best back-drop of a prison scene, and lost the competition. One critic ascribes the publication of Piranesi's early engravings, including the first of his famous prisons, to the artist's desire to vindicate himself. In the nineteenth century be-medalled members of the French Institute and the Académie des Beaux Arts, as well as equally important German academicians, turned their hands to stage settings from time to time. Isabey, pupil of David, designed for the Paris Opéra. Daguerre, both painter and architect, better known for his discovery with Niepce of the daguerreotype, painted the settings for one opera, and for the Théâtre de l'Ambigu, a back-drop of moonlit moving clouds which critics at the time found "astonishingly real and natural." Chasseriau designed a set of theatrical costumes. At Lugné-Poë's experimental Théâtre de l'Œuvre, between 1890 and 1900, we find Vuillard designing settings for *Rosmersholm,* Carrière for Maeterlinck's *The Intruder,* Burne-Jones and Rochegrosse for Bataille's first play, *Sleeping Beauty,* and Toulouse-Lautrec and Odilon Redon collaborating as well. When another art theatre was founded by Rouché in 1910 the list of his designers reads like a catalogue of important contributors to the most modern annual exhibition of the day, the Salon d'Automne. The later seasons of the Russian Ballet employed the next generation of innovators, now the gilt-edged stock of leading picture-dealers: Matisse, Dufy, Bracque, Chirico, Derain, and Picasso. The Swedish Ballet enlisted Laprade, Foujita, Bonnard, and Picabia.

The Renaissance tradition of transferring to the stage the technique of the easel-picture has thus survived to the present day. Any number of innovations in scene-painting are nothing more than the experiments already accepted by critics and collectors within picture-frames, magnified to fit the frame of a stage. Delaunay's reeling arches of the Salon d'Automne in 1919 reappear in Moscow as a revolutionary stage setting seven years later. Russian designers have displayed extraordinary ingenuity in costuming actors in cubes and cones so that they resemble a Cubist portrait, and the Habima Theatre developed a form of make-up which gave the faces of its players the appearance of being constructed in triangular planes. For a Berlin production of

Savonarola in 1923 the actors were clothed in brass tubing and sheets of tin. The foliage forms of Rousseau's jungles reappear in Covarrubias' forest where Shaw's Androcles finds his lion. The broken or divided pigment of the Impressionist palette is now regularly applied in scenic studios; stage skies palpitate according to much the same system of applying paint that is used in Monet's wheat-fields. Most of our atmospheric gauzes and transparencies, like the park scene in *Liliom,* are modified Whistler nocturnes. The dramatic chiaroscuro and the deliberate use of shadow to simplify and emphasize form, now so typical of modern stage lighting, were first seen in Meryon's etchings and Daumier's paintings. I can remember how novel my back-drops for *Pierre Patelin* seemed in the Bandbox Theatre of the Washington Square Players, although their flat colour masses were nothing more than an application of the technique for making modern posters in use everywhere in Europe. Another little theatre made its little sensation with a black-and-white ballet that was an enlarged Beardsley drawing.

Scene-painting has remained the painter's holiday. The modern back-drops of art theatres in the 1890's or the 1920's repeated the pictorial conventions accepted as art outside the theatre, just as the back-drops of the 1820's or the 1870's reproduced the formulas of neo-classic or romantic painting then in vogue. Nevertheless not one of the successive innovations that revolutionized modern art, once transported to the theatre, succeeded in creating a tradition that could revolutionize the art of stage setting. Despite the occasional collaboration of a number of important painters, what we call modern stage-craft has been born of a realization that painting itself is a minor part of stage setting and that the kind of aesthetic insight that may be important in creating an easel-picture is often negligible and more often pernicious as an element in a stage picture. Paint, even when applied by the greatest pictorial genius of an epoch, by itself had no magic power in the theatre. The same methods of painting that

263

created the illusion of a world in a painted picture helped to destroy it on a painted stage. With the treasury of modern painting to draw upon for four centuries, at the end of the nineteenth century scene-painting went bankrupt.

3. CAVEAT PICTOR

This result can be understood by analyzing the distinctive contribution of the Renaissance to scenic design and the causes of its decay. Before the Renaissance every stage had striven for the illusion of reality and succeeded in creating it piecemeal. The Renaissance invented a complete illusion: painted perspective. Every theatre had had its feints and tricks, but the illusions achieved were a fragmentary imitation of nature. At best no more than a part of the stage could be transformed. The laws of perspective proved to be the greatest stage trick of all. Any stage could be made to seem larger than its actual dimensions. The eye had been momentarily deceived before by an actual descent from on high, actual smoke and flame, water and blood. Now the human eye could be continuously deceived for hours on end. For the spectator's vision inside the theatre, functioning exactly as it did outside it, stimulated by the same organization of receding lines and planes, accepted the stage as a world with a certainty that had never before been possible. The stage-designer was able to simulate the widest horizons and burst the theatre's walls while remaining within them. A stage fifty or one hundred feet deep, as the case might be, was effectively miles deep, rimmed with the sea if necessary, and reached to heaven. The stage setting could be made a self-contained pictorial unit, presenting the same kind of unity that the eye gave to any aspect of the world it focussed on.

Is it surprising that no one doubted that a magic formula had been discovered? Now that we have formed the habit of seeing in perspective, it is difficult for us to experience the exhilaration afforded

by the sight of perspective painting in a theatre unless we can recover
it by looking at some of the prodigious architectural back-drops designed by the Bibbienas. But having acquired the habit of vision that
sees lines and planes receding to a vanishing point on the horizon,
we may wonder why every trick of perspective drawing was so furiously exploited by the theatre that for more than two hundred years
it seemed the most indispensable element of theatre art. We forget
that laws of perspective were once a sensational scientific discovery
and had all the importance and impressiveness of the newer scientific
laws promulgated today. The art of perspective drawing formed an
essential part of every treatise on architecture. Its principles became
a separate field of research where careers were made and reputations
established. To praise a painting because of its correct perspective
drawing would today be very faint praise indeed. But during the
Renaissance such praise was an accolade. Vasari cites a picture by
Carpaccio "for the perspective view of landscape which diminishes
very finely" and another by Gentile Bellini for a vista of galleys and
fighting men in a sea battle, "seen in perspective and diminished with
the most correct proportions." Piero della Francesca's position as an
authority on perspective, including a "knowledge of Euclid" and "all
the most important properties of rectilinear bodies," all but equalled
his reputation as a painter. A knowledge of perspective was in fact as
important a part of a painter's equipment as a knowledge of anatomy.
Artists had to train themselves to reproduce the illusions of fore-
shortening in space, just as painters recently had to school themselves
to use a new palette in order to give the illusion of sunlight. It was
originally as difficult for the general public to realize that they saw
objects in perspective as it was only yesterday for them to accept the
fact that shadows in the open air are violet in hue and objects not
bounded by a wire-drawn outline.

Scenery painted in perspective might have remained a spacious style of stage setting "entirely real and of noble extent," had it been able to retain its original balance of architectural and painted forms and the scale on which they were first projected. Two developments prevented this: the increasing shallowness of the stage itself and the tendency, in order to make spectacular scene-shifting easier, to paint everything and build nothing more than flat stretches of canvas, which could be given a semblance of form by the scene-painter's brush. The most striking difference between a typical theatre plan of the eighteenth century and one of today is that the proportions of the stage and the auditorium have been reversed. Today the stage space is rarely more than half the depth of the space occupied by the audience. In the older theatres the stage is at least as deep as the auditorium, often half again as deep. In the eighteenth century the stage at the Royal Theatre of Turin was 115 feet in depth, at the Paris Opéra 105 feet, at Versailles 96, and at the Montpellier theatre 70. Their auditoriums varied from 51 feet in depth to 65. In 1760, Jacopo Fabris, who designed settings for the court theatres of Frederick the Great and the court of Denmark, compiled a manuscript treatise on theatrical architecture and scenic design. His ideal theatre has a depth of 236 feet. Of this, on its central axis, the auditorium occupies only 49 feet but the stage 145. In such distances, architectural or landscape perspectives could be scaled to some degree of plausibility, recede gradually, and merge almost imperceptibly with a painted back-drop. But once the average stage became so shallow that an actor moving twelve or fifteen paces up stage had the sky at his elbow, the entire structure on which the illusions of scene-painting were based collapsed and the very semblance of reality that mathematically determined perspective had been able to create became an obvious artifice.

The professional scene-painters were of course the last to realize the fact because the popularity of scene-shifting gave them a position of crucial importance. Palaces and porticos, entablatures and cornices, cliffs and hills, if carpentered were heavy. To move them quickly was all but impossible. But a flat piece of canvas could be painted with every shadow accurately cast on it to trick the eye completely; at least so scene-painters and theatre-managers believed. Solid walls were equally cumbersome even when made of canvas. Why not in the interests of easy scene-shifting break them up into small pieces? This was done, and the side of a building or a room became a series of narrow flats, set along the sides of an elongated equilateral triangle, rows of columns for the inside or outside of every building, tree-trunks for every scene in the open air. To a spectator in the mathe-matical centre of the auditorium, where the scene-designer always imagined himself to be sitting, each capital or beam, jutting out slightly behind the next, did give some illusion of a receding wall But to every one else, whose eyes raked the stage at an angle, every room was entered by twelve alleys and every forest by as many parallel paths. A certain semblance of distance could nevertheless persist on stages that remained from 80 to 100 feet deep. But when they became shallower, the system, instead of maintaining the optical illusion it originally set up on a mathematical basis, became its own caricature. And this painted caricature of Renaissance intentions persisted to the end of the nineteenth century. Painted scenery could be turned out so much more quickly; it was lighter; above all, it was cheaper. Why not paint everything? Theatre-managements lent a ready ear. Except for a few pieces of furniture on which the actors had to be seated from time to time, everything was painted—pots, pans, stair-ways, leaves, flowers, pictures, fire-places, bric-à-brac. In 1808 Wilhelm Schlegel complained:

Our system of decoration . . . has several unavoidable defects . . . the breaking of the lines on the sides of the scene from every point of view except one; the disproportion of the player when he appears in

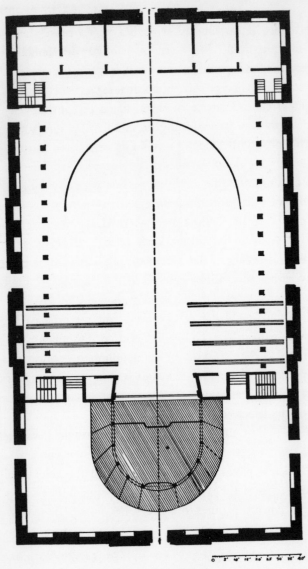

FABRIS' IDEAL STAGE, 1760. AUDITORIUM 49 FEET IN DEPTH,
STAGE 145 FEET IN DEPTH

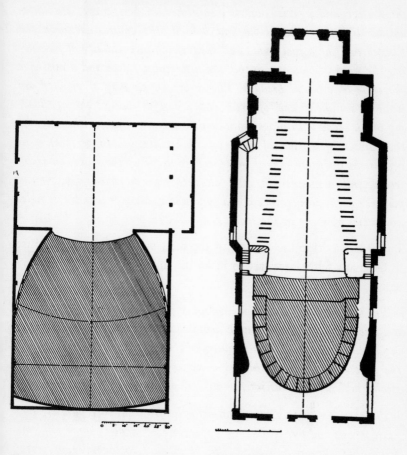

THE GUILD THEATRE, NEW
YORK. AUDITORIUM 72 FEET
IN DEPTH, STAGE 49 FEET IN
DEPTH

PALAIS ROYAL THEATRE, LATE
18TH CENTURY, RE-DRAWN
FROM DIDEROT'S ENCYCLO-
PAEDIA. AUDITORIUM 50 FEET
IN DEPTH, STAGE 110 FEET
IN DEPTH

the background against objects diminished in perspective; the unfavorable lighting from below and behind; the contrast between the painted and the actual lights and shades; the impossibility of narrowing the stage at pleasure, so that the inside of a palace and a hut have the same length and breadth. The errors which may be avoided are want of simplicity and of great and reposeful masses; the overloading of the scene with superfluous and distracting objects, either because the painter is desirous of showing off his strength in perspective or because he does not know how otherwise to fill up the space; an architecture full of mannerism, often altogether unconnected, nay, even at variance with, possibility, colored in a motley manner which resembles no species of stone in the world.

But as late as 1870 the director of the most enterprising court theatre in Germany felt it necessary to make the following notes for his company:

The actor must never lean against painted scenery. If his gesture is a free and easy one, he cannot avoid shaking the setting and destroying the illusion of whatever it portrays. If the actor is preoccupied with the necessity of not touching the scenery, his gestures acquire a restraint which makes his intentions obvious.

Pieces of scenery on which an actor leans or supports himself such as doorposts and tree trunks must therefore be made of some solid material, that is to say be made plastic (a practice, incidentally, becoming more common in our better theatres).

The simultaneous use of painted and plastic objects on stage must be managed so that the difference of material is not disturbingly apparent.

There is no more inartistic effect than that of plucking a rose which is the only artificial flower among a lot of painted ones or, in the workshop of the Violin Maker of Cremona, *seeing on the rear flat among half a dozen painted violins with their painted shadows, the actual violin that has to be used, casting an actual shadow.*

A common failing of directors is that they are not sufficiently careful in relating the actor to architectural forms, such as trees painted in perspective, buildings, etc. . . . The actor should never get too near upstage streets or the back-drop, otherwise his proportions in relation to the scenery must seem preposterous. He should not, for example, as he so often does, station himself in front of a painted house where the door only reaches to his hips and where he can, without extending himself, look into the first story window, or, if he raises his arm, touch the chimney on the roof.

An art of stage setting that invited such juxtapositions had obviously reached the height of the ridiculous. The fact was realized by the director who penned these notes. He was the Duke of Saxe-Meiningen, who between 1873 and 1890, after marrying an actress and training a Jewish stage-manager, so completely revivified the technique of production that he laid the basis of modern stage-craft.

CHAPTER II

ROYAL INNOVATIONS:
GEORGE II, DUKE OF SAXE-MEININGEN

I. MOTION AND MEANING

THE Duke of Saxe-Meiningen's claim to the title of theatrical innovator rests upon two accomplishments: he established the dramatic value of the stage picture as an indispensable factor in interpreting a script and he demonstrated that scenic effects must be fundamentally related to the actor. The human figure in movement was made the pictorial unit. Instead of first making a picture and then letting his actors wander about in it as best they could, taking care not to lean on canvas tree-trunks and to keep free of the painted gables under their elbows, he planned his setting to fit their movements both as individuals and as groups, movements carefully planned before the work of stage setting was begun. His career inaugurated a new epoch in theatrical production and made the subsequent development of modern stage-craft possible because he eventually convinced every important director in Europe, including Antoine and Stanislavsky, that the fundamental problem to be answered by the scene-designer is not, What will my setting look like and how will the actor look in it? but, What will my setting make the actor do? More than this, he made plain that the dramatic action of a performance was an organic whole, a continuous pattern of movement, complex but unified like the symphonic rhythms of orchestral music. At the end of his career the dynamic relation of a mobile actor and an immobile setting in continuous interaction was an accepted axiom. And it is upon this assumption that experiments in production have proceeded since his day.

George II was for his time an accomplished painter and draftsman. He designed every detail of his productions, including the costumes complete to the minutiae of hats and head-dresses and such accessories as swords, canes, pikes, and helmets. The settings used were enlarged from his own pencil-drawings. Their graphic method would be classed today as tight and academic, but they were revolutionary drawings nevertheless, for they are not pictures of settings but almost always of settings filled with human beings, grouped as they were to be at climactic moments. The Duke of Saxe-Meiningen's pictures demonstrate that stage pictures can have no independent existence, that a stage setting is not complete until the actor has taken his place in it. The lines of one cannot be set until the movements of the other are determined.

How fundamental and far-reaching this insight was it is difficult for the layman, even the habitual theatre-goer, to realize unless, by sitting in at rehearsals, he has learned how directly the motions of actors, not only particular gestures, but also their movements back and forth across the stage, affect the meaning of what they say. We think of plays of action as distinguished by the violent movements of murder, combat, flight, despair, love-making—raising of swords, parrying of blows, embraces on a bench or a balcony. But even in plays of violent action such extended gestures occur only occasionally. The action of a play is continuous. The cumulative effect of human movements on a stage is equally decisive when they are casual and consist of nothing more than rising from one chair, sitting down on another, moving to a door, looking out of a window, moving from left to right and back again. For the actor must not only speak and gesticulate; he must move from one spot to another. And it is precisely this succession of movements that makes a performance out of the process of speaking the words of a script. Directing a play involves not only directing vocal inflexions and the individual gestures that centre in the actor's body; it involves also directing motion, moving bodies from one position to the next. Leave actors rooted in a single spot and the most dramatic scene ever penned becomes not drama but a recitation.

Imagine that you are about to rehearse a comedy, the first act of *Arms and the Man*. Forget Shaw's stage-directions for the moment and take the act after Bluntschli has broken into Raina's bedroom and she has decided not to rouse the house. Do not consider the scene beyond the moment that she leaves to call her mother. Here are two people quietly talking to each other. Now select your ideal players: Bernhardt in her youth and Coquelin cadet, Katharine Cornell and Roland Young, Alfred Lunt and Lynn Fontanne. Keep them seated. They may recite the lines flawlessly, achieve every comic innuendo, laugh and weep to perfection. But keep them seated. The effect will be not of an incident lived but of a reading, a perfect piece of elocution with gestures attached. Keep them standing but never allow them to move from the same spot, and the effect will be the same.

You meet what seems to be a simple problem by telling your two players to move about as they have a mind to. Immediately you discover how subtle the problem is. For they cannot move about aimlessly unless you wish to convey a general impression of restlessness and nothing more. But if they move, where are they to move to? You find yourself obliged to set the essential parts of your scene: a window leading from a balcony (through which the artillery officer can break in), the young lady's bed, a door leading to the rest of the house, a table or tables to hold two essential properties, a candle and a photograph of the young lady's fiancé. Now begin to move your actors, and it will not be long before you discover that the positions of these two openings and the few pieces of furniture determine not only how your actors move but also the implications of everything they say, and after a while, the entire mood of the scene.

Analyze the problem more closely and consider at the outset only the relative positions of the balcony window, the door, and the bed. And assume that you get no more help from Shaw than Shakespeare or Molière gives a director. Raina blows out the candle and goes to bed. Where will the candle be? Next to the bed seems the obvious place. But that cannot be set until the director has made up his mind what Raina does when she discovers a man silhouetted against her window and lights the candle again. If the candle is within easy reach the lady will be discovered in bed by the soldier. If the rest of the act were purely melodramatic this might be an excellent arrangement, for the soldier could then threaten the lady at the pistol's point. It might do equally well if the act were entirely romance of the blood-and-thunder variety, and Bluntschli a long-lost lover, banned by the family and determined either to force himself into Raina's bed or to drag her off with him down the balcony. But the act is nothing of the sort. Its words are a comedy of *rapprochement* between a terrified young woman and a terrified young soldier, who find they have both been needlessly afraid of each other and finally take each other for granted. Even an amateur director would discover that this cannot be conveyed if the two continue to talk eye to eye on the bed or immediately plump themselves down on a near-by settee. Hence it becomes important to separate the lady and the soldier as soon as possible. The position of the table with the candle on it is therefore decisive. If it is not next to the bed but half-way across the room, Raina can leap out of bed to light it and she and Bluntschli can face each other, he on the opposite side of the stage as he locks the door to the room. But until a director is certain of these positions of his actors he cannot set the position of a bed or a night-table.

Until he is equally certain of their positions in what follows he cannot fix the relative distance of his window and one door, or set the remaining pieces of furniture. The lady and the soldier come to an understanding when she realizes that he is not a military brute but a gentleman and he perceives that she is romantic enough to be chivalrous, after which it is plausible that they sit down and talk the situation over. But that can be accomplished in several ways, each of which will determine or be determined by the position of two chairs or a settee. A settee may be near enough to Raina for her to reach it first while Bluntschli is still at the door uncertain of what he is in for. In that case Raina will take command of the situation and the comedy of their uncertainty will be played with the soldier tottering on his feet with fatigue but all the while proving that he has the instincts of a gentleman by not sitting down until he is asked to, eyeing the empty bed longingly but not going near it. Or the settee may be near enough to Bluntschli for him to drop into it with a sigh of relief the moment he sees he has only a frightened girl to deal with. This leaves the man in command of the situation. He must then convince her that he is a gentleman although he does not behave like one, and the lady capitulates when she finds him a harmless chocolate-cream soldier. If it strikes the director that sitting down beside a grimy stranger on a settee really makes it plain that Raina has been won over, there will be no other furniture in the room. If this seems unimportant there may be several other chairs and they may talk to each other across the room, both gradually edging nearer each other as their mutual panic subsides. On the other hand it is not inconceivable that the director might have Bluntschli throw himself on the bed—his fatigue makes this plausible enough—and play the entire scene with deliberate disingenuousness, knowing that the lady, feeling herself more compromised every minute, must come to terms with him if she is not willing to have him shot. The bed will then have to be brought more or less prominently down stage, whereas before it could be left up stage, as it is needed only for a moment at the beginning and the end of the act. In each case the humour of the scene has a different overtone and different implications. I have by no means exhausted the possibilities of the simplest kind of setting or the dramatic consequences of placing a door, a window, a bed, a table, and a settee. But until a director visualizes them and places them so that he is sure of their effect on the movements of his actors, no amount of characteristic detail of Bulgarian architecture is of any importance whatsoever.

This visualizing of motion, and the planning of a setting that will induce it, may be done for a director by the author, it may be inadequately done, it may have to be added to, or it may have to be invented from start to finish. But in no case can the job be avoided. The kind of imagination involved in anticipating the connection between the physical properties of a stage setting and the kind of acting that is to take place within it, and the inventiveness necessary to relate the two, are an essential part of every director's equipment. For the implications of certain lines, the ability of others to provoke a laugh, the very meaning of certain words, will depend on what the actors do at the moment of speaking them. Their meaning will depend on the way two people stalk each other about a room, converse side by side, the precise moment when they stop doing one and begin doing the other, and also whether the transition is abrupt or direct. For the effect of a single line may be changed by the kind of physical motion that accompanies it.

Take the moment when Raina shows Bluntschli the portrait of the Bulgarian major whom he has been ridiculing: "That is the photograph of the gentleman—the patriot and hero—to whom I am betrothed." Shall the lady rise, get the photograph from across the room, and present it with a great flounce and flourish? The effect of this is to underline her romantic heroics and the next instant to spoil her attitude completely when Bluntschli stifles a laugh. This is what Shaw calls for and it undoubtedly heightens the effect of Bluntschli's amusement more than if Raina, without getting up, did nothing more than reach for the picture on a near-by tabouret. But if at this point in the scene Bluntschli were still standing and Raina seated, her gesture of confidently playing her trump-card as she showed the photograph of her fiancé might be the very thing to make Bluntschli capitulate on the lines:

> *I'm really very sorry. Was it fair to lead me on?*

However, the way he crosses to her as he says these words can colour their implications. The printed speech with its stage-directions reads:

(Looking at it.) *I'm really very sorry.* (Looking at her.) *Was it fair to lead me on?*

But even these directions do not fix the way this single moment is to be acted. Its effect has still to be determined by the precise timing of the cross. It makes a decided difference whether Bluntschli says, "I'm really very sorry," and then crosses to Raina, or whether he goes over to her before saying anything. Shaw doesn't direct him to speak "with sincere remorse" until a few seconds later. But if he does so now, if immediately upon seeing the photograph of the major he is genuinely apologetic and crosses to Raina on that impulse, what registers is the fact that he sympathizes with her predicament. What becomes important is his look at the photograph, not his look at her. That can be quick and casual. But if his apology is the usual polite and colourless formula and he goes to her only after having seen the look in her eyes, what registers is the fact that it is the genuineness of her feelings that moves him, not the mere fact that she is engaged. His look at the photograph is therefore casual, not the look into her eyes. And if that is prolonged only a second more than seems necessary, it conveys to the audience that Bluntschli, without knowing it, is beginning to fall in love. His laughter a few minutes later is, in spite of himself, kindly, because an undercurrent of sympathy has been established. If this is not established his amusement may sound malicious and leave him a cynical professional soldier laughing at a romantic young girl, condescending to her to the end of the act. On the other hand a director may find at a much earlier moment in the act an opportunity for the two to be naturally drawn together. They may already be seated side by side by the time the photograph is shown and the scene can then be played against the tableau of a tête-à-tête. Precisely because their most violent differences of opinion do not separate them, their unconscious attraction for each other will be emphasized. It then becomes important to avoid a cross on the words "I'm really very sorry," whereas with another way of playing the scene it was important to plan it to the second.

Such niceties involved in co-ordinating motion and meaning in the theatre are called stage business. The nuances I have been describing are not confined to realistic comedy or realistic playwrighting in general. They are as necessary for a production of *Hamlet,* as decisive on a larger and more complicated scale, in building the mood and qualifying the emotions expressed by any particular scene. The total effect of a production depends very largely on the cumulative force of the business that a director is able to invent. A play's action often consists less of its overt acts than of the movements (not specifically called for by the text) that accompany speeches in a way that enlarges or underlines their import. The subtleties of stage business are what prevents a play's being ready for performance the moment that the actors know their lines. Most of the time consumed in rehearsal goes to relating a continuous pattern of movement that must accompany words if they are to be acted and not simply spoken. Moments of violent action rarely offer any problems. The business of hiding Bluntschli behind the window-curtain, when a Bulgarian officer enters to search the house for fugitives, can be easily set in ten minutes, like the business of Hamlet stabbing Polonius behind the arras. But movements that will be significant when Hamlet shows a miniature of his father to the queen have to be searched for, precisely like those needed when Raina shows Bluntschli a photograph. When Hamlet sees Ophelia gone mad there is nothing in the text to indicate which lines are spoken "with genuine remorse" and between which lines he looks at her. The climax of the players' scene depends on where Hamlet crouches spying for the first sign of terror in the king's face, how he leaps forth in accusation, where and how he moves until that moment, and every movement of the queen, the court, the players, throughout the scene until they break up in confusion.

The term "production" as opposed to "performance" has come to be used in an honorific sense, because a production is taken to include the process of integrating the movements of actors, as individuals and as groups, and building them into stage pictures that have the power of interpreting a script. If a director mounting *Hamlet* or *Macbeth, Peer Gynt* or *Danton's Death,* were to rely wholly on the readings of his company and did not sustain them with a characteristic pattern of movement that bound one scene to another, he would be asked why he had attempted to produce the play. A director who did nothing more than have his actors execute the printed stage-directions of a script, even though these were the legacy of the greatest of dramatists, would seem almost as anomalous as a Stokowski or a Toscanini interpreting the Ninth Symphony of Beethoven and relying on his strings or wood-winds to give accent and symphonic colour by following the printed tempi of the score.

The plasticity of a theatrical performance, now taken for granted, was before the Duke of Saxe-Meiningen's productions almost unknown. Between 1870 and 1890 acting in almost every leading theatre consisted very largely of reading lines; the action that accompanied them was as much a matter of traditional routine as the acting of operatic rôles still is today. The prevailing ideas of technique were very largely inherited from operatic performances; the more serious a play, the more likely it was to be declaimed as a series of arias without music. An actor joining a troupe to play in *Hamlet* or *Macbeth* needed almost as little rehearsal as a tenor nowadays, who might, if necessary, leave one performance of *Tosca* in Berlin and appear in another at Milan an hour after his train arrived. In London during the 1840's, Madame Vestris was considered a crank because she insisted upon careful rehearsals and superintended them herself, "a custom so unusual . . . that when Macready as a young actor had tried . . . to do it for himself, he was almost thrown out of the company." How little the kind of ensemble that we now expect and demand was dreamed of even by the Prince of Players is indicated in the memoirs of Katherine Goodale, then Kitty Molony, a juvenile in Edwin Booth's touring company in 1886: "That first morning we rehearsed *Richelieu* and *Hamlet*. The second day we did *Hamlet, Richelieu,* and *Macbeth,* and were out of the theatre by three o'clock. Many of the company had played together with Mr. Booth and some . . . were of Booth Theatre casts. These veterans did not wait for instructions, but tackled their scenes with the sure touch of knowledge. . . . Three tragedies in a four-hour rehearsal was nothing to them." It is therefore not surprising to learn that "ten days proved enough to get the company letter-perfect in *Richelieu, Hamlet, Macbeth,* and *Othello.* The repertoire consisted of these four tragedies, and in addition, *Richard III . . . , Katherine and Petruchio, Merchant of Venice, The Fool's Revenge, Brutus, Don Caesar de Bazan, King Lear,* and *A New Way to Pay Old Debts.*" Presumably the lot was rehearsed in twelve hours. Lines and cues were rehearsed and seemingly very little else. "As an actor, Mr. Booth came down to cues. When the scene demanded that the supporting actors have the full speech, Mr. Doud [the stage manager] read it." It was not thought necessary that any actor practise in advance of a public performance his or her reactions to Booth's performance. The company started out letter-perfect in three tragedies and added the remaining seven on the road. But Booth did not trouble to appear at these rehearsals. "I do not remember another rehearsal the entire season that he attended." I suspect that the effect of these performances on a present-day spectator, apart from Booth's acting, would be very like the impression made by the members of the House of Commons on a character in one of Masefield's novels, who described them as buns throwing their currants at one another.

A similar theatrical régime existed in France. It was after seeing the Meiningen players in Brussels in 1888 that Antoine's eyes were opened and he was able to formulate the technical details of his programme of theatrical reform in his open letters to Sarcey. He gives a ludicrous picture of performances at the Comédie Française and elsewhere: a bourgeois interior as large as a room in a palace, one leading lady who paces about like a tragedy-queen while she is embroidering, two actresses who declaim obliquely into the audience during an entire performance and never once during the course of their conversations look each other in the eye, stage business arranged without reference to the text in order to give leading actors the most conspicuous entrance or exit. He speaks of the hypnotic power of the footlights, and inveighs against the practice that allows actors to walk out of any scene, come down to the prompter's box, and address the audience, leaving the rest of the company planted up stage behind them. He tells one story of a theatre that had gas footlights, with the result that the actors' trousers were always singed, and another of an actor at the Palais Royal who, having to hang up his hat, paraded across the footlights and with the greatest seriousness went through the pantomime of looking for a peg in the invisible fourth wall. He admits his own difficulties in trying to get a few of his own company to walk without falling into a typical theatrical strut and confesses that he abandoned rehearsals of one play because he was unable to make two actors cross the stage naturally or sit down at a table without striking an attitude and staring into the audience. It was almost impossible, Antoine admits, to get an actor to remain seated if he had to deliver a speech of any length. After the first few lines he invariably asked, "This is where I get up, isn't it?" "The stage is a tribune and not an enclosed space where an event occurs." It is the ensemble playing of the Meiningen troupe that Antoine holds up as an example for the French theatre to follow—its actors who play to each other, its supernumeraries who are so absorbed in the scene taking place that they turn their backs to the audience if necessary. The mere fact that an actor occasionally turned his back to the audience was in 1888 a revolutionary novelty. Antoine describes one detail of the last act of *William Tell*. Tell, waiting for Gessler, finds his path blocked by a beggar and his two children, who play a long scene of supplication at his feet with their backs to the audience. "Could you have seen it you would have been as enthusiastic as I was . . . and admitted that a back turned to the audience at the right moment can convince spectators that there is something more important in the theatre than paying attention to them." When an actor today turns up stage to play a scene we think of it as part of a new technique of a recent school of naturalistic acting, whereas the innovation is only one of the details of the Meiningen technique of ensemble playing, originally an incidental part of the production of a heroic play by a romantic poet.

In contrast to Antoine's picture of the French theatre in 1888, compare Stanislavsky's description of a single scene in another Meiningen production of Schiller, which he saw when the duke's company visited Moscow in 1885:

I can never forget a scene from "The Maid of Orleans." A skinny, piteous, forlorn king sits on a tremendous throne; his thin legs hang in the air and do not reach the floor. Around the throne is the confused court, which tries with all its strength to uphold the semblance of kingly ritual. . . . Into this picture of the destruction of a king enter the English ambassadors, tall, stately, courageous, and impudent. . . . When the unhappy king gives his demeaning order, which insults his own dignity, the courtier who receives the order tries to bow before he leaves the king's presence. But hardly having begun the bow, he stops in indecision, straightens up, and stands with lowered eyes. Then the tears burst from them and he runs in order not to lose control of himself before the entire court.

With him wept the spectators, and I wept also, for the ingenuity of the stage director created a tremendous mood by itself and went down to the soul of the play.

2. PLAN OF ACTION

The theatrical value of stage business not mentioned in a script, the dramatic importance of the total stage picture as established by the Duke of Saxe-Meiningen, was built up not only by actors but by a stage setting directly related to them. His work as director-designer is an irrefutable demonstration of the fact that scenic design is fundamentally related to architecture, not because it reproduces architectural forms, but because it is based on architectural plan and, like the plan of a building, directs whatever human activity it shelters. As sightseers we may identify architecture with façades but as householders we hold the architect to account if he has planned the layout of rooms that do not help us through our daily routine. Any housewife knows that the placing of a sink, a kitchen cabinet, a stove, a pantry, and a broom-closet, if correctly spaced, directly affects the ease with which she can cook for the family; if incorrectly placed, they can make it difficult to keep a servant. A real-estate agent would have difficulty renting an apartment where bedrooms opened directly into the dining-room, which had to be crossed in order to get to the bath. The most perfect Georgian detail in window-frames and panelling would not reconcile a single tenant to the fact that two sets of activities had not been segregated, those of sleeping and getting dressed, those of eating and entertaining. The first and the most important question that an architect, like a scene-designer, puts to himself is, "What will the people who inhabit my building do?" He often spends far more time developing the plan of his building, invisible underfoot, but nevertheless directing every future step to be taken in it, than he does in elaborating the ornament of his façade, obvious to every passer-by. In larger structures, such as banks, hotels, office buildings, and railway terminals, the arrangement of the main units of a ground-plan is of crucial importance. It organizes the circulation of crowds, prevents them from doubling on their tracks, leads them without detours to the objects that bring them into the building, sets up a current of activity and controls it almost as directly as a traffic-light does a stream of automobiles. A single mistake in the relation of entrances and exits to a main lobby or a bank of elevators can create a traffic-jam as quickly as too narrow a street placed between main thoroughfares. It is the plan of a building, not its façade, that helps people to achieve their purposes or impedes them.

The value of a building depends upon the architect's ability to plan intelligently, and this ability to plan depends in turn upon his capacity to anticipate the typical movements made in carrying out the purpose that brings the average person to an art museum, an office building, or a railway terminal. The museum visitor must be guided without a guide. The commuter, without bucking streams of people going in opposite directions, must be led on the shortest axis to the train platform, picking up his evening paper, an extra ticket, or a new timetable on the way. The mediocrity of its neo-classic ornament does not prevent the Grand Central Terminal in New York from being so excellently planned that the commonest rendezvous is the information desk, where any two people can find each other easily even at the peak of a rush hour.

The vertical planes of architecture that carry its ornament are rooted in its horizontal ground-plans. The historic styles of such monuments as cathedrals, temples, and mosques grow out of a typical arrangement of space made to direct the path of a votary towards a priest or a god, hidden or revealed, a characteristic pattern of worship made up of a certain sequence of steps, genuflections, ablutions. The design of the ground-plan organizes this sequence about a point of central interest. The design of the enclosing walls attempts to symbolize or enhance the emotion that is supposed to accompany the typical progressions of each form of devotion. The design of a stage setting is built up by a strictly analogous process. Its plan, unseen by the audience, controls the pattern of movement made by a group of players; its façade, which immediately strikes the audience's eye by its choice of shapes and colours, expresses the prevailing emotions of the players as they move through this pattern. This is what is meant by the current dictum, "A setting should express the mood of the play," a thoroughly superficial statement unless one realizes that the basis of stage setting is architectonic. Whatever mood is evoked by its pictorial effect is created by a fundamental relation of façade and plan. A stage setting can be best defined as a plan of action.

The great contribution of the Duke of Saxe-Meiningen to the development of stage-craft was his insistence on the continuous and direct relation between the design of a setting and the actor's movements within it. His power of imagination lay in his ability to conceive this interaction to its last detail and develop both elements of it simultaneously. If his conceptions seem realistic to us today, it is only because we have foolishly restricted the field of imagination in the theatre to the creation of stage pictures that have the tenuous and slightly ambiguous quality of dreams. The effect of this school of stage-craft, at present so fashionable, is often to make the event enacted on the stage more remote. The effect of the Duke of Saxe-Meiningen's methods was to achieve an intensified reality and give remote events the quality of actuality, of being lived for the first time, so that a Frenchman, Antoine, was intensely moved by the assassination of a Swiss tyrant, and a Russian, Stanislavsky, reduced to tears by the degradation of an inconsequential French king. In an era whose culture was far less affected by its industrialism than by the increasing eclecticism and internationalism of its taste, Hamlet's conundrum was answered. The performance of a play was given a new kind of unity; it became an organic and dynamic whole. No innovator is wholly original. Possibly many of the specific innovations of the Meiningen theatre had already been attempted. Like spearmen's shields they had been in battle before. But at Meiningen they were assembled into a phalanx that gathered the momentum to achieve an epoch-making victory which determined the subsequent direction that the art of the theatre was to take.

The details of the Duke of Saxe-Meiningen's settings were therefore significant, even when literal, because so directly related to dramatic action. Five studies were made for the opening scene of *The Maid of Orleans,* involving the relative positions of a chapel and an ancient tree. In the same play an abandoned wagon, piled high with military paraphernalia, was dragged on stage, not only for its value as an accent in a pictorial composition, but also to hide the approach of the French troops whose surprise attack is the climax of the scene. In the scene in *Macbeth* in which Macduff's children are butchered, the room where they were seen playing with their mother was entered by a long stairway from a balcony. The assassins were discerned there in half-shadow by the audience and the horror of the moment was immeasurably heightened by their slow, silent descent, waiting for the moment to strike. This stairway is the prototype of many that have been used since, including the staircase in Copeau's masterful production of *The Brothers Karamazov,* where Smerdiakov darted up and down like a malignant spider. Much of *The Merchant of Venice* was played on a bridge over one of the Ghetto canals. On it the masqueraders danced in a frenzy of excitement as Jessica eloped, hidden in a gondola below it. This same scenic scheme formed the basis of Reinhardt's revival of the play some thirty years later. The doge's courtroom was enclosed by a loggia balcony, not only for the decorative effect of its characteristic architecture, but also to hold a crowd of on-lookers who watched the trial and added to its excitement by reacting to Gratiano's jibes and Portia's casuistry. Silence was dramatized as well as sound: the scene of conspiracy in Brutus's garden was played almost entirely in whispers. Light and colour were used to achieve dramatic climaxes: Brutus's tent was deep vermilion, lighted only by a candle, filled with deep shadows. The actor playing Caesar's ghost, clad in a vermilion toga, was lost in them until one of the then new electric spot-lights, shot through the tent's flap, struck his face. His vermilion robes still merging with the colour of the tent gave him the appearance of hanging in the air, and the ghost disappeared as uncannily into the murky shadows when the spot-light was turned off. The duke seized every opportunity to play with varied intensities of light; in one scene he lighted a loggia with the gas-light still in general use, then had a tapestry drawn and showed a garden brilliantly lighted with electric lamps, thus achieving an effect of sunlight. For the scene in *Mary Stuart* where Elizabeth signs Mary's death-warrant, the table was lighted by four candles and the rest of the stage lost in shadow. But directly back of the table, dimly caught by reflected candlelight, was a copy of Holbein's portrait of Henry VIII, who seemed to preside smiling over the occasion. Antoine cites one lighting effect that he saw in Brussels as an example of "epic naïveté": a shaft of sunlight, coming through a high window, strikes an old man at the very moment that he dies. But such a deliberate timing of stage lighting to accent the pathos of a scene, like all of the duke's lighting effects that I have described, are now the commonplaces of staging. The interpretative value of varying intensities of light and the contrast of light and shadow are assumed by every director and designer. But they were almost apocalyptic revelations of the possibilities of stage-craft at a time when every other stage was filled with a bland radiance and actors singed their trousers at the footlights in order to be seen.

Another interesting aspect of the Meiningen productions was the duke's consistent effort to add to the plastic possibilities of stage setting by breaking the monotonous surface of the stage floor into different levels. In the *Hermannsschlacht* where a delegation of Roman generals comes to parley with a German chieftain in his native forest, the primeval world which they are invading was emphasized by the unevenness of the stage itself, the hummocks and fallen logs that had to be clambered over in order to reach the chieftain's hut. In *Fiesko* the movement of a court fête was carried up and down a double stairway in a palace courtyard. Antoine complained that the Alpine paths in *William Tell* resounded like wood and thought that the use of platforms was overdone. We should probably find that they were not used often enough. For an entire range of movement, valuable dramatically, is lost when actors are kept shuttling back and forth on an unbroken stage floor. The vertical relationships of higher and lower have the capacity to symbolize purely emotional relationships of one person to another and even of a person to an idea. The yearning of lovers is heightened by the use of the traditional balcony. A king or lawgiver pronounces his judgments more appropriately from on high and his figurative fall is symbolized when he falls from an actual throne or a rostrum. The pull of gravity suggested by the act of climbing a height emphasizes the pull of tradition, the burden of matter opposed to the élan of spirit. These physical ups and downs are important aids to interpretation in the theatre because outside of it we respond to them with mimetic responses often so subtle that we are only half aware of them, as when we look up to a President on a balcony or a preacher in a pulpit, whom we are supposed to look up to as a political or a moral superior. The sight of an aeroplane rising from a field gives us a sense of elation, of release from our bondage to earth. We soar with a bird in flight. We rise with the sky-rocket, involuntarily say, Ah! as it bursts, and then sigh as though we were fluttering down with its tinsel stars. Dramatic performances have always exploited similar devices. The Greek gods appeared above the palace roof. In the mystery at Mons, Pilate does not go to the upper of his two thrones until the climactic moment when he condemns Christ. But the Duke of Saxe-Meiningen's originality lay in his ability to show how movement up and down could be used to dramatize scenes where the possibility of utilizing it had not been suspected, how much more often it could be effectively used than on the few occasions where a playwright called for it. On this intuition alone the dogmas of various modern schools of production have been founded, so that an entire play is now often performed up and down staircases, terraces, plinths, and trestles.

3. CROWDS

One aspect of the organization of a performance completely realized by the Meiningen productions, which made a sensation wherever the troupe appeared, was the handling of stage crowds. The super has always been the bane of every director, the butt of every critic. He usually looks exactly like his other title, an extra, thrown in at the last moment in the ragtag and bobtail remnants of the wardrobe, and repeats a few set evolutions like a green recruit on his first parade, terrorizing the actors around him with the fear that he may at any moment set the house snickering. He was made an important part of productions at Meiningen by the characteristic thoroughness with which the duke integrated every detail of a performance into an ensemble. He was rehearsed as regularly as any actor, costumed as carefully, trained to carry armour or to handle weapons. The regimental air of a stage mob was destroyed at its source by breaking up every large crowd into smaller groups. A definite rôle was assigned to each group and words improvised for them, so that their combined murmuring and muttering had the impact of a crowd of people actually expressing its convictions and not imitating a uniform sound. Each group was led by whatever actors were not cast for the leading parts on a particular evening; they were expected to alternate in the mobs of the same scenes where they had often played important rôles. Mob duty was required of every member of the company; there were no exceptions. When Von Bülow's wife refused, trading on the influence her husband could exert as the royal Kappelmeister, she found herself obliged to resign.

General symmetry of arrangement was avoided, stage centre made a forbidden refuge, even parallel crossings banned. The attack on symmetry was carried to such details as uniformity of posture. Every extra was trained to watch his neighbour and to avoid falling into the same position, to concentrate on the scene being played and never under any circumstances to stare at the audience. The duke never lost an opportunity of pointing out that soldiers on the march were not on parade, had individual gaits, and did not carry their spears, muskets, or halberds at the same level. The characteristic stance of every period was carefully studied. One of the duke's favourite theories was his belief that the habit of standing with heels together was spread by the vogue of the minuet in the eighteenth century. Supers in plays of an earlier period were taught to stand with their legs planted apart, as the sixteenth century engravings of *Landsknechte* showed them. But the power of suggestion was not neglected. No stage mob, as the duke was fond of asserting, could possibly be a mob in point of actual numbers. If the audience was to get the impression of size it must be unable to see the edges of the crowds, which should always disappear into the wings or be massed behind an opening. If this were not practical the whole set would have to be contracted to give the same effect. These methods are now, like others of the Meiningen company, the truisms of stage practice. But the duke was the first to make them an acknowledged part of theatrical routine.

In the opening scene of the *Hermannsschlacht,* the invading Roman legionaries enter a primitive German village. At royal theatres elsewhere it was the rule to send twenty or thirty supers, bright as tin Caesars, marching with the precision of Prussians on parade against a landscape back-drop. At Meiningen the invaders debouched through a narrow lane that barely allowed them to pass four abreast. Their bronze armour was dulled to a brown-black as if by months of campaigning. They entered down stage and disappeared up stage into the alley between the house-fronts. What the audience saw most of the time was not a succession of faces but the sombre repetition of the backs of bucklers and helmets; the total effect was that of an almost impersonal, a relentless, military machine. The power of an invader was dramatized as the play began.

In the last act of Schiller's *Fiesko* a bastion guarding the harbour of Genoa is captured in a surprise attack. The obvious way of staging this scene is to show the harbour in moonlight and then bring on the usual soldiery from the wings to clash swords on an open stage for two minutes in fake fury. For the Meiningen production the stage was contracted to a shallow courtyard under the bastion wall, closed by an enormous iron-studded gateway. The stage was dim, faintly flecked with moonlight. The bottom of a tower was a guard-house; a few soldiers sprawled on its steps. Others dozed on a near-by fountain. Two narrow alleys led off stage. The night-watch passes. Silence of night. Peace. Suddenly from the other side of the gate the sound of distant alarm-bells growing louder mingles with the ground-swell of an approaching mob. The guards pile out of the tower and grab their weapons as the attack on the portal begins. Thunder of weapons on wood. The iron ribs of the door hold up. The wood splinters. One sees the first besiegers, the moonlight at their back glittering on their pikes thrust through the breach. Hand-to-hand fighting through this narrow opening. A petard explodes. The gateway is sprung, the door tumbles. The attackers wedge the defending garrison into the narrow alleyways, where the mêlée continues, and finally drive them off stage, where the noise of sword-play dies away. The harbour glitters in full moonlight through the ruined gateway, and provides the background for the concluding moments of the act.

In such staging imagination reveals itself—in the contrast of silence and the first distant sounds of danger, the suspense as these rise to a crescendo, the heightened suspense as the violence of the attack is heard but not seen, the clash of iron, the ripping of splintered wood, the concentration of hand-to-hand fighting over key positions, the sudden contrasts of moonlight and shadow, first on the points of swords and halberds as they pierce the gate and then on the harbour for which the battle has been fought. By such means the audience is aroused to accept the reality of a battle and instead of watching a few ragged foils that would disgrace the name of Agincourt, is carried into the conflict, is able to share in its excitement, to be engaged in it with the characters of the play whose fortunes are involved in the same struggle.

Perhaps the most celebrated of the Meiningen mob scenes was the coronation procession of the dauphin in Schiller's *Maid of Orleans*. The crowd packed a shallow square under the portals of Rheims Cathedral. The stage was too small to hold them as they waited for the first sight of the cortège; they disappeared off stage, strained against soldiers trying to keep a lane free, climbed on each other's backs, stood on tiptoe, hopped up and down, packed every spare ledge on a fountain, jammed the stairways of near-by houses, leaned over window-sills on each other's shoulders. The mounting excitement was carefully timed as the royal procession crossed the stage into the cathedral and increasing bursts of cheers greeted each notable, such as Dunois, when he was recognized. The crescendo of jubilation swelled at the sight of the dauphin under his canopy. All the while trumpets repeated a single theme adopted from one of Brahms's chorals, with clarion insistence that mounted higher and higher until at the appearance of Joan it reached a climax of frenzy that usually incited an echoing ovation from the audience.

4. SOURCES

The mathematical axiom that the whole is the sum of all its parts was first applied at Meiningen with a full realization of how many details are involved in a theatrical performance and combine to produce a final unity of effect. It was supplemented by the duke's unerring sense that the chain binding one scene to another, or even one moment of a scene to the next, was no stronger than its smallest link. No detail was too small to be planned, studied, and rehearsed. In applying this principle to stage costumes the duke established another revolutionary precedent. Costuming actors was almost as haphazard and as slipshod as the rehearsing of extras, and the effects achieved were either dowdy or gaudy. Any consistent attempt to relate the style of costumes to the general style of a production was almost unheard of and any attempt to bring them within a hundred years of the period portrayed by a play almost always unsuccessful. In 1859, when crinolines were the height of fashion, one German director posted explicit orders that they could not under any circumstances be worn under antique costumes. But pictures of leading German actresses of the period survive showing Iphigenia's and Medea's classic overgarments obviously held out with crinoline petticoats. A few stock styles and a few materials, known as theatrical goods, were stretched to include the whole range of repertory. Stanislavsky gives a picture of the state of theatrical costuming that prevailed in Moscow at the time that the Meiningen company played there. "There were only three styles in vogue at the *costumiers'* shops: 'Faust,' 'Les Hugue-nots,' and 'Molière.' . . . Have you some sort of a Spanish costume, like 'Faust' or 'Les Huguenots'? was the question usually asked of the *costumiers.* 'We have Valentines, Mephistos, and St. Bries of all colors,' was the usual answer." Like every other department of theatrical production, costuming followed operatic tradition. No leading actor would think of wearing a ruff or a high collar. The neck must be free or one's voice was strangled. Leading juveniles played their love scenes in one adaptation or another of the Byronic shirt. And every actor wore pretty much what he or she pleased. At best the general effect achieved was that of the usual costume-ball.

At Meiningen costumes were designed for a play with the same care as its settings, and the drawings made for both at the same time. For the first time audiences in the theatre became aware of the differences in line and silhouette that distinguished the modes of the Renaissance in Spain, France, and Italy. Verrocchio, Dürer, Holbein, Raphael, Velasquez, or a Roman statue supplied the models, instead of a theatrical tailor. The full flare and scale of historic modes were recovered, whether in a coronation robe, a farthingale, or a toga. The draping of a toga occasionally required as much as thirty yards of material. One guest player who came to Meiningen to play Brutus had to have several yards of his costume cut out before he was able to rehearse without tripping over his own feet. The regular company had no such difficulties, for the wearing of costumes was part of the business of rehearsing until an actor grew accustomed to the typical stance and the typical gestures that each historic period of costume induces. Supplementary sketches were made for the details of wigs, of shoes, for the placing of jewels or medallions. Each costume was delivered to a dressing-room with a slip of written instructions as to how it was to be worn. No actor was privileged to change a fold or a button without the duke's approval. When typical brocades and velvets could not be found, they were especially woven. The characteristic differences of arms and armour of different periods were as carefully distinguished. Theatrical armour that could be purchased being almost as grotesque as the usual theatrical costumes of the day, an armourer was installed as part of the Meiningen workshop.

We are apt to deplore such concern with authenticity as the beginning of a trend toward archaeological exactitude, which is supposed to have hampered the growth of improvisation and hindered the development of a "theatre theatrical." The costumes used by David Belasco and Beerbohm Tree are usually cited as instances of the deplorable consequences of the Duke of Saxe-Meiningen's researches. As a matter of fact their costuming was invariably full of grotesque and glaring inaccuracies, for which they were never called to account because knowledge of costume is still rudimentary. I found by chance in an obscure classical dictionary the description of a Roman toga which when cut out of one piece could be easily worn and fell naturally into classic folds. It was far more beautiful because inevitable and expressive of the body underneath it than any drapings that I might have pinned on. The style of a historic costume, like that of a modern gown by Poiret or Chanel, depends on the way it is cut and sewn together. A good cutter, still the mainstay of any London tailor, has always been the mainstay of costume design. The basis of any costume is always the cutter's pattern that fits it to the human body when worn. A designer begins to learn the elements of the art of clothing the human body by studying sources, until he understands how the weight and texture of the material used combine with the pattern on which it is cut to give a garment its particular character. It is the cut of a Persian robe, an Egyptian kaftan, or an East Indian skirt that lends it expressive grace when it moves with a human being.

Historic styles, like modern styles, are often silly and arbitrary but they are as often the product of dressmakers' ingenuity, of invention and experiment, tested and corrected in use by generations of native craftsmen. Like a stage setting, a stage costume must be related to a pattern of action; it is designed not only to be seen but to be worn. A knowledge of what this relation involves can often be best acquired by research and reconstruction. A costume-designer begins his apprenticeship by learning how perfectly the cutter's pattern of a Japanese court robe, the slightly starched silk and the points at which it is fastened, combine with the traditions of Japanese court ceremonial; why an Arab robe pieced together according to the system still used by Arab tailors can give an actor walking across a stage the impressiveness of a caid crossing a Moroccan market place. The weakness of much of so-called imaginative costume design in the theatre is that it is most effective on paper and is less imaginative than what has already been invented. It is as easy to exaggerate and heighten a historic silhouette in a costume drawing for the theatre as on a modern fashion-plate. This does not insure its exaggerated lines being visible when executed. If the result is not based on a sound knowledge of dressmaking and the relation of materials to dressmaking pattern, an Arab chieftain on the stage is more liable than not to look as though he had escaped from a Turkish bath in an exceptionally large and slightly damp bath-towel, and a Japanese princess in her flapping kimono seem more like a girl on her way to a boarding-school bath-room than a counterpart of Utamaro's or Harunobu's aristocrats. Imagination that cannot digest knowledge, fancy that cannot root itself in fact, more often than not produces empty conventions that very soon become formulae.

The lesson taught theatrical designers by the Duke of Saxe-Meiningen was the same lesson that Matisse once gave a class of students who, thinking to please him, had proceeded to fill their canvases with abstract splotches of colour. He brought out the cast of a Greek head and asked the astonished innovators to paint it. "You must not think you are committing suicide by adhering to nature and trying to picture it with exactness. In the beginning you must subject yourself to the influence of nature. After that you can turn your back, motivate nature and perhaps make it more beautiful." The study of historic costume sources made by the Duke of Saxe-Meiningen was, like all his other efforts, pioneer work. No adequate volume on the history of costume existed. His research antedated the collections of Racinet, Hottenroth, Hefner-Alteneck, and the immense reference library on the subject that has since been built up.

In another respect costume-designing at Meiningen brought a valuable lesson to the theatre. When one discovers how even the most preposterous historic styles, seemingly clumsy and unwieldy, were actually constructed, including even the widest farthingale, they can be easily worn. And so long as dramatists persist in laying their plays in the past, this knowledge is of immense help to the actors playing them. Even Queen Elizabeth was able to sit down—and the chairs of the period were not five feet wide. Her attendant nobles might look like overstuffed pincushions, but they were not immobilized by their doublets and jerkins, were in fact violent men of action who got about as nimbly as we do in long trousers and fought duels even if they did not play golf. One can learn why by studying an actual costume of the period preserved at the South Kensington Museum. Watteau's and Boucher's belles danced the minuet in an elaborate outfit of trains, frills, and ruffles and, as the gallant engravings of the period prove, made love impromptu without disrobing. Unless a designer can recover the deftness of French dressmaking of the period, actresses in eighteenth-century costume today are forced to totter about like badly articulated dolls. The grace of any period of costume depends on purely technical tricks of tailoring and dressmaking. The obvious way of holding an 1840 skirt in its bell-like shape is to line the bottom with some stiff material such as tarlatan. But the shape of these skirts was actually preserved by being lined with a soft material, cotton wadding, sewed loosely in a deep bottom hem. I learned the fact from an actual costume of the period that I once picked up at an antique-dealer's in New Haven after a football-game. Use this knowledge on the stage and how much more grace is lent an actress, with what flowerlike ease the bell enclosing her sweeps and sways! I can remember how appalled I was at the prospect of the problem of costuming *Silas Lapham* in the mode of the seventies. How could actresses with these enormous bustles bobbing behind manage even to sit down? Fortunately in a back number of *Harper's Bazaar* I discovered an illustrated advertisement of a "lobster-pot" bustle of the period. When I got a seamstress to reproduce the light articulated whalebone ribbing, not only was the enormous cascade of material sprouting from the waist easily held, but the actresses frisked and swished about, even jumped up on tables while waiting for cues at rehearsals. Had I got the effect by stuffing the tops of their skirts with padding or horse-hair, their movements would have been as inhibited as though each of them had carried a small sack of flour tied to her waist.

The value of the Duke of Saxe-Meiningen's costumes consisted not only in showing how essential a basis for design authentic sources can be, how much they can add to the so-called atmosphere of a historic play, but also how necessary the authentic construction of costume is to the actor—a fact proved by comparing the original costume-drawings with the photographs of members of the company. The tragedy-queens are not slightly overblown matrons got up for a masquerade; they have some of the authority of queens as court painters once saw them. The knights and squires seem to be Dürer's and Schongauer's come alive. The flamboyance of one period contrasts with the clinging elegance of another, such as the costumes for Molière's comedies. Intentions, however limited, were realized. Costumes became clothes; they were constructed so that they could be worn and, combining with every other element of a production, dramatize action. The Duke of Saxe-Meiningen did not exhaust the scope of costume design in the theatre, or indicate its imaginative goal. But he laid the foundation for both.

5. SUM OF DETAILS

The immense complexity added to a production at Meiningen would have been worse than useless if the details of costumes, crowds, and individual stage business had not been integrated. The process of welding them into a whole was accomplished by incessant and tireless rehearsal—also a revolutionary innovation for its day. The Meiningen company was endowed with one form of capital as necessary as money and even rarer in the theatre—time. Every play was rehearsed until it was ready. It was not produced until it was ready. Rehearsals when the company was not playing began at four or five and continued past midnight. At one the duke stopped the company for an instant, called out, "My friends, I wish you a happy New Year!" and continued the rehearsal well into the morning. Its general supervision, the idea and scheme of a production, were in the duke's hands; questions of interpretation in the reading of lines were handled directly by his wife. Chronegk executed decisions as a combined assistant director and stage-manager. He was a relentless disciplinarian, his motto equivalent to one I have heard so often from Philip Moeller: "There are no excuses in the theatre." At a rehearsal in Moscow which Stanislavsky witnessed an actor was a few minutes late. Chronegk promptly deprived him of every leading rôle for the rest of the engagement and assigned him to playing in the mob scenes. Settings and costumes were ready for the first rehearsals, also essential properties such as furniture or weapons and armour that might prove unwieldy in handling. There was no costume rehearsal—that invariably grotesque occasion when whatever unity and rhythm of life a production has achieved up to that moment is shot to pieces by distracting actors with costumes that do not fit, shoes that pinch, swords that dangle between their legs, steps that they trip over, wigs too tight, furniture too high or too low, too large or too small, so that unity and rhythm have to be recovered in a last-minute frenzy for the opening night. Actors were expected to learn the business of their parts at the outset and were not allowed to forget. No written record was kept, a production was always a living and expanding thing, to be re-rehearsed, given new meanings and fresh nuances, after its first performance. And every member of the company was expected to remember a production to its last detail. Stanislavsky was present also when an assistant stage-manager failed to bring in a group of robbers on cue. Chronegk called on a stage-hand at random, who recited the entire monologue that preceded their entrance.

The spirit of experiment kept these rehearsals from becoming a depressing routine. The company was invited to contribute its ideas. When differences of opinion developed and the triumvirate did not agree, the different versions were tried out in succession. Nothing was too difficult to attempt, no attempt was abandoned before it had been tried again and again. At one rehearsal an actor waiting for his cue with a candelabra of four immense tapers found, when his scene was reached, that they were burnt out. Eleven lines in the preceding scene had been rehearsed for two hours. The duke had the defects of his qualities. Hours were once wasted in attempting to co-ordinate the flashes of musketry volleys on a distant hill with the off-stage noise of gun-fire—a back-drop being perforated for the purpose. For another battle scene, the duke insisted on a dead horse for Talbot's death, in order to avoid the inevitable dying-gladiator pose and so give the actor a position in which he could die in convincing fashion and at the same time turn his face to the audience. Hour after hour the stuffed lummox was dragged to every possible position and in every one its four rigid legs made acting between them or over them ridiculous. But the duke persisted and finally solved the problem by turning the legs up stage so that Talbot died in an effective pose supported by the animal's caparisoned back.

The ensemble effects that the Meiningen theatre laboured to get were not always mob scenes and the grandiose tableaux involved in the historic dramas, then a popular part of German repertory. A complete change of timbre and pace was achieved for Molière's *Le Malade Imaginaire* and for *Twelfth Night*. The pillow-fight in the former and Maria's laughing-fit in the latter were bits of comic invention that later became traditional in other German theatres. The company's comedians were found better by contemporary critics (including Antoine) than its tragedians. But the company's success in both fields was a triumph of ensemble playing, for they succeeded without the aid of a single player recognized as an actor of the first rank. The directorate was not always satisfied by the invariable popularity of their mob scenes, which on tour were always the talk of the town, nor by the critics' amazement at that complete investiture of every play. This was natural at a time when Antoine was supposed to have been financially as well as artistically reckless because, during his fourth season, he persisted in building new sets for every play instead of using the stock scenery that belonged to the house. Chronegk complained bitterly to Stanislavsky: "I brought them Shakespeare, Schiller, and Molière, and they are interested in the furniture. What kind of taste have they, anyway?" But the duke persisted in believing that the soul of a play had to have a body, and that the smallest break in its texture might let its life-breath escape like a hole in one's windpipe. The least detail of a performance remained important to him because a single ridiculous detail could in a moment destroy a mood that had taken half an hour to create. It is typical that when the company left Meiningen for Berlin for their first performance in any other theatre—a crucial moment, with their reputation and future at stake—his only worry was about a certain Pfutz, who had worked out an elaborate death-agony for himself in one of the final battle scenes of *Julius Caesar*. His telegram delivered on the opening night contained nothing more than "Good luck to all. Tell Pfutz not to be too long dying."

6. SCHOOLMASTER TO EUROPE

May 1, 1874—the date of the first performance of the Meiningen company in Berlin—can, I think, be considered the May-day of a revolution in the modern theatre. Saxe-Meiningen was a minor principality, Meiningen then a town of only eight thousand inhabitants. Berlin was incredulous. What was this small-town repertory company and why had it presumed it had anything to show the *königliche-kaiserliche* centre of German *Kultur*? The first-night audience came to sneer and remained to cheer a kind of dramatic performance that they had never dreamed of. The triumph was repeated the following year not only in Berlin but also in Vienna and Budapest. Between 1874 and 1890, in addition to 385 performances in Berlin, 2,206 were given in tours that carried the company to all the leading German cities and to London, Amsterdam, Rotterdam, Copenhagen, Stockholm, Basel, Warsaw, St. Petersburg, Moscow, and Odessa. The company became the first theatre of Europe, a school of the theatre for every theatrical centre. None escaped its influence. Every tradition of routine repertory based on opera was discredited and a method of bringing plays to life on the boards was everywhere recognized as nothing less than a new art. Insurgents everywhere were stimulated to redouble their efforts and to clarify their programmes. The lessons that Antoine learned in Brussels—the handling of stage crowds, the creation of mood and atmosphere in stage setting, the flexibility and subtlety of stage business, the effectiveness of interpretation carried through every detail of performance—he accepted as a model, and carried into the programme of his own Théâtre Libre. The organization of the Meiningen company and its methods formed the basis of his own *Plan for an Ideal Theatre,* published a few years later, which, could it have been carried into execution, might have revitalized the French stage and created a national theatre in fact as well as in name.

The first performances of the Meiningen company in Moscow were given in 1885. Their effect on Stanislavsky, then at the end of his amateur period, was profound. "Their performances showed Moscow for the first time productions that were historically true, with . . . fine outer form and amazing inner discipline. I did not miss a single one of their performances, I came not only to look but to study as well." Chronegk for a time became his model. "When it was necessary to bring all to one common denominator, I was saved by the despotism of stage direction that I had learned from the methods of Kronek with the Meiningen Players." "Very soon the majority of Russian stage directors began to imitate me in my despotism as I imitated Kronek." Not only Chronegk but the ideal that his despotism expressed served as a model for the subsequent programme of the Moscow Art Theatre —the necessity for a commanding director who could visualize an entire performance and give it unity as an interpretation by complete control of every moment of it; the interpretative value of the smallest details of lighting, costuming, make-up, stage setting; the immense discipline and the degree of organization needed before a performance was capable of expressing "the soul of a play." These elements of the Meiningen tradition in turn became a tradition at the Moscow Art Theatre, including the endless rehearsals and the practice of making leading actors play in stage mobs. But it was Stanislavsky's particular genius that enabled him to see that the outer discipline imposed by the director was not enough. "The stage director can do a great deal, but he cannot do everything. The most important thing is in the hands of the actor, whom one must help, who must be guided in the proper direction." It was Stanislavsky's intuitive understanding of the needs of the actor, and the subsequent inner discipline for the actor evolved, that, added to the Meiningen methods of production, in turn made the Moscow Art Theatre the first theatre of Europe for the next generation. It was Stanislavsky's insight into the art of acting that saved him from becoming nothing more than one of the directors "of the new type . . . mere producers who made of the actor a stage property on the same level with stage furniture, a pawn that was moved about in their *mise-en-scènes*. . . . Only with time, as I began to understand the wrongness of the principle of the director's despotism, I valued that good which the Meiningen Players brought us, their director's methods for showing the spiritual contents of the drama. . . . My gratitude to them is unbounded and will always live in my soul."

In 1890, during a second tour of Russia, Chronegk collapsed and never recovered his health. The duke, already an old man, could not face the prospect of carrying on without his veteran lieutenant. Friends urged him to give a final gala season at Berlin by way of crowning his career. He waved aside the project with the words: "It is not necessary. The German theatre has learned everything it had to learn."

Had the word "German" been omitted the statement would none the less have held true. When a director today plans a production, he fills in a concept originally established by a royal amateur. No important director since the duke's time has failed to be a disciple of one aspect or another of his theories and his practice. His principles of stage-composition have been elaborated in Reinhardt's *The Miracle* and *Danton's Death,* imitated in productions such as *Saint Joan* by the Theatre Guild, intensified in *The Tidings Brought to Mary* and *Man and the Masses.* All our experiments are based upon the cardinal doctrines established at Meiningen: the essentially plastic relation of the actor in movement to the stage space he moves in, the forms he walks on, the shape of the stage setting enclosing him, and the dynamic relation between an actor in motion and an immobile setting so fundamentally planned as architecture that it determines the whole pattern of a play's movement and at the same time intensifies its meaning. No director since the Duke of Saxe-Meiningen has combined his dual capacities as director and designer. But because he demonstrated so convincingly how every detail of scenic design can affect every moment of a performance, the director now insists on a designer as an indispensable collaborator. And the designer not only follows the routine established by the Duke of Saxe-Meiningen in planning and painting his settings, but also assures the unity of his pictorial scheme by carrying it through to the details of wigs and weapons, the galloon on the hem of a garment, the line of a chair, a bit of bric-à-brac on a mantelpiece. But no director alive except Stanislavsky seems aware of his indebtedness to an innovator who made plain that the life of a play did not become more real by imitating surfaces or by isolating the actor at the footlights, but by relating the actor so fundamentally to the backgrounds he moved in, to every object he touched, that these in turn refracted his presence and heightened his dramatic importance. The unity achieved is not that of an outline, of the simple melodic line in duets and trios, in arias of oratorios answered by choruses. It is analogous to the less symmetrical pattern that characterizes all other forms of modern art, like the unity of painting that makes a richer whole of complex colour-contrasts and opposing forms, the unity of polyphonic musical compositions where the intricacies of counterpoint enrich simple harmony, where dissonance is related to melody and an immense range of timbres combines to make an orchestral whole.

Nine years after the last performance given by the Meiningen company at Odessa, a Swiss philosopher, Adolphe Appia, completely analyzed the aesthetic principles of the new stage-craft. But he made the mistake of publishing his findings in German, a language little read by American or English critics, who assume it to be incapable of expressing any truth about any art. Apologists of the new stage-craft, eventually convinced of the creative importance of the German theatre, witnessed the productions of the Duke of Saxe-Meiningen's successors without suspecting their source. His name is not considered important enough to be included in the index of Sheldon Cheney's review of three thousand years of drama, acting, and stage-craft, although one finds Raquel Meller and Mounet-Sully. It is not surprising that for more than twenty years Gordon Craig has been able to pose as the darling of the gods and to arouse universal pity because no one would give him a king's ransom to achieve the unity of a theatrical performance controlled by his master mind, a unity that had been successfully demonstrated by a German prince a few years after Craig was born. Even now, in an epoch of endowed research and cultural exchanges of all sorts, no Carnegie or Guggenheim Foundation considers the archives of the Meiningen theatre worthy of its attention. No graduate of any of our universities, where courses on modern drama are a new field of learning, has laid the perishable laurel of a doctor's thesis on the Duke of Saxe-Meiningen's tomb. But the duke, could he be aware of the fact, would undoubtedly be as indifferent to it as he once was to the prospect of being acclaimed at a farewell season in Berlin. The theatre has learned what it needed to learn, nevertheless.

CHAPTER III

DAY-DREAMS:
THE CASE OF GORDON CRAIG

I. TRANSLATION

WHAT designer has not, at one time or another, on seeing one of his scenes set up, felt like Quince when he beheld his friend in ass's ears and exclaimed, "Bless thee, Bottom! bless thee! thou art translated!" When scenic projects are carried out they are in the literal sense of the word translated, carried over from one medium to another. In this process lie all the unavoidable technical problems of stage-craft which have preoccupied the designers of every epoch in the theatre's history. The technical problem in its fundamentals is always the same: How are the form, colour, texture, atmosphere, and light of a design to be preserved when enlarged and erected in a theatre? A scenic drawing is no more than an intention; it is no better than the methods eventually used to embody it. Paper, as the Germans say, is patient. A swirl of the brush can create atmospheric distance in a water-colour, the sense of physical liberation that a landscape gives when one walks in it. But the space evoked by a water-colour wash or perspective drawing is the very quality most easily lost when the design is translated to a board floor that meets a canvas back-drop or a plaster wall. Space was never more convincingly evoked than by the perspective scenic drawings of the nineteenth century, which caricatured their intentions when executed. Any number of designs that as drawings seem to express the spirit of a play, once in the theatre, are transformed into something as grotesque as a donkey trying to make love to a fairy queen.

The dramatic poet evokes the full sweep and scale of nature at every turn, lifts up his heart to the hills, testifies to the glory of the firmament, opens his window on the foam of perilous or silver seas. A playwright can say, with Edna St. Vincent Millay:

> *All I could see from where I stood*
> *Was three long mountains and a wood.*
> *I turned and looked the other way*
> *And saw three islands in a bay.*

A designer can project the scene and recapture the mood in which such a scene is viewed, in a drawing that may be worth preserving in an art museum. But if an audience in a theatre must share this vista with Iseult at Tintagel or Ariadne on Naxos, all that it sees from where it sits will, in all probability, be something very like the enlargement of a lithographed calendar advertising the advantages of spending the summer in Maine. The overwhelming chances are that the audience will not see massiveness and mobility of natural forms, the downward thrust of cliffs and headlands interlocked with the upward thrust of mountains, holding the sea in their arms. Iseult or Ariadne will command the vista, so dramatically appropriate for love in exile, on a wrinkled hummock of padded canvas that has lost all semblance to the elastic tension of a hillside and the easy undulations of the earth. It is of course a simple matter to solve the problem by evading it and to say that an audience need see nothing more than a woman on a flight of steps looking into a void. But, as I have pointed out, both playwrights and audiences for more than twenty centuries have been insistent in their demand that the stage be a world and that the backgrounds of action be visualized. If a designer decides that the problem is insoluble, he finds himself in the position of Bernard

Shaw at a lecture when a solitary hearer booed him while the rest of the house applauded furiously. "I agree with you," said Shaw, "but what can we do against so many?" The designer who declares that the technical problems presented to him every day in the year by every dramatist, whether poet or realist, genius or hack, have nothing to do with art, decrees his own exile. If he cannot invent a technical method more certain to create beauty in the theatre than the prevailing one and put it into practice, he does nothing more than surrender the field to those who manufacture ugliness. The technical problems of stage-craft may never be satisfactorily solved until playwrights and audiences become what they never have been. But in a living theatre the technical problem of finding ways and means to embody a microcosm of the natural world has to be solved daily.

Every stroke of the designer's pencil or of his brush must be enlarged at least twenty-four times on the stage. And the scene-designer's art consists not in being able to record his intentions as skilfully as the painter of easel pictures, but in being able to make a picture that, once it is enlarged, retains its original values of texture, colour and form. Mathematical enlargement by itself is of no use because in every square inch of a drawing colour, form, and texture are inextricably combined. They can be translated to the stage only by being disintegrated and then recombined. How can this be done so that they retain their original effect? In a sketch a plaster wall scintillates in sunlight. The plaster surface must be translated into canvas, wood veneer, or some composite building-board solid enough to be carpentered, light enough to handle. The modulations of white have to be organized in entirely different scale if the wall is not to be as monotonously flat as the side of a newly painted barn. The light that was part of a brush-stroke becomes actual light that hits a surface so painted that it will vibrate as the original sketch did. In a scenic sketch "little aspens dusk and shiver," we find ourselves in a gloomy wood astray or in Philomel's bower. How are we to recapture the resilient massiveness of clumps of trees so that on the stage they can seem an appropriate refuge for a poet or two lovers? Cut down a grove; transport it; it becomes a collection of dead limbs and faggots. Reproduce each tree with canvas stretched over wire frames and hung with imitation leaves, and each becomes a bedraggled mummy of a living tree. Suggest a forest with columns of canvas hung in folds and you lose the grace and lightness of the kind of grove that a given scene calls for. Project the grove with a stereopticon; you keep a semblance of its palpitant life but lose the essential forms that gave the original drawing its design.

In a scenic sketch a hero meditates on a hill-top crowned by a soaring cumulus cloud. How impressive as a picture! It might be as effective on the stage if one could find a way of translating the cloud. Paint it on the back-drop and it loses its effulgence. Cut it out of cardboard and hang it on a wire; it has a wire-line edge and soars no more freely than an angel on a Christmas-tree. Project it with a lantern-slide. How then, precisely because it has some of the ambience and transparency of a cloud in nature, are you to avoid making it seem conspicuous because its forms are paralyzed and do not dissolve and then rebuild themselves? At the same time you discover that if the cloud projection is to be seen, the rest of the stage will have to be dark; enough light on your actors will wipe it out of the heavens. Resolve these difficulties with a moving-picture machine and project a cloud in motion; your stage heaven seems a photograph that has no relation to the other parts of your stage setting.

Renounce the attempt to translate landscape forms to the stage and limit your effort to translating the forms of architecture. You have restricted the number of your problems but you have not made solution of any one of them easier. The actual forms of architecture can be approximated by stage carpentry. But their actual scale cannot be absolute even on the largest stage ever planned; and once scale is made relative, the very proportions that make an architectural drawing dramatic are often lost. The actor cannot be led up a flight of a hundred steps, down the immense depth of a cathedral nave; the eye cannot be led into the soaring heights of its groined arches, or through an entire temple colonnade. These distances can of course be suggested, but in the process much of the effect of a total architectural pattern is sacrificed. The base of a column or of one archway can be given its full scale but the rest of the architectural picture, so easily indicated in a scenic drawing, must be stunted or truncated. Throw the carpenter out of your theatre, call back the painter. Let him paint in perspective or in flat formal patterns; both will seem transparent artifice as soon as the first actually three-dimensioned actor, an organic piece of nature, appears.

Drawings for the theatre are desires. They should all be signed with a question-mark, for they are, even the best of them, pretences until they are fulfilled. A designer for the stage is a pretentious counterfeit of the Creator in miniature. Not being a god, he must attempt to create a world by one system of mechanics or another—each inadequate, each more or less clumsy—which tries to hide its inherent defects by striking a new balance between fact and illusion, truth and deception. And every attempt, whether its aim be reproduction or illusion, must be translated into materials that may in themselves easily destroy the aesthetic quality of the original design. The life of a scenic idea is inextricably bound up with the search for the purely mechanical means by which it can be projected on the stage without being destroyed in the process. The drawing of a stage setting is largely a dream. Its realization is often nothing less than a nightmare.

2. AMATEUR'S HEAVEN

The sense of liberation that Craig brought to workers in the theatre was largely a delusion; he succeeded in making any number of them forget the mechanics of execution by the simple expedient of ignoring technical problems altogether. The designer had only to dream nobly, aspire, expand, let his line go up and up—it could not go high enough. Nothing had weight or substance. Make a towering cliff and set a cloud at its summit. Matter would ultimately obey the spirit somehow, somewhere, sometime. The designer was a veritable god. Drawings did not need to be proved in practice. A sketch was in itself sufficient proof, a divine revelation. The effect of Craig's words was often magical because he made the theatre seem a magical place; assertions had the power of incantations, prophecy replaced experiment, dreaming and drawing were the only forms of labour.

As soon as one dream was shattered by actuality, the designer could take refuge in another. Did the flesh-and-blood actor destroy the aesthetic unity of the stage picture? Lo, the flesh-and-blood actor was himself destroyed in a paragraph; he no longer existed. The super-marionette was called forth and existed before it had been invented. Did any one deny that this docile mechanism was a superman? A new religious ritual would presently be founded on its antics. Was the stage a shoddy place of paint and tinsel? Let the theatre borrow the marble and gold of the Catholic Church; the designer, *ipso facto,* had these precious new materials in his hands, and could make the theatre a church in short order. Was the stage a black box? Let it live in the sunlight under an open sky. A moment's thought was enough to prove that true drama had never been played anywhere else. However, the flexibility of electric light was in itself magical. Craig said, "Let there be light," and for the first time in centuries the actor stood revealed. But was it not also true that no performance in any theatre could adequately express the greatest dramas, such as Shakespeare's? Another flash of revelation showed the playwright to be an interloper in the sacred precincts of the theatre. He was banished, and it became apparent that the theatre had never discovered its true subject-matter, which was itself like a dream that could unveil thoughts to our eyes in mystic pantomimes. The pitch of prophetic utterance rose higher and higher, like the chorus of angels in the mystical Heaven where Faust was finally welcomed. The ineffable was experienced, the indescribable achieved.

Craig's heaven was a welcome refuge for every one beaten by the difficulties of expressing ideas in a recalcitrant material. Here at Craig's feet, will and deed, idea and embodiment, were one. The happy tyranny of childhood was recovered. For the artist, who preserves something of the directness and the purity of a child's desires, is cradled by the child's day-dream of a world that magically responds to every wish. The artist emerges by dominating the child in him and begins the actual conflict of imposing some of his ideas on a world existing outside of his private heaven. But Craig, after his first attempts at staging in London in 1902 and 1903, took refuge from the actualities of theatrical production in a Florentine villa.

In the course of twenty-five years he has emerged to do only six productions, of which not one was epoch-making and one, his American production of *Macbeth,* an acknowledged artistic débâcle that not even his disciples were able to defend with any conviction. But his magazine *The Mask* and his successive volumes redoubled his assertions, ramified his contradictory theories, and presented his ideas as no more than hints of what he could do with a theatre were he put in absolute control of one. His readers were never allowed to forget that he alone was the Master capable of transforming the theatre of today and founding the veritable theatre of tomorrow. With Craig in his heaven all seemed well with the theatre, at least to its theologians. They wel-

315

comed a prophet who could invent new panaceas for a new theatre as fast as the latest one had been proved a nostrum, and commenced to extol Craig as the one source of every innovation in stage-craft, the unmoved mover, who like a god could set a world in motion and direct its subsequent course from his retreat in Italy by the modern magic of remote control. Evangelists themselves, they needed a source of divine inspiration, and Craig supplied its perfect simulacrum. His manner was oracular, therefore he seemed a prophet. His statements were sufficiently cryptic and vague to recall the utterances of historic oracles. A murky penumbra of meaning blurred his doctrines, which gave disciples the opportunity of becoming apostles. The new theatre was shoved into a more and more remote future, where it became alluringly mysterious. To explain Craig's consistent failure to perform his promised miracles when called upon, it was pointed out that even the foremost art theatres of Europe were too materialistic to reflect his pure and perfect spirit. A legend of martyrdom was promulgated. Craig was declared to be the victim of a world-wide conspiracy by theatres which welcomed every other form of experiment, encouraged and developed a host of modern designers, but singled out Craig and kept him in exile in order to pilfer the ideas that he never adequately expressed. The theatre's theologians continue to hail Craig, moving toward him in genuflecting sentences over long stretches of eulogy extending like a ceremonial carpet to a pontifical throne or a wonder-working shrine. And in almost every volume on modern scenic design one seems to hear, at the mention of his name, the echoes of Isaac Watts's hymn:

> Let the Redeemer's name be sung
> In every land by every tongue.

In the face of this continued *Te Deum,* I venture to assert that Craig's relation to the development of the modern theatre is primarily that of a demagogue of decided literary gifts. Trained originally as an actor, he has remained an exalted mountebank, declaiming nobly and drawing crowds to the door of an aesthetic side-show. His habits of mind are essentially lazy and rhetorical; he has the talent of a sensational journalist for summarizing an artist's problem in a provocative head-line. But he has never shown the slightest capacity, either as a critic or as a designer, for the work involved in pushing to a solution a single problem that he has posed. Long before that point was reached he struck another attitude and, in order to conceal his failure, strutted once again in the mantle of a prophet, which he manipulates with the skill of an eighteenth century tragedian playing in the grand manner. He can bare his breast to the "slings and arrows of outrageous fortune" and present a perfect picture of a misunderstood genius who has never been given an opportunity to execute his dreams. He has not been prevented from doing so by a mean and jealous world but by his own lack of authentic creative power. He has all the superficial attributes that we associate with a romantic and disordered type of genius but he has not the essential force of genius, the sullen determination to come to grips with the material difficulties of his instrument and so arrive at the creative pitch that turns dreams into their embodiments.

As a result Craig does not know the theatre. He does not understand the theatre as those who have worked in it and conducted its experiments do. When he makes a pretence of planning the theatre of the future he has not the architect's gift for precise visualization. He does not possess the concrete imagination of a director who can organize all the elements of a performance into a living whole. His one valid doctrine—the necessity for a single directing mind that can give a production artistic unity—had been enunciated and demonstrated by the Duke of Saxe-Meiningen before Craig wrote or drew a line and was amplified by Stanislavsky while Craig was publishing his pseudo-revolutionary volumes. His one technical innovation, the use of screens, in his own hands became a somewhat clumsy and inflexible formula. His other supposed innovations are belated discoveries of theatrical expedients already discovered by others. His few drawings whose aesthetic qualities are relevant to the stage are echoes of the conceptions of an indubitable creator, Adolphe Appia, that in every case antedate his own. Craig lacks the one faculty that distinguishes the artist from the amateur; the French describe it as *la volonté de faire*—the will to do. Like every other person of genuine artistic endowment who does not succeed in evolving a successful technique of expression, Craig consoles himself with the strident technique of exhibitionism known as the artistic temperament. He remains today what he was at the outset of his career, essentially an amateur, with a capacity for intense appreciation, soaring enthusiasm, and facile improvisations. Like the amateur's his projects are radiant but vague, full of glowing possibilities but possessing so little inherent structure that he himself cannot embody them.

Craig's first pamphlet, *The Art of the Theatre,* published in 1905 and enlarged into a book in 1911, did not open a new era. It opened a theatrical heaven to the thwarted amateur. The workers who established the modern theatre in Europe and America were originally amateurs when they entered it. Stanislavsky worked as an amateur for twenty-one years before founding the Moscow Art Theatre with Dantchenko. Antoine, although he had once been a pupil at the French Conservatoire, was a clerk in a gas-company when he inaugurated his Théâtre Libre. The Duke of Saxe-Meiningen started his career as a royal dilettante. The Volksbühne of Berlin, which now rivals the State Theatre in importance, was originally an amateur society that gave performances only on Sunday afternoons. The Washington Square Players, who developed into the Theatre Guild, were amateurs at the outset, who performed only Friday and Saturday evenings. The Provincetown Theatre, which established Eugene O'Neill as a playwright, was organized and directed by amateurs when it began. But these amateurs were amateurs only through lack of experience, not, like Craig, amateurs in spirit. Their theories, as revolutionary in the eyes of the established theatre as many of Craig's, were a prelude to action. These groups did not prophesy; they hired a hall and started to demonstrate their ideas, no matter what makeshifts they had to utilize. The Duke of Saxe-Meiningen attacked the rococo traditions of the court theatre in a royal opera-house. The Théâtre Libre gave its first performances in the auditorium of a private club and rehearsed them in a billiard-room back of a cabaret. The Washington Square Players rented an out-of-the-way theatre, so small that it was called the Bandbox, abandoned by a troupe that had given shoddy musical comedy in German. Stanislavsky's first theatre was improvised in his own home. The Moscow Art players rehearsed for their first season in a country barn. The Provincetown Theatre's first stage was on a remodelled wharf. Every one of these groups made theatrical history because it was animated by the knowledge that nothing can be accomplished in the theatre, whether great art or the most transient claptrap, except as a result of a devouring determination to tame a public—to battle with it, tempt it, taunt it as one might a lethargic animal and finally arouse the roar of its allegiance. Every veritable artist in the theatre, as well as its charlatans, is consumed by that passion. Craig lacks it completely. He could dream nobly on paper. But in almost every instance when he transferred his dreams to a stage, their water-colour beauty evaporated.

3. PROSPERO WITHOUT ARIEL

Isadora Duncan's enthusiasm gained for Craig the commissions to design *Rosmersholm* for Duse in 1906 and *Hamlet* for the Moscow Art Theatre in 1910-11. In each Craig revealed his inherent incapacity to control an actual production. "No scene that I have worked at," he declares, "was worked at for its own sake. I thought solely of the

Drama . . . of the actors . . . of the dramatic moments." But because his settings were conceived primarily as pictures, difficulty began the moment that actors were put into them. According to Isadora Duncan's account of the setting for Rosmer's sitting-room: "Craig had been pleased to see the high interior of a great Egyptian temple with enormously high ceiling, extending upwards to the skies, with walls receding into the distance. Only, unlike an Egyptian temple, at the far end there was a great square window. . . . Craig had been pleased to see this in dimensions of ten metres by twelve. It looked out upon a flaming landscape of yellows, reds, and greens which might have been some scene in Morocco." In order to persuade Duse to use Craig's conception, Isadora, who acted as interpreter, lied whenever necessary. "I hope some of the lies I told . . . may be forgiven me, for they were in a holy cause. . . . Eleanora, looking rather disconcerted, said: 'I see this as a small window. It cannot possibly be a large one.' To which Craig thundered in English: 'Tell her I won't have any damned woman interfering with my work.' Which I discreetly translated to Eleanora: 'He says he admires your opinions and will do anything to please you.'" In consequence the window thirty feet square in a sepulchral room was completed. In rehearsal it was "a vision of loveliness." In her performance, Duse managed to adapt herself "to every great line and to each shaft of light that enveloped her. She changed all her gestures and her movements. . . . But when the other actors came on—Rosmer, for instance, who put his hands in his pockets—they seemed to be like stage hands who had walked on by mistake." Very naturally, despite a moment of enthusiasm, Duse abandoned the setting after a single performance.

There is of course no reason why Rosmer's home should not be abstractly and mystically conceived. But there is every reason why a mystic and abstract setting should be related to the kind of performance that is to take place within it. A beautiful picture can easily be achieved at the rise of the curtain. However, a preliminary picture that fails to relate itself to the entire development of a play and makes one of the leading players seem by contrast a stage hand is no better than any blatantly painted, old-fashioned back-drop that was also continually at odds with the actor in front of it. Had Craig been a "Master of Drama" as he pretends to be, his first impulse would have been to throw his window, not Duse, out of the theatre.

Not even Stanislavsky's indubitable genius as a director, nor his enthusiastic co-operation and that of his entire staff, could bring Craig's ideas for *Hamlet* to the point of realization. The gap was particularly noticeable in the scene for "To be or not to be." "In his sketch," writes Stanislavsky, "Craig expressed himself in the following manner. There was a long corridor, gray and gloomy. The walls were blackened, and hardly noticeable shadows crept up these walls from beneath. These shadows personified the earthly life that had become hateful to Hamlet. . . . The other side of Hamlet was pictured on the sketch by a bright swath of light in the sunny rays of which appeared and disappeared the silvery figure of a woman who tempted Hamlet to come to her. This was what Hamlet called, 'Not to be' . . . The interplay of darkness and light was to symbolize the struggle in Hamlet between death and life. All this was wonderfully pictured in the sketch." But, when he attempted to stage it, Stanislavsky is forced to admit: "But I, as stage director, could not bring it to life on the stage. . . . With the use of ordinary theatrical means the interpretation suggested by Craig looked like a piece of hokum. . . . Finding no scenic means for the showing of the dark shadows of life as they were drawn in the sketch we were forced to deny ourselves Craig's plan."

Stanislavsky blames the "coarseness of theatrical means of production" for his failure. "May a time come when newly discovered rays will paint . . . the shadows of color tones and the combinations of lines. May other rays light the body of man and give it that indefiniteness of outline, . . . that ghostliness which we know in our waking and sleeping dreams." However, Stanislavsky, in staging *The Blue Bird* three years before producing *Hamlet,* had already succeeded in sustaining the atmosphere of a waking dream with all its necessary ghostliness and indefiniteness of outline. It is a common mistake to identify the Moscow Art Theatre entirely with the realistic precision of *The Cherry Orchard* or *The Lower Depths*. I happened to see a revival of *The Blue Bird* in Moscow in 1926. It successfully utilized every trick of modern stage-craft—gauzes, transparencies, fluctuating coloured light—and gave amazing visionary quality even to its painted settings. No method of lighting could transfigure the essential bathos of a silver temptress beckoning Hamlet. It is hokum—the sort of hokum that spectacular music-hall revues have regularly made part of their "vision of loveliness." The production as a whole, according to Stanislavsky, had the very defects of decoration from which Craig was to save us; it was "grandiose, affected to such an extent that its beauty attacked the eye and hid the actors in its pomp. . . . The more we tried to make the production simple, . . . the more it seemed pretentious and displayed its showy naïveté."

Craig's scheme for making and manipulating the screens that formed the background of every scene also proved abortive. His original idea was that "they were to be . . . organic . . . as near nature as possible, and as far from being artificial as we could have them." Craig suggested the use of stone, fresh lumber, metal, and cork. As any one but Craig could easily have foreseen, the use of any such materials in the theatre was preposterous. "We could not find a natural material for the making of the screens. . . . We tried everything—iron, copper, and other metals. . . . To use such screens we would have been forced to rebuild the entire theatre and to install electric scenery shifts. We tried wooden screens and showed them to Craig, but neither he nor our stage hands desired to move the terrible and dangerous walls. We tried cork screens, but even these were too heavy. In the end . . . we had to make peace with simple theatrical unpainted canvas on light wooden frames."

Even when made of canvas, "the great screens could not stand up well and would fall. If a single screen fell, all the others followed it. . . . The shifting of the screens demanded many long rehearsals with the stage hands. For a long time we were unsuccessful; now a workman would unexpectedly jump to the forestage and show himself . . . now a crack would form between two moving screens and the audience would see the life backstage; now the back of the scenery would show; now a screen would become stuck in one place." The original plan called for moving the screens before the spectators. But "one hour before the first-night performance there was a real catastrophe. . . . Suddenly one of the screens began to lean sideways more and more, then fell on the screen next to it, and the entire scenery fell to the floor like a house of cards." Only a frenzy of last-minute effort and "the help of the traditional theatrical curtain which coarsely but loyally hid the hard work of the stage hands" made the opening performance possible.

Craig was so singularly helpless during all these proceedings that it is not clear whether or not he was actually present. Certainly he showed none of the authority of a master. He had left his drawings behind him the year before with instructions that gave no clew as to how his effects were to be obtained. The solution of every problem has to be found for him, the results shown to him. He does nothing at a time when every other artist who has any sense of the theatre would have fought to realize his intentions by supervising every detail of his work. Craig remains helpless through all the final rehearsals and to the night of the opening performance, when his invention collapses before his eyes. Nevertheless Craig refers patronizingly to "the little Art Theatre of Moscow" and in 1913 writes of *"Hamlet* as it was pro-

323

duced by me with Mr. Stanislavsky's assistance." Ten years later, in *Scene,* he has the effrontery to announce as his epoch-making contribution to the art of the theatre the ultimate scene. "I come to my Theatre and my large screens and lamps . . . I now pass each scene through its drill . . . at each appointed cue a single or a double leaf of my screen moves . . . at each cue another leaf or other leaves turn—advance—recede—fold up or unfold . . ." Has Craig, since his retreat from Moscow, solved the technical difficulties involved in his pirouetting scenery? By no means. It is, as usual, not necessary. "After this small scene of screens . . . is adopted, I will pass on to the developing of this larger scene shown to you in the twenty etchings. . . . But to ask to see it put in practice while the small version of *something* like the same thing remains to be carried out for the English Theatre—and in a theatre of my own—is, I think, looking a little too far ahead." It was of course also out of the question to look backward and mention the small version that had tumbled in the Russian theatre. One is forced to wonder how much nearer an artist can approach the line that divides a visionary from a charlatan. Two sentences from Stanislavsky's memoirs—"All this was wonderfully pictured in the sketch. But I, as the stage director, could not bring it to life on the stage"—need only Craig's signature to be his epitaph.

4. ABANDONED PUPPETS

If one traces the development of a few of Craig's reputedly great ideas, the laziness of his mental processes becomes evident. The fate of the supermarionette is typical of so many of Craig's innovations, which all, sooner or later, become puppets in his hands. He pulls the strings for a minute and then lets them drop. It was, of course, sensational to distort the obvious implications of Eleanora Duse's exasperated cry: "To save the theatre the theatre must be destroyed, the actors and actresses must all die of the plague"; and to assert: "Do away with the real tree, do away with the reality of delivery, do away with the reality of action, and you tend towards doing away with the actor. This is what must come to pass in time . . . Do away with the actor, and you do away with the means by which a debased stage-realism . . . flourishes. No longer would there be a living figure to confuse us into connecting actuality and art; no longer a living figure in which the weakness and tremors of the flesh were perceptible. The actor must go and in his place comes the . . . Über-marionette."

But after this preliminary jerk nothing more was heard of the super-mechanism. The use of life-sized marionette angels in mystery-plays at Dieppe beginning about 1443 is mentioned by Bapst and other historians. In another one of these performances a marionette of the Virgin raised its arms to Heaven. A similar use of marionettes in a German mystery-play occurred at Lubeck a few years earlier. A certain De Grille established a puppet opera at the Théâtre du Marais in 1676; the puppets were spoken of as pygmies because they were four feet high. They were such successful performers that Lully, afraid of their possible competition with the Royal Opera, had the theatre closed. Marionettes were so much the rage in Paris during the middle of the eighteenth century that Boucher and other well-known painters of the day designed and painted puppets that collectors acquired at high prices. The use of marionettes is still wide-spread in Asia and the great dexterity with which they are manipulated is a matter of common knowledge. But if the marionette were to replace actors such as Duse, it would have to be given an incomparably more supple mechanism than it had acquired in centuries of use.

Had Craig been an innovator, a man of the theatre and not a pamphleteer, he would have tackled the problem. If Craig had not simply got hold of an idea, if an idea had got hold of him, would he not have conducted an extensive research among records and documents, travelled to the East, but above everything attempted to design, construct, and manipulate his supermarionette? If he really did believe that it was destined to save the theatre, could he have delayed throwing himself into a frenzy of experimental labour? Craig had a workshop in Florence, also student assistants. But there is no evidence that he ever did a stroke of sustained experimental work on the project. He has not recorded a single improvement either in the construction or in the manipulation of marionettes and presumably to this day knows no more about building or using marionettes than a number of German puppeteers or our own Tony Sarg, who makes no pretence of revolutionizing the theatre but succeeds in entertaining children.

Grant that Craig is not a man of the theatre and examine his idea purely as theory; it becomes, like his projected mechanism, nothing more than resounding, unsubstantiated assertion. To do away with the reality of action and delivery is not to do away with the actor. The actor has always been of central importance in theatres classified as formal and non-realistic—the arena of Greek tragedy, the Noh dramas of Japan, and many types of dance-dramas still current among Asiatic peoples. Noh players and Greek tragedians utilized masks. But this concealment of the tremors of the flesh is not a necessary adjunct of a non-realistic technique of acting. Mei Lan-Fang, without a mask, demonstrated how dominant the actor is in the traditional Chinese theatre, which is formal in movement, symbolic in costuming, and so little given to real trees or any other imitation of nature that the same two stools can in turn become a boat, a mountain, or a nuptial couch; actors circle the stage, which then becomes another room, and generals elaborately dismount from invisible chargers.

It suited Craig, for the sake of making a sensational statement in 1908, to ignore the same facts of theatrical history that he invoked in 1913, when he extolled the formal open-air theatres of the past as patterns for the theatre's salvation and offered as another panacea formal arrangements and rearrangements of blank screens as an ideal background for the actor. Twelve years after announcing the Savior Marionette he was declaring that "In creating a scene for a Drama . . . we have never to forget what the spectators require. One of the first of their demands is that they shall . . . see and hear the actor as he performs before us." No other worker or theorist in the modern theatre had ever forgotten that obvious fact except Craig himself.

Consider another of his revolutionary proposals, the proposal to banish not only the player but the playwright, summarized in the statement: "When the theatre has become a masterpiece of mechanism, when it has invented a technique, it will without any effort develop a *creative art* of its own." Observe that the theatre of Aeschylus, Sophocles, Euripides, Aristophanes, Shakespeare, Racine, and Molière to the unerring and prophetic eye of the then young Mr. Craig had somehow failed to create an art of its own. "Let me repeat again that it is not only the writer whose work is useless in the theatre. It is the musician's work which is useless there, and it is the painter's work which is useless there . . . let them keep to their kingdoms, and let those of the theatre return to theirs. Only when these last are once more reunited there shall spring so great an art . . . that I prophesy that a new religion will be found contained in it. That religion will preach no more, but it will reveal. It will not show us the definite images which the sculptor and painter show. It will unveil thoughts to our eyes, silently— by movements—in visions."

It is not apparent what persons are left to be reunited in the theatre after the playwright, the actor, the musician, and the painter have been banished, except perhaps the component parts of Craig's personality. Nor is it obvious how visions can reveal thoughts to eyes without using some form of imagery analogous to the painter's and sculptor's, nor how movement is to be observed if there are no definite images of one sort or another which move. The only element left in the theatre for the eye to seize would be rays of light. Performances consisting of the amorphous shapes of coloured lights projected on a screen were achieved a few years ago by Thomas Wilfred's colour organ. No one found in them either a new religion or a substitute for the production of plays on a stage, least of all Mr. Craig, who by that time had probably forgotten his prophecy, just as at the time of making it he failed to consider the implications of his own words. His statement sounded well; he had made his little effect. Was that not enough? He has since then failed to indicate any sort of visions except those sketched in his drawings, composed, like all drawings, of the very definite images of the painter and the sculptor, drawings which become so preoccupied with sculptural forms that one series published in 1923 resembles nothing so much as views of abandoned marble-quarries.

Had Craig been genuinely creative he might very easily have given the theatre productions that had the implicit meaning of visions rather than the explicit meanings of spoken drama and have created a new species of masque with masked actors, symbolic mass movements, and the interplay of colours and abstract forms. It required nothing more than genius. Had Craig been that genius, nothing could have prevented him from pouring out his visions and accumulating a monumental body of work, just as Ibsen and Shaw persisted in completing plays when no management would risk their performance. Inigo Jones and Ben Jonson had once lifted the masque form to an amazing pitch of technical and artistic perfection and revolutionized English stage-craft. There is no reason why Craig, with his literary gifts, could not have played Jonson to his own Inigo—no reason except that it is so much easier to prophesy than to create, and instead of embodying ideas to announce them in sonorous words. Craig has published nothing more than a few unrelated drawings for a "drama" of *Hunger,* supplemented by a fragmentary synopsis. Having by the most superficial kind of verbalism achieved the position of a prophet, he preferred to settle down to demonstrating the essential art of the theatre by sketching stage settings for plays written at a time when, according to his own definition, the theatre had not yet acquired a veritable theatre art.

5. BELATED DISCOVERIES

In 1931 Craig made an amazing statement in *Fourteen Notes* printed by the University of Washington. "I am told by a student that every design in my book *Towards a New Theatre* can be worked out in practice on a stage, and that the stage need not be larger than is an average-sized stage. I always thought that most of them could be done, but I am not displeased to hear from a younger man that I was not wrong in my supposition." The master who rails at England for not giving him a theatre of his own does nothing more than suppose that his designs are capable of execution. It never occurs to him to reach for a scale ruler, to make working drawings, to build a model where the proportions of his intentions could have been verified. He waits eight years and then takes a student's word for it. The creator proceeds by guesswork, and the unsupported assertion of a beginner is convincing proof. The tableau of inexperienced maturity supported by inexperienced youth should perhaps bring tears to the most sceptical eyes. But it so happens that a year before *Fourteen Notes* was printed I had several of the designs in *Towards a New Theatre* analyzed to scale and a model built of one—the setting for *Macbeth,* Act I, Scene 5—using as the basis of measurement either the treads of a stairway or the human figures indicated. Unless the use of painted perspective is resorted to—an old-fashioned practice that Craig repudiates—the setting for *Macbeth,* Act II, in order to have the scale and depth indicated by the drawing, would require a stage opening a hundred feet wide and ninety feet high—as high, that is, as the average eight-story building. In Act I, Scene 5, of *Macbeth,* the castle walls prove to be more than fifty-three feet high—the height of a five-story building—and extend back for another fifty-three feet. (See page 503.) And these are only two scenes for a play that has many more. How the walls of stage palaces are to be built five stories high, of the lightest stage material known that can simulate solid forms, namely, canvas, and how, once set, they are to be shifted, are problems that Craig obviously never thought of. It is of course possible to translate these designs to the stage by reducing their proportions. But it is precisely this grandiose scale which makes them as drawings distinctive and impressive.

In another drawing for *A Scene for a Play by Shakespeare,* published in 1905, the towers of a castle front are fifty and seventy feet high, its façade is eighty-eight feet across, and the depth of the scene a hundred and forty-four feet. The quarry-like etching (Plate 14 in *Scene*) contains rectangular columns approximately seventy feet high. The stairway in another project from *Macbeth* winds about a column that is twenty-seven feet in diameter (therefore more than eighty-four feet in circumference) and which towers so high that it is cut off by a proscenium opening more than fifty feet in height.

These stupendous proportions are not in themselves impracticable. If the theatre of the immediate future requires settings of such depth and height in plays calling for incessant changes of scene, then the art of the theatre consists not only in making scenic sketches, but also in devising the machinery to sustain and to move tons of scenery; a working knowledge of engineering becomes part of the technical equipment necessary for the complete director such as Craig pretends to be. Elaborately mechanized stages raised and lowered on hydraulic plungers, sliding forward sectionally and descending to the cellar for ponderous scene-changes, were designed, built, and successfully operated in Dresden, by Hasait at the Royal Opera House and by Linnebach at the State Theatre. Both had trained themselves to be not only architects but hydraulic and electrical engineers as well. Craig never analyzed his projects to the point of realizing the necessity for such apprenticeship. As with the supermarionette, it was more convenient

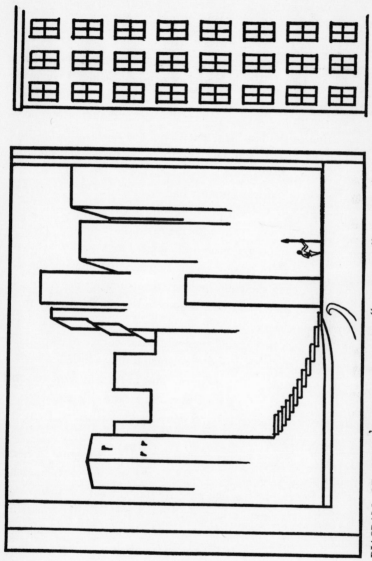

DIAGRAM OF CRAIG'S DRAWING FOR "MACBETH," ACT II, FROM "TOWARDS A NEW THEATRE," COMPARED WITH AN EIGHT-STORY BUILDING

to state the super-setting as an intention and to leave the technical problems of execution to a conveniently remote future.

Many Germans besides Linnebach have designed such stages, each with different mechanical means for setting, constructing, and shifting scenery. Frank Lloyd Wright and Norman-Bel Geddes have made complete architectural drawings for a series of modern theatres, every one an experiment in the construction of stage and auditorium, accurately projected to the last inch. But Craig, continually dogmatizing in regard to The Theatre and The Theatre of the Future, has not published an accurate drawing of a single playhouse. His only concrete project is for a long stairway entrance-hall of a theatre; he is concerned with it entirely as the pedestal for a fashion parade.

"I hope the ladies will agree with me that I have made it possible for quite a number of persons beautifully dressed to be seen at the same time. I can picture them passing up the staircase first showing the left side of the dress, then showing the back, then showing the right side of the dress, then they could turn round, and we could see the front part, then we should see the back again, then we should see the left side again, and then they would disappear. And as they passed up the steps they would be placed against that which is only a little less beautiful than they are, some golden statue or statue in ivory by a master, and these little golden and ivory statues would mark the different stages of their progress as they ascended and descended. . . . Ladies, I am entirely at your service."

Craig as usual gets no farther than the threshold. I venture to assert that he has not published the design for the interior of this or any other theatre because he has never clearly thought out the shapes and relation of the stage, auditorium, dressing-rooms, lighting apparatus, and scene-shifting equipment, nor been able to organize them about a definite type of production or direction. He reveals a tendency to dwell upon the inessential in theatre architecture, which produced the grand stairway of the Paris Opera House and those of a dozen other royal opera houses throughout Europe, studded with marble, if not ivory and gold, statuary.

Gordon Craig has spent a lifetime serving his apprenticeship, not in the sense of perfecting his art, but in achieving the most elementary understanding of the necessities of theatrical production which every beginner accepts and after a few years' work makes part of his daily routine. The sketches for *The Pretenders* at Copenhagen in 1926 are spread large on the pages of a *de luxe* portfolio. Here is elaborately recorded the fact that Craig at last understands that scenery must be moved swiftly if a production is to be successfully played. He discards one project for a ponderous church doorway because it "would have been a trouble to shift." He notes with satisfaction of other settings: "It took fifteen seconds to set"; "half a minute to set"; or was "taken off in a few moments." In every art theatre in Europe and America speed of scene-shifting is so much a prime element in determining any design that it is taken as a matter of course. It would not occur to any one but Craig, who still thinks of himself as the centre of the theatrical universe, to record his most elementary mistakes for the enlightenment of his contemporaries.

His general scheme, the unit set, has in one form or another been standard for more than forty years. Craig feels himself an innovator because his designs involve the casting of shadows as part of the accent and pattern of a scene and startle the Royal Theatre's chief electrician, who prides himself on having perfected lighting apparatus that removes every vestige of shadow from the stage—an ideal abandoned long since in every modern theatre of importance. The play of shadow in stage lighting is now so commonplace that no one thinks of commenting upon it as a novelty. Craig is astounded to see the columns of his church projected by the Linnebach lantern. "I had," he admits, "never used any projection by light on a great scale until then";

333

and he adds: "I was delighted to see with what precision these electrical apparatuses could project a design and how much more interesting it was as a light design than when painted." Germany had reached the same conclusion more than five years previously and had put no fewer than three separate systems of projecting scenery on the market. In 1921 I saw settings projected by light successfully used at the Stockholm Opera and the Stuttgart Theatre. They were already a common occurrence in other German playhouses. In 1922 I introduced the practice to America in *Back to Methuselah,* and later in *The Insect Comedy* and *From Morn to Midnight.* Craig cannot free himself from his congenital megalomania of believing that nothing exists until he perceives it and pontifically approves.

The *Pretenders* folio concludes with another summary of the needs of the ideal theatre, including such "novelties" as a director with moral courage, sound financial structure, and a permanent staff of administrators—trained actors, designers, costumers, electricians, and their technical assistants—as though theatres with precisely such organizations had not been in successful operation since 1870 at Meiningen and since 1890 in every important German state theatre and opera-house, in Reinhardt's, Stanislavsky's, and Meyerhold's organizations, and for briefer periods in Granville-Barker's in London, Copeau's in Paris, and at the Theatre Guild in New York for more than ten years. As a summarizing insight into the lesson of this production the reader is offered such truisms as "One works to find the most useful, not the most decorative scene—that scene most useful to the play and the players," and "The stage is a place to act in, not a picture to act against." Craig brought no new theatrical conception to the production; he reverted to a variation of the screens used in Moscow fifteen years previously. He brought no more knowledge of his craft to Copenhagen than he did to Moscow. The stage of the Danish Royal Theatre was conventionally but well equipped with the type of machinery used to modernize German stages between 1880 and 1900. In Poulsen, the director, Craig found a father-substitute who, according to Craig's own account, foresaw all difficulties, acted as a buffer for every personal contact, and was largely responsible for the success of the performance because both he and his large technical staff took the entire burden of execution off Craig's shoulders. Craig the self-acclaimed leader had to be led; the director who was to change the theatre's destiny was himself directed.

The instability of Craig's mind, its fundamental lack of integrity, has prevented his work from acquiring that indubitable unity of style which marks the work of every great artist. Its lack was never more evident than in his designs for *Macbeth,* which he sent to this country to be lighted and painted by others. What artist with the least pretensions to being the creator of a unique kind of stage setting could have treated his ideas as so much merchandise, like a barbed-wire fence or a chicken-coop, sent out by a mail-order house to be unwrapped and erected by the ultimate consumer? Any one who knows the theatre knows that it is the one place where there is always the maximum opportunity for the proverbial slip because so many disparate motions of speech, pantomime, scenery, electric light, animate human beings, and inanimate objects must be completely co-ordinated in a single rhythm. The greatest directors cannot always avoid the slip that spells failure, even after months of planning and weeks of rehearsal. But Craig, with a reputation so hedged from contact with the world that it has acquired an air of divinity in his own eyes, could not risk failure. He remained in Europe and allowed *Macbeth* to proceed to inevitable fiasco, as ghastly a travesty of an artist's intentions as the modern theatre has ever witnessed.

But with every allowance for loss of quality due to slipshod execution and divided responsibility, the complete failure of the production was due to the fact that as a conception it had no unity. It was, like Craig's books, a medley of methods, a hodge-podge of guesses. One scene was excellent school of Reinhardt. Because of Craig's inability to think in terms of actual spatial relationships, another scene was played on a stone bridge as squat as the rural bridges one finds spanning a weedy stream in Sussex. The distant castle that was to be seen first almost as a mirage was suggested on a back-drop in the usual grand-opera manner and seemed a picture postcard. Back-drops flapped down stage to cover scene-shifts. Interiors were painted canvas that might have been taken from Henry Irving's or Augustin Daly's storehouse. Macbeth's costume was a Norse warrior's that could be made by appropriating the bearskin on the hearth and tying it with thongs. It showed less capacity for improvisation than the costume sketches for the Duke of Saxe-Meiningen's production of *The Pretenders* in 1874. The banquet scene suggested an Italian fête on a decorated bridal chest of the cinquecento and repeated the banquet setting for Craig's production of *The Pretenders* at Copenhagen. The final scene at Copenhagen was also repeated, formal terraced steps bounded by a straggling rustic fence. The one setting that had any tragic intensity was the interior of Banquo's castle, for which Craig reverted to his formula of screens, originally destined to save the theatre, which here could not be used consistently enough to stylize a single play. After such an exhibition of artistic incompetence the rest of Craig's career might very well have been silence. But he had been so successful in inculcating the doctrine that scenic art is too noble, lofty, and mysterious to be capable of execution that his disciples welcomed another demonstration of the inevitable martyrdom of the artist touched with divinity, in the theatre tainted with original sin.

6. THE ROMANTIC ILLUSTRATOR

Craig's partisans defend his importance by declaring with Glenn Hughes that his drawings "are consciously ideal, and their purpose is not to provide working plans for stage-craftsmen of the world, but to instruct them in the principles of design . . . although they are intended chiefly to inspire, most of the designs can be realized literally in a certain kind of theatre—one whose stage is sufficiently large and adaptable." It is evident, I think, from the model made for *Macbeth,* that an ideal stage large and flexible enough to handle Craig's scenery would be not an expression of a purified theatre but a gigantic monument to present-day engineering, a stage that would exaggerate the need for ponderous, costly, and complicated machinery, and, instead of liberating theatre art, chain it irretrievably to mechanism. But even if one looks at Craig's designs apart from any questions of execution, purely as ideals, as embodiments of the principles of design, as sources of inspiration, it should be apparent that they are nothing more than the irresponsible improvisations of a romantic water-colourist. These designs are based not upon principles, but upon the repetition of a few grandiose proportions; the pictorial ideal that they are supposed to inspire is irrelevant to the essential purpose of dramatic production.

So many forms of liberation have now become romantic that it is difficult to isolate the pictorial equivalents of the romantic mood. Santayana has perhaps best suggested its essential component as one that makes us "feel the magic of strangeness and distance" and gives us "a certain sense of homelessness in a chaotic world." The magic of distance that awakes this feeling of isolation is in itself a product of the combined glamour and pathos that distance evokes. Any past becomes romantic when we view it consciously through the mist of time and remind ourselves that if we thrust out a hand we rend a magic veil and lose what we reach for. Remoteness is inherent in romantic forms; they are never too clearly defined, their edges are blurred by dawn or dusk or are given an imposing scale by the larger erasures that night can make. Romantic abodes are not constructed, they arise; they are not grounded in a manual world but are called forth and are easily dissolved into silhouettes. Even the stone pile of a cathedral becomes tracery and is buttressed by its shadows.

The romantic attitude breeds the cult of the picturesque, whose devotees see the Middle Ages as the Dark Ages, find the beauty of classic antiquity most easily in its dilapidated monuments, prize an ancient bronze because of its accidental patina, prefer everything to be weather-beaten or tarnished by use. Thus relics and fragments come to be recognized as romantic in themselves and a fallen temple or a ruined castle is felt to be appropriate to a romantic landscape. Because the romantic soul is a homeless soul it has so often found refuge in gloomy woods and shadowy thickets, grottoes and caves, barren heaths and lonely stretches of sea-coast, that we now identify these sites as typically romantic places. A suggestion of decay and disintegration tinges the romantic palette. To flirt with death is a form of romantic gallantry, and a well-arranged rendezvous with death is as fitting a form of consummation as finding one's true love. In a truly romantic love-story suicide is always an alternative to passion.

Much of the strangeness and mystery of death lurks in the shadows of the romantic world. By the preference of its poets it is sheltered from the sun and they feel their most direct contact with its significance not at noon but at night, when graves yawn, spirits rise, ghosts walk, witches dance on the Brocken, a poodle turns into the Devil, a raven croaks "Nevermore!" The favourite time for romantic meditation is near midnight, when a clock striking the hour, chimes sounding from a belfry, or a stranger knocking at the gate send forth ominous reverberations. The chiaroscuro of the romantic's vision is created by constantly juxtaposing life and the shadow of death, by contrasting the pulse of living with the paraphernalia of doom—the skull on the study table, the funeral urn under the flowering laurel, love among the ruins, in a churchyard, in a forsaken garden. The supernatural creatures of romantic imagination live in gloom, arise out of vapours, vanish in smoke. Its gods exist in a Norse or a Celtic twilight. The romantic young lady sighs behind drawn curtains and her disappointed lover cries that life is a dream.

The glamour of Craig's drawings is due to their graphic qualities, which can arouse a purely romantic mood. They are not visions of a new theatre where the conflicts of life can be intensified but project instead some of the loveliest refuges ever offered to the typically furtive, romantic soul. The poetry of Craig's designs is a survival of the poetry of the mauve decade, the 1890's, an echo of the deliberately exquisite and tenuous cadences of Yeats's *Shadowy Waters,* Verlaine's *Fêtes Galantes,* Dowson's *Pierrot of the Minute.* Craig's palaces and porticos need to be peopled with actors like Verlaine's maskers in *Clair de Lune:*

> *. . . delicate and dim*
> *That play on lutes and dance and have an air*
> *Of being sad in their fantastic trim.*

> *The while they celebrate in minor strain*
> *Triumphant love, effective enterprise,*
> *They have an air of knowing all is vain,—*
> *And through the quiet moonlight their songs rise . . .*

The light suffusing Craig's settings is, like Verlaine's moonlight and Mallarmé's mistress, *triste et beau*—beautiful and sad. As on Yeats's *Shadowy Waters* it seems to

> *. . . have fallen in the dreams the ever-living*
> *Breathe on the burnished mirror of the world,*
> *And then smooth out with ivory hands and sigh.*

The light of day does not penetrate Craig's romantic world. A pale mixture of dawn and dusk seems to have taken its place. Everything is hushed; a footfall would make no sound; the shock of dramatic conflict has no place here. Craig's scenes seem ideal retreats for the new drama to those temperaments that instinctively recoil from the shock of action and experiment, for in them, as in a romantic grotto, they can mope and moon and vicariously rest their tired wills and tired eyes. In the diaphanous distances and veiled heights of Craig's sketches they recover a sense of the freedom that they cannot win for themselves. The homeless soul recognizes itself in the human figures who move among towering forms that are not oppressive because they have no weight or substance. Nothing is decisive; every contour is slightly softened. The walls of Macbeth's castle are not stone or plaster that could support itself erect for any length of time. They are made of compressed snow. Everywhere a too solid world seems about to thaw and resolve itself into dew. Contemplating it, a certain number of artists who would like to be revolutionaries without going into battle declare themselves to be inspired; and an equal number of theorists whose concepts are so vague that they have to be sheltered in a shadowy future declare that their ideas have been freed from bondage to the past.

Craig's drawing for *Julius Caesar,* Act II, Scene 2, is a perfect Whistler nocturne. Its beauty is a film applied, like the dusk that clothed the Thames water-side with poetry. As a water-colour sketch it is a subtle rendering of a Florentine campanile at twilight. As a setting it would be an appropriate asylum for a monk or a recluse. It is absurd as a background that should heighten the mood in which Caesar declares his determination to unmask the face of danger.

> *Caesar shall forth; the things that threatened me*
> *Ne'er looked but on my back; when they shall see*
> *The face of Caesar, they are vanished.*

What Craig has dramatized is not the psychic atmosphere of the scene but its physical atmosphere, and he has pictured night in so lyric a fashion that it becomes useless as an interpretative background. This Florentine night would be expressive only if Caesar sighed and swooned. The silvery temptress beckoning Hamlet proved to be hokum in the Moscow Art Theatre because it was an attempt to foist upon profound tragedy the romantic imagery of the 1840's, including Undine and shadows that rippled like water. As Stanislavsky pointed out, Craig's conceptions cannot be realized by theatrical means. But even if Prospero could rear them before our eyes they would be irrelevant to the dramas for which they were intended. For the poetry of abiding drama is robust; its aim is not to make reality a dream but to imbue a dream with reality, to make even a legendary past so immediate that we are drawn into it and live it again as our own. The romantic qualities of Craig's scenic sketches can express romance everywhere except on the stage, for the theatre is the one place where the past does not become romantic in the sense of being remote, but as soon as it is made dramatic, takes on actuality. Both the scale and the tonalities of Craig's drawings, could they be made part of stage settings, would not liberate the theatre but would consign it to limbo.

The veiled distances of Craig's theatre are meant to catch whispers or to echo songs but not to back the assertions of speech. These vaults could hold cascades of sound. These vast spaces can best be paced to the rhythm of music. Their grandeur would be most appropriate for grand opera. Craig's first productions were for opera—Händel's *Acis and Galatea,* Purcell's *Dido and Aeneas,* and *A Masque of Love.* His greatest mistake has perhaps been that he forsook the field of opera for that of spoken drama. He often looks to opera for his models. His project for *Macbeth,* over which such to-do has been made because it calls for the entire play to be performed up and down a rock capped by clouds and swathed in mist, is borrowed from Appia's drawing and description of the Walkyries' crag where Wotan casts his spell and Brünnhilde falls into an enchanted sleep. The gigantic rose-trellis intended to screen the opening scene of *Caesar and Cleopatra,* if used there, would have no dramatic value whatever. But how fitting it would be to hide a slightly corpulent prima donna singing *Aïda!* The rectangular alley for *Macbeth,* Act II, Scene 1, needs only to be sealed with a slab in order to make it a tomb where Aïda and Rhadames could die in unison.

Craig has a very feeble plastic imagination. Speaking of a setting as "a world to walk in and out of," he writes: "Theoretically, ruined architecture would always be better for the actor than a perfect palace, because when a building is ruined it becomes more dramatic, less stilted, and you can see right through two, three, or four rooms and five passages to the furthest wall." The idea of the advantages of arches seen in perspective is borrowed from Serlio's Renaissance treatise— "Therefore choose or make houses which show well, as an open gallery or lodge [loggia] through which you may see another house." But Craig's feeling that ruins are dramatic is a characteristically romantic attitude. Because he cannot compose in three dimensions nor conceive architecture except in pictorial terms, the grandiose quality of his drawings is obtained by a monotonous repetition of height, until a human being becomes a lonely and romantic figure winding his way round billowing draperies five times his bulk, and under walls ten and twenty times his height. In a sketch for *Caesar and Cleopatra,* Cleopatra's "dear little kitten of a Sphinx" is so inflated that Cleopatra is herself reduced to the insignificance of a kitten climbing the trunk of an elephant. The comic intimacy of the scene that follows, when Caesar finds her lying asleep between the statue's paws, would be lost in such a monument. How is the mood of satiric comedy intensified by proportions so colossal?

In commenting on another design for the same play, Craig declares that the moment he thinks of the scene it makes him think of the actor. But it is the actor whom Craig cannot keep in mind for five consecutive minutes. Once he takes his pencil in hand, his romantic itch to achieve a grandiose effect gets the better of him. What reason is there to suppose that an actor can be helped to dominate a scene by being invariably reduced to the size of a fly on a window-pane, or that a repertory of drama can be served by engulfing human beings? An infinitely greater variety of forms is needed in order to dramatize action—the oppressiveness of horizontal masses as well as the release of vertical ones, corners where the actor can be caught and hemmed in, low windows and squat arches that emphasize his human scale instead of immense portals that continually dwarf him. Craig has almost no conception of the variety of plastic relationships that can be established between an actor and his environment. His mind being essentially rhetorical, his drawings get their effect by repeating a single trick of exaggerated emphasis.

The comparatively few designs of Craig that have enough inherent structure to be used on a stage, like his screens, are borrowed from scenic ideas that have already been used in the theatre. The model for *Hamlet* shows the most striking analogy to Sabbattini's seventeenth century perspective diagram of how to make a junction of streets. (See page 504.) The celebrated spiral staircase for *Macbeth* echoes the essential forms of one of Appia's earliest drawings, made for *Tristan and Isolda* in 1896. (See page 506.) Craig is important as an innovator only in so far as he succeeds in being an imitator. Most of his supposedly daring innovations repeat what has already been done. *Towards a New Theatre,* published in 1913, contains three "moods," sketches of a stairway on which three brief moments of a dance take place. But in 1910 at Munich I saw Reinhardt stage *Lysistrata* on a single stairway that stretched across the entire stage and play most of *Hamlet* around a single column that was dramatically effective although it was not thirty feet in diameter nor one hundred feet high. How limited Craig's architectonic imagination is, can be readily seen

343

by comparing the limited number of his variations of plinths and pilasters with the progressive variety of Norman-Bel Geddes' purely architectural compositions for *Joan of Arc, Lazarus Laughed,* and Dante's *Divine Comedy.* The truth is that had Craig's drawings been originally published as illustrations to a *de luxe* edition of any volume of romantic poems, no one would have suspected that they had any connection with the theatre. They have no vital connection with the theatre, despite the fact that they were printed with pretentious comment that attempted to prove them a new form of theatre art.

Craig's original ideal of the theatre, which once created such a stir, is also a typically romantic refuge, so remote that its drama becomes nothing more than an agglomeration of mute shapes and shadowy movements. "The über-marionette will not compete with life—rather will it go beyond it. Its ideal will not be the flesh and blood but rather the body in trance—it will aim to clothe itself with a death-like beauty while exhaling a living spirit." "If the form be that of the living, on account of its beauty and tenderness, the colour for it must be sought from that unknown land of the imagination, and what is that but the land where dwells that which we call Death?" These are the typical vapourings of a wounded romantic who flirts with the thought of dissolution and suicide. They revive the greensickness of the romantic movement, the sentimental morbidity of the 1840's when with pallid brow, in a darkened room, the truly poetic wept inconsolably for a dead love and renounced the light of day. How could Craig ever have been expected to lead the way in the theatre, which is eternally dedicated to affirming the significance of life even under the shadow of catastrophe? Of that essential affirmation from which drama springs Craig knows nothing.

7. THE ROMANTIC ACTOR

Craig is essentially an actor. He began his career as a minor member of Irving's company in 1889 and remained there for eight years without distinguishing himself, despite Irving's friendliness and the additional advantage of being Ellen Terry's son. Craig never recovered from the chagrin of that first failure. His later career in its totality is a compensation for a youthful defeat. His books, pamphlets, drawings, are all moments in a successful impersonation. Craig has not been a creative artist; instead he has acted the rôle of the unappreciated genius as conceived in the romantic manner of *La Vie de Bohême* or *Trilby,* complete even to the cape, and so well acted that a comfortable villa in Italy was made to seem as pathetic as a chilly garret. Craig's victories are all verbal. Nothing was proved but everything was made plausible. He has dramatized his disappointments as part of an unhappy love-affair with the theatre, making his points in tirades played to the gallery scattered across two continents. Despite his incompetence as an artist, Craig, because of his ability as an actor, has succeeded in imposing himself as an artist-hero.

The kind of theatre that Craig instinctively admires is the old-fashioned theatre, and the kind of acting which thrills him is not some new and purer form of the art, but old-fashioned acting with all its virtuosity and sure-fire tricks. There were signs of this as early as 1908, in one of the first numbers of *The Mask,* when he allowed John Balance—probably a pseudonym for himself—to say:

In Sarah Bernhardt we have the perfect actress. She seems to have set out to become perfect in her work and we find she has accomplished the task. This can be said of no other woman upon the stage, and, now that Irving is no more, it can be said of no man. Therefore she stands alone in being alone able of all living persons to give a perfect exhibition of acting.

345

Craig's enthusiasm for the bravura of a star actor ignores every new standard that he tried to set up as a theorist and reformer, because his theories were thrown off from the top of his mind; they never engaged his emotions. What he writes of Irving's Lyceum comes from the core of his temperament. In his biography of Henry Irving, Craig at the age of sixty speaks like a stage-struck youngster. His idolatry of Irving becomes hysterical. Irving did not walk, he danced. He did not speak, he sang. His movements were dances perfectly fitted to the language of Shakespeare. Irving, Craig is certain, never failed to feel regret that his actors were flesh and blood and not puppets. "Irving was the nearest thing ever known to . . . the Uber-marionette."

Craig writes as though the theatre had never developed during the last fifty years, as though it had never evolved a conception of production in which acting is not an exhibition but one element in the organization of all the elements of a performance so complete that the total result has the unity of a work of art. Craig, the seer, acclaims the value of the melodramatic claptrap that can serve as a vehicle for a star and reprints the last act of *The Bells!*

The biography is less valuable for its picture of Henry Irving than for the clew it gives to Craig's divided loyalties. Craig is the son of Edward William Godwin, an architect and on occasion a stage-designer, one of Ellen Terry's husbands. But by a curious short-circuiting of mental associations, which is not uncommon, Henry Irving becomes Craig's father-image and imposes himself as the archetype of everything supreme in the theatre, a lawgiver, a demigod. As the younger man matures he feels the natural impulse to resist Irving's authority and to assert his own, and then finds himself in the predicament that invariably confronts the ambitious son of a famous father: the son is impelled to rival his father, to excel him if possible, but feels no confidence that he can do so. The contradictions and vagaries of Craig's theories of the theatre result from transferring this conflict to an ideal theatre and finding an outlet there for his struggle with a father-image. The ideal theatre has not a living actor in it! Irving is killed in effigy. The supermarionette is born of Craig's desire to revenge himself on the actor who haunts him and to avenge his own mediocrity as a mime. There can never be another Irving to do what Craig could not do. There can never again be a young actor who will suffer as Craig suffered. The actorless theatre is not ideal for the rest of mankind, but it is for Craig, for Craig can rule it more absolutely than Irving ruled the Lyceum. "Irving in his theatre was what Napoleon was in the midst of his army. Irving was sole ruler of the Theatre of England, from 1871 till his death." Craig will be an even more absolute monarch than Irving, for even Irving had to wait upon the playwright, and Craig bans even this source of possible opposition. The ideal theatre will have for its plays pantomimes dictated by a tyrant, Craig himself, whose word is aesthetic law. He will be the sole ruler of the theatre of tomorrow and he constructs it so that the task will be easy; like a child in its nursery, he will rule over mechanical dolls.

But Craig is haunted by the memory of his deed, like the stage murderers in the melodramas which he so admires. It is not wholly an accident that one of the scenes he selects to reprint is from *The Bells*. Irving's memory continues to jangle in Craig's mind. His protestations that the moment he starts to design a scene he thinks of the actor, that he has never forgotten drama and dramatic moments, are all addressed to Irving's ghost. He abandons his original theories by way of penance; by way of atonement he will serve the actor, bring him into greater prominence than ever with spot-lights and screens.

But once in a theatre, the conflict reasserts itself. He threatens to throw Duse out of her own theatre. He dwarfs her with an enormous window. He dwarfs the actors in his drawings with the enormous height of his settings. His difficulties in getting to the point of accepting commissions and his difficulties in executing them, apart from his technical ignorance, arise from the fact that any director who controls a theatre becomes a substitute for Henry Irving, and Craig instinctively recoils from repeating the humiliation of his first unsuccessful apprenticeship. But once at work the buried loyalty reasserts itself; Craig becomes the beginner who is delighted by being praised in playing a small rôle to Irving's satisfaction. Stanislavsky and Poulsen become kindly mentors who encourage him, remind him that he is a great man, solve his problems for him, lead him to eminence. With extraordinary perversity Craig keeps himself in a state of technical ignorance so that this situation, which he dreads and yet at the same time desires, must be repeated every time he undertakes a production. But once the production is over he must compensate his sense of defeat and therefore calls the Moscow Art Theatre a little theatre and speaks of Stanislavsky as his assistant. However, for the Copenhagen production of *The Pretenders,* Craig originally planned to do no more than a few scenes and stage-manage one. It was difficult to persuade him to undertake the entire production. "I was happy to be an assistant," he writes for the first time. But he does not dedicate his memorial volume to Poulsen, who carried him through the production, but to an actual monarch, Christian X of Denmark. And in the same year he makes his final obeisance to the Napoleon of the Lyceum Theatre by publishing a eulogy of Irving which ignores or negates every theory of the theatre that Craig had spent a lifetime promulgating as gospel.

The shock of another early defeat completed Craig's introversion, when his productions of Purcell and Händel failed to bring the English public to his feet as Irving had done when he first appeared in *The Bells.* Craig's subsequent laziness is neurotic in origin, the sensitiveness of a grown man who at heart remains a favourite child after the shock of an early defeat when he cannot, at the first blow, reduce the world to the status of an admiring father and a doting mother. He continues to demand the equivalent of a mother's love or a father's admiration, which a sceptical world usually fails to provide for self-acclaimed genius. In self-defence a flight from reality begins, a morbid fear of failure develops, and the mind, with the cunning of an armourer, forges a protective cuirass of soundly riveted reasons for a will afraid to meet the test of combat. In Craig's case this process of rationalizing fear took the form of extravagant demands: he must have fantastic sums of money; he must first have a specially constructed theatre, also requiring a fortune to build, before he could start; he must be treated as a dictator or a king before giving the first sign of what he proposed to do; he must have a school where he could, for years if necessary, train his company and his technical assistants to carry out his ideas. No one else alive was fitted for that esoteric task. In one way or another the event was postponed and Craig's pretensions escaped being put to the test. Is it wholly an accident that Steichen's celebrated photograph of Craig shows him huddled in a cape, apparently on the point of furtively stealing from the room?

That Craig is neurotic is in itself no indictment of his capacities. An artist has been defined as a neurotic who continually cures himself with his art. But Craig has never been able to cure himself; his inhibitions block the true development of his ideas and prevent him from dominating his material. Both Craig's theories of theatre art and his actual practice of it are irrelevant to the theatre's growth, because they do nothing more than dramatize a flight from the realities of life and the actualities of the stage. His conception of the purity of theatrical art is vitiated by a kind of impotent gentility, the gentility of persons whose ideal of love is so pure that they cannot risk the dissatisfactions of a mundane love-affair, remain pure because they evade any purification that passion can bring, and then, as middle-aged celibates, use their sterile purity as a standard by which to test the passions of others. Like Craig they invent new calendars of sin. Had Craig even been able to accept the discipline of experience and work with one director continuously for five or ten years, his drawings for stage-settings that had vindicated themselves often enough before an audience would possess a beauty far more significant than those which he has already bequeathed with such a grandiloquent gesture to posterity. Craig's work is immature because it has never outgrown the mentality of childhood in which it was originally conceived, where wish and will are identified in the magic satisfactions of day-dreaming. Ideas and ideals, however noble in intention, are wasted in the theatre unless they can be treated as so much raw material to be refined in the crucible of experiment. No artist has ever served the theatre who did not possess the unaffected humility of a workman. Craig has no place in a living theatre of today or tomorrow because the theatre continues to live by remaining a workshop.

CHAPTER IV

AESTHETIC PRINCIPLES:
THE IDEAS OF ADOLPHE APPIA

I. MUSIC AS LAWGIVER

A PASSIONATE Wagnerite, music was to Appia, as to Pater, the ideal art to whose condition all the other arts aspired. He found in Wagner's music-dramas of the Niebelungen hoard the key to the scenic artist's liberation. As a philosopher Appia longed for the consolation of the Absolute and found it in a new kind of operatic score, a novel cohesion of music and dialogue; once its secrets had been penetrated, its musical intervals, tonalities, and rhythms deeply felt, these could supply an unerring clew to their scenic interpretation, determining not only the form of the stage-setting itself but the movements of actors within it down to the smallest detail of stage business and the fluctuations of light that illuminated them. As an artist Appia found release in music because its emphasis was emotional rather than factual and so supplied a norm which an artist could approximate until his settings were equally expressive. Stage pictures were to be freed from the necessity of reproducing backgrounds of action; they were to be transfigured until every element in them embodied the emotions that it was to arouse as an integral part of its form, its colour, and its total design. *Ausdruckskraft*—the force of expression, expressiveness—was one of Appia's favourite terms, and became the corner-stone on which most of the later doctrines of theatrical expressionism were reared. "Music finds its ultimate justification in our hearts," he wrote, using that traditional term to summarize the emotional core of our being, "and this occurs so directly, that its expression is thereby impalpably hallowed. When stage pictures take on spatial forms dictated by the rhythms of music they are not arbitrary but on the contrary have the quality of being inevitable."

The theories that elucidated the basic aesthetic principles of modern stage design, analyzed its fundamental technical problems, outlined their solution, and formed a charter of freedom under which scenedesigners still practise, appeared in two volumes under two quasimusical titles: *La Mise en Scène du Drame Wagnérien* (*The Staging of Wagner's Music-dramas*) and *Die Musik und die Inscenierung* (*Music and Stage-Setting*). The first was published in Paris in 1895 as an inconspicuous brochure of fifty-one pages, the second as a full-sized volume, translated from a French script, in Munich in 1899. Neither was ever widely enough read to warrant reprinting, nor has either ever been translated, a fact which immensely aided Gordon Craig in imposing himself as a prophet on the English and American theatre. Both the book and the booklet are now so difficult to procure that they have become collector's items. But their influence was immediately felt, for Appia was that rare combination, a creative artist of exceptional imagination and at the same time a rigorously logical theorist. Many of his ideas are blurred by an appallingly clumsy German translation, which, like most philosophical German, straddles ideas, so that catching their meaning becomes rather like trying to hold a greased pig running between one's legs. Fortunately *Music and Stage-Setting* contained eighteen illustrations of projected settings for Wagner's operas, which embodied Appia's aesthetic principles with such finality that they became a revelation of a totally new kind of stage-setting and stage lighting, then as strange as the outlines of a newly discovered continent at dawn and now so familiar. These drawings revealed a unity and a simplicity that could be made an inherent part of stage-settings in a way that no one had hitherto conceived, Wagner least of all. Practitioners of stage-craft were converted by a set of illustrations to a gospel which most of them never read.

There is in Appia much of the *Schwärmerei* typical of German music, and at times a mouth-filling grandiloquence, a bewildering mixture of philosophic concepts such as "inner reality" and the transcendentalism of German metaphysics, expressed in romantic and mystic imagery (also typically Teutonic) used to beatify Art, Nature, and the Poet. Art is an inner something, eternal, ultimate, hidden behind appearance, another *Ding an sich,* which only a particular kind of poet, like Wagner the creator of music-drama, can clothe with meaning. The demands of Music become a kind of categorical imperative which, if obeyed, will lead to the universal laws of the universal work of art:

The loftiest expression of the Eternal in Man can only be reborn and forever renew itself in the lap of Music. In return Music demands that we have implicit faith in her. . . . This book was written in the service of Music and for such a mistress no experiment is irrelevant, no labor too great. . . . In order to express the inner reality underlying all phenomena the poet renounces any attempt to reproduce their fortuitous aspects; and once this act of renunciation has taken place the complete work of art arises. . . . Then Wagner appeared. At the same time that his music-dramas revealed a purely expressive form of art, they also confirmed, what we had hitherto dimly sensed, the omnipotent power of music. . . .

Music and music alone can co-ordinate all the elements of scenic presentation into a completely harmonious whole in a way which is utterly beyond the capacity of our unaided imagination. Without music the possibility of such harmony does not exist and therefore cannot be discovered. . . .

353

Music-drama will become the focus for all our highest artistic accomplishments and will concentrate them like rays of light converging through a lens.

Such prophecies and pronunciamentos resound through Appia's theories, at times with Wagnerian sonority. There are times also when his theories seem the scenario for another music-drama in which the artist-hero, guided by the goddess of Music, will wrest a treasure from its crabbed guardians, not a cursed treasure but a beneficent one whose magic touch is capable of transfiguring not only the artist but the theatre and all the world. Two thirds of *Music and Stage-Setting* are devoted to a lengthy speculation on the future of music-drama. Appia accepts Bayreuth as the ultimate expression of German culture, indulges in an elaborate analysis of French culture, shows how German music can arouse the religious nature of French musicians, how the French artist's sensitiveness to essential form can wean Germans from their instinctive dependence on realism. At Bayreuth, in an international poet's Elysium, the two nations are to conduct jointly a presumably endless cycle of music-dramas which will carry Wagner's original inspiration to the expressionistic heights implicit in his music.

At the same time Appia shows a thoroughly Gallic capacity for objective analysis, which he uses to explain the aesthetic problems of the scene-designer and the technical means available for solving them. Here with amazing directness and clarity he dissects the plastic elements of the stage picture. In doing so he anticipates in detail the present technical basis of stage lighting and outlines precisely the way it has since been used, not only as an indispensable means of unifying stage settings, by suggesting mood and atmosphere, but also as a method of emphasizing the dramatic values of a performance and heightening our emotional response to them. The first hundred and twenty pages of Appia's volume are nothing less than the textbook of modern stage-craft that gave it both a new method of approaching its problems and a new solution.

2. THE PLASTIC ELEMENTS

The aesthetic problem of scenic design, as Appia made plain, is a plastic one. The designer's task is to relate forms in space, some of which are static, some of which are mobile. The stage itself is an enclosed space. Organization must be actually three-dimensional. Therefore the canons of pictorial art are valueless. The painted illusion of the third dimension, valid in the painted picture where it can evoke both space and mass, is immediately negated when it is set on a stage where the third dimension is real.

The plastic elements involved in scenic design, as Appia analyzed them, are four: perpendicular painted scenery, the horizontal floor, the moving actor, and the lighted space in which they are confined. The aesthetic problem, as he pointed out, is a single one: How are these four elements to be combined so as to produce an indubitable unity? For, like the Duke of Saxe-Meiningen, he was aware that the plastic elements of a production remained irretrievably at odds if left to themselves. Looking at the stages about him he saw that the scene-painter of his day merely snipped his original picture into so many pieces which he stood about the stage, and then expected the actor to find his way among them as best he could. The painted back-drop was the only part of an ensemble of painted scenery that was not a ludicrous compromise. Naturally the scene-painter was interested, being a painter, in presenting as many stretches of unbroken canvas as possible. Their centre of interest was about midway between the top of the stage and the stage floor at a point where, according to the line of sight of most of the audience, they attained their maximum pictorial effect. But the actor works on the stage floor at a point where painted decorations are least effective as painting. So long as the emphasis of stage setting is on painted decoration, the inanimate picture is no more than a coloured illustration into which the text, animated by the actor, is brought. The two collide, they never meet nor establish any interaction of the slightest dramatic value, whereas, in Appia's phrase, they should be fused.

"Living feet tread these boards and their every step makes us aware of how meaningless and inadequate our settings are." The better the scenery is as painting, the worse it is as a stage setting; the more completely it creates an illusion of the third dimension by the pictorial conventions of painting, the more completely an actually three-dimensional actor destroys that illusion by every movement he makes. "For no movement on the actor's part can be brought into vital relation with objects painted on a piece of canvas." Painted decorations are not only at odds with the actor but also with the light that illuminates them. "Light and vertical painted surfaces nullify rather than reinforce each other. . . . There is an irreconcilable conflict between these two scenic elements. For the perpendicular, painted flat in order to be seen, needs to be set so as to catch a maximum amount of light." The more brilliantly it is lighted, the more apparent the lack of unity between it and the actor becomes. "If the setting is so placed as to refract some of the light thrown on it its importance as a painted picture is diminished to that extent."

For Appia there was no possibility of compromise by keeping actors away from perspective back-drops where doors reached only to their elbows, or by warning them not to lean on flimsy canvas cut-outs down stage. He denied painted simulation of the third dimension a place in the theatre with a finality that gave his analysis the air of a revolutionary manifesto. He was the first to banish the scenic painter and his painted architecture from the modern stage. To Appia the actor was *massgebend*—the unit of measurement. Unity could be created only by relating every part of a setting to him. He was three-dimensional, therefore the entire setting would have to be made consistently three-dimensional. The stage setting could have no true aesthetic organization unless it was coherently plastic throughout. Appia's importance as a theorist is due to the consistency and the practicability of the methods he outlined for achieving this result.

One began to set a stage not in mid-air on hanging back-drops, but on the stage floor where the actor moved and worked. It should be broken up into levels, hummocks, slopes, and planes that supported and enhanced his movements. And these were again not to be isolated—a wooden platform draped with canvas here, a block or rock there, planted on a bare board floor, a "chaise-longue made of grass mats." The stage floor was to be a completely fused, plastic unit. Appia in this connection thinks in terms of sculpture. In order to make a model of a stage floor as he described it one would have to use clay. He considered the entire space occupied by a stage setting as a sculpturesque unit. The solidity achieved by setting wings at right angles to each other to imitate the corner of a building seemed to him feebly mechanical. He conceived much freer stage compositions where the entire area could be modelled as a balance of asymmetrical, spatial forms, a composition in three dimensions, that merged imperceptibly with the confining planes that bounded the setting as a whole.

Appia expressed in dogmatic form much of what the Duke of Saxe-Meiningen had demonstrated pragmatically. But in promulgating his theory of a stage setting he completed its unification by insisting on the plasticity of light itself, which no one before him had conceived. He demonstrated in detail, both as a theorist and as a draftsman, how stage lighting could be used and controlled so as to establish a completely unified three-dimensional world on the stage. Appia distinguishes carefully between light that is empty, diffuse radiance, a medium in which things become visible, as fish do in a bowl of water, and concentrated light striking an object in a way that defines its essential form. Diffused light produces blank visibility, in which we recognize objects without emotion. But the light that is blocked by an object and casts shadows has a sculpturesque quality that by the vehemence of its definition, by the balance of light and shade, can carve an object before our eyes. It is capable of arousing us emotionally because it can so emphasize and accent forms as to give them new force and meaning. In Appia's theories, as well as in his drawings, the light which in paintings had already been called dramatic was for the first time brought into the theatre, where its dramatic values could be utilized. Chiaroscuro, so controlled as to reveal essential or significant form, with which painters had been preoccupied for three centuries, became, as Appia described it, an expressive medium for the scene-designer. The light that is important in the theatre, Appia declares, is the light that casts shadows. It alone defines and reveals. The unifying power of light creates the desired fusion that can make stage floor, scenery, and actor one.

Light is the most important plastic medium on the stage. . . . Without its unifying power our eyes would be able to perceive what objects were but not what they expressed. . . . What can give us this sublime unity which is capable of uplifting us? Light! . . . Light and light alone, quite apart from its subsidiary importance in illuminating a dark stage, has the greatest plastic power, for it is subject to a minimum of conventions and so is able to reveal vividly in its most expressive form the eternally fluctuating appearance of a phenomenal world.

The light and shade of Rembrandt, Piranesi, Daumier, and Meryon was finally brought into the theatre as an interpretative medium, not splashed on a back-drop, as romantic scene-painters had used it, but as an ambient medium actually filling space and possessing actual volume; it was an impalpable bond which fused the actor, wherever and however he moved, with everything around him. The plastic unity of the stage picture was made continuous.

If one looks at reproductions of stage settings before Appia—and the history of stage setting might almost be divided by B.A. as history in general is divided by B.C.—they are filled with even radiance; everything is of equal importance. The stage is like a photograph of a toy theatre; the actors might be cardboard dolls. In Appia's drawings for the first time the stage is a microcosm of the world. It seems to move from "morn to noon, from noon to dewy eve," and on through all the watches of the night. And the actors in it seem living beings who move as we do from sunlight or moonlight into shadow. Beneath their feet there is not a floor but the surface of the earth, over their heads not a back-drop but the heavens as we see them, enveloping and remote. There is depth here that seems hewn and distance that recedes infinitely further than the painted lines converging at a mathematical vanishing point. In attacking the conventions of scene-painting Appia created an ultimate convention. For the transparent trickery of painted illusions of form he substituted the illusion of space built up by the transfiguration that light, directed and controlled, can give to the transient structures of the stage-carpenter. The third dimension, incessant preoccupation of the Occidental mind for four centuries, defined by metaphysicians, explored by scientists, simulated by painters, was re-created in terms of the theatre, made actual. The stage more completely than ever before became a world that we could vicariously inhabit; stage settings acquired a new reality. The light in Appia's first drawings, if one compares them to the designs that had preceded his, seems the night and morning of a First Day.

359

3. LIGHT AS THE SCENE-PAINTER

Light was to Appia the supreme scene-painter. "The poet-musician," he declared, "paints his picture with light." Although at one moment Appia announces that his book is dedicated to the service of the goddess of music, at another he says: "It is precisely the misuse of stage lighting with all its far-reaching consequences which has been the chief reason for writing this book in the first place. . . ."

Only light and music can express "the inner nature of all appearance." Even if their relative importance in music-drama is not always the same, their effect is very similar. Both require an object to whose purely superficial aspect they can give creative form. The poet provides the object for music, the actor, in the stage setting, that for light.

In the manipulations of light Appia found the same freedom that, in his eyes, music gave the poet. Light controlled and directed was the counterpart of a musical score; its flexibility, fluidity, and shifting emphasis provided the same opportunity for evoking the emotional values of a performance rather than the factual ones. As music released the mood of a scene, projecting the deepest emotional meaning of an event as well as its apparent action, so the fluctuating intensities of light could transfigure an object and clothe it with all its emotional implications.

Light with its infinite capacity for varying nuances was valuable to Appia for its power of suggestion, which has become for us the distinguishing mark of everything artistic. He points out how in *Das Rheingold* one can give the impression of water through the sensation of depth by keeping the stage dim, filling the scene with "a vague obscurity" where contours are not defined. For *Die Walküre* the open air will be felt only if the summit of a mountain detaches itself clearly against misty distances. The flames of the *Feuerzauber* are not to be continued an instant beyond the time allotted to them in the score. Their intensity will be emphasized by contrasting them with "a limpid night sky vaguely pierced by stars." The light in Alberich's cavern, which is illuminated by his forge, is to have an entirely different quality: "The general feeling given will be one of oppression and a lack of light. The proportions of the setting will contribute to this sense of oppressive weight. Reflections of spurts of flame will intermittently illuminate now this detail of the setting, now that one; and the setting itself, in blocking the source of light, will cast shadows that produce an ensemble chaotic in effect of which, it goes without saying, the personages in the scene will be a part." The *Waldweben* in *Siegfried* is to be accompanied by a wavering play of fluttering sunlight and leaf shadows. The forest is to be made with the barest indication of a few tree-trunks and branches. Siegfried will seem to be in a forest because he is tinged in the vaguely green suffusion of light filtering through leaves and bespattered with an occasional sun-spot. The audience will then see a wood even though it does not see all the trees.

The flexibility of stage lighting, as Appia envisaged it, relates it fundamentally to every movement that an actor makes; the whole setting by fluctuations of light and shade moves with him and follows the shifting dramatic emphasis of a particular scene or sequence of scenes. Appia shows how, in the first act of *Siegfried,* Hunding and Siegfried are to be alternately in light and shadow as their respective rôles become more or less important. And he points out also that any portion of a setting—a building, a tree, the background of a room—can actually be brought forth or wiped out as its dramatic importance in the scene increases or diminishes.

4. LIGHT AS INTERPRETER

Light in Appia's hands became a guiding principle for the designer, enabling him to give to a setting as the audience sees it the same reality that it is supposed to have for the actors in it. In an appendix to *Music and Stage-Setting* he shows in detail how the control of stage lighting makes this possible for a production of *Tristan and Isolda*.

Act II: As Isolda enters she sees only two things: the burning torch set as a signal for Tristan and enveloping darkness. She does not see the castle park, the luminous distance of the night. For her it is only horrible emptiness that separates her from Tristan. Only the torch remains irrefutably just what it is: a signal separating her from the man she loves. Finally she extinguishes it. Time stands still. Time, space, the echoes of the natural world, the threatening torch—everything is wiped out. Nothing exists, for Tristan is in her arms.

How is this to be scenically realized so that the spectator, without resorting to logical reasoning, without conscious mental effort, identifies himself unreservedly with the inner meaning of these events?

At the rise of the curtain a large torch, stage centre. The stage is bright enough so that one can recognize the actors clearly but not bright enough to dim the torch's flare. The forms that bound the stage are barely visible. A few barely perceptible lines indicate trees.

By degrees the eye grows accustomed to the scene. Gradually it becomes aware of the more or less distinct mass of a building adjoining the terrace. During the entire first scene Isolda and Brangäne remain on this terrace, and between them and the foreground one senses a declivity but one cannot determine its precise character. When Isolda extinguishes the torch the setting is shrouded in a half-light in which the eye loses itself.

Isolda is submerged in this whispering darkness as she rushes to

Tristan. During the first ecstasy of their meeting they remain on the terrace. At its climax they approach [the audience]. By almost imperceptible degrees they leave the terrace and by a barely visible flight of steps reach a sort of platform near the foreground. Then, as their desire appeases itself somewhat and only one idea unites them, as we grow more and more aware of the Death of Time, they finally reach the extreme foreground, where—we notice it for the first time—a bench awaits them. The tone of the whole secret, shadowy space surrounding them grows even more uniform; the forms of the terrace and the castle are submerged, even the different levels of the stage floor are hardly perceptible.

Whether because of the contrast of deepened darkness induced by extinguishing the torch, or perhaps because our eye has followed the path that Tristan and Isolda have just trod—however that may be, in any case we feel how softly they are cradled by every object about them. During Brangäne's song the light grows still dimmer; the bodily forms of the people themselves no longer have a distinct outline. Then (page 162, first ff, of the orchestra) suddenly a pale glimmer of light strikes the right side of stage rear: King Mark and his men-at-arms break in. Slowly the cold colourless light of day increases. The eye begins to recognize the main outlines of the stage setting and its colour begins to register in all its harshness. Then as Tristan with the greatest effort at self-mastery realizes that he is after all among the living, he challenges Melot to a duel.

In the setting, cold in colour, hard as bone, only one spot is shaded from the dawning day and remains soft and shadowy, the bench at the foot of the terrace.

This was written in 1899!

I know of no single document in the theatre's history that reveals more completely the rôle that creative imagination plays in staging a play nor one that demonstrates better how inevitably the imagination of a creative artist is specific and concrete. The passage, as well as its continuation and the similar analyses that follow it for the production of the *Ring of the Niebelungen,* are the measure of Appia's genius. In comparison Craig's dark hints and his windy pretensions show him, more than ever, to be an inflated talent. Appia can himself be windy in prognosticating the future of German and French music. But once he focuses upon the theatre he is the master and the master craftsman, completely aware of his methods and materials, certain of how they can be organized, certain too of their effect to the last detail. The semi-obscurity of this second act of Tristan is dictated by a vision where, as in the words of the stage-manager of Mons, all is clarity and light.

The chiaroscuro of Appia's drawings is shadowy like Craig's; its misty envelopments, its dissolving silhouettes and vaporous distances, are characteristically romantic. But this picturesque atmosphere is made an integral part of stage pictures that, instead of dwarfing the actor, are directly related to him as a human being. Despite the shadowy shapes around him the actor remains the centre of our interest, the focus of dramatic emphasis. Appia's stage pictures are not conceived as effects into which the actor is put; they spring from the actor and are complete expressions of his assumed personality and passions. Appia, designing for the opera, evolved a type of stage setting so compact, so directly related to the emotional flux of drama, that he anticipated the development of scenic design in the theatre. Craig, designing for the theatre of the future, made settings so emptily grandiose that they have no future place except in grand opera. Appia staged even fewer productions than Craig did. His contacts with the actual theatre were less frequent. But his sense of the theatre was so concrete, so technically true, that his drawings, like his stage-directions, were capable of being translated to a stage as soon as he had made them.

Light fluctuates in Appia's drawings as it does on the stage of a theatre; it fluctuates on stage settings today as it did in Appia's drawings, and gives to canvas forms just such simplifications of mass and outline as Appia indicated. At one moment or another the lighting of any modern production, whether Jones's *Richard III* or Geddes's *Hamlet,* Reinhardt's *Danton's Death* or Jessner's *Othello* (and I could add the names of a hundred others that I have seen as well as my own), are dramatized with light and shadow in ways that repeat, however much they may amplify, Appia's original methods and effects—the same use of shadows to dignify and to envelop form, to translate emotion into atmospheric moods, to define by suggesting. The modern stage is filled with the light that was always to be seen on land and sea but never in the theatre until Appia brought it there. Craig's belated attempt to emphasize the actor with light against an ambiguous neutral screen, the declaration of Arthur Kahane, Reinhardt's assistant, in 1919, "Lighting is the real source of decoration, its single aim being only to bring the important into light and leave the unimportant in shadow," do nothing more than paraphrase the ideas and the doctrines of Adolphe Appia.

Appia's light-plot is now an accepted part of every modern production. It parallels the plot of a play and is a visual comment upon it as continuous as a musical score. It is separately rehearsed, memorized by the stage-electrician, and is part of the stage-manager's prompt-book. The fewest of its changes are dictated by actual stage-directions, such as the extinguishing of a torch; the vast majority are an accompaniment to action and aim to emphasize the atmospheric qualities of a stage setting in a way that can project variations of dramatic mood and thereby intensify the emotional reaction of an audience.

Appia's supreme intuition was his recognition that light can play as directly upon our emotions as music does. We are more immediately affected by our sensitiveness to variations of light in the theatre than we are by our sensations of colour, shape, or sound. Our emotional reaction to light is more rapid than to any other theatrical means of expression, possibly because no other sensory stimulus moves with the speed of light, possibly because, our earliest inherited fear being a fear of the dark, we inherit with it a primitive worship of the sun. The association between light and joy, between sorrow and darkness, is deeply rooted and tinges the imagery of almost every literature and every religion. It shows itself in such common couplings as "merry and bright," "sad and gloomy." How much less lonely we feel walking along a country road in a pitch-black night when the distant yellow patch of a farm-house window punctures the darkness! The flare of a camp-fire in a black pine forest at night cheers us even though we are not near enough to warm our hands at it. The warmth of the sun or of a flame does of course play a large share in provoking the feeling of elation that light gives us. But the quality of light itself can suggest this warmth effectively enough to arouse almost the same mood of comfort and release, as when, after a dingy day of rain and mist, sunlight strikes our window-curtains and dapples the floor of our room.

Between these two extremes of flaming sun and darkness an immense range of emotion fluctuates almost instantly in response to variations in the intensity of light. The key of our emotions can be set, the quality of our response dictated, almost at the rise of the curtain by the degree and quality of light that pervades a scene. It requires many more moments for the words of the players or their actions to accumulate momentum and to gather enough import for them to awaken as intense and direct an emotional response. And as the action progresses our emotions can be similarly played upon. It was the singular limitation of Appia's temperament that he could find no basis for the interpretation of drama except that dictated by the tempo and timbre of a musical score. His imagination could be stimulated in no other way. But in indicating both theoretically and graphically the complete mobility of stage lighting he has made it possible for any play to be accompanied by a light-score that is almost as directly expressive as a musical accompaniment and can be made as integrally a part of drama as music was in Wagner's music-dramas.

5. LIGHT ORCHESTRATED

The amazingly concrete quality of Appia's vision is again made apparent by the fact that he predicted the present technical set-up of our stage lighting systems. With nothing more to guide him than the rudimentary systems of his day he understood their inadequacy. He divided light-sources on the stage into two systems—diffused or general light, which merely flooded the stage with an even radiance, called flood-lighting today, and focussed, mobile light, now known as spot-lighting. It was this almost neglected source of light which Appia pointed to as the important one.

Without doubt, as soon as scenery is no longer painted canvas set up in parallel rows, all lighting apparatus will be used in a radically different fashion from what it is today, but the basis of the construction will not change greatly. The mobile [spot-light] apparatus will be utilized to create plastic light and its mechanical perfection will have to be made the object of the most careful study. In conjunction with the more or less stationary flood-lighting apparatus, screens of varying degrees of opacity will be used; their purpose will be to soften the oversharp definition of light thrown by lamps on parts of the setting or on actors in close proximity to any particular light-source. But the major portion of the spot-lighting apparatus will be used to break up light and diversify its direction in every way possible. These lamps will be . . . of the greatest importance in maintaining the expressive effect of the total stage picture.

The development of stage lighting apparatus has followed Appia's prediction. For a while lamps were moved on bridges above the stage and literally followed the action of a play. But the spot-light has been perfected so that it can be equally mobile while its source remains fixed. Lenses of varying sizes—six or eight inches giving a varying maximum spread in combination with electric lamps of 250, 500 or 1,000 watts—are focussed to cover overlapping areas or concentrated into a "spot" the size of a face. Each is controlled by a separate dimmer that regulates its intensity over a range of a hundred fixed points varying from full to out. For a modern production as many as a hundred such spot-lights may be in use, each covering a particular area of the stage floor, hundreds of shafts of light criss-crossing from iron stanchions at each side of the stage, from one or more pipes overhead, casting funnels of light of different colours and intensity which the actor walks into or out of. They are in continual flux, ebbing and flowing, merging and separating, but always slowly and subtly enough so that there is never a jump by which a spectator can become directly aware of the changes that are imperceptibly taking place before his eyes. He feels their effect before he realizes that the changes have occurred.

A light-plot of this sort is separately rehearsed and is then known as a light-rehearsal. For a large production a rehearsal often takes several days of consecutive work that is an important part of a designer's job. Conducting a light-rehearsal is very like conducting an orchestra. Every lamp is a separate instrument carrying its own thread of symphonic effect, now carrying a theme, now supporting it. A certain proportion of these lamps are directed at scenery, part are concentrated on actors' faces. Appia insisted that the "plastic power of light" was as important for the actor as for the set. He inveighed against the flattening effect of footlights on actors' faces and ascribed the overloading of make-up to the fact that an even brilliance from below wiped out all expression from human features, whereas focussed light could model faces and carve expression into them like a sculptor. "But," he adds, "light will not be used merely to strengthen or to weaken the modelling of a face; rather it will serve to unite it or to isolate it from the scenic background, in a natural way, depending on whether the rôle of a particular actor dominates a scene or is subordinate to it."

At a light-rehearsal Appia's assertion holds true. Diffused light that merely shows a setting is, as he said, a simple matter. Plastic lighting that dramatizes its meaning is all-important and a matter of complex adjustments. "The difference in intensity between the two kinds of light must be great enough in order to make shadows perceptible; above this minimum an infinite variety of relationship is possible." It is this infinite variety, this continually shifting balance between light-sources, which occupy hours of experiment at light-rehearsals.

6. LIGHT AS SCENE-BUILDER

Appia even envisaged one of the most recent developments of stage lighting—the projected scenery that Craig was astounded to discover at Copenhagen.

Light can be coloured, either by its own quality or by coloured glass slides; it can project pictures, of every degree of intensity, varying from the faintest blurred tonalities to the sharpest definition. Although both diffused and concentrated [spot] light need an object to focus on, they do not change its character; the former makes it more or less perceptible, the latter more or less expressive. Coloured light in itself changes the colour of pigments that reflect it, and by means of projected pictures or combinations of coloured light can create a milieu on the stage or even actual things that before the light was projected, did not exist.

Light became for Appia not only a scene-painter but a scene-builder.

The stage setting will no longer be as now a combination of right-angled flats ... but will rather be arranged for a specific purpose, a combination of varying planes extending into space. This principle gives colour an entirely new meaning; it no longer needs to embody any specific thing on a flat stretch of canvas or to create a factitious reality; it becomes "colour in space," capable of reconciling and combining all the elements of a setting into a simplified whole. ...

These continually changing combinations of colour and form, changing in relation to each other and also to the rest of the stage-setting, provide opportunities for an infinite variety of plastic combinations. They are the palette of the poet-musician.

They are the palette and the chisel of scene-designers today. Appia's vision has made even the third dimension itself completely flexible on the stage. Space is no longer absolute. Distance, as far as the eye of the spectator is concerned, can be created as effectively by the different intensities of intersecting volumes of light as by actual spacing measured in feet. An actor stepping from a brilliant funnel of light into half-shadow may recede far more perceptibly than if he walked fifteen feet up stage through even radiance. The sky beyond the platform of Elsinore can be infinitely remote although it may be almost within reach of Hamlet's outstretched hand at the rampart's rim. Light can contract the deepest stage or extend a shallow one. The heaviest piece of scenery appears flimsy until it is reinforced with shadows that suggest its mass and weight and veil the actual material of its linen surface. A designer knows how quickly at light-rehearsal a flood of light from the wrong source can literally blow a setting to pieces, flatten out the heaviest column; an electrician's mistake in bringing on a single extra lamp during a performance can be as disastrous.

For a production of *Don Juan* I made a cathedral of a single column, the silver grille of a *reja,* and a black back-drop. The light had to strike the column principally from stage right, and his supposed funeral, which Don Juan had come to witness, was supposed to take place off stage right so that he faced the principal light-source. The opposite side of the column was left in shadow in order to exaggerate its mass, for, heavy as it was, it was only half the scale of a cathedral pier. Enough light had to be concentrated at the base of the column to illuminate the principal scenes of the act; too much would have destroyed the column's solidity. Just enough light had to spill on to the silver grille to make it gleam, but none could spill too far beyond it, for there was no more than six or eight feet between it and the black back-drop. Even then one sensed the shallowness of this space until I shot a ray of light angled downward, from a point out of sight overhead, so that it seemed a ray coming from an unseen cathedral window. The brilliance of this light-ray was such that by the time the spectator's eye had penetrated it it was slightly dazzled; he could no longer tell whether he was looking into six feet of depth or sixty.

The silhouettes of factories seen through the railroad viaduct in *Liliom* were not more than eight or ten feet back of its opening. The trees on the gauzes of the park scene in the same play were no more than four or five feet apart. Nothing but the balance of light-planes gave them depth and distance and kept them in place so that they seemed hundreds of feet away. It is comparatively easy to light actors to the exclusion of their surroundings, even when they move through a dozen positions in as many minutes, and in the process distort the setting; it is a simple matter to light a setting and obliterate the actors in it. The designer's incessant problem is to keep both in the right relation throughout the course of a play. Nothing but the complex manipulation of light makes a satisfactory solution possible. No scene painted or built through scenic design is completed until it is finally lighted. The designer is today more dependent on the electric filament than he ever was on the brush.

The lighting of the last act of *Elizabeth the Queen* can serve to illustrate how not only the building and painting of a stage setting but even its costuming can be designed almost entirely for their values when lighted. The germ of the scene was the lighting of its final moment: Elizabeth, after Essex had descended the trap-door to his death, was to be seen rigid on her throne-chair, like a bronze statue, staring forever at her fate. Over her head the light was to catch two royal-red banners so that they hung like bloody fangs in the glow of dawn striking through turret windows. Accordingly Elizabeth's gown was made of a copper cloth. But as its metallic brilliance was to be seen only for a final tableau, it was covered with black chiffon stitched to it with a design of black and gold thread almost imperceptible except as its glints gave a sense of encrustation. During most of the act the black film dulled the fabric so that it took no light from Lynn Fontanne's face. The room was an empty cylinder; four narrow windows in an ascending line suggested the spiral ascent of a tower. It was painted in greys and blue, for the turret was to be shadowy with the breath of approaching death. But a fine spatter of dull-red paint was spread on just the portion of the wall behind the throne-chair, invisible until caught by the final light of dawn. The banners overhead were completely lost in shadow at the top of the set. A single candle placed on a chest motivated the general light of the scene. The chest was placed near the trap-door where Essex was to ascend. There were only two areas of light—one around the throne, the other between the chest and the trap-door, at first dim, as no important action took place there for the first part of the act. In each area the light was kept off the walls, raised just high enough to catch the actors' heads. The rest of the stage was in half-shadow. When the players came on to do a scene from *The Merry Wives,* they emerged from shadow only by accident, for they were nothing more than a momentary foil to the queen's mood as she paced back and forth waiting. When the trap-door opened and Essex entered, the lights on it were increased, but the change was imperceptible because none of the added light struck the walls; its slightly increased intensity could not be seen except on Essex's face. During the final colloquy the light grew dimmer everywhere except in the small space where Essex and the queen played their farewell. Just before they parted the blue of night through the windows began to fade to the pink of dawn. As Essex descended, the added light vanished with him, leaving nothing more than a flickering candle. A faint tinge of cold blue light stole up the walls. The light through the slits of windows became brighter, almost red. And as Elizabeth straightened in her chair the first shaft of warm morning sunlight struck full upon her, turning her to bronze and at the same time plucking the banners out of the shadow, turning them into bloody fangs that seemed to drip over the queen's head as the curtain fell.

7. LEGACY

Such a bit of stage lighting is a fraction of Appia's legacy to the modern stage. I do not imply that the designers of this generation read an out-of-print German volume and then rushed into the theatre to apply its precepts. They were already in the air, already being projected by spot-lights, already part of a modern tradition and its technique. Modern designers accepted a torch without knowing who lighted it; our experiments amplified Appia's theories almost before we knew his name, had seen his drawings, or had heard a quotation from his published work. Appia's first two volumes contain the germinal ideas that have sprouted, almost without exception, into the theories of modern stage-craft that we listened to—the necessity of visualizing the mood and atmosphere of a play, the value of presentation as opposed to representation, the importance of suggestion completed in the mind of the spectator, the effectiveness of an actor stabbed by a spot-light in a great dim space, the significance of a "space stage," and the more abstract forms of scenic art.

It was Appia who first said:

Our stage is a vista into the unknown, into boundless space, and this space for which our souls long in order that our imagination can be submerged in it, is given no added value by making our settings part of the structure of the whole theatre building. . . . The Greeks identified the scene of the play with the boundaries of the theatre; we, less fortunate, have extended it beyond that limit. Our drama, thrust into a boundless realm of the imagination, and our roofed-over amphitheatres, into which we are packed, are related only by a proscenium arch; everything beyond it is fictitious, tentative, and bears every evidence of being without any justification except as part of a particular performance.

It was Appia who first emphasized the distinction between the aesthetic values of classic formality and those of modern scenic illusion.

The antique stage was unlike ours, not a hole through which the public was shown in a constricted space the combined effect of an infinite variety of media. Antique drama was the event, the act itself, not a spectacle.

The passage of which these statements are a part gave the cue which prompted our present efforts to dislodge the proscenium arch and to unite the audience with the play by making the stage a part of the auditorium.

It was also Appia who, as a theorist, first insisted on the dominant importance of the director as a dictator controlling every element of a theatrical production.

The man we call director today, whose job consists in merely arranging completed stage sets, will, in poetic [music] drama, play the rôle of a despotic drill-master who will have to understand how much preliminary study stage setting requires, utilize every element of scenic production in order to create an artistic synthesis, reanimate everything under his control at the expense of the actor, who must eventually be dominated. Whatever he does will to a great extent depend upon his individual taste: he must work both as an experimenter and as a poet, play with his scenic materials but at the same time be careful not to create a purely personal formula.

Only an artist and an artist of the first rank can accomplish such a task. He will have to test his own imagination conscientiously in order to free it from every stereotype, above all from anything influenced by the fashion of the moment. But his principal effort as a director will be to convince the individual members of his acting company that only the arduous subjection of their personalities to the unity of the production will create an important result. He will be very like the leader of an orchestra; his effect will be a similarly magnetic one.

This conception of a master artist in the theatre is Craig's "Master of Drama" and, with Appia's contempt for the scene-painter, supplied the theme for Craig's first dialogues on the art of the theatre and most of their subsequent variations.

The art of the theatre today finds its full freedom within the boundaries of Appia's original concepts in a stage setting that is completely plastic—plastic in the sense of being infinitely malleable, plastic also in the sense of being consistently three-dimensional. More recent experiments in production continue to play with our sensations of space and our emotional reactions to projections, either actual or implied, of the third dimension. We accept the dynamic relations of a three-dimensional actor moving through a third dimension, whether constructed or indicated, as the greatest aid that can be given to the expressiveness of a play in performance. Light itself has come to have the character of a form in space. The illumination focussed and projected through the lens of a modern spot-light is a funnel of light that has the shape of a cone. Its outlines, when sharply focussed, are often discernible and are often made part of the pictorial pattern of a stage setting. At one extreme, we make stage space absolute, the stage setting purely architectonic, and depend entirely on the movements of actors, singly or in mass, to create the stage picture. Light then acquires, in our eyes, a classic purity of definition. At the other extreme the stage becomes murkily romantic and the dynamics of light is used to create the illusion of an actual extension of the space played in; it is extended until it seems infinite and is filled with every possible combination of shadowy masses related by atmospheric planes that have every degree of opacity.

Like every other form of scenic effect, modern stage lighting is an illusion. It too deceives the eye. But completely controlled, in the way that Appia indicated, it is the most subtle form of deception yet discovered. It is tactile in effect. The modern stage setting is thereby given unity by evading a conflict between illusions of different kinds. Even at its most vaporous moments a modern setting is three-dimensional, continually relates the actor to the space in which he moves, is an extension of his body as well as a symbolic projection of his state of mind. Our emotional reactions to drama when acted are intensified by an aesthetic emphasis upon extension in space, either reproduced or suggested, expressing dynamic patterns of human beings in action, who move through fluctuating planes of light; and these in turn create a dynamic interplay of contours and forms.

The aesthetics of modern stage setting, like the aesthetics of modern art in general, accepts tactile value as the supreme value and the basis of significant form. In the frame of the theatre, as in the picture-frame, we can find no other test of expressiveness. The modern art of theatrical production, "the art of the theatre," was completely organized, as a medium of expression, when the doctrines that Appia outlined and illustrated were added to the technique of rehearsal and presentation established by the Duke of Saxe-Meiningen's experiments. The unity thus established remains an aesthetic norm. Most of what we call innovation or experiment is a variation of Appia's ideas, deduced from his original premises—the refinements of acting evolved by Stanislavsky, the refinement in the control of electric lighting now being perfected by electrical engineers.

No genuine aesthetic novelty is possible on the modern stage until simulating the third dimension becomes less important to us as an emotional stimulus. For the time being the forces that can contribute to the growth of play-giving as a modern art lie outside the theatre's walls.

PART FOUR

ALTERNATIVES

CHAPTER I

THE THEATRE AND ITS PLOT OF GROUND

1. GAMBLER'S PARADISE

WHENEVER the talk turns to the future of the theatre, it is the fashion for the speaker to draw up his legs, take a grasshopper leap over a century or so, and, whirring victoriously, ask every one to follow him into a theatrical Elysium. At such moments I am always reminded of Valentine's exclamation when he finds himself falling in love: "What's this place? It's not heaven: it's the Marine Hotel. What's the time? It's not eternity: it's about half-past one in the afternoon." It is undoubtedly exciting for us to fall in love with the theatre's future. But our courtship, whatever our plans for the honeymoon, must take place in a theatre that resembles the Marine Hotel in this: It is a commercial enterprise that must pay its way; it is rooted on a plot of ground that has to meet taxes and throw off rent, and these taxes are likely to be high because, although the building may shelter an occasional love-affair, its situation has to be either central enough or attractive enough to draw a steady clientèle who come to admire the view. The theatre's ability to do this depends on its ability to compete with other forms of leisure in a competitive society for the profits offered to private enterprise by a competitive organization of industry.

To talk of the theatre's life as though it depended solely on its ability to create forms that clothe ideas is a disastrous policy. Any possible development of theatre art is a mirage unless the theatre is able to survive as a profit-making business or to be endowed as a non-profit-making institution. The vitality of any type of theatre that can be conceived has no meaning except as part of the organized life of a typical community. The theatre cannot be taken up bodily and transplanted to an ideal site without taking the community along with it. The theatre can be given no new impetus by being spelled Theatre, or by talking of it as though it could, like certain species of orchids, exist while clinging to a decayed stump, deriving its nourishment from the air—the intellectual atmosphere of our age, the *Zeitgeist*. The theatre of today can neither be transplanted nor be transported without first tracing the roots of its economic life. It is earth-bound. What prevents its development as an art, in spite of an extraordinary fertility in inventing new methods of expression at present, is the fact that as a business enterprise it is nothing more than an adjunct to a gambler's paradise.

Bernard Shaw has pictured the actual state of affairs with his usual lucidity: "Theatrical business is not like other business. A man may enter on the management of a theatre without business habits or knowledge, and at the end of forty years of it know less about business than when he began. The explanation is that a London West-End theatre is always either making such an enormous profit that the utmost waste caused by unbusinesslike management is not worth considering, or else losing so much that the strictest economy cannot arrest the process by a halfpenny in the pound." Transpose London West End to Broadway, halfpenny and pound to cent and dollar, and the statement is an accurate account of the economic basis underlying the hysteria and chaos of play-producing in New York.

The profits of putting on a successful play are so fabulous, and the losses of putting on a failure are so catastrophic, that a theatrical producer is not in the business of putting on plays but of finding and producing "smash hits." If he does not, he is forced to take the play off and follow Whistler's advice to the owner of a decrepit cab-horse: "Rub him out and begin all over again." The basic principle of theatrical financing is the gambler's double or quits, for the profits of the smash hit can easily wipe out the losses of a string of failures and leave in a single season a margin of profit that would satisfy a large-scale operator on the stock exchange. The chances of picking a hit may be one in twenty, but the smash hit pays at a rate of a thousand to one.

If we bar the additional expenses incident to Glorifying the American Girl and parading the choruses of musical comedies or revues rehearsed with large orchestras, the curtain can be raised on the average theatrical venture for a sum between $10,000 and $20,000, including the necessary amount of preliminary touting in the form of press-agent stories and advertising. Twenty to twenty-five thousand dollars is usually an ample figure, and this insures a competent cast, well-built sets with as much furniture or window-dressing as may be required, period costumes if necessary, a first-rate scenic designer, and an experienced director. A thousand dollars in advance royalties will secure almost any play. Actors, organized in a powerful labour-union, supply four weeks of rehearsing free for the assurance of only two weeks' salary. A designer of established reputation rarely commands a fee of more than $2,000 even for an elaborate production, and a director is usually satisfied with $500 a week during rehearsal and a small percentage of possible box-office receipts after the play opens. These initial expenses may seem high considered as actual cash outlay. But what do they amount to compared to a possible gross intake of more than a million dollars in the course of a single year?

Dwell upon the bookkeeper's balance-sheet of *Journey's End*, announced under the caption "A War Play Celebrates Its Birthday" in the New York *Times* of March 16, 1930. This play by an amateur, Mr. Sherriff, had opened at Henry Miller's Theatre in New York, March 22, 1929. It was originally produced in London as a little theatre experiment in January of the same year after having been rejected by Sir Barry Jackson, Basil Dean, A. H. Woods, and unfavourably commented upon by Bernard Shaw when the play was submitted to him in manuscript.

	Performances	Gross Receipts
North America		
New York	401	$819,873.43
Chicago company	222	348,367.65
Canadian company	207	277,224.75
Southern company	118	113,416.72
Eastern company......................	100	168,275.08
Total as of March 1..................	1,048	$1,727,157.63
Other Countries		
London (to March 8)...................................		$560,000.00
3 British tours (to March 8)...............................		360,000.00
Australian tour (to March 1)..............................		185,000.00
Continental-English tour (to Feb. 25)......................		70,000.00
Far Eastern tour (to March 8)............................		45,000.00
		$1,220,000.00
Total		$2,947,157.63

"It is impossible," said Maurice Browne, the English producer, "to gauge the prospective earnings. An African tour opens in August." But the total of gross receipts of nearly $3,000,000 in the course of a single year, with more to come without counting movie-rights, is sufficient to arouse the envious attention of a stock-broker or a "big business" man. Net profits cannot of course be deduced from these figures but they are without doubt within the dreams of avarice. Calculating the author's royalties at the prevailing American rate of 5 per cent on the first $5,000, 7½ per cent on the next $2,500, and 10 per cent on everything over that, and averaging the receipts of the American season on the basis of eight performances a week, Mr. Sherriff's American earnings for the year (although as a beginner he may have accepted a lower rate at the start) amount to the satisfying total of about $132,000, without counting added receipts from holiday and special matinées. Allowing a proportional sum for the English and Continental gross business, $93,000 is added, making a total of author's royalties estimated at approximately $225,000. Which leaves a gross return of about $2,722,157. Although from one-third to two-fifths of this sum must be deducted for theatre rentals, the owners of the enterprise have reaped a very satisfactory profit on their original investment particularly when one remembers that the play called for only one inexpensive setting—the interior of a dug-out at the front—a minimum crew of stage-hands, a small cast, and standard military costumes. The expense of reproducing the show and sending it out ten times could not have exceeded $100,000. And the first year, as Mr. Browne pointed out, was only a beginning.

Such possible profits in the theatre are not exceptional or typical only of post-war inflation in boom times. The total profits of *The Count of Monte Cristo* and those of *Uncle Tom's Cabin* are estimated to have run into millions. Testifying before the House committee on patents against the new copyright bill on April 11, 1930, Mr. William Klein of the Shubert Theatrical Enterprises listed authors' royalties as follows: *Potash and Perlmutter,* $378,285; *The Trial of Mary Dugan,* $312,650; *Broadway,* $300,000; *The Bat,* $300,000; *Friendly Enemies,* $232,331. The royalties on musical comedies ran to higher figures: $410,000, $573,000, $595,000. These figures explain why playwrighting is so popular a profession and why theatres crowd one another in side-streets running off Broadway until they form a theatrical ghetto a mile and a half long and not more than half a mile in width. I do not doubt that if the pecuniary outlook of a modern playwright were as uncertain as that of a painter of modern easel-pictures, we would still find artists dedicating themselves to writing nothing but plays and

385

see managers producing them, like Antoine, in club-rooms or rehearsing them in cafés. But any one may be pardoned for suspecting that if the maximum profit of play-producing were a certain 20 per cent on the capital invested, which would seem lucrative to any other form of commercial enterprise, as for instance taxicab companies, playwrights might be no more numerous than coachmen and theatres no more conspicuous than livery stables.

The producer is of course not left alone to exploit so rich a field; the landlord exacts his toll here as everywhere in modern life. With enormous gambler's stakes being played for, and a frantic competition, until very recently, for theatres in which to win them, building and owning theatres became one of the most lucrative forms of real-estate investment. A three-story theatre could return a rate of interest to its owner beyond the possible expectations of the owner of an apartment-house, office building, or hotel. There were, before overbuilding had caused its inevitable reaction, about 72 theatres in New York. The landlord got his share of the stake by taking 40 per cent of the gross box-office receipts. He thus played for hits like every one else in the theatrical business and dispossessed on two weeks' notice any play that did not show a satisfactory return. How satisfactory the landlord's gamble can be is made plain in another report from the New York *Times* of September 27, 1931, under the caption, "The Music Box Stops to Count Up." The receipts of the first *Music Box Revue,* which opened the house in 1921 and ran for fifty-four weeks, were "something more than $1,500,000 in that time." Forty per cent of this sum is $600,000, a very ample return to the landlord within one year on a theatre of a type that, with its plot, could at the time be built for $1,000,000 or less. But this was only the first year. During the second season the *Second Music Box Revue* played to a gross of $1,000,000. Thus within two years the owners had taken in a sum that equalled their original investment in land and building. In what other kind of real-estate speculation would such a feat be possible? Since that time the theatre has housed the following successes:

Third Music Box Revue	46 weeks
Fourth Music Box Revue	23 "
Cradle Snatchers	59 "
Chicago	20 "
The Spider	29 "
Paris Bound	29 "
Paris	24 "
First Little Show	40 "
Topaze	20 "
Once in a Lifetime	35 "

A total of 325 weeks in eight seasons. If one averages the weekly intake of such successes, many of them the smash hits of their seasons, at the moderate figure of $20,000 per week, this single theatre yielded a gross rental of $6,500,000, or nearly six and a half times its original cost in eight years of operation. In comparison the profits of that supposed real-estate Shylock, the slum landlord, seem paltry and the erection of a sky-scraper nothing less than a charitable bequest to New York City's sky-line. But failure to corral successful plays can also ruin a theatrical landlord. There are at present several theatres in New York that can be purchased, it is reported, for the price of their arrears in mortgage interest and taxes.

2. BREAK-DOWN

The results of basing the production of plays on gambler's expectation and not on the average profits of an average production have, in New York, resulted in such an inflation of values that even before the present deflation was felt the theatre business as a whole developed unmistakable symptoms of a chronic financial break-down. The typical New York playhouse is a boarding-house run by a landlord who often has no interest in the theatre whatsoever except to the extent that it returns him an exceptional rate of rental. Was it Dumas who said that he needed nothing more to stage a play than three boards and a passion? The present-day theatre landlord is the only person in the theatre's history who has taken that declaration literally. He needs to sell nothing more than site value to gamblers. As a result theatres are jammed into the smallest possible assemblage of New York building-plots of 20 x 100, resulting as a rule in a total plottage of 80 x 100 or 100 x 100, a shape that affords the worst possible basis for the satisfactory architectural planning of the relation of stage to auditorium. But the theatre landlord is selling the opportunity of selling seats to the highest bidder. As many seats as possible are jammed in, sight-lines are disregarded, the stage is cramped in width and made as shallow as possible, often less than twenty-five feet in depth. No more electrical equipment is provided than is needed to control the house footlights and the lights in the auditorium. Hours of expensive rehearsal-time are spent dragging in and setting up all the other lamps needed to light a play and plugging hundreds of feet of cable into portable switchboards. If a production requires more than three or four sets, the shallow stage creates a jam that wastes more hours of the time required to set them up or get them hung. As a producer often never knows until the previous tenant has defaulted what theatre he will be able to move into, he frequently gets one where the stage is so much shallower than even the average that he has to cut down his sets and rebuild them at the last moment. His greatest item of the expense is for labour, the cost of overtime for union stage-hands during scenic rehearsals. But this he cannot reduce by a single cent with any effective labour machinery for speeding up scene-shifting or for unifying the control of electric switchboards, because it does not pay the theatre landlord to install a scrap of such equipment. He is being paid for the value of his site and is too good a gambler to load himself down with any needless fixed-capital charges or unnecessary forms of overhead. As a result, for a stage that often doubles his rehearsal expenses and his crew of stage-hands, makes rehearsals a needlessly protracted agony, and subjects his actors to every kind of unnecessary nervous strain, the producer pays as much as $8,000 per week or more in rent after his play has opened—if he is lucky enough to keep it running at a profit.

The increasing wails of theatrical managers that the industry is being slowly ruined by the competition of the movies and the high cost of production are like the hard-luck stories that one hears from hangers-on at racetracks. They simmer down to the universal complaint that it costs so much to back the wrong horse. If the manager had to risk only $10,000 instead of $25,000 at each throw, that would mean a loss of $30,000 instead of $75,000 before the profits of a million or a million and a half might be pocketed. We are asked to believe that if scene-builders, scene-painters, scene-designers, and scene-directors would only reduce their charges all would be well in the theatre.

Every form of reduction in costs is advocated: 10 per cent of this or that at times becomes a magic figure. But no one will face the necessity of reorganizing the entire economic basis of the industry. The piteous plight of the managers of failures or quasi-successes, being slowly devoured by the ogre of organized labour, is paraded like one of Madame Tussaud's more horrible waxworks. But none of the gentlemen who invite the public's pity is equally vocal when he finally achieves a smash hit grossing a million or more a year. Having sold the motion-picture rights, he is usually to be found keeping his own counsel at Palm Beach or on the deck of the *Europa* or the *Aquitania* en route to London or Paris. Every attempt to organize theatrical managers into a unit that might direct the theatre industry as a whole has failed. The stumbling-block is often a new-comer who occupies a commanding position because he happens to be the owner of the biggest hit in town. Life for him is so roseate that he cannot concern himself with technical details; he is dallying with dreams of retiring for life "if the business keeps up another six months." He cannot take seriously an extra $300 per week on a crew-bill or a possible extra thousand dollars or two on the original cost of production. This is the small change of life, almost too small to notice, part of the original chip that won him the pot. One effort of the theatrical managers to turn themselves into a National Theatre collapsed of its own ineptitude. A more recent one, despite honest efforts by its few courageous members to improve conditions for both themselves and the public, ended with the group being unable to hold out for more than a few months against the practice of selling seats in a block to ticket-speculators, thus making the cost of playgoing as well as of play-producing prohibitive. The theatre public was sold out by one set of gamblers to gamblers of another kind. The managers could find no better way of saving themselves as a group than by squeezing an extra margin of profit out of even their certain successes in order to recoup past gambling losses a bit more quickly and to accumulate a fresh stake that could be risked at new odds. The picture, sordid as it is, would be comic if it were not so ominous an augury for the theatre's future in this country.

Nevertheless it would be unfair to see the theatrical manager melodramatically as a deliberate villain. He is forced to such expedients very largely because, as an individual in an unorganized industry, he often has no other choice. If his play is not an immediate hit he runs the risk of being dispossessed unless his weekly gross reaches a substantial figure. If his production requires more than two weeks to be built into a success, he can keep it open only by sinking more capital in it, and in most cases his capital is depleted when he opens his play in New York. The ticket-speculator who guarantees him a four or six weeks' "buy" is therefore his necessary ally and often performs the same function as the banker who advances money to merchants and manufacturers so that they can meet the expenses of their weekly overhead and pay-roll until their profits accrue. When Mr. Lee Shubert, also testifying against the new copyright bill, stated that fully 70 per cent of all plays produced were failures and that the producer must look to moving-picture rights to make up his losses, he also asserted, according to newspaper report, that the playwright took no risk in the deal, receiving much of the profit, and that the producer had the little end of the pay horn with the big chance to lose. Mr. Shubert's estimates should be authoritative, for the Shubert theatrical enterprises are at present in receivership. But the industry as a whole will not be saved a similar fate by convincing playwrights that they are not good enough gamblers and for the theatre's good should play for longer odds with the theatrical manager.

These chronic financial difficulties of the theatre industry are due to the habit of organizing play-production around the long chance of the occasional hit. Why should stage-hands volunteer to reduce their wages? The greed of theatrical landlords forced them to work for years on stages so badly equipped that overtime during rehearsals into the small hours of the morning became the rule. They therefore exacted punitive rates for overtime. Having grown used to this as the mainstay of a yearly income, they naturally resist the belated introduction of labour-saving machinery and occasionally insist on minimum crews much larger than a given production needs. They have never been shamed by having coals of fire heaped on their heads in the form of a weekly bonus voluntarily offered by some manager who is making a fortune out of a smash hit. Actors' salaries are high, being largely unemployment insurance collected in the form of two weeks of work guaranteed them. Carpenters and truck-drivers, reading of weekly grosses of $25,000, $30,000, and $35,000, are very naturally determined to get their proportionate share of the pickings. The tendency of wage-scales throughout the theatre is therefore to rise to a rate where only phenomenal success can carry them.

The situation is further complicated by the fact that often only a fraction of the original investment in a production is the producer's own; he may exact 50 per cent of the possible profit as the price of management, the funds being supplied by fellow gamblers from other industries who are willing to risk $10,000 or more on a possible hundred-to-one shot. The business practices of the American theatre are not typical of sound financial organization, but are those that prevail everywhere when large-scale enterprises are financed with insufficient capital and inadequate reserves. Most of the present effort of business management in the theatre goes into haggling, driving hard bargains, and encouraging all kinds of sharp practices, the most common of which is to evade or delay the final payment due scene-builders, scene-painters, and scene-designers. They too, like everybody else, are expected to wait for the next hit. I know of scene-painters and scene-builders who have uncollected balances of nearly a quarter of their business on their books, due from managements that have not gone into bankruptcy; and of one scene-designer unable, at the end of last season, to collect the final payment on four productions, one of which had been successful enough to go on tour after a New York run. The necessity of extending credit and of continuing it beyond a point that any other industry would countenance inflates the cost of scene-building and scene-painting to such a point that the few managements who do settle their bills within thirty days as a rule pay the overhead charges of carrying their rivals who have gambled less successfully.

For some inscrutable reason these practices are considered typical of the "commercial theatre," whereas the only theatres in New York that are commercial in any sound sense of the word are its "art theatres," and by these I mean not only the Theatre Guild but also the Neighborhood Playhouse and Winthrop Ames's, although both have closed, Arthur Hopkins's since its inception, the Provincetown Theatre during its best years, and Eva Le Gallienne's at its best moments. These art organizations put into practice the rudiments of business common sense observed in every other kind of business. They planned organizations that had a sound relation to their product and to their rate of production. Simplifications and ingenuities of all sorts cut their scenic budgets; careful planning, able scenic designers, and competent technical staffs avoided last-minute confusion and waste. Programmes were budgeted without an extravagant amount of capital; when an art theatre could afford a production costing no more than $5,000 it did not put on one costing $15,000 to mount. Productions were made in one theatre wherever possible, and its equipment was built into a permanent asset. In some cases a nucleus of a permanent acting company accepted lower salaries in return for the prospect of a season's steady employment. These theatres were organized, and as organizations were out not to take a long chance on a smash hit that might cram half the theatre-going population in New York inside their doors, but to produce a certain kind of play for a particular type of audience, exactly as a manufacturer produces a line of goods for the expected needs and taste of a certain section of the public. As a result they maintained standards of output and enlarged their clientèle by making their name a trade-mark synonymous with the kind of reputation and goodwill that a "hard-boiled" manufacturer on taking over a hardware concern is willing to pay for in hard cash.

However, such businesslike art organizations could not in the long run evade the economic problem of play-producing which the majority of unbusinesslike commercial managers created. Art theatres at the outset avoided some of the burdens of Broadway by producing in little theatres off the beaten track, where rents were low, and by budgeting their programmes so that a moderate-sized audience coming regularly enough would return a small margin of profit. But the increasing scale of costs dictated by Broadway very soon upset any such initial advantages. Steadily mounting union wage-scales doubled the cost of building, painting, and rehearsing. The cost of even simplified stage settings increased to a point that made the purely experimental play an almost impossible risk. Young actors who were willing to accept lower salaries for a few years, while making a reputation, had to ask for higher ones according to a standard set by Broadway and with the rising cost of living were obliged to cash in on their reputation with the best Broadway could offer them. The nucleus of a company of first-rate actors grew more and more expensive to maintain. The standard of salary tended to become what a manager with a hit could afford to pay his cast. The small houses, even when filled every night, could not yield a sufficient margin over a minimum budget. And the moment an art theatre planned the move to larger quarters it was faced with real-estate values and taxes fixed by Broadway managers and their landlords.

The growth of experimental theatres in this country has been blocked by the same economic conditions that make all privately owned theatrical enterprises hazardous. In the long run, unless some of the art theatres' artistic successes occasionally proved to be a hit with almost as high a rate of profit as a Broadway producer looks for, they could not accumulate sufficient reserves to survive their artistic failures. Winthrop Ames is said to have sunk more of his personal fortune in his productions than he ever took out of them. The standard of Arthur Hopkins's productions, remarkable as his best ones always are, is not so uniformly high as it was a few years ago, when he produced *The Devil's Garden, The Jest, Richard III, Hamlet,* and *Macbeth,* and the same has been said of several seasons of the Theatre Guild. Eva Le Gallienne's repertory, according to report, is made possible by an annual subsidy, and her theatre has had to shut down for the seasons 1931-32 in order to allow its director to search for new material. The Provincetown Theatre and the Neighborhood Playhouse have disbanded their organizations. As a whole the promise of artistic insurgence in the American theatre of ten years ago has not been realized. Despite innumerable little theatres, experimental stages, and fireside players that dot the country, there is not one that gives certain promise of growing into an important professional organization.

The reasons for this comparative failure are primarily economic and not artistic. That the Theatre Guild has survived more successfully than any other group of insurgents who started out at about the same time is due not only to the ability of its directors or to the number of its subscribers, which enables the Guild to ignore Broadway standards, but also to the fact that more of the Guild's artistic experiments proved to be hits in the Broadway sense than those of any other art theatre. Fortunately the public often wants the kind of play that has never been wanted before and patronizes drama that it never thought it could enjoy. Such hits as *Liliom,* early in the Guild's career, or *Strange Interlude,* more recently, were unpredictable and unexpected. But it was these hits as well as its artistic standards, its executive ability, and its sound business organization, that endowed the Guild Theatre. The Guild was indirectly endowed at the outset by Mr. Otto Kahn, who not only leased it the Garrick at what was a low annual rental for a theatre outside the regular theatrical district, but also said that the rent could be paid not when due but when earned. The rent was promptly paid during the first season of 1919-20 because *John Ferguson* proved such a success at a few preliminary performances in May that it ran all summer. Similarly *Jane Clegg* redeemed the losses of the first winter and *Liliom* those of the third. It became a practice to move such successes as *They Knew What They Wanted* from the little Garrick Theatre, with a seating capacity of five hundred and thirty, where they could be allotted only a portion of a subscription season of six plays, to Broadway theatres where they could run for the entire year and play to a much larger public than would subscribe in advance to an entire Theatre Guild programme. The profits that the Theatre

Guild's hits provided might of course have been dissipated by unwise management instead of being accumulated in a reserve fund. But it was this fund, as well as an increasing number of subscribers, which enabled the Guild to plan its own theatre and to raise the additional capital needed by a publicly subscribed bond-issue of half a million dollars.

However, the new site in order to attract a larger theatre-going public had to be near the theatrical district. The present tax-assessment of land and building is approximately $860,000; interest is paid on the usual first mortgage. Fifty per cent of each year's profits are allocated to redeeming the bond-issue and a special reserve is maintained for paying the interest on bonds that have not been retired. The success of the Theatre Guild does not make its financial responsibilities lighter to carry. Despite the advantage of owning its own playhouse, it labours under the economic burdens of any other theatrical manager or theatre-owner. Its artistic problem if anything grows more difficult. In order to preserve its artistic integrity it must continue to find and to produce plays that are not ear-marked as popular successes and are experimental in quality; but unless a proportion of them prove to be commercial successes and a few of them smash hits, the Guild cannot thrive indefinitely. If the Guild were to discover a new school of American playwrighting, acting, and directing so novel that for two or three seasons its theatre housed nothing but box-office failures, it would not be long before the Guild as a producing organization went the way of the Provincetown Theatre and the Neighborhood Playhouse. The moment an "art theatre," however soundly organized as a business, succeeds as a theatrical enterprise it finds itself facing much the same economic dilemmas that the "commercial theatre" faces. It may not be in the business of producing hits, but unless it does now and then, it too must go to the wall ultimately, if not quite so quickly as its commercial rivals.

I am attempting no last-minute Jeremiad. The last ten years of

American playwrighting and play-producing have been an indubitable renaissance. If occasionally we gnash our teeth like shipwrecked mariners watching the fleeting sail of art disappear over the horizon's rim, it is because we forget that even in the heyday of the great historic periods of drama, there were never more than one or two theatres in any theatrical centre that produced work of consistently high quality. Time flatters the historian and gives him the illusion of great perspicacity by discreetly rubbing out the enormous quantity of theatrical rubbish that once strode the boards and is no longer worth recording, except as a curiosity, between the covers of a book. If any one doubts this let him compare the quality of such recent Broadway successes as *The Green Pastures* and *Once in a Lifetime* with *Uncle Tom's Cabin* and *The Lion and the Mouse,* or let him compare any of the successes of the last decade with the specimens of typical American drama of the previous twenty years in Montrose Moses's compendium, *Representative American Plays.*

The commercial theatres have in fact aped both the tone and the material of the art theatres as fast as these won popular acceptance. The successes of the commercial theatre repeated and often cashed in on the successes of experimental playhouses. Indeed the present plight of Broadway is very similar to the predicament of its remaining art theatres. Nothing but smash hits can keep them going and smash hits, with an occasional exception like *Abie's Irish Rose,* are more and more often made from plays so novel both in point of view and treatment that ten or twenty years ago they would never have been picked as having the slightest relation to anything that the public could be supposed to want. The obvious stereotypes and the easy money have been drained off into the movies, for as Gilbert Seldes points out: "Every new form of entertainment drains off the cheap and accidental elements of its predecessor, a notable example being the complete disappearance of the matinée idol from the stage, his place being taken by the sex appeal . . . of the movies. The bad talkies in turn are based on silent movies, just as the early silents merely reduplicated the old melodrama." Present-day hits have a validity of characterization and an amount of criticism of life that would have sent the old-time theatrical manager gibbering to the nearest saloon for a bracer. Hits grow harder to write and harder to pick. The usual diatribes against the competition of the movies are very largely based on the fact that the success of the motion-picture has forced the theatre to be original both in the choice and in the treatment of its material. Playwrights have abandoned their old subject-matter to the moving picture, but they have appropriated much of its technique, so that a play like *Grand Hotel,* a superficial heightening of the sentimentalities and pathos of old-fashioned melodrama, requires, in order to be successful, a coordinated technique of presentation entirely beyond the imagination of old-time producers who knew when to turn on blue moonlight and to play soft music. Commercial managers are beginning to suffer financially because the average Broadway theatre is not equipped like the former German state theatres at Dresden, Berlin, or Stuttgart. They hang on to the lapels of their favourite authors and beg them to write a "sure-fire hit" in one set and for a cast for three people. But modern playwrights with extraordinary perversity continue to write successes in eleven acts or twelve and fifteen scenes that cannot be put over by a single high-priced star, and in addition to casts of thirty-five or fifty, require three or four leading players of the first rank. The result is that the successful manager, even when he has picked a hit, often has to face a salary-list and a production-expense that make his risk greater than ever. The irony of the present state of the theatre in New York is that every influence which is forcing the improvement of its product is also making its financial basis more and more precarious, so that the American theatre, despite its indubitable artistic progress, seems to be strangling in a clutter of side-streets that we call Broadway.

CHAPTER II

FIRST STEPS TOWARD TOMORROW

I. THE DOOR TO YESTERDAY

THE former prosperity of the theatre as a commercial enterprise was based on its ability to avoid complete concentration in New York by exporting its surplus to the entire country. The public for plays was not a fraction of the population in one large city but a fraction of the population of every State. This was "the road," and its potential purchasing power provided the American theatre's financial reserves. The American producer used to be prosperous because he was able to subsidize the risk of his new ventures by the royalties that continued to come in from his travelling companies, who rolled merrily along not only to all the larger cities but to towns so small that they were "one-night stands." As the receipts of *Journey's End* show, the profits of duplicating success with a number of road-companies can exceed even the profits of a long run in a theatrical capital. Every manager dreams of finding a play that can be sent to South Bend or South Africa. The practice of touring plays twenty years ago was so general that the standard dimension for building scenery is still a flat five feet nine inches wide. This dimension seems arbitrary until one learns that the doors of American baggage-cars are six feet high; each section of scenery, in order to be stood on its side and shoved through the door, had to allow a margin of three inches for clearance.

The organization of the theatre as a factory for smash hits has wiped out the possible profits of the road even faster than it has wiped out the chance for profits in New York City. The "road," except for musical comedies, where it can listen to the song hits of the year before they are heard from every hotel orchestra or on every other radio programme, prefers to see plays that are established successes and have the prestige of a season's run in New York behind them. Not only are there no longer enough of such successes to keep the road supplied, but the risk of sending out anything that has been talked of for less than six months in syndicated newspaper columns is so great that fewer and fewer managements can afford to take it. In addition to the higher costs of reproducing scenery and costumes and of running with unionized crews, there are the greatly increased costs of railroading, as compared to those of twenty years ago, and the increased cost of living, which sends up road salaries for actors. Many, revolting against being imprisoned in one rôle for more than a year, refuse to go on the road at any price. Furthermore, the success of commercial hits depends so much more on ensemble acting than formerly that the second-line company is in itself a risk, particularly as the "road," which can see a perfect facsimile of Greta Garbo or Charlie Chaplin around the corner, demands the original New York casts and complains that it is being cheated if it does not get them. Successful plays are no longer set in flats and borders that can be hung in a few hours, but depend on an amount of scenery and a degree of technical complication that often bars the one-night stand; even if the house could be sold out the stage could not be got ready.

The easy success of road-companies in the past was based on the lure of the star actor; the backwoods turned out to see the leading actor or actress and took the play for granted, so that Sarah Bernhardt playing in French could fill a circus-tent. But the disappearance of the star and his or her personal "box-office draw" has wiped out one of the major sources of certain profits. In addition the very originality of present-day successes makes them liable to offend established taboos and prejudices that survive behind the lace curtains of Main Street long after they no longer show their faces in Brooklyn or the Bronx. A certain proportion of Broadway successes are poor road risks precisely because of their subject-matter. Occasionally a play such as *The Green Pastures* or *Strange Interlude* can triumph over all these obstacles. But *Once in a Lifetime* had to abandon its tour and return to the storehouse. Sure-fire successes for the road grow rarer than sure-fire successes for New York. The movies have absorbed not only the appeal of the matinée idol but also that of his or her material—the hypocrisies, sentimentalities, and evasions, the fairy-tale stereotypes, the life-lies and sex-lies. The small city's local theatre, relic of the days when Booth and Barrett turned up regularly—its single trap-door is still called the Hamlet trap, being placed where convention required for the grave scene—has become a frowsy and musty place which it hardly pays to renovate because owning and running "legitimate" theatres outside of New York became an unprofitable form of real-estate investment long before the present theatrical slump in New York began. The "legitimate" theatre manager or his landlord, who cannot cover his risks or recoup his losses with tickets at two dollars and a half and three dollars, very naturally whines when he sees the crowds travelling to the nearest movie palace, where for a dollar or less they swallow the hokum that the theatre-owner can no longer purvey, where they can fall in love with the star, and, on the way in, can get almost as great a thrill from a military usher as if they were being shown around West Point by a brass-buttoned cadet.

"Revive the Road and Save the Theatre" has for the moment become a popular slogan. But how this is to be done unless by incantation and prayer is not apparent. Do theatre-managers plan to revive the star actor and actress or the matinée idol? Are they going to cut the cost of railroading or refuse to send out any plays except those in one set? How is the dramatic material that is a sure-fire hit in New York going to become sure-fire hokum, once on the road, so that it can compete with the talkies? How is the cost of production going to be cut in general and the financial risks of failure be reduced? How is the supply of smash hits, now too few to tap the purses of the theatre-going public of a single metropolis, to be enlarged so that it supplies dramatic fare to an entire nation? No plan has as yet been evolved that faces, much less meets, the inherent difficulties of the problem. Theatrical managers prefer to delude themselves into thinking that, like a camel going through the eye of the needle, they can recover their palmy days by ducking their heads and clearing by a margin of three inches the door of a baggage-car.

2. THEATRES AS CIVIC CENTRES

It may very well be that a single metropolis has heretofore always been the heart of theatrical enterprise. But economic conditions are now so changed that the pulse of play-production in New York, like a heart muscularly diseased, functions spasmodically and barely keeps a part of the body of the theatre alive. The arteries of communication have hardened or been totally destroyed, so that it is useless to speculate on how a hopelessly centralized theatre can supply the blood-stream of living drama to the whole country. The entire commercial basis of theatrical production will have to be radically displaced before the theatre can revive. If and when the "road" finally dies, the American theatre may indeed be reborn in co-ordinated but self-sustaining theatrical centres.

The highest general level of theatrical production in the modern theatre was reached in Germany from 1900 to 1914 and continued for some years after the close of the World War. It was made possible by the fact that every large city was a self-sufficient centre of theatrical culture. Munich, Stuttgart, Dresden, Darmstadt, Leipzig, Cologne,

Bremen, or even such small cities as Weimar, Posen, and Stettin, did not wait for Berlin to ship them whatever shop-worn successes it could spare but built superbly equipped theatres that were civic monuments. They did not rely on a single star like Moissi, who happened to have a "road draw" and could tour Europe. A play was not necessarily consigned to limbo because its original performance was a failure; it was often repeated and made a success in another state or civic theatre a few weeks or months later. The possibilities of a script were often tested not by one but by a dozen different directors; classics of all sorts were kept alive by continual reinterpretation. Parochialism was avoided by a frequent interchange of leading actors and occasionally by arranging for the repertory of important foreign companies, who were invited on a *Gastspiel* as guest players. Private theatrical ventures were not discouraged; they were on the contrary stimulated by the wide-spread encouragement given to theatre-going everywhere. Fortunes were lost and also made in private theatres, including Reinhardt's own Deutsches Theater, which made Berlin the theatrical capital of the country and for a time of Europe. But cities that were not cosmopolitan centres, and could not draw upon a transient population, were able to have a theatre without being mulcted by speculators gambling on the immediate profits of phenomenal successes. The entire theatre industry was established on a broad foundation, with the result that until 1921 or so the only building of importance that attempted to solve any of the problems involved in relating an adequate stage to a well-designed auditorium was done by German architects who did not have to limit their imagination to the cupidity of a local real-estate market. The only real technical progress made in reducing the labour and lengthy rehearsals by scene-shifting machinery and switch-boards that embodied the advances of electrical engineering was first made in Germany. The first successful electrical apparatus for projecting scenery was the result of German research. I remember

403

visiting in 1921 the works of Siemen-Schuckert at Siemenstadt in the suburbs of Berlin. It was a small city in itself, where giant electric dredges, cranes, and dynamos were turned out. But it also contained a laboratory devoted to perfecting electrical equipment for theatrical use. The building in relation to the expanse of the rest of the works seemed no larger than a switchman's hut. Nevertheless it paid one of the largest manufacturers of electric machinery to maintain a department devoted to theatre lighting because every perfected device had as potential purchasers all the state and municipal theatres, whose policy it was to improve their equipment rather than to keep it at an obsolete minimum.

The development of the theatre is directly related to the economic rent of land, because the theatre is not only an exhibition-room but a factory, a plant to produce plays. Productions have to be assembled in a workshop; unification of plant equipment is no less essential to the theatre than to any other form of modern industry. The proper size for a theatre that is to be efficiently run requires a plot of ground invariably much larger than any lot in a congested district that an individual investor can afford. By the time an adequate plot is assembled, its initial cost, in competition with other forms of real-estate investment, is so great that any possible rental from it is too low to attract private capital, and the same holds true of its mechanical equipment. When the Theatre Guild was planning its new theatre, its directors considered the possibility of installing a single labour-saving device to facilitate scene-shifting and stage-setting—electric elevator-stages. They found that a minimum of three would have cost at least $75,000, involving carrying charges that could not be risked. Any number of German theatres have completely mechanized stages with five times that amount of elevator equipment. The Theatre Guild, like every other American theatre, because it cannot afford the ground-rent involved in having its stage, carpenter-shops, and scene-painting studio under one roof, must spend a considerable amount every year in order to have its settings hauled several miles from the carpenter to a painter, then to the theatre, and finally to the storehouse. The average production requires four truck-loads of scenery, which cost $35 per load to haul, an item of approximately $2,500 a season. The switch-board specified for the new Guild Theatre called for a system of unified control that not one of the largest manufacturers of electrical equipment was prepared to produce or could produce except at a prohibitive figure. Switch-boards of this type are now being marketed because the larger movie palaces can afford to pay for them. The unavoidable wastes of a plant that cannot be made mechanically or electrically efficient, added to the unavoidable costs of cartage, the overtime of protracted rehearsals, and the separate profits that have to be paid to firms of scene-builders and scene-painters, I estimate to be from $15,000 to $20,000 a year for a schedule of six plays alone. And similar wastage is unavoidable for any theatre that produces steadily throughout the season. Nevertheless the Guild Theatre is exceptionally well equipped as American theatres go, and its directors were willing to make the stage fifteen feet deeper than the average although this added space alone involved an additional investment in land of about $45,000. German theatres were saved similar financial burdens by states and cities that considered the theatre no less a civic monument than an art museum or a public library.

It is not beyond the bounds of possibility that the general level of culture in this country may eventually rise to a point where a group of wealthy citizens will feel that it is no less important to provide their city with a theatre than with a museum or a concert-hall. The American theatre may yet become as honorific an outlet for private benefaction as art, music, and literature have been. Detroit or Cleveland does not rely on a road-tour of the Philadelphia or the New York Philharmonic orchestras in order to hear symphonies by Brahms and Beethoven, nor do they wait for a loan exhibition by the Metropolitan Museum in order to see important examples of old and modern masters. Detroit and Cleveland, New York and Philadelphia, are within a few hours of each other by rail and each pair of cities could conceivably share a single symphony orchestra between them. But because the performance of musical symphonies is felt to be of the highest importance, each city maintains the best orchestra that can be assembled and the ablest conductor it is possible to secure. When the performance of plays is felt to be equally important, these cities will provide whatever endowment is needed in order to have permanent acting companies of first-rate players, as they do now to maintain first-rate players of violas, tubas, French horns, and kettle-drums; and they will be directed by leaders comparable to Golschmann, Gabrilówitsch, Goossens, Koussevitsky, Sokoloff, Stokowski, and Toscanini. Until the interpretation of a script by a great playwright is felt to be as important as the interpretation of a score by a great composer, the pretence that the American public wants better plays is, if not hypocritical, at least disingenuous. When playwrighting and play-acting are thought to be worth the local millions now lavished on the installation of painting and sculpture and the performance of orchestral music, the leading industrial centres in this country will have theatres of the first rank. Until then the answer to their perennial plaints is, I am afraid, the vulgar one: Put up or shut up.

The Puritan suspicion that the theatre, however nobly disguised, is a side-door to Hell, survives among our best minds. It is felt that the public benefactor who endows an art museum, an orchestra, an opera-house, or a university is certain of a place in Heaven. But to endow a theatre is not yet considered a sound first mortgage on immortality. The one million dollars given to Yale so that Professor Baker could conduct a school of the theatre there, and the lesser sums allotted to courses in play production at ninety-four universities, train graduates most of whom cannot find opportunities on an already over-crowded New York Rialto. No opportunity for sound growth and development is offered them in most of the meagrely equipped local amateur groups and little theatres. We have the ironic picture of our leading educational institutions turning out hundreds, and before long thousands, of directors, designers, and theatre technicians who have no better future than to remain teachers and to teach amateurs to teach other amateurs to be content to remain amateurs.

The new civic centre at Cleveland presents an equally ironic picture. Grouped about a park one finds an art museum and a new symphony hall; the next building to be erected is to be a museum of natural history. Thus the coming generations of Cleveland will be assured of seeing a collection of well-stuffed anthropoid apes, superbly displayed in stage settings that imitate a tropical jungle. But they have as yet no assurance of being able to see a cycle of Shakespeare's comedies in their chronological order, played by the biological successors of the anthropoid ape in settings that might illustrate the imagination of the greatest English poet. If a new bust of Aeschylus were discovered and presented to its art museum, its director would congratulate himself on the acquisition, notify the newspapers, and issue invitations to a private showing. But a performance of a tragedy by Sophocles can wait until Broadway managers or the Theatre Guild get round to it. Cleveland is of course no exception; its best minds, like those of Philadelphia, Detroit, Chicago, or San Francisco, will probably be content to accept as a substitute a performance by the local orchestra conductor of an inadequate scenario of *Oedipus Rex* done into Latin by a minor French poet, sung by opera stars and a college glee-club chorus to the music of a Russian composer. Meanwhile the local humanists will publicly deplore the waning influence of Greek classics in a jazz age. They will attempt to counteract our intellectual syncopation by going to hear a superb rendition of Mozart's overture to *The Marriage of Figaro,* but they will make no plans to ensure a performance of Marivaux's comedies or any of Molière's. These are reserved to demonstrate to high-school students, most of whom will never learn to speak French, the niceties of French syntax. After which the best minds, having done their full duty as educators, will seat themselves on reproductions of historic furniture made by enterprising manufacturers from the museum's best examples; and thus seated, surrounded by similarly evolved upholstery and bric-à-brac representing periods of perfect taste, they will digest the latest diagnosis, recommended by a book club, deploring the low level of American culture.

On a recent visit to Cleveland, before lecturing at its art museum I spent an afternoon studying the switch-board at its symphony hall. It is the latest marvel of electrical engineering, as compact as the usual organ console, easily manipulated by controls no larger than organ-stops, which can direct the interplay of hundreds of electric lamps. From it lights can be played like a musical score, but its only immediate function is to send the lights of the auditorium through the cycle of the spectrum in order to match the mood of a musical programme. The system of magnetic contacts and electric rheostats that makes such subtlety and unification of control possible occupies an entire subcellar and is reported to have cost close to $100,000. Not much more than twice that sum could have equipped a theatre where a turn of the switch would have converted the stage into a platform for a symphony orchestra for its comparatively few annual performances and given the city the added opportunity of seeing drama for part of every week in the year.

While I was attempting to understand the manipulation of this switch-board—a mighty brain feeding a rudimentary nervous system —an extraordinary demonstration filled the auditorium, packed with selected delegations from high schools and adult study-groups who had come from all over the state to compete for the best score in identifying unnamed excerpts from well-known composers. A small orchestra played fifteen or twenty bars and stopped. Was it Brahms, Berlioz, Respighi, or Verdi? The silence was broken by the combined scribbling of a thousand pencils scratching printed score-cards. Monitors stood watching each group in order to avert cheating. The final score-cards were to be turned in, checked, and judged. The winning groups of adolescents and adults would then be awarded prizes, be publicly acclaimed, and return home to clip their group pictures from the rotogravure section of Sunday newspapers and hang them alongside the picture of their graduating class banked on the steps of a chapel or of a gymnasium. It is no doubt a desirable accomplishment to be able, without the help of a programme, to distinguish Mozart's music, Mendelssohn's, Strauss's, from Stravinsky's. But why has it occurred to no one that if such training is an important effort in education, it is equally important to enable these same groups to distinguish by ear a scene of Shakespeare from one by Marlowe, a tirade by Shaw from one of Molière's, an apostrophe by Euripides from one of Racine's?

The danger of relying on the beneficence of the American millionaire is due to the fact that in bestowing his benefactions he wishes to feel like a king and so repeats the patterns of royal patronage to the arts. Museums were originally collections of royal taste, housed in abandoned royal palaces such as the Louvre or the Pitti. From the first, in order to satisfy the regal tastes of their original donors, American museums were made to look as much like royal palaces as possible. Their directors have recently begun to realize that paintings, statues, and bric-à-brac can neither be seen nor be studied to the best advantage in halls so imposing that Louis XIV might have held court in them or Napoleon I have been acclaimed there by his marshals. Royal opera-houses having often been an appendage to the courts of Europe,

American millionaires are willing to agree that unless their native city boasts an opera-house it is not a civic centre of the first importance. In return the millionaire donors are accorded several tiers of horseshoe boxes where they can publicly preen themselves. The resulting architectural design of opera-houses in this country has made even endowed opera financially precarious, because the lower orders of society, with whom opera is genuinely popular, have had to be shoved into galleries remote from the stage. When New York's millionaires founded a New Theatre, this same snobbery encouraged a fashionable architect to reproduce an outmoded opera-house plan and provide horseshoe boxes for a theatre, thus hoisting the common people, to whom the enterprise was ostentatiously dedicated, into balconies where they could neither see nor hear. A recent attempt to build a new opera-house in New York had to be consigned to the scrap-basket because Joseph Urban, in order to plan a rationally constructed auditorium, reduced the number of possible box-holders. Nothing but the commendable spirit of abnegation on the part of the potential box-holders of Philadelphia's projected opera-house, who consented to be placed in a less conventional position, made it possible to plan an auditorium that would bring three thousand spectators into effective relation with the stage.

Strangely enough, despite the fact that there has been no sign within the last decade that this country can breed an important operatic composer, the opera-house remains the golden goal of private endowment when it considers theatrical enterprises. The American composer of opera must be enticed out of his hiding-place at all costs. But American playwrights who have already proved themselves to be among the original and creative artists of this generation must either write smash hits or revive their dramatic talent in Hollywood. Whenever that tenderest of annuals, an American opera, opens at the Metropolitan Opera House, the New York *Times* fills columns, often on the front page, with ecstatic eulogies and prognostications. Here obviously is the theatrical event for which America is waiting. But when a play without music, such as *Strange Interlude* or *Mourning Becomes Electra,* opens, the *Times,* with the aid of a convenient directory on its last page, enables the habitual theatre-goer to find its critic's comments wedged in the usual column on page 24 or 31.

The first step toward rehabilitating the theatre in this country will be made when the wealthiest citizens of such centres of wealth as Philadelphia, Chicago, Boston, Detroit, Cleveland, St. Louis, San Francisco, and at least ten other large cities decide to devote as much money and energy to building and running a theatre as they now do to running art museums and symphony orchestras. No great amount of research would be needed in order to plan these theatres and their technical equipment. Twenty years of experiment in Germany have made plain what combinations of sinking, sliding, elevator-stages are the most efficient aids to scene-setting and scene-shifting. Given any first-rate architect in each of these cities and an advisory board consisting, let us say, of designers such as Jones, Bragdon, Urban, or myself, such technicians as Monroe Pevear of Boston or Stanley McCandless of Yale, the representative of one or more manufacturers of remote-control switch-boards, and one foreign technical director of the type of Hasait or Linnebach, not many months would be required in order to establish the structure of a playhouse that could be easily converted to suit the needs of any school of direction or stage-setting, where with the minimum of manual labour one could stage realistic or poetic spectacles that ran to forty scenes if necessary behind a proscenium or on a forestage that projected into the audience. This forestage, being the platform of an electric elevator, could be sunk out of sight when not in use or raised for symphony concerts, visiting recitalists, dance programmes, pageants, and spectacles. A large auditorium seating two or three thousand and a smaller one seating between five hundred and one thousand persons would make every variety of experiment or revival possible in repertory.

Such theatres could be run on strictly professional lines. They would attract the surplus of able actors now chronically unemployed in New York and directors as capable as our present orchestra conductors. These theatres' workshops for designing, building, and painting stage settings would very quickly become class-rooms for the nearest university where courses in dramatic production were given, then training-schools where graduates could develop professional assurance, and eventually laboratories for aesthetic and technical experiments of every kind. If twenty such playhouses existed New York's art theatres as well as its best Broadway producers would bid for the privilege of playing to assured audiences on stages so well equipped that they did not have to drag along on tour tons of unnecessary equipment. A central board of directors for this group of theatres could take its pick of each season's Broadway successes and set a standard of production that it would pay the most commercial manager to shoot at. They would also have a commanding influence in the play-market provided they organized their audiences on a season's subscription basis as they now do for opera and concerts and as the Theatre Guild has done in New York. For they would then be able to assure any playwright of twenty to forty weeks of performances in a chain of civic theatres. We might within a few years see plays tested on this new "road" and then come to New York if they were successful enough to warrant the increased production-costs and the high rentals of Broadway. The best Broadway successes would tour twenty cities, and successes discovered in Detroit or San Francisco could move to Broadway for a lucrative run. In any case there would be a continuous and healthy circulation of drama throughout the country.

Winthrop Ames first outlined to me such a basis for a genuinely national theatre, but unfortunately, and mistakenly I think, at the time he no longer felt himself young enough to organize the project himself. But he too was well aware of the fact that the theatre is none the less an art because it is forced to survive as a modern industry. For that reason standardization of these allied theatres would be essential as far as their electrical and mechanical equipment is concerned. A successful production in one city could then be sent to another after its first run of a few weeks by shipping nothing more than the stage settings. Whatever system of scene-shifting was adopted would be uniform throughout all these theatres and thus reduce both rehearsal time and rehearsal costs to a minimum. A light-plot could be reproduced on identical lighting apparatus already in place and be rehearsed in a few hours. The pooling, not only of these but of all other resources, if intelligently planned and controlled, should result in economies great enough to make large sections of good but cheap seats available at every performance or allow a certain number of popularly priced performances per week that would bring back into the theatre the thousands who are already bored with the routine repetition of eroto-priggery in the talkies. In fact the directors of this chain of civic art theatres would be in a strategic position not only in regard to plays but also in regard to films. They could easily fill their houses one or two nights a week with moving pictures like *Le Million, Prince Achmed,* or Eisenstein's *General Line,* which a local distributor would not dare to risk putting on for a week's run.

This would not be heaven. It would still be half-past one in the afternoon. No miraculous rehabilitation of the theatre would be accomplished overnight or even in the course of a few years. At the outset the level of taste displayed by the directors of endowed civic theatres in regard to new material might easily be worse than Broadway's at its best. Hypocrisy is still a national virtue; mass production of bigots is the one American industry that seems to thrive through every economic depression. The belief is still current outside

413

of our largest cities that the theatre must pay no more attention to unpleasant facts than propagandists hired by the electric power trust devote to concealed assets, that plays can uplift the morals of a community by resolutely pretending that the sexual act is practised in a state of amnesia automatically induced among those members of the community legally entitled to set up housekeeping. The taboos and timidities, the pruriences and pseudo-purities, of clergymen, temperance advocates, Christian sewing-circles, moralists, evangelists, and uplifters of all sorts, who have bedevilled local politics with false issues, might for a time fasten on the theatre. The present stranglehold of Catholic censorship on the Boston theatres, exercised through Irish office-holders, is a sample of the worst that we can expect. The organized browbeating of every generous social programme that has been carried into the endowed university might be felt in the endowed theatre. Magnificent stages, once built, might be given over to national security pageants and anti-communist pantomimes, or be filled with the dances of high-school nymphs who never fled from a satyr.

Nevertheless the theatre by appealing to its audiences with a uniquely direct and pervasive eloquence has a way of circumventing dogmatic restraints, in common with the other arts. Endowed art museums do show nude statues with impunity; the programmes of endowed orchestras are not limited to Handel's oratorios and Bach's *Passion;* Rabelais as well as Ruskin can, with more or less difficulty, be obtained at endowed public libraries. Rationally organized opportunities to hear music, see paintings, or read books, freed from the cupidities of private competition, tend to get better music performed, better paintings appreciated, and better books read. It is the opportunities for private speculation that keep alive the smutty peepshows and the sex-story magazines. *Strange Interlude* did play to a profit in towns not usually considered on the theatrical map. College schools of the drama often give "radical" plays that shock college faculties, but they are often less easily intimidated than professors of "radical" theories of economics. The potential directors bred by the present interest of our universities in dramatic production are likely, when called to civic theatres, to prove Pauls among the Corinthians. Once theatre-going is organized and encouraged, and audiences typical of a complete cross-section of our population get an appetite for play-going, those audiences will probably prove as eager for novelty, as impatient at transparent hypocrisy, as other theatre audiences have often been. Give two thousand local suit-and-pants cutters or cotton-spinners, who have been through strikes and lock-outs, an opportunity of filling a civic auditorium at fifty cents a seat, and the management will probably find it more profitable to put on *Man and the Masses* or *The Weavers* rather than to produce *Peter Pan* or *Pollyanna*. A nation-ally organized theatre would eventually acquire its own momentum and give vent to the criticism and dissent of vast sections of our popu-lation that are at present inarticulate because they have no ready outlet for expression. The hypocrisies of our present-day political, economic, and religious codes might easily be discredited in a circuit of civic play-houses before a public that is now listless or confused after listening to the debates of State senates, city aldermen, and local trade-unions.

The vitality of present-day American playwrighting is such that it may possibly survive every present handicap. To many *laissez-faire* will seem the wisest policy. But it has been found disastrous as a means of assuring us of a regular quota of food and shelter. The theatre, if it is to escape its cycles of hysterical inflations and de-pressions like those of farming and manufacturing, will have to or-ganize itself and relate itself to the community as a whole on an economic basis so sound that American plays can be produced regu-larly enough to nourish a national culture. American playwrights will not suddenly develop the vigour of Aeschylus or of Shakespeare because they are given the opportunity to fill an architectural stage

415

designed by Oskar Strnad or Frank Lloyd Wright. Like the play-wrights of every other country, they write not for theatres but for audiences. They will not react to the presence or the absence of a proscenium arch as they will to the stimulus provided by assured audiences of two thousand a night in twenty or thirty cities of the country, for whom they can write in one set or forty, for a cast of five or a cast of several hundred, without being inhibited by the thought of production-costs that cannot yield a speculator's profit on the in-flated values of congested building-lots in the country's largest city. If poetry is to be reborn in the American theatre it will, I believe, rise to the opportunity of addressing permanently organized, nation-wide audiences who have been made habitual theatre-goers. In the smaller auditorium of each civic theatre the American playwright who is creative would have an opportunity to experiment with both form and subject-matter that he can find nowhere at present. In the larger auditoriums he would be tempted to raise his voice in order to be heard and in the process become something less of a reporter and something more of an orator. He might at the outset resort to bombast and rant, but in the end he would probably be driven to invent new myths if only to reach the gallery gods of established people's play-houses. He would, I think, do this more quickly by attempting to keep the interest of an actual, national audience than by attempting, as he does today, to satisfy the individual taste of a handful of New York theatrical managers, most of whom hope to make a fortune in six months.

3. THEATRES AS COMMUNITY CENTRES

However, a co-ordinated chain of theatres in the larger cities of this country is not a broad enough basis for an American theatre, which cannot be established until theatrical production reaches across city lots and becomes the centre of an entire country-side. An indication of how this can be done has already been given in the Community Centre of Westchester County, which, as organized and run by the county's recreation commission, is an augury of the American theatre's future growth. The county includes such towns as Yonkers, White Plains, and Peekskill. But not one would be considered a one-night stand by a New York manager sending a play on tour, nor could one of them support a third-rate local stock-company. But by pooling their resources with twenty other townships and several hundred incorporated villages, their inhabitants have been able to enjoy a building constructed at a cost of nearly one million dollars, paid for by a bond-issue, and to support the two theatres it contains, one seating five thousand and the other four hundred and fifty. The building stands on the Bronx River Parkway, one of the finest examples of landscape road-building in the East, which connects the northern end of New York City with the Hudson Valley at Peekskill. And several hundred thousand commuters, without scurrying back on the last midnight local, are able to ride in comfort to hear the Metropolitan Opera Company, a revival of *Orpheus* with Matzenauer in the title-rôle, recitals by Paderewski, Percy Grainger, and Paul Robeson. Such star attractions have been so profitable that the income from rentals was over $25,000 during 1930, and for the first eight months of 1931, despite the financial depression, had netted $10,000, thus reducing the cost of running the building, met by county taxes. A number of private organizations, ranging from a Trails Association to a School of the Theatre, use the building as their headquarters and contribute to their share of its upkeep by dues and gifts. The enterprise began with an annual programme by a community chorus. The county Choral Society now contributes $27,739 annually and has united all the scattered local choirs, including those of its Negro churches, into large choruses that give expert and impressive performances. The county supplies a representative cross-section of population: millionaires on country estates, suburbanites on half-acre plots, small-town shopkeepers, clerks, truck-gardeners, servants, and factory-hands. Snobbery and prejudice are happily absent; the disfranchised and delinquent are not excluded. One of the smaller halls is open to Negroes every Thursday night, the only "respectable" dance-hall where they are welcome. There are classes of all sorts, including two for boys and girls who are out on probation.

A typical week's programme (December 12 to 18, 1931) consists of Chekhov's *The Cherry Orchard* on Thursday, Friday, and Saturday, with a cast of professional players directed by Leo Bulgakov, formerly of the Moscow Art Theatre; on Sunday, a Westchester County Peace Meeting; on Tuesday, White Plains Fire Department Ball; on Friday, Don Cossack Russian Male Chorus; in addition to an exhibition of wood-carving during the week. For the week of December 28, for four evenings and two matinées, Ben Greet and a group of English actors in *Julius Caesar, As You Like It, Macbeth, Twelfth Night, A Comedy of Errors,* and *Hamlet;* and on December 30 a tennis exhibition-match between William T. Tilden and Francis Hunter.

No doubt some of my readers grin at this point and ask how American drama is to be liberated by sharing the limelight with a fireman's ball or rubbing shoulders with tennis champions. My answer is, Why not? The financial weakness of the American theatre at present is very largely due to its exclusiveness, paid for by the colossal economic waste of playhouses limited to one form of public entertainment, which are used only twenty-four hours a week and rarely for more than forty weeks of the year. During one visit of the opera to the Westchester Community Centre, a poultry show occupied the basement. A possible catastrophe was avoided by covering all the roosters' heads with improvised cardboard boxes in order to prevent them from crowing and so interrupting the prima donna's arias. However, such juxtapositions are far less ridiculous than the risks run by insisting on the exclusive tenancy of an expensive building. The American drama might more easily greet a new day in theatres where poultry occasionally clucked in the cellar rather than in theatres that cannot pay the cost of upkeep unless they house a smash hit, or are forced to stand empty for lack of one.

Unfortunately the idea of giving theatrical performances in the West-chester County Centre was accepted as part of its programme only after the building was half completed. As a result the stage of the small theatre is hopelessly cramped for lack of space, without adequate light-ing or scene-shifting equipment. The larger stage, laid out originally for choral performances and concerts, is too shallow for the best pos-sible use to be made of it, despite a modern switch-board. Nevertheless this county centre can serve as an indication, if not a complete model, of how a theatre can be made a centre and can also begin to pay its way by being related to a programme of recreation for an entire com-munity. Not only artists of the theatre but also painters and architects have recently come to realize that they cannot grow except as part of planned communities. The painting of easel-pictures is a moribund profession, because pictures have to be stacked in studios or dealers' storerooms, waiting a chance to entice the occasional wealthy patron, and are produced with no relation to the habits or the habitations of any substantial proportion of the population, who cannot afford space in which to hang the paintings that they might want to buy. Archi-tects have discovered that the haphazard building of sky-scrapers, im-posing enough to be catalogued as monuments, blocking each other's light, siphoning the tenants out of one district and pumping them into towers in another, has reached a point of congestion that paralyzes every form of traffic and helps to make urban life physically exhaust-ing and spiritually intolerable. Every programme that attempts to en-visage the future of architecture accepts as its unit not the individual building but a city plan, not the individual house but the housing programme of a regional plan. Nothing is more certain than that we shall be forced to organize not only American industry but all of American life according to plans that more and more eliminate the wastes of private speculation and supplant them with the co-ordinations of collective effort. We have already begun to face the necessity of eliminating dead men's curves in our road-building and substituting landscape parkways for the superfluous hot-dog stands and filling-stations that now clutter the margin of our highroads. There is every evidence that American cities will eventually be linked with farming and suburban communities by such systems of automobile parkways. Along them community playhouses that were community centres like Westchester County's should have an inevitable place as subsidiaries to a chain of endowed city theatres that were civic centres.

Drama could be housed there with every other form of recreation. Craft-shops for metal work, painting, and wood-carving, machine-shops and electric laboratories for the amateur, would throw off as by-products the scenery, painted or projected, furniture, ornaments, or whatever other properties a local stage needed. Local choruses and dancers could be drafted and trained for revivals of Greek tragedies or for the insurgent masses of whatever new choral dramas might be written. The local amateur theatre would have the opportunity of studying visiting professional companies, and its most talented members be given both the training and the contacts that develop professional skill. These playhouses should exist in gardens of which an open-air arena might easily be made a part, where local gardeners could compete for annual prizes, where lovers could meet and children play. Every such community centre would tap a population on a radius of sixty miles that could reach it by automobile and so serve a territory of approximately eleven thousand square miles. If the American theatre is to have a larger life it will be, I believe, in a co-ordinated network of such theatrical centres that are a part of integrated communities. If playwrighting is to achieve new vitality, it will be helped to do so by sharing a playhouse that welcomes every other type of recreation. It might thrive there as it never has in a side-street, even though it share its quarters, from time to time, with firemen on a holiday, athletic champions, lions of the keyboard, and prize roosters.

CHAPTER III

THE PLAYWRIGHT
AND THE SPOKEN WORD

1. YEAH? OH, YEAH!

IF WE continue to speculate on what the American playwright may accomplish, once he is freed from subservience to theatrical landlords and individual managers, it is important to remember that the necessity for providing exaggerated private profits is not the only form of bondage to which he is subject. If he is to recover the masculine vigour of dramatic poetry for which the theatre's theologians pray, he will also have to free himself from the present tyranny of colloquial speech.

Like every other form of literary effort, playwrighting seems to be muted by a desire for the gentility that has so often fastened itself on American literature and subdued it like a maiden aunt come to keep house for her widowed brother. Our prevalent standards of literary style appear to be set for us by the well-bred woman and the well-dressed man and to be transmutations of precepts originally instilled by female school-teachers and fashionable tailors. We must be reticent at all costs. To be too emotional in prose writing is vulgar; it is comparable to talking too loud in public. One too many relative clauses in a sentence is the equivalent of a frill on one's evening shirt; too bright a simile is an evidence of bad taste, like a diamond stud. If a metaphor is used it must be discreetly added to a sentence, like a scarf-pin in one's necktie. Advice on the cultivation of literary style often echoes the old

Sunday-school lesson: the self-indulgent writer, if he continues to flaunt patches of purple prose, will presently be marked with a stigma like the drunkard's ruddy nose.

Where reticence is not the ideal of elegance, a kind of deliberately cultivated inarticulateness is sought for as a sign of strength. It is the equivalent of the small boy's self-consciousness. We too as writers want to be "regular fellers," quick to "call down" the next fellow's pretensions by shouting, "Show-off!" We desire to grow up to be "regular guys," strong, silent men, captains of our souls, of course, but the literary counterpart of a sea-captain on his bridge or a railroad engineer in his cab who issues commands through his teeth and punctuates them with a squirt of tobacco-juice. Hemingway conceals his essential romanticism in sentences whose monotonous accent glints at regular intervals like high-lights on rifle-barrels stacked at an arsenal. His imitators seem inclined to take as a standard of sentence-structure the ten-word telegram. The staccato dialogue of German Expressionist playwrights was at one time dubbed "telegraph style" by German critics. Faulkner "writes like an angel" but his chosen mouthpieces are morons and half-wits. And most of us attempt to maintain a cheerful informality in our private conversation that tends to make it resemble the conversation of two morons, Chuck and Flora, in Cleveland's juvenile court as reported by its referee, Eleanor Wembridge, in *Life Among the Lowbrows*: "If Chuck remarked, 'There goes a white horse,' she shouted with laughter, and said, 'Hot dog!' If he said, 'That's a Ford,' she agreed, murmuring, 'You said it!' and snuggled closer. She could also say, 'Ain't it so?' 'You're a fright,' 'I'll say,' 'Hell's bells,' and 'You're crazy with the heat.'"

The universal fear of seeming verbally elaborate or pretentious has made conversation, like letter-writing, a lost art. No one will take the time that it requires; if he does, it is taken as a sign of weakness of character and his social or business career can be ruined by spreading the rumour that he talks too much. The cult of the "low-brow" infects even our intellectuals. If one of them were to take five minutes to qualify an opinion with verbal nicety he would embarrass his friends almost as much as if he had arisen to recite "The Wreck of the Hesperus." It is considered better social form to confine critical approval to "swell piece," "a wow," "great stuff," and disparagement to "lousy," "phony," "hooey," or "tripe," and so keep in tune with a casual "Okay" or "So long." In his fantasy on American *mores, Juan in America,* Eric Linklater gives a few moments of conversation overheard at a speak-easy.

An argument, animated but monotonous, was in progress at a table near to that occupied by Juan and Mr. Cohen.

"Oh yeah?" said the man.

"Yeah," said the woman with him.

The first yeah *had a rising inflexion, and the man's voice was exaggeratedly bitter, sarcastic, and incredulous. The responsive female* yeah *declined and deepened in tone, and the woman spoke harshly, combatively, and doggedly.*

"Is zat so?" enquired the man, and seemed marvellously sceptical.

"Yeah, that's so," replied the woman.

"Well, that's too bad," said the man. "That's just too bad." His sarcasm sharpened to an almost metallic edge.

"Oh yeah?" said the woman, in her turn incredulous.

"Yeah," replied the man, and his voice was harsh and dogged.

A few minutes later:

"Yeah," said the woman at a nearby table.

"Is zat so?" enquired the man.

"Yeah, that's so" . . .

The argumentative man and his controversial companion had relapsed into a sullen silence. From a further group came a voice, heavy with emotion, asserting with singular intensity, "He's a swell guy when you get to know him," and some one else, lauding a hero equally anonymous, shrilly declared, "Well, he just kicked the pants off him. Yes, sir. Just kicked the goddam pants off him."

This picture of the conversational habits of our leisure class seems to me both complete and accurate. If the standard for the written sentence is the telegram, we seem to be in the process of accepting as the ideal form of the spoken sentence a subtly inflected grunt.

The explanation usually given of such familiar attempts at abbreviation is that they represent an effort to adjust our speech to the rhythms of a machine age. We are supposedly impelled to simulate the heightened pace of life around us and, in speaking, to imitate the regularly spaced clatter of a railway train, the tapping of automobile valves, the clacking of a typewriter, the click of a ticker-tape. The assumption although plausible is untenable. The speed of modern life may tend to excite us emotionally, but it tends to paralyze us physically. We are surrounded by objects that flash or fly by at forty or fifty miles an hour, whirr and hum at hundreds of revolutions per minute. But surrounded by them we sit more continuously than any previous generation has done. Collectively we break all speed records; individually we are so constipated that every grocery-store stocks laxative breakfast-foods. Our tendency to make "Yeah" a substitute for a sentence and a sentence a substitute for a paragraph is the result of watching so many objects race past us—from automobiles, train windows, aeroplane cabins, or on the moving-picture screen—that we have lost the capacity for concentrated attention for more than a few seconds or at most a minute at a time. Our abbreviated colloquialisms are nothing more than another symptom of our weakened power of observation that vitiates not only speech but every other form of expression which requires a degree of reflection for its exercise and enjoyment.

We are inclined to decide that whatever will not yield its meaning at first glance or during the first half-minute is not worth the effort. Recently an investigator, Professor E. S. Robinson of Yale, used a stop-watch as a check on *The Behavior of the Museum Visitor*. Sixty were observed in a museum that contained one thousand paintings hung in forty rooms. The longest time spent in front of any one picture was sixty seconds. But only one visitor concentrated to this extent. Eight satisfied their interest in twelve seconds, thirteen in eight seconds, eleven in six seconds, and seven in two seconds. The average time spent in observing any one painting by sixty people who had enough interest in art to visit an art museum was nine and two-tenths seconds, and they looked at only fifty-six out of the one thousand paintings displayed.

The same kind of mental lethargy is so prevalent that it has to be catered to by the way ideas are presented in print. The reader has to be whipped into attention if he is to behave very differently from the museum visitor. Even that fraction of the book-buying public known as serious readers cannot be trusted to push their way unaided through a sustained piece of critical analysis. A philosopher these days needs to be something of a journalist in order to hold his reader's interest. It is obvious from any number of recent volumes that even our so-called intellectual classes rely to a great extent on the equivalent of newspaper head-lines. Essays in magazines that extend to over three or four thousand words are subdivided by numerals 1, 2, 3, 4, and so on. "Whirl Is King," "Sorties and Retreats," "Deep Dissolution," "The Children of the Rock," "The Children of the Sun," "A Lost Leader and a House," sound like the picturesque chapter-headings of a romantic historical novel. They are actually chapter subdivisions in two of the most serious books recently published, one on national culture, the other on religion, by two critics totally dissimilar in temperament, neither of whom can be suspected of compromising for an instant with the degree of intelligence expected from his readers. The example seemed to me a wise one to follow. I have made my chapter subdivisions as picturesque and as provocative as possible and carefully avoided calling this book, as I might have had I been writing it a century ago, *An Enquiry into the Present State of the Theatrical Arts, Their Scope, Technique, and Purpose, with Especial Reference to Their Relation to the Prevailing Tastes of the Most Civilized Inhabitants of Europe and America.* The need for catering to a prevalent demand for abbreviation affects much of our typography. In a recent volume of reminiscences of London of the nineties by an English painter, the average paragraph consists of two, three, or four short sentences. The material itself is subtle and witty and addressed to the taste of sophisticated book-buyers; the volume is priced at five dollars. But the large type and the short paragraphs make each page typographically reminiscent of a First French Reader, where beginners have a foreign language broken up for them so that it can be easily bitten off and assimilated.

2. DEFLATED SPEECH

The necessity for breaking language into short and easily digested groups of words in response to a popular demand is even more keenly sensed by playwrights than by other authors. For a reader may lay a book down when he is momentarily bored; if he finishes it later he may help to make the book a success. But the one thing a playwright cannot do is to run the risk of having any one "walk out on his show." A book can wait for its audience, a play cannot. A playwright is therefore bound to be abnormally sensitive to the possibility of fatiguing an audience and, with the notable exceptions of Shaw and O'Neill, playwrights in general pander to our incapacity for sustained attention. Meredith, James, or Conrad might with impunity invent a form of conversation that no one habitually uses, for unless their dialogue is read aloud, a practice that few readers indulge in, it does not immediately seem unusual. But in the theatre the average ear seizes fifty times more quickly upon any rhythm of talk that is an uncommon kind of talk. This makes the persons using it seem unnatural and gives an air of unreality to dialogue, which, during a performance, must hold its audiences by seeming, momentarily at least, real and lifelike.

The impulse of playwrights at present is to meet the difficulty by surrendering to it completely. The easiest way to please audiences is to reproduce the speech of people who have no interest in sustaining intelligent conversation, since the latter is considered a pedantic form of exhibitionism by the literate and unnecessary by the illiterate, for whom the various inflexions of "Yeah? Oh, yeah!" are a sufficient means of communication. The simplest way of "putting a play over" is to let audiences hear the kind of speech they have just been indulging in at cocktail-parties, speak-easies, or over bridge-tables, to give them in the theatre the kind of talk that they are in the habit of hearing from their friends. The mouthpieces of plays that deal with the polite dilemmas of the upper classes tend to be characters whose conversation is so restrained that it is almost colourless; the struggles and the quandaries of the lower classes are revealed to the extent that they can be expressed in language overheard at a street corner or in a domestic relations court of a "tough" district. Emphasis is obtained by interpolating "lousy bastard," "goddamsonofabitch," or "what the hell" at appropriate intervals. No similes or metaphors are possible except those that can be made to seem plausible in the mouth of a débutante, a night-club hostess, a man about town, or a gangster.

Such reproduction of the timbre of contemporary life is in itself nothing to deplore. A fresh eye, the ability to see at first hand, is as important for the playwright as for the painter. A return to nature is always a preliminary excursion for any art that wishes to invigorate itself. The danger at present is that the plausibility and effectiveness of colloquialism in our theatre will be considered not a mere beginning but an end in itself, a significantly modern method instead of so much raw material from which a distinctively modern dramatic style will have to be made. For drama in order to be interpretative must sooner or later face the necessity of making articulate ideas and aspirations that are usually inarticulate, and so achieve an intensification of habitual speech. The American playwright today is handicapped by his inability to use any subject-matter that has not already found expression in a ready-made vernacular of a kind that can be cut up into crisp, short speeches easily spoken by the average actor.

The actor feels the tyranny of colloquialism no less directly than the playwright, for dramatic critics are also converts to the cult of reticence and easy abbreviation. Unless an actor becomes expert in a kind of fashionable, tight-lipped subtlety he will be damned for overacting, whereas the highest praise that can be accorded him is the announcement that he is "restrained." He lives in terror of being dismissed as rhetorical and old-fashioned, of being branded as a "ham" and declared eligible only for Shakespearean revivals, which is equivalent to being consigned to limbo, for Shakespeare's plays, like the Greek tragedies, are revived less and less frequently as it becomes increasingly difficult to assemble a company that can sustain their lines for five consecutive minutes. A premium having been put on mimicry, many of our best actors become superlative mimics. But when they cannot imitate the rhythms and inflexions of colloquial speech they are usually at a loss. When intensified utterance is called for they fumble, having nothing to fall back upon as an alternative but the oratorical methods of a discredited "What ho! Avaunt thee!" school of playwrighting. Having trained themselves to make no motions more violent than those involved in smoking cigarettes, shaking cocktails, slipping in and out of rooms or on and off furniture, jerking a thumb, or pulling the trigger of a pistol, the general run of able actors begin to feel that acting begins at the neck and extends upward, that facial expression is of paramount importance, that a play, like the Battle of Bunker Hill, cannot begin until every one in the audience sees the whites of the actors' eyes. The majority of actors' bodies are atrophied from lack of use. The dejection of a beggar seated at a curbstone may be apparent to passers-by at ten yards long before his features are distinctly seen. The fear of a mother expressed by the way she bends over the crib of a sick child can be felt by any one seeing her through a window, although her back be turned and she herself little more than a silhouette against a night-light. But the ability to attain this totality of bodily expression has become almost a lost craft. As a substitute the actor carefully droops an eyelid, drops the corner of his mouth, or indulges in some more subtle facial contortion, none of which can be clearly seen by the majority of his audience, seated forty or fifty feet back of the curtain line. When gestures that accompany violent emotion are called for, they are usually so clumsily done that an astute director modifies them into a series of minor convulsions or gulps that can be praised as free from the taint of "ham."

It is amazing that our theatres are so often crowded. For not only is it difficult for audiences to see the subtleties of present-day acting but also it is increasingly difficult to hear them. A few nights ago I emerged from a seat in the tenth row of the orchestra with a temporarily stiffened neck, due to the continued strain of trying to hear the ends of sentences that two accomplished players persisted in swallowing during three acts of witty dialogue. It is idle to talk of a possible revival of poetry in the American theatre, to invoke glibly the vigour of some dramatic poet of the past, until we face the dual problem: How is the American playwright to graft sonorous and rhythmic speech on to his indigenous material? How is the actor going to learn to speak it when written? If a script were to be written tomorrow that rang with the cadences of Sophocles' choruses to *Antigone,* it would be far less likely to be rejected by a theatrical producer than to be abandoned in rehearsal, because no cast could be assembled capable of projecting its language in performance.

3. DEBASED CURRENCY

The revival of poetic intensity of utterance would not be so urgently needed if the American temperament were naturally laconic. In that case the elisions and condensations of our colloquial speech might become an expressive dramatic style. But we happen to be a particularly garrulous people. The news in our newspapers is written by the garrulous for the gullible. Size—the number of columns, the number of pages—is the criterion of journalistic importance. No other nation encourages journalistic verbosity that makes a twenty-six-page daily edition of an American newspaper, when spread out, form a rug of printed paper 12 feet by 5 feet 7½ inches. The Sunday edition of another newspaper that I measured recently contained 459 square feet of printed matter and weighed 2 pounds 6½ ounces. Except for critical and autobiographical columns, journalists are so uncertain of reporting anything with finality that repetition becomes the most commonly accepted form of emphasis. Any event thought to be important news is told three or four times—by an anonymous reporter, by a special writer, and by two rival news services. Adventurers have always been tall talkers; sailors and hunters usually spin the longest yarns. But we no longer wait for the adventurer to return. American newspapers encourage him to begin talking as soon as he starts. The transatlantic flyer contracts for his autobiography before he takes off and relays the first instalment by wireless from mid-ocean. Byrd's antarctic expedition never stopped talking; every morning an arctic waste of words blanketed some page of the New York *Times*.

Such verbosity is wide-spread enough to be regarded as typical. The popular American short story has been lifted out of the mould used by Bret Harte, Stephen Crane, and O. Henry; it is no longer short. Its most highly paid practitioners fill our most popular magazines with lavalike narratives that overflow through several pages of advertising columns. A President who condensed his annual message to the Congress into thirty-five hundred words would probably run the risk of being impeached for frivolity in the conduct of high office. Coolidge, reputedly our most taciturn President, exceeded many of his predecessors in the length of his congressional messages. When he became a journalist and attempted to summarize the significance of current events in a few hundred words daily, he was able to do this only by repeating platitudes. The stream of his thought was clear but shallow; unlike the trout-streams that he occasionally angled in, it made no pools that hid ideas worth fishing for. Most of our simple, clear thinking is of the same transparent kind; it evaporates quickly and leaves no residue. When experts are summoned to analyze economic or social problems, their findings usually run to such length that they are never widely enough read to influence public opinion.

Having as a result of our mental laziness refused to understand or to employ the emotional overtones of the written or spoken word, and having promulgated a monotonous form of unemphatic, simple declarative expression, which we delude ourselves is particularly fitted to express the truth and nothing but the truth, we are easily taken in by the stalest tricks of rhetoric and the most shop-worn oratorical formulas. Of all literate nations we are the most easily victimized by catchwords and head-lines; by slogans, whether applied to cigarettes or to candidates for public office; by third-rate campaign orators, high-pressure salesmen, patent-medicine fakers, medical quacks, bogus-stock swindlers; by propagandists and publicity agents of every kind, who exploit us annually by the hundred thousand and earn fortunes with the greatest ease on the strength of being fervid and highfalutin before a population that has largely forgotten how to use words or how to test their value.

Our habitual form of expression, written or spoken, runs past like machine parts on a giant belt, a monotonous assembly of prose so uniformly unemphatic and so mechanically put together that as a whole it is inexpressive and has a minimum of interpretative power. In order to seem contemporary the playwright is impelled to repeat its flaccid rhythms and its colourlessness. Because he accepts a convention of speech that makes analysis or reflection "high-brow" and ostentatious, he is rarely able to utilize characters intelligent enough to make comments of any importance on the meaning of the dramas that they take part in. Theatre audiences are likely to learn no more of our typical economic, religious, and political struggles than can be overheard by listening to their slightly bewildered victims—rural preachers, district leaders, tenant-farmers, miners on strike, convicts awaiting their turn in the electric chair. It is of course true that people in the grip of a catastrophe rarely know "what it is all about." It is equally true that regicides and parricides of former epochs who had just assassinated a rival did not stop, as they wiped their daggers, to summarize the meaning of good and evil, the nature of sin and retribution, or the relative values of life and death. The dramas of the past that we class as poetic became so by adopting a convention which enabled their heroes to be capable of searching thought and profound reflection, touching the depths of human experience and defining its goals, at moments when in actuality they might have done nothing of the sort. And they were capable of doing this in the theatre because they were given a form of utterance that crowned heads never habitually used in the Greece described by Homer or in England and Scotland as chronicled by Holinshed. The convention of didactic debate and choral odes in Greek tragedies, the convention of the soliloquy in Shakespeare's, is an integral part of the structure of poetic drama; without these formally constructed gaps in the dramatic sequence of

433

events, the traditional poetry of poetic drama could not have found an opportunity for expression.

Until an equivalent modern convention is evolved, dramatic poetry cannot become an integral part of American playwrighting. Some way remains to be discovered of organizing a concatenation of events that, without destroying their dramatic force, will give an opportunity for the kind of comment on the meaning of the events enacted that cannot be expressed by the rhythms of colloquial idiom and the vocabulary of current conversation. The importance of O'Neill's attempt to revive the use of the soliloquy in *Strange Interlude* did not lie in the fact that the soliloquy is in itself inevitably poetic, but in the fact that it enabled a college professor, a novelist, a biologist, a small-town belle, and a conventional business man to interpret, as they could not do in talking to each other, the inner significance of their loves and hates bred by the typical relationships of father and daughter, husband and wife, lover and mistress, in present-day society. Poetry is always an interlude in drama and remains a strange interlude until it is technically made an integral part of the structure of dramatic writing. Without this integration the intensifications of poetic imagery and poetic rhythm seem artificial and superficial ornament, a decorative encumbrance instead of an inevitable means of heightening the reality of a play's theme.

However, no poetic convention such as the soliloquy will by itself revive the writing of dramatic poetry. It is an empty chalice until it is filled with a distillation of poetic speech. It is comparatively easy to take a sensitive, introspective young man, Henry Elsin, or let us say, Henry Elgin, suffering because his still buxom mother has married again, set him down in the back-yard where some children have left a snow man, and allow him, hunched in his overcoat, to ruminate as follows:

Henry: *Damn my stepfather; lecherous old bastard. If I could only kill him. But I'm a snivelling introvert. All I can do is complain. I can't do anything.* . . . *Mother—mother's nothing but a whore. No! I shouldn't have said that. Forgive me, mother.* . . . *But it drives me almost mad to think of it. God! if I could only kill myself— get away from it all. There's nothing to live for.* (He hunches more deeply into his coat collar.) *I'm afraid! Afraid to do anything. Afraid of death.* (He shivers.) *Spooks. What they told me when I was a kid. Just afraid of the dark—but it sticks. It gets me.* (Looking at the snow man.) *I'm just so much mush—mush like you.* (He breaks into bitter laughter, takes off the battered derby from the snow man's head and salutes him elaborately.) *If I could only thaw with you tomorrow—thaw, just dissolve, trickle into the earth—run off into the sewer, etc., etc.*

It would be possible, following the current tradition of poignant in-articulateness, to continue in this vein, to add to the pathos of the scene by having two care-free children come out and cover the young man with snow until he too seemed another snow man. One could bring on a cook, who in sweeping off the back-yard sang an Irish tune with a refrain to the effect that life could be taken easily, "as the leaves grow on the tree." Or one might achieve a symbolic climax by having the snow man melt before the eyes of the audience. None of this, how-ever, would alter the transparent fact that Henry's pathetic confession contains the sum and substance of two of Hamlet's soliloquies, and because it is not couched in the language of supreme poetry is, by just that enormous gap, inferior as drama to Shakespeare's tragedy.

Psychologically we are far more certain than Shakespeare could have been that the young man in the back-yard is a neurotic, suffering from a well-defined mother complex, that he wishes to kill his stepfather (as the London psycho-analyst Ernest Jones pointed out some years ago) because, having been jealous of his own father and desiring to displace him by sleeping with his own mother, he has transferred this childish hate to the man who has taken his father's place as his mother's bedfellow. One might continue my improvisation and motivate beyond the possibility of dispute any subsequent degree of neurosis or psychosis that could afflict Henry, any bloody deed, whether murder or suicide, of which he might be capable. But because he did not express himself in language comparable to Hamlet's he would be, for that reason alone, a less dramatic expression of the fundamentally tragic conflicts of the human ego. The disability that the modern playwright suffers under is this: Although he may trace unerringly the conflicts of the libido or the psyche (if we prefer these words to the older one, soul), although he may envisage just as clearly as any of his predecessors essentially tragic stories, he cannot make them incandescent and illuminating at their climactic moments because of his inability, or his unwillingness, to employ the intensifications of poetic speech.

4. THE ENFEEBLED WORD

This disability is so fundamental that it is evident in plays dramatically feeble as well as in plays that are dramatically powerful—at one extreme *1931*, by Claire and Paul Sifton, withdrawn after a week, a failure according to both critics and public; at the other, O'Neill's *Mourning Becomes Electra*, acclaimed by both critics and public as a masterpiece and playing to packed houses. *1931* depicts the disintegration of Adam, a freight-handler, a typically healthy, brawny, and optimistic American day-labourer, unable to find a job. No one has denied that he was made a typical figure, that the total picture of the degrading effect of unemployment was true and convincingly observed to the last detail. The play, inspired by generous indignation and compassion, was an attempt to stir audiences to a realization of the tragedy of an individual caught in a social catastrophe. Yet audiences were not moved, although they knew that every word and every situation was undeniably typical of the experience shattering hundreds of thousands of men in New York City alone. *1931* may have been weakened as a story because its authors adopted the chronicle form of loosely related incidents. But they provided an abundance of situations that were obviously dramatic—Adam's quarrel with the foreman, his attempt to get money by a hold-up that he could not carry through, his desperate surrender when he made his fiancée his mistress, his equally desperate escape to join a rioting mob when he finds her again, a diseased prostitute. According to J. Brooks Atkinson: "By virtue of Franchot Tone's beautifully tempered acting of Adam, the material of *1931* has a torturing dramatic vitality. . . . Mordecai Gorelik has designed a memorable setting—the monstrous exterior of a factory. . . . To see the whole cycle of unemployment resolve into the tragedy of one man, to see him in gaunt perspective against the heedless, impersonal background of a thundering city is to have the present crisis in tangible form. What you have read here and there in the newspapers, what you observe in fragments as you prowl inquiringly around the streets, becomes complete and vivid in the theatre and fills you with anguish."

Why then were audiences at *1931* not purged by the pity and terror that are supposed to satisfy them when they watch tragedy in the theatre? Mr. Atkinson assigns as a reason the inherent weaknesses of theatrical pamphleteering: "The pamphleteer's worst fault is his inefficiency. He does not know how to squeeze drama out of dramatic material. He dissipates his theme across a multiplicity of scenes that would worry a movie director. Having no instinct for form, he produces his story in dry stencil snippets. He has no real affection for the truth of his characters. *He writes dialogue with his fingertips. He has only an intellectual approach to a medium that is emotional or nothing.*" The italics are mine, for I feel that deficiency of style is the clew to the failure of *1931,* rather than its lack of formal dramatic structure.

Many plays in the last decade have achieved dramatic power although snipped into ten and twenty scenes. *1931* lacked emotional power because of its language; it could not arouse any profound or lasting reaction in audiences already filled with some of the horror, the compassion, and the indignation that moved its authors, because their verbal style was itself a succession of dry stencil snippets. Owing to the tradition of more or less inarticulate poignance, not a character in the play was much more capable than an actual foreman, newsdealer, or unemployed factory-hand of expressing the meaning of anything he saw or suffered. The emotion lacking throughout was the heightened emotion that poetry can give to a statement of experience. The problem that was fuddled was not one of form in connecting a series of incidents, but a problem of style in connecting a series of words. The problem could have been solved if the Siftons had not been unable, like so many other American playwrights, to devise a form of dramatic speech by which the typical labourer, his sweetheart, and his employer, while remaining in character were yet able to voice all the implications of their individual fates that related them to a social tragedy. Because no one could speak dramatically, the vision of tragedy was implicit in the stage setting, with its clanging iron shutters cutting off mute and discouraged mobs from the promise of work. It was not explicit in the leading players, and because anything that they were able to say remained verbally trivial, their story eventually became insignificant.

When Adam, after weeks in hospital, stumbled past an unfinished building and propping himself against an ash-can tried to voice his despair and his ultimate agony, we looked on, we sympathized, we were prompted to give him a quarter, half a dollar, even a dollar. But this moment, which should have been apocalyptic, scorching us with blinding revelation, terrifying us with the thunders of judgment, revealing as in a vision flaming about one human being the floundering cruelty of a desperate industrialism, this moment remained merely pathetic because Adam could say nothing more than might conceivably be overheard in a lodging-house or a bread-line. What might have been the dramatic climax of the play failed because Adam was not made a new Adam, faced with a new doom, denied a paradise where he could earn his living by the sweat of his brow. It left him another typical case, a jobless man, a convalescent who needed post-hospital care that he could not afford, a convincing exhibit among the data of a district nursing service. Here was a play potentially momentous in theme, inherently tragic in import, that dribbled away its tragedy. Its audiences were able to derive no more emotion from meeting its protagonist in the theatre than from meeting him on a street corner, because he was not conceived by a poet. Adam was doomed as a theatrical personage because he lacked a poetic vocabulary.

Turn to *Mourning Becomes Electra* at the other end of the dramatic scale. We may agree with Joseph Wood Krutch when he writes, "It is like all supremely great pieces of literature, primarily about the passions and primarily addressed to our interest in them. Once more we have a great play . . . which does mean the same thing that Oedipus and Hamlet and Macbeth mean—namely that human beings are great and terrible creatures when they are in the grip of great passions and the spectacle of them is not only absorbing but also at once horrible and cleansing." But it is also possible to admit the force of Mr. Krutch's qualification: "To find in the play any lack at all one must compare it with the very greatest works of dramatic literature, but when one does compare it with 'Hamlet' and 'Macbeth' one realizes that it does lack just one thing and that thing is language—words as thrilling as the action which accompanies them. Take, for example, the scene in which Orin (Orestes) stands beside the bier of his father and apostrophizes the body laid there. No one can deny that the speech is a good one, but what one desires with an almost agonizing desire is

439

something not merely good but something incredibly magnificent, something like 'Tomorrow and tomorrow and tomorrow . . .' or 'I could a tale unfold whose lightest word. . . .' If by some miracle such words could come, the situation would not be unworthy of them. Here is a scenario to which the most soaring eloquence and the most profound poetry are appropriate, and if it were granted us we should be swept aloft as no Anglo-Saxon audience since Shakespeare's time has had an opportunity to be. But no modern is capable of language really worthy of O'Neill's play, and the lack of that one thing is the penalty that we must pay for living in an age which is not equal to more than prose. Nor is it to be supposed that I make this reservation merely for the purpose of saying that Mr. O'Neill's play is not so good as the best of Shakespeare; I make it, on the contrary, in order to indicate where one must go in order to find a worthy comparison."

In *Counter-Statement* Kenneth Burke says, "The contemporary audience hears the lines of a play or novel with the same equipment as it brings to reading the lines of its daily paper. It is content to have facts placed before it in more or less adequate sequence. . . . As a striking instance of a modern play with potentialities in which the intensity of eloquence is missing, I might cite a recent success, Čapek's R.U.R. Here, in a melodrama which was often astonishing in the rightness of its technical procedure, when the author was finished he had written nothing but the scenario for a play by Shakespeare. It was a play in which the author produced time and again the opportunity, the demand, for eloquence, only to move on. . . . The Adam and Eve scene of the last act, a 'commission' which the Shakespeare of the comedies would have loved to fill, was in the verbal barrenness of Čapek's play something shameless to the point of blushing. The Robot, turned human, prompted by the dawn of love to see his first sunrise, or hear the first bird-call, and forced merely to say 'Oh, see the sunrise,' or 'Hear the pretty birds'—here one could do nothing but wring his hands at the absence of that aesthetic mould which produced the overslung 'speeches' of Romeo and Juliet."

It does not follow that poetry is the antithesis of realism, that dramatic dialogue must revert to the symmetries of established verse forms or the processional pace of iambic pentameters. The realistic approach is no less valid in the theatre than in a painting or a novel. But in no field can it be expressive until it rigorously reorganizes its observed material according to a predetermined pattern or rhythm. Even when nothing more than an imitation in nature is aimed at, an imitation remains feeble unless observation is sharpened by deliberate analysis, and relations not apparent are searched for, established, and emphasized, that is, until some method of selection is applied consistently enough to create what is called a style. An art student trying to copy a nude figure exactly, a portrait-painter attempting to get a literal likeness, must practise some degree of the selection and simplification which Rembrandt intensified in painting a side of beef or a self-portrait. The lack of vitality in the present realistic tradition of American playwrighting is largely due to its inability to achieve a style capable of transcending the clumsiness and feebleness of current talk.

The alternative does not consist in forcing coal-heavers and washer-women to speak as grandiloquently as the kings and queens of classic tragedies. Dramatic dialogue can have the intensity of utterance characteristic of poetry and at the same time avoid tirades and apostrophes and be written for plays that can be acted on kitchen chairs. But the modern playwright will have to devise an equivalent for traditionally poetic speech if he is to become genuinely eloquent. Playwrights need to begin the kind of experiments with word rhythms which Whitman or Robert Frost or Vachel Lindsay carried through, and the effort will have to be made deliberately and consciously until it is recognized as an integral part of the playwright's job. Any attempt to uplift modern drama to the plane that its most fervent partisans describe, or to give it a larger dimension, will necessarily be futile so long as it is directed at the playhouse instead of being concentrated on the play. The problem to be solved does not centre about the architecture of the stage but about the verbal style of playwrighting. Projected reforms in the style of stage-settings will remain very largely irrelevant until dramatic dialogue attains a style that can release the cumulative emotional force of poetry. Until the modern dramatist becomes an effective poet, the hands of his designers, like the tongues of his actors, are tied.

5. POETS AS PHILOSOPHERS

The consequences of our present traditions of playwrighting are unfortunate not because they restrict the designer to realistic stage-settings, but because they restrict the playwright in the selection and treatment of his material. Despite the indubitable progress made in bringing relevant themes into our theatre, our plays as a whole do little more than touch the fringes of American life. The typical struggles that have shaped American society are dramatized by critics and social historians, and are to be found far more frequently between book-covers than in the theatre. American playwrights have not yet compassed any of the bloody struggles of capital and labour to be found in Adamic's *Dynamite—The Story of Class Violence in America,* the tragicomedies of our imperialist orgies such as those recounted in Millis's *The Martial Spirit,* or our recurrent religious hysterias reviewed in Seldes's *The Stammering Century.* When such themes are touched in the theatre, our playwrights for want of poetic power fail to suggest the magnitude of the forces involved, the scope or the significance of the struggle. They resemble miniature-painters attempting to depict the Last Judgment. At best they resurrect an incident or isolate a single figure that loses dramatic power because it is not related to the scale of a larger composition, and we are given no more insight into martial or religious hysteria than can be implied in the eccentricities of a single revivalist or the lecheries and profanities of a handful of doughboys under fire. When an attempt is made to retell the fate of Mooney or of Sacco and Vanzetti, the plays fail for the same reason that *1931* did; the significance of their themes cannot be expressed in words powerful enough to dramatize them.

When acknowledged poets such as Paul Green or Lynn Riggs take to playwrighting, their verbal felicities achieve by turns memorable characterization, subtlety, poignance, humour, pathos, and, as performed, a boyish optimism. But they add little to the scope and depth of our prevalent methods of dramatizing experience. *The House of Connelly* depicts the relics of an epoch in American history which Claude Bowers chronicled under the title *The Tragic Era.* But the essential tragedy of those years of blundering reconstruction is not re-created in retrospect. The most powerful moment of the play, when the hero indicts his ancestors as the cause of their own degradation for having bred bastards with their slave wenches, touches a central and tragic theme that is never again related to the play nor resolved. The struggle of an intransigeant South is not apparent in the portraits of its indigent survivors. With slight changes they might be made equally typical of any other decayed landholding aristocracy. Because the original ideals that made a vanquished civilization something to fight for and to cling to are never adequately projected, the suicide of the old Southern colonel, although genuinely pathetic, is not tragic. We are never certain whether or not in his prime he was an aristocrat rather than the windbag we see in old age. The sight of gentlefolk fallen into poverty is always pathetic, particularly when as individuals they are made so living. But how much do they convey of the real values of a high-spirited and gracious culture that our uncontrolled growth as a nation was unable to save? How is one to accept as a happy ending the spectacle of the young lord of the manor who marries a daughter of the people and dedicates himself to the same grinding frugality and unremitting toil that has brought bankruptcy to the farmer everywhere else in the United States? Are we to accept it as a symbol of the effort that is to redeem the South or as an assurance that any young man who finds the right wife can make the old farm pay? As a Northerner I get no further insight into the South, its past or its future, than is afforded in the recognition that down-at-the-heel aristocrats invoke lost glories, become corrupt, die but do not surrender; and that their heirs, without money enough to live like aristocrats, had better take off their coats and get to work. A true story well told, but at the same time how inadequate an interpretation of the deeper implications of its material—the doom of an entire generation that does not know how to save itself and is in many ways still an alien people unable to attach itself to the life of a nation of which it cannot become an integral part.

The break-down of the pioneer spirit is more lightly told in *Green Grow the Lilacs,* but again the play presents nothing more than the pathos of another picturesque era which disintegrates more gaily to the echoes of its folk-tunes. The happy ending again consists of the young man who finds the right wife, a cowboy who renounces his broncho, also takes to the plough and looks forward to breeding more farmers, who are presumably to save the country when they are not being saved by the campaign promises of the Republican and Democratic parties.

One can salute the promise of both these writers, recognize their genuine gifts, and yet find that they echo foreign literary models more directly than they interpret American life. *The House of Connelly* seems a retelling in an American environment of Chekhov's *The Cherry Orchard,* and *Green Grow the Lilacs* a blander and less mischievous echo of *The Playboy of the Western World.* This in itself could be lightly granted; young artists, however original, usually begin by following accepted models. What is disquieting is the fact that the exceptional sensitiveness of both these writers is so wholly descriptive, and results in the heighening only of characterization and episode. They show no sensitiveness to the social implications of their chosen subject-matter and seem almost naïvely unaware of the forces which made and unmade the societies that they evoke, apparently content to play at their periphery, somewhat as children playing at being explorers might halt at the edge of a dark wood. One can acknowledge the qualities of both these plays that made them exceptional and well worth doing, one can be moved or delighted by them in the theatre, and nevertheless find their poetry immature and, though genuine, superficial. It is capable of painting charming or pathetic genre pictures; it is tender and shy; but the stories it tells are like ballads of sad or true love, sung to the accompaniment of a country fiddle that rasps faintly. What such colloquial poetry can give to the contemporary theatre is not much more valuable as a medium for dramatic expression than colloquial prose. It lacks dramatic power because it lacks eloquence; it lacks eloquence because it lacks vision; it lacks vision because, although it can describe the conflicts of the individual, it cannot conceive the larger conflicts of society. It has nothing to reveal or to proclaim that can illuminate the world we live in.

"Take eloquence and wring its neck," exclaimed Verlaine. On the basis of that injunction he produced many subtle, plaintive, and exquisite poems, but they are conceded to be minor poetry. The poetry that finds its way into the American theatre at present is minor in the same sense. A new theatre for a new society may be a mirage. It may be an immediate goal. But it will not be reached by erecting model playhouses unless they can be filled by poets capable of relating theatres more fundamentally than at present to the society that builds them. Even community playhouses will not serve communities until playwrights contribute to the growth of community life by seeing society steadily and seeing it whole. The ability to create human beings who can take on life in the theatre and the ability to make them vehicles of important ideas, the ability to describe and the ability to interpret, may be capacities that are destined to be permanently sundered by the trend of our times, which makes specialization and the division of labour the basis of every other form of production, from assembling an automobile to deducing a biochemical theory. Possibly the enormous scope of modern learning, the difficulties of fact-finding in a highly mechanized society, and the growing intricacies of scientific research may make the discovery of any truth so difficult that its propagation will have to be left to technicians and experts. The artist may be unable to assimilate sufficient knowledge for achieving syntheses of any kind; those that he is able to work out may inevitably be superficial, or at best brittle didacticism, the tapping of a school-teacher's pointer on a black-board. The playwright of the immediate future may be precluded from making valid judgments as to the value of any experience whatsoever. Perhaps his present disinclination to attempt such judgments is a sound intuition on his part. If this be true, then all talk of a new theatre that will have greater importance and wider influence than the theatre has heretofore had is wasted breath. Unless modern playwrights can become poets who are also philosophers, as dramatic poets have been before them, the theatre of tomorrow, however unique its architecture, will remain a monument to yesterday.

6. POET AND PEASANT

The difficulties inherent in reviving a poetic form of speech are apparent if one considers a single element of poetic effect—imagery. Figures of speech are a traditional poetic expedient because, as a matter of psychological fact, a comparison that establishes an analogy between one object and a seemingly dissimilar one heightens our perception of the first object and intensifies our experience of it. The same holds true of analogies that compare a subjective state to a visible occurrence, such as rising anger compared to a thunder-storm. The speech of primitive peoples is picturesque because it is so full of pictures that are used to make experience more vivid in the telling. The poetic image is originally a means of emphasis and an aid to communication. Folklore and folk-song are packed with imagery reflected in the speech of peasants who have never studied prosody, just as Yankee farmers refer to something that "spread like wildfire," was "quick as a streak of greased lightning" or "slow as molasses in January," whether or not they have been taught at the little red schoolhouse to classify such phrases as similes. The conversation of rural communities collects figures of speech as farmers' trousers collect burrs when walking through a field. One township a few hours outside of Vienna, where rolling hills fall away on every horizon, is called by its inhabitants "the hunchback world" (*die buckeliche Welt*); they would be astounded to be told that they were embryonic poets and had used a metaphor. Peasants and children probably anticipated both poets and botanists in christening their native wild flowers Dutchman's breeches, adder's tongue, jack-in-the-pulpit, love-in-a-mist, bleeding heart, just as they anticipated geographers in naming local mountains Giant, Saddleback, Le Lion Couchant (Crouching Lion), Die Jungfrau (The Virgin), Iztaccihuatl (The White Woman), and describe local waterfalls as Bridal Veils, neighbouring crags as Devil's or Lover's Leaps. Educated people are taught to recognize poetry and to support poets. Uneducated people often talk poetry themselves without knowing it.

Word pictures tend to be common and to be used without self-consciousness as part of everyday speech, so long as language remains the most important form of communication. The most effective method of telling what some one has seen or some one else has done is then to heighten the telling of it by the emphasis that verbal rhythm and word pictures can give. Some one has been more adventurous than the rest of his fellows and has seen a bigger mountain, a stranger flower, a wilder beast, surprised a god or a sprite. Something of his wonder and his sense of self-importance is given to the object as it is being described. And this impulse to brighten, heighten, colour, and exaggerate experience persists in conversation so long as there is no other ready way of conveying the importance of an experience. Poetry is originally spoken; it is addressed to a listener; it is the invention of a speaker to make his tale impressive and important. Poetic imagery tends to become sporadic as the printed word and the printed picture gain currency. The word that had to be illustrative is in turn illustrated; the spoken word is no longer the sole repository of experience or the only avenue of communication. Traffic on it drops off and moves more quickly, as it does on a main street when a new thoroughfare is opened. The making of poetic phrases is at first diverted from common speech to the printed page and becomes the prerogative of a specialist who stamps poetic idiom at a recognized mint with an official value, thus establishing a literary currency that takes the place of original tokens of verbal barter. So long as printed matter does not become too common, the writer retains some of the uniqueness of the original story-teller and makes his reports with metaphoric emphasis. At first the gap between the poet consciously declaiming poetry and the less self-conscious teller of tales is not great. Thus in the Elizabethan accounts of sea-voyages one reads: "The seas were rolled up from the depths . . . as if it had been a scroll of parchment." Or, "The sea swelled up above the clouds and gave battle to Heaven. It could not be said to rain; the waters like whole rivers did flood in the air." Such passages would not be inappropriate in *The Tempest,* beside

> *. . . the fire and cracks*
> *Of sulphurous roaring the most mighty Neptune*
> *Seem to besiege, and make his bold waves tremble,*
> *Yea, his dread trident shake.*

The writer who is not lost in a flood of printed matter is aware of a direct contact with his reader as though addressing him, and utilizes not only word pictures but the emphasis of rhythm and sonority. Until readers' ears are dulled by the sight of too much print, the printed word has aural associations. The reader hears the sound of what he reads. It is a common experience to find that most prose from the sixteenth through the eighteenth century can be read aloud with enjoyment, whereas any number of important modern novels are unendurable if read aloud for more than a few minutes. As books, pamphlets, and newspapers increase, this habit of aural association, which slows up the process of reading as it does that of writing, becomes atrophied. The science of exact measurement is used to improve our knowledge of the world, and language becomes more precise and colourless in use. The individual eye or ear is no longer to be trusted. To emphasize the value of experience by poetic means requires more and more bravado and self-assurance, becomes in fact a slightly ostentatious act, like pinning a flower in one's buttonhole, and flowery language becomes the mark of the literary dandy. Authors in the early phases of literary history write as men talk. We end by talking like an army of writers who no longer listen to the sound of what they have written. The swagger and savour of speech disappears in private talk and stage dialogue. Words become a debased currency; as with Chinese coppers, it takes a yard or two of them to complete a transaction of any importance and when some one attempts to sell us an idea with the single coin of a metaphor we suspect him of being something of a swindler or a charlatan; we pause suspiciously, bite the gold piece, or ring it against the nearest established fact in order to be certain that we are not accepting counterfeit money.

For the same reason the gap between daily speech and dialogue in the theatre can become too great. It is difficult for audiences habitually to accept a form of conversation on the stage that is widely different from their own. If statistics are to be trusted we are better educated than our great-grandfathers. But they turned out yearly to hear a repertory of Shakespeare's plays, whereas today we require national endowments to make regular performances of his plays possible. I suspect it was because our forefathers relished the opportunity of carrying life off with an occasional flourish in twirling their moustachios or bowing deeply and preferred to say, "Madame, your most obedient and humble servant," rather than to wave two fingers and say, "So long." I also suspect that they enjoyed Mark Antony's oration for the same reason that they enjoyed many of Webster's or Sumner's. They indulged in elaborate love-making and high-sounding amorous epistles themselves and so enjoyed high-sounding amours in the theatre, although their bookshelves probably held fewer anthologies of the world's best poetry than our own. Poetry is uncommon in the theatre at present, not because we cannot breed poets, but because we lack the desire for a kind of leisure in which we might dwell on the echoes or the colour of the spoken word. It is a strain for us to listen to rhythmic, accented, or eloquent speech since we no longer consider it important to achieve rudimentary accents and emphases ourselves and have no criterion of judgment. The poet in the last century often confined himself to "closet dramas" that were never intended for performance in a theatre and in consequence lost his inherited skill for telling stories in dramatic form. He rarely attempts even that today. Playwrights who have won an audience by learning to write plays often try to become dramatic poets. But very few poets who have won an audience by their poetry attempt to become playwrights. They are aware that their audience no longer exists in the theatre. They are encouraged to write poetry upon condition that they do not speak it out loud.

The metaphoric exuberance of Elizabethan drama, which we hark back to as a symptom of theatrical health, was not due to a lack of painted scenery that forced audiences to see with their ears. Equally florid dialogue existed in Italian and French theatres of the time and was spoken in front of elaborately painted stage settings. The prevalence of a poetic form of speech in the theatres of the sixteenth and seventeenth centuries was due to the fact that the spoken word was still the most readily available repository of experience. Audiences who could not experience Rome, for example, in the Sunday rotogravure sections of newspapers, illustrated outlines of the world's history, Everyman's encyclopaedias, or cheap text-books, if they wanted to know classic pomp and magnificence, relied upon a spoken account of it. They got it most easily in the theatre, where they could listen to Rome made alive in the speech of human beings who presumably lived there, just as they got their knowledge of the New World while listening at the neighbourhood tavern to a sailor just back from the Gold Coast or the Americas telling of savages and strange beasts. Every extension of experience for audiences the vast majority of whom could neither travel nor read very widely depended upon speech packed with every rhythm and image that could give it vividness and force. But we go to the theatre without any such expectancy. We go to hear only such things about Rome as we have not already learned from a trip to Europe, paintings, novels, histories, or newsreels. The modern playwright has no incentive to load his sentences; they are no longer argosies sailing home filled with plundered treasure. To modern audiences apostrophes to Rome or to anything else, however well written, seem to impede drama rather than to heighten it. Instead of listening like our ancestors, we are likely to be bored and to wait impatiently for "something to happen." We are as disinclined to turn to the theatre for the kind of enlargement of experience that spoken poetry can give as to turn to the Bible for our knowledge of the elephant or to be content with assurances that the Behemoth moves his tail like a cedar, that his bones are like bars of iron, and that he can drink up the River Jordan.

In the bare stubble of our speech a few backwaters of poetic diction survive. They are the vocabularies of backwoods communities that have remained remote enough to escape education by the printed word. Their conversation is still primitive in its naïve use of poetic imagery and offers to the playwright who reproduces it an opportunity to write poetic plays without seeming to be conscious of deliberately writing poetry and so estranging his present-day audiences. A poet is often made by discovering such a vocabulary. Yeats has told how he found Synge at loose ends in Paris and induced him to visit the Aran Islands, from which Synge derived the idiom of the plays that made his reputation as a poet-playwright. The speech of our Western frontiersmen or that of our Southern Negroes has occasionally been of similar value in the American theatre. But the lilting lingo of cowboys and darkies cannot be applied successfully to other subjects than folk-themes, and these are not inclusive enough to serve as a basis for interpreting a wide range of American life. The hidden treasure found in the abandoned slave-quarters or on the lone prairie cannot be hoarded indefinitely. Sooner or later it is dissipated in being exchanged for a debased verbal currency and the folk-lore playwright, after a respite, is forced to face the same problem that confronts any poet who attempts to write for the American theatre.

7. REVALUATION

Poetry cannot, I believe, be lured back into the theatre by inviting it to preside over "unrelated miracles of staging and lighting" or by urging it to invent the equivalent of religious ritual for "the human-divine intimacies" of an age about to be born. The means of its rehabilitation lie outside the theatre for the time being. Until the spoken word is revaluated as an important currency of communication in daily intercourse, until conversation begins to be cultivated as an intelligent pastime, dialogue on the stage will not arouse the kind of reaction in its audiences that induces the intensifications of style which make poetic speech an integral part of drama. The necessary preliminary to such a development is the rehabilitation of leisure to a point where it cultivates reflection rather than distraction.

The slightest breeze on a breathless summer afternoon is apt to be taken as a sign of an approaching thunder-storm that will clear the air. Similarly, I am probably predisposed to see, in the first puffs of scepticism now stirring, the vanguard of cleansing winds of doctrine. Present indications of a change in our standards of value taken singly seem feeble, but viewed collectively they indicate that the pattern of American life is about to be altered and that the American stage, along with every other form of expression, will benefit by the change. The process has been immensely accelerated by the booming collapse of the "new economic order." The promised land is no longer seen as a valley dotted with one-family houses, each in secure possession of a front lawn, where, reconciled to the loss of a few picturesque waterfalls, we are to live happily ever after among the tributaries of the General Electric. Our household gods may still be the vacuum-cleaner, the electric toaster, the electric stove, and an annual crop of new electric gadgets, but we no longer accept them as the symbols of our final liberation nor do we envisage the garage as the stable of a magic steed that will free us by rushing us over two hundred miles of crowded roads on a Sunday afternoon. We have begun to question whether all the efficiencies of labour-saving machinery have freed us for anything worth having. It is symptomatic of this impending revolt against our present culture that of the many books recently published about Mexico, the one to become a best-seller was written not by Ernest Gruening or Carleton Beals, the Americans who can describe the country most intimately and can speak with the greatest authority as the result of a long sojourn there, but by Stuart Chase, a statistician who had already indicted the wastes of mass production and mass merchandising. He makes his account of the battle of Aztec and Spanish cultures an eloquent homily on the happiness of an Indian population who have not yet submitted to the technique of machine industry, a convincing plea for the spiritual satisfactions of primitive agriculture and peasant handicraft. A new code of values, already being established, threatens to make Mexico a romantic American refuge and to substitute the Mexican Indian for the noble savage. Our popular monthlies, whose circulation is large enough to guarantee the fact that their readers are not told anything to which they are not predisposed to listen, are filled with attacks on our present standards of living, such as "A Declaration of Independence" or "A Search for the Center." It has begun to dawn upon a good many thousand Americans that when the efficiency expert has performed his last miracle they are free on their extra afternoon off to return to themselves and to invite their souls. They have discovered, without re-embracing any revealed religion, that they possess souls (although they may prefer to call them egos, psyches, or libidos), and have become aware that the soul has needs that can be as directly experienced as those of the stomach, that it cannot be invited without being fed. In searching for nourishment they begin to discuss the most ancient and philosophic problems: What is the Good Life? and, Why is it Good? and to argue with Lucretius about the nature of things—*de rerum natura.*

I do not imply that there is to be an outburst of amateur sonneteering on the subject or that the small investor will try to forget the tarnished gilt edges of his stocks and bonds by crowding theatres to hear didactic dramas on The Happy Indian done in heroic couplets. But we have begun to explore our age for a catalyst rather than for the philosopher's stone, to search for some standard of value other than gold which can sustain a truly civilized state of society. And as a bourgeois mother once remarked of her daughter's trip to Europe, it will help to make conversation. If we are interested in the problem of values we will talk about it and begin to accept words not as a means of killing time but as a means of revealing ideas that are vital to us. Conversation, as it does in all societies seeking to define the standard of value and to recognize the pattern of a new culture, will again become the green-room where ideas are rehearsed before they make a public appearance. As a result of such practice we will learn to reappraise the values of verbal style; after experiencing the need of expressing our convictions eloquently we will be ready to listen more easily to the heightened eloquence and the added meaning that poetry can lend to theatrical dialogue.

This will not be heaven; it will still be half-past one in the afternoon. The theatre even then will have to face as many experiments as it does now in order to find successful dramatic forms. No automatic adjustment of play to audience will occur of its own accord. But audiences will be prepared by their employment of leisure to be potential spectators for poetic drama to a degree that they are not now. The retreats of leisure are already being created. In numerous valleys in New York State and New England, the forest has begun to climb the hillsides from which it was originally driven, has begun to cover abandoned pastures where small-scale farmers can no longer scratch a living. One friend, on his Vermont hill-top, complained to me that his favourite view of rolling fields had in the last ten years turned into a young wood. Walter Prichard Eaton has described how the wilderness has recently reconquered whole townships in the Berkshires. But these abandoned acres have found a new class of tenant, pioneers of our new leisure who build week-end cottages or country homes and, in both the literal and figurative sense of Voltaire's injunction, cultivate their gardens. To increasing numbers of people reflection and meditation are no longer the prerogative of the professional philosopher.

The same opportunities are being created for the less affluent. Projects for the architecture of tomorrow are less concerned with aggrandizing sky-scrapers, which have already reached the point of diminishing returns, than with devising housing schemes for entire communities so that co-ordinated planning will bring decent living-conditions, where leisure can be used and enjoyed, within the means of a larger proportion of our population. A colossal effort is getting under way to reduce the unit cost of housing by the use of new materials, the economies of mass construction, and the technique of machine assemblage of standard parts. It is typical of all these attempts that they banish the constricted back-yard and the private carpet of a front lawn, and center about the communal and so maximum use of garden courtyards or small parks. The largest apartment-house in the immediate vicinity of New York, just completed, where the monthly rent of a room has been reduced to sixteen dollars, is constructed about a courtyard set with flowering shrubs and trees that twenty years ago would have been thought appropriate for a millionaire's country estate. In such surroundings we are likely to talk more freely and to better purpose.

Conversation is only one of the many fields to which we can restore a conscious cultivation of taste and to that extent prevent life from losing its savour. The opportunity given to a workman to grow petunias on his own balcony or to see a flowering hawthorn-tree at his back-door will not in itself make him an enlightened amateur or a patron of any of the arts, whether painting, poetry, or drama. But it is indicative, I think, of a wide-spread recognition among our leaders, who will determine what forms American life is to take in the near future, that there is something more to be filled than the dinner-pail. An organized theatre that has renounced gambler's profits, is spacious enough to welcome every form of recreation, and is no longer the tenant of a landlord who looks forward to a 100 per cent profit annually, is likely to find an intelligent audience among tenants of other landlords who are content with 6 per cent annual return or less and provide the maximum rather than the minimum setting that the act of living no less than play-acting needs in order to be well performed. The theatre of tomorrow cannot develop in isolated splendour. It may rise temporarily out of competitive greed like the shining towers of our sky-scrapers; like them it will be strangled by the accumulated waste, the congestion, and the misery at its foundations. The design of theatre art and theatre architecture, if it has any quality worthy of being hailed as new, will be related to the design of society. The civic theatre can become a civic centre only in decentralized and rationally planned cities; the community theatre can be a community centre only in integrated communities.

The hope for a new theatre and a new theatre art is something more than an aesthete's day-dream to the extent that it is typical of a collective effort, already begun, which is setting the stage for a new social order where, as workers and citizens, we shall be stimulated to play our individual rôles more successfully. If the effort succeeds, theatre-managers who direct a chain of national community or civic theatres will ultimately find themselves sitting at the same conference table with the architects of garden cities and regional plans. They will be both the leaders and the servants of a society consciously organized to test the values of experience, to adjust all our available means to desirable ends, to preserve a perpetually reinvigorating relation between labour and leisure. Such a society will not be humourless or grey with the dour determination of the reformer and the uplifter. Its plays will often be shows as well as revelations. It will relax by watching slap-stick comedy and vaudeville and will be less impressed than we are today by the trick of calling them a revival of

457

commedia dell' arte. It will escape from its momentary bewilderments, fatigues, and frustrations by listening to romantic fairy-tales in the theatre and sympathizing occasionally with Cinderella stenographers. But its capacities for enjoying the theatre will not be so speedily exhausted at this threshold. It will be a society that can stimulate the playwright to adventure with it and so recover his lost authority as a poet-interpreter.

8. ENVOI

No doubt it seems presumptuous for a designer to venture so far into the fields of sociology and literary criticism or to demand the poet-seer as a collaborator. I have done so in order to make plain that the development of scene-designing as an art must wait upon the arrival, in sufficient numbers, of dramatic poets capable of interpreting life profoundly. Until they appear the scene-designer, whatever his graphic gifts may be, can do little more than mark time. So far as I can see my own work objectively, I find that my best work has been done for plays that have expressed poetic insight—those of Goethe, Shakespeare, Claudel, Toller, Werfel, and O'Neill. If I were asked to contribute to an anthology of contemporary American scenic design and limited my contribution to settings for plays that were important as dramatic poetry, I would have automatically recorded my most important stage settings, even if they were to be judged not for their value in performance but entirely for their aesthetic values as designs. The same distinction holds true in judging the relative value of different scenes for the same play. The best setting in *Marco Millions* was not the spectacular Chinese court nor the Mohammedan or East Indian temple courtyards, but the scene aboard the princess' ship, where the poetic rather than the satiric values of the script reach a climax. And the same is true of the final setting for *Elizabeth the Queen;* the empty room in the Tower where the lovers, bitter-wise in renunciation, part under the shadow of a scaffold, was more nearly beautiful than the decorative throne-room where they argue and match wits.

A designer is more truly creative when he fails with the poet, as I did with O'Neill in *Dynamo,* than when he succeeds with the playwright who is nothing more than an observer. I have never shared more directly the excitement, the adventure, and the power of the modern theatre than in following the trail of O'Neill's mind from a power-house on a Connecticut river to the play that it inspired. When I first read the script, how incredible the singing, crooning dynamo seemed, how strained the effort to apostrophize it as a god whose commands could be interpreted! I visited the power-house. I heard the swish of water in the sluice below, a rushing accompaniment to the one dynamo that happened to be running at so many hundred revolutions per minute. It had a distinct musical note. I noticed that the recording dial was not working. "How can you keep track of it?" I asked the superintendent. "Oh, I know by the sound," he replied. Here was a technician, like a violinist tuning his instrument, relying on his sense of musical pitch to control a machine whose fluctuations had to be mathematically exact. I passed the transformers where the lazy current of a river had been transmuted into an electric current of thirty thousand volts. The heat generated by the change was so great that water could no longer cool the transformer; it had to be jacketed in cylinders of the heaviest oil. I passed a switch-board where tiny red and green lights blinked and winked, signalling changes of load that released enough energy to turn the wheels of entire factories or to light a small city. I stood in front of the condensers on an upper story where the thirty thousand volts of current were fed to the main transmission-line. I was warned to keep ten feet back of a protecting rail. The electric energy streaming through a copper wire at this point was so great that a static spark might jump across the gap and burn me severely. No insulation invented could protect me from those copper wires. If I touched one I would flame like a match and be consumed in an instant to my very bones. I noticed that the porcelain insulators had much the same form as certain ceremonial vases in Chinese temples. I listened to accounts of the terror of one thunderstorm when lightning struck a power-line miles away and the immense flow of current, short-circuited, shot back, and burned out one dynamo as if its windings had been so much paper.

Here was water that became fire, energy that sang a monotonous tune, that did croon like a lullaby and then became incandescent light. Here was power that could give man the strength of a god able to move mountains, the source of blind energy that could execute his commands over a network of metallic nerves beyond the reach of his eyes, that could light his way through darkness, reclaim him from toil, and, if not propitiated, consume him with flame. As I left a commonplace bare brick and steel power-house, I was touched with a terror and a veneration for the invisible forces controlling modern life that are potentially its salvation and its destruction, its heaven and its hell. I have left many cathedrals less awed and humbled. I had been at a shrine where an invisible miracle was daily performed, a transubstantiation no less miraculous than that of the Mass. And the purely mathematical calculation of engineers had given porcelain insulators the same beauty of form that ancient artists had given to temple vessels.

Rereading O'Neill's script, I seemed to understand for the first time the myth of Prometheus the fire-bringer. I understood why primitive peoples had cringed in terror before thunderbolts and erected altars to invisible gods. I had experienced, through a poet's insight, the wonder, the humility and pride, the hunger for power, the ecstasy of calling it forth, in which religions are born.

I do not for a moment pretend that I succeeded in putting any of this into my setting. The play itself failed at its climax when O'Neill's dynamo became an archaic god that could exact nothing more than an almost pathological desire for sexual purity. The theme of the play was short-circuited before it reached expression. Nevertheless I continue to hope that the play will be rewritten and that the projected trilogy of which it was to be a part will be completed. I continue to feel that in *Dynamo* O'Neill touched the sources of modern faith and despair more nearly than in exploring so much more successfully the insatiable desires of one modern woman for satisfaction in sex or in tracing the meaning of fate and retribution through the forbidden passions of one New England family. For *Dynamo,* despite its failure in performance, was more nearly the kind of success that the theatre needs today than hundreds of its present successes. In setting *Dynamo,* in sharing a poet's intuition, in accepting his symbols, in attempting to make the commonplace mechanical shapes of our industrial environment significant of the forces for good and evil that they released, in building them into a rostrum on which the hope and despair of our effort today to dominate ourselves and the world about us could be voiced—I understood how the designing of a stage setting could be made a creative act, whether or not I myself could make it one.

That road is the road which the modern designer must follow if he is to mature as an artist. He suffers most today not in being forbidden to experiment with colour, light, and form, but in not being called upon often enough to share the conceptions of playwrights who have creative imagination. As a group, American designers are in danger of becoming virtuosi. I begin to wince when I see by the morning paper how infallibly another one of us has caught the mood of a play. We are almost too sure of our results. We are not forced to grope often enough, to search for form, as other artists have had to do, to dig it out of ourselves, in frenzy, in agony if need be, and bring it forth at first only in fragments, broken, piecemeal. Our

461

fingers begin to seem like the well-protected digits of concert pianists. Despite every effort to preserve our integrity we seem to say, as the curtain rises and the expected burst of applause comes: Watch us now. There is nothing that we cannot do on our instrument—*legato, staccato, glissando, sostenuto—adagio, andante, vivace—con mobile, con amore, ma non troppo.* No, never too much. The rhythm will be just right, exactly what the moment needs to dance to.

Alas, it usually is. I have heard of designers who returned scripts to producers because they were trash and I have applauded their decision. I should be more encouraged if I heard of a designer who returned a script in despair because the problem of finding an appropriate scenic form for it was momentarily beyond him. Instead, in four weeks, three weeks, two weeks if necessary, we produce the commendable result. There are times when I wish our taste was not so certain and when I wonder whether we are much better than parlour magicians practising sleight-of-hand. Name your epoch, gentlemen! We are both prestidigitators and men of the world. We have travelled with our eyes open, on two continents and in our libraries. There will be no picture postcards. Everything will be skilfully interpreted, whether based on our own observations or on a document. Tragedy, comedy, history, pastoral-comical, historical-pastoral, tragical-historical, tragical-comical-historical-pastoral, scene individable, or poem unlimited—nothing is beyond us.

As designers we need the discipline of apprenticing ourselves to playwrights who can explore modern life under the light of the poetic imagination. Its light is needed, for the deductions of science, which are supposed to have instituted a new age of reason, bring us only fitful enlightenment. Our present-day scientific rationalizations so often become instruments of misery and oppression because they are so often divorced from human values. The same dispassionate knowledge, cleansed by the sterile impartiality of laboratory experiments, can breed babies hygienically or wipe out a thousand of them with a whiff of poison gas. Our technology that can endow us with machine-made plenty requires multitudes to starve periodically. The task of reason may well be to discover unsuspected relationships and to record them regardless of the consequences. Imagination is reason coloured by the emotions that its discoveries arouse and in the hands of the artist relates them to human needs and human desires. Where can they be more convincingly related than in the simulacrum of life which the theatre provides? Certain savages in the upper reaches of the Amazon make a nourishing food out of a root that in its raw state is a deadly poison. The dramatist has a similar function to perform in present-day society.

We have up to now achieved the framework of poetic drama rather than its substance. We need poets who can make us experience the sins that we connive at as well as those that we commit and share the dooms which we decree for others as well as those that we suffer individually. The heartbreak of tragedy might then purge us more completely than at present of the terrors that afflict us as living beings. We need poets who can also, in the laughter of comedy, reconcile the pretentions of modern wisdom with the emotional satisfactions that it can give. I do not see the poet reverting to a traditional rôle and, like a flounced and ruffled Apollo at the end of an eighteenth century ballet, mounting in gilded glory to a theatrical empyrean. The spoken word is too valuable a medium of expression to be squandered in refurbishing abandoned myths or in investing with a fresh nimbus gods who have abdicated. It need not be wasted in giving resonance to the voice of Fate conceived as a sibyl speaking through an ancient mask. There could be no more appropriate site for tragedy than the street corners of *1931*, the death house of *The Last Mile*, the Negro cabin of *Never No More*. The impact of realism need not be sacrificed because the naked fact is clothed with language radiant enough to fill us with something more than terror and brings us a peace less fugitive than pity. The

463

starving workman, the condemned criminal, the Negro mother watching her son being lynched, need only the force of poetic expressiveness to become our Hamlets and our Hecubas.

In the modern theatre, as in every other, the beginning is in the word. The actor cannot be reanimated until he is given the task of animating language so enriched in texture and so resonant with implications that it requires for its expression the entire range of modulations of which the human body and the human voice are capable. Only speech that soars can fill the undecorated forms of our most formal stage settings with enough significance to make them more than barren architecture and, at the same time, prevent our ambient patterns of colour and light from becoming empty decoration. Stage scenery may then reflect not only the subtleties of electric illumination but the light of ideas striking it from beyond the theatre's walls, and the forms of our stage settings acquire symbolic force, like the art forms of other epochs, by becoming images of good and evil.

As designers we cannot perform the functions of dramatic poets, but once they enter the theatre we are their indispensable collaborators. We cannot call them forth. It is they who must summon us. Meanwhile we wait and work.

ILLUSTRATIONS

JEAN FOUQUET   *Scene from a Mystery Play*   MID 15TH CENTURY

L. BURNACINI

Il Pomo d'Oro 1068

HELL SCENE

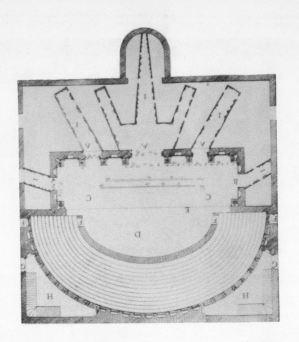

TEATRO OLIMPICO   PLAN

TEATRO OLIMPICO – ORCHESTRA   VICENZA 1584

TEATRO OLIMPICO – STAGE LATE 16TH CENTURY

STREET SCENE LATE 17TH CENTURY

471

S. SERLIO 1545   SCENE FOR COMEDY

MODEL OF   THE SAME SETTING

PAGEANT STAGE   ANTWERP 1582

OPEN AIR THEATRE   AMSTERDAM 1609

475

OPEN AIR THEATRE

477

AN ITALIAN PAGEANT

PAGEANT AT PRAGUE

1723

UNIT SETTINGS   MID 17TH CENTURY

UNIT SETTINGS

Marco Millions

UNIT SETTINGS

PERUGINO – DETAIL 1482

STAGE SETTING 1608

MANTEGNA   CA. 1497

STAGE SETTING   17TH CENTURY

JACOPO FABRIS – 1760   DESIGN FOR STAGE SETTING

PIERO DELLA FRANCESCA   1416-1492

PIERO DELLA FRANCESCA   1416-1492

SETTING FOR *Andromeda*   PARIS 1650

CLAUDE LORRAINE, 1600-1682 LANDSCAPE

SETTING BY TORELLI 1654

DESIGN FOR STAGE SETTING

F. IUVARIA 1676 – 1736

PARIGI 1637

INIGO JONES 1640

SCENES FROM *Le Bourgeois Gentilhomme*

FIGURE 42. A THEATRICAL OF MOLIÈRE'S *La Princesse d'Elide*

PRODUCTION AT VERSAILLES OF MOLIÈRE's *Le Malade Imaginaire*

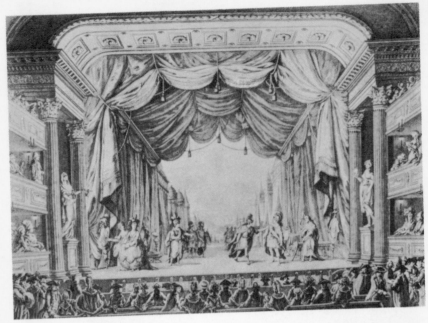

SETTING AT AMSTERDAM   1772

SETTING BY BURNACINI   1668

SETTING AT DROTTNINGHOLM 1784

SETTING AT DROTTNINGHOLM 1784

DESIGN FOR SETTING   FRANCE 17TH CENTURY

STAGE SETTING   AMSTERDAM 18TH CENTURY

SETTING AT DROTTNINGHOLM, SWEDEN   1784

SETTING AT DROTTNINGHOLM, SWEDEN   1784

DROTTNINGHOLM, SWEDEN

STAGE SETTING 1784

498

STAGE SETTING

SETTING FOR *William Tell*

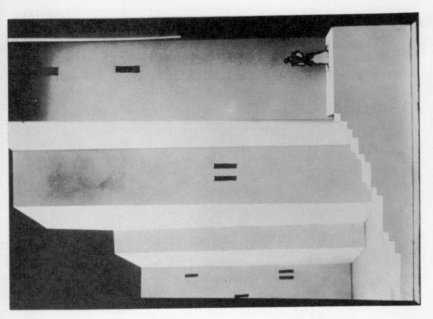

AUTHOR'S MODEL OF SAME SCENE

G. CRAIG

DESIGN FOR *Macbeth*

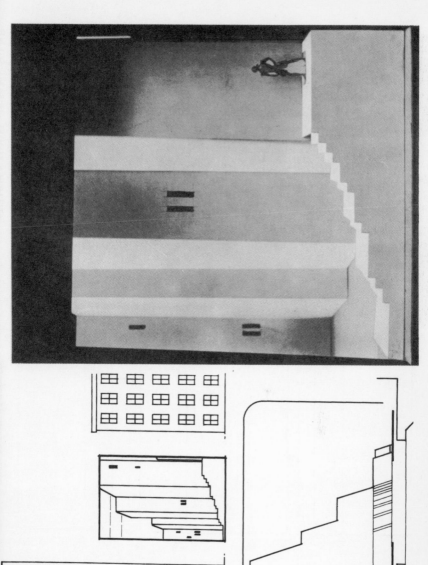

SAME MODEL WITH 35 FOOT PROSCENIUM OPENING

DIAGRAM OF MODEL TO SCALE

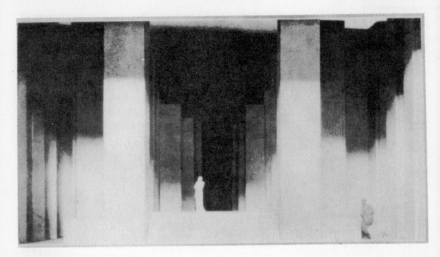

G. CRAIG 1912   MODEL FOR A SETTING

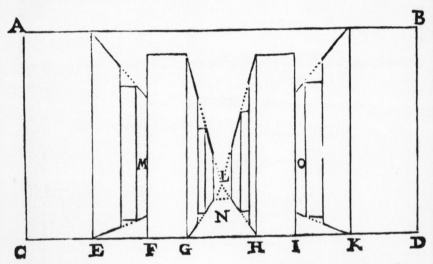

SABBATTINI 1638   DIAGRAM FOR *Street Scene*

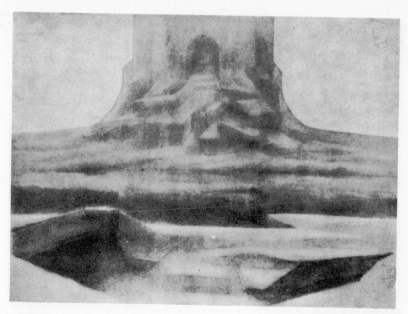

A. APPIA

Rheingold 1892

A. APPIA

Little Eyolf 1924

A. APPIA

Tristan 1896

A. APPIA

Tristan 1923

A. APPIA

Tristan 1923

A. APPIA

Tristan 1923

DUKE OF SAXE-MEININGEN

FOUR STUDIES 1875

FOR *Fiesko*, ACT V

509

L. SIMONSON

"STRIKE"

"REVOLUTION" SCENES FROM *Man and the Masses*

DEFEAT

THE SETTING USED

L. SIMONSON 1924

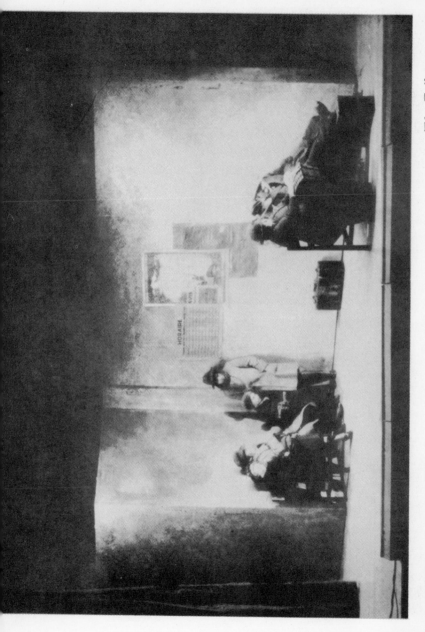

SCENE FOR *The Failures* 1923

L. SIMONSON

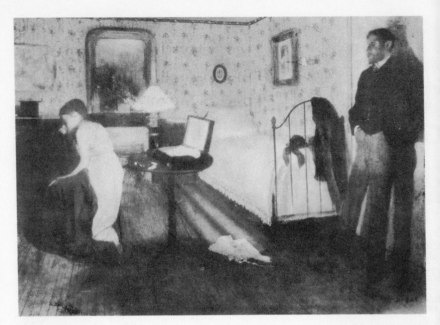

DEGAS INTÉRIEUR 1874

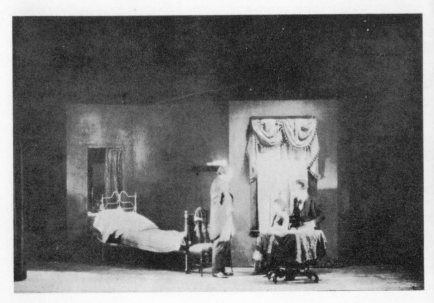

The Failures 1923

HENRI-ROUSSEAU   SNAKE CHARMER 1907

M. COVARRUBIAS 1925   *Androcles and the Lion*

TOWER OF LONDON   FROM A PHOTOGRAPH

R. E. JONES   DESIGN FOR *Richard III*

R. E. JONES' SETTINGS FOR *Richard III*   AS LIGHTED

INTERIOR POWER HOUSE

STEVENSON, CONN.

POWER STATION

L. SIMONSON   SETTING FOR *Dynamo*

Hairy Ape, MOSCOW 1926

Hairy Ape, NEW YORK 1920

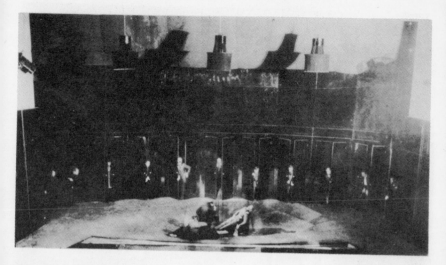

MEYERHOLD, MOSCOW   *The Inspector General* 1928

MOSCOW ART THEATRE   *The Inspector General* 1908

G. PITOËV

SETTINGS FOR *Liliom* 1923

L. SIMONSON

SETTINGS FOR *Liliom* 1921

DUKE OF SAXE-MEININGEN   DESIGN FOR *The Pretenders* 1876

R. E. JONES   DESIGN FOR *Hamlet* 1923

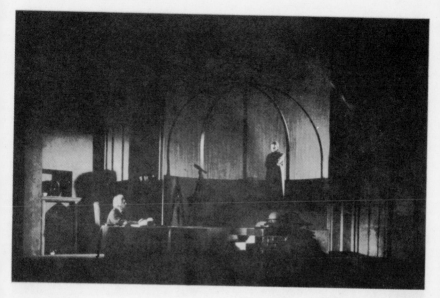

L. SIMONSON

Faust: STUDY. 1928

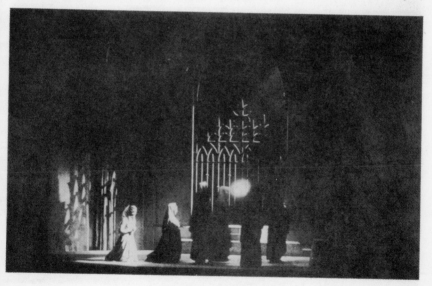

L. SIMONSON

Faust: DOM. 1928

L. SIMONSON

SETTINGS FOR *Marco Millions* 1928

528

DETAIL

Marco Millions

LAMPS IN USE

A CRITICAL BIBLIOGRAPHY

A complete bibliography of the history of stage-craft would demand a chapter in itself. I have limited my list to the books in my own library, indicating books out of print by an asterisk (*) and volumes costing from twenty to fifty dollars and up by a dagger (†). The booksellers I have found to be of the most assistance in procuring theatrical material are E. Weyhe, New York City; B. Westermann, New York City; Francis Edwards, London; E. Wasmuth, Charlottenburg-Berlin, and K. Hiersemann, Leipzig. The Gotham Book Mart and the Drama Book Shop, New York, which I do not happen to have used, also specialize in books on the theatre.

GENERAL HISTORIES

From the point of view of completeness, documentation, and illustration the best available general history in English is A. Nicoll's *The Development of the Theatre* (Harcourt, Brace, New York, 1927), which describes with great technical exactness methods of staging from Greece to modern times and includes theatre architecture and costuming as well as scenic design. The chapter on the modern theatre is, however, inadequate. Of particular interest are the extracts from Somi's dialogues (1550) in Appendix B. **A History of Theatrical Art* by Karl Mantzius, the first five volumes translated by L. von Cossel (London, Duckworth, 1903-21, 6 vols.), has been superseded by more recent works as far as its first three volumes on the theatres of Greece, the Middle Ages, and Shakespeare are concerned. Vol. IV on *Molière and His Time* and particularly the portion of Vol. V, *The Great Actors of the Eighteenth Century,* that deals with the development of the German stage, contain material not readily available in English. Mantzius's emphasis is almost entirely on acting and direction. The volumes are not very fully illustrated. Sheldon Cheney's *The Theatre: Three Thousand Years of Drama, Acting and Stagecraft* (Longmans, 1929) is valuable for its attempt to present in a single volume a complete history of the theatre's development by co-ordinating the plays and acting of every epoch with theatre architecture, costume, and stage setting. It is well illustrated and the modern stage is treated fully. Unfortunately Mr. Cheney's evangelistic conviction that the modern theatre will go to heaven by eschewing realism affects both his selection and his treatment of evidence. Nothing cited seems in itself inaccurate. But as a result of the author's *parti pris* the book as a whole is out of drawing, a fact which becomes evident if one compares Mr. Cheney's account of the Greek or mediaeval theatres with Flickinger's, Decharme's, or Cohen's. In contrast Germain Bapst's †* *Essai sur l'histoire du théâtre* (Hachette et Cie., Paris, 1893, illustrated) is far more authentic, a mine of first-hand material running from the Middle Ages to the latter part of the nineteenth century. Particularly valuable are the complete lists of scene-painters and their principal productions in the sixteenth, seventeenth, eighteenth, and nineteenth centuries. Rosamond Gilder's *Enter the Actress* (Houghton Mifflin, 1931, illustrated) in recounting the careers of leading ladies from the sixteenth to the nineteenth century gives a fresh picture of the acting and staging typical of historic theatres. Joseph Gregor's *Wiener scenische Kunst: Theaterdekoration* (Wiener Drucke, 1924, 60 full-page plates) analyzes the development of the various styles of stage setting from the seventeenth century to the present day. His *Wiener scenische Kunst: Das Bühnencostüm* (Amalthea, 1925) is a companion volume dealing with the development of costume design. The best inexpensive bird's-eye view without text of the successive phases of stage setting from the Middle Ages to the end of the eighteenth century is a folio picture-book of 52 reproductions (including two of the mediaeval stage in colour), *Das Bühnenbild,* by C. Niessen (Klopp, Bonn, 1927). † *Denkmäler des Theaters* (R. Piper, Munich) is a monumental and expensive work in twelve folios of engravings and drawings—from the Middle Ages to the twentieth century—of theatrical productions, pageants, festivals, costumes, etc. from the extensive collection in the National Library, Vienna, reproduced with the extraordinary facsimile printing, particularly in the colour plates, for which the Vienna State Press is famous. A portable private museum for the specialist.

THE GREEK THEATRE

In addition to A. E. Haigh's *The Attic Theatre* (3rd edition, Clarendon Press, Oxford, 1907) and R. C. Flickinger's *The Greek Theater and Its Drama* (3rd edition, University of Chicago Press, 1926), the best corrective to the cult of the pseudo-Greek is P. Decharme's *Euripides and the Spirit of His Dramas,* translated by James Loeb (Macmillan, 1906).

THE MEDIAEVAL STAGE

Far more informative as to the details of the staging of mysteries and passion-plays than E. K. Chambers's *The Mediaeval Stage* (Clarendon Press, Oxford, 1903, 2 vols.) are Professor Gustave Cohen's equally authoritative volumes: *Histoire de la mise en scène dans le théâtre religieux français du moyen age* (new edition, H. Champion, Paris, 1926) and (same publisher, 1925) *Le livre de conduite du régisseur et le compte des dépenses pour le mystère de la Passion joué à Mons en 1501,* from which I have cited excerpts in Part II, Chapter II. The general reader will prefer Professor Cohen's shorter volumes, *Le théâtre en France au Moyen Age:* I, *Le Théâtre Religieux* (Rieder, Paris, 1928, 59 illustrations from mediaeval miniatures) and II, *Le Théâtre Profane* (same publisher, 50 illustrations, 1931).

RENAISSANCE AND ELIZABETHAN THEATRES

An indispensable preliminary to understanding the development of the pictorial stage setting, its Renaissance sources, and its development through Inigo Jones to the beginning of the eighteenth century is L. B. Campbell's *Scenes and Machines on the English Stage During the Renaissance* (Cambridge University Press, 1923, illustrated), a model doctor's thesis if there ever was one, scholarly but thoroughly readable, fit to gladden the heart of Abraham Flexner. It is compact and complete, with vivid description of technical details, particularly of Inigo Jones's scene-shifting devices, and well-organized source material from contemporary documents. The actuality, as opposed to the myths, of staging in the Elizabethan theatres and their immediate successors is best studied in W. J. Lawrence's * *The Elizabethan Playhouse and Other Studies* (Second Series, Shakespeare Head Press, Stratford-upon-Avon, 1913); *The Physical Conditions of the Elizabethan Public*

Playhouse (Harvard University Press, 1927); and *Pre-Restoration Stage Studies* (Harvard University Press, 1927). The standard reference work for the period is *The Elizabethan Stage,* by E. K. Chambers (Clarendon Press, Oxford, 1923, 4 vols.). The chapters on the masque and the court play in Vol. I, those on staging in the theatres, sixteenth and seventeenth centuries, in Vol. III, including the stage-directions cited, are the portions of greatest interest to designers. Appendix G to Vol. IV reproduces an extract from Serlio's treatise in Italian, with three illustrations and two diagrams.

The English translation of Serlio's treatise is procurable in † * *Architecture* (first five books published by Robert Peak, London, 1611). A facsimile of Nicola Sabbattini's * *Practica di fabricar scene, e machine ne' teatri* (Ravenna, 1638), with a complete German translation, has been published by the Gesellschaft der Bibliophilen, Weimar, 1926.

Excellent reproductions of Italian Renaissance stage settings are contained in V. Mariani's picture-book history, *Scenografia italiana* (Firenze, Rinascimento del Libro, 1930); it has 128 plates, which also illustrate the development of Italian scenic design to date. C. Ricci's *La scenografia italiana* (Fratelli Treves, Milan, 1930) covers the same ground, but devotes more space to the appalling settings for Italian operas of the last century, which the Metropolitan Opera House of New York still does its best to perpetuate.

SEVENTEENTH AND EIGHTEENTH CENTURIES

The most complete record of Inigo Jones's work, chiefly from the Duke of Devonshire's collection, is to be found in Vol. XII, Publications of the Walpole Society, * *Designs by Inigo Jones for Masques and Plays at Court: A Descriptive Catalogue of Drawings for Scenery and Costumes* (Oxford, printed for the Walpole and Malone Societies, 1924). *The Masque of Queenes,* by Ben Jonson (London, The King's Printers, 1930), contains 16 page plates: 2 of sketches for the setting, and 14 of drawings for costumes.

For the development of French stage decoration from Italian models see L. Celler's * *Les origines de l'opéra* (Didier, Paris, 1868), H. Prunières' *L'opéra italien en France avant Lulli* (Champion, Paris, 1913), Romain Rolland's * *Les origines du théâtre lyrique moderne: histoire de l'opéra en Europe avant Lully et Scarlatti* (E. Thorin, Paris, 1895) and his *Musiciens* *d'autrefois,* translated as * *Some Musicians of Former Days* (Henry Holt, New York, 1915).

The simultaneous settings of the Hôtel de Bourgogne and the Comédie Française in the seventeenth century are reproduced (49 plates) with the stage-directions and those of stage-managers in *Le mémoire de Mahelot, Laurent et d'autres décorateurs,* with notes by Henry Carrington Lancaster (Champion, Paris, 1920). L.-V. Gofflot's *Le théâtre au collège* (Champion, Paris, 1907) gives a detailed account of theatricals at the French Jesuit colleges. John Palmer's *Molière* (Brewer & Warren, New York, 1930, inadequately illustrated) in dealing with the productions of Molière's plays gives descriptions of the manner in which they were staged. The short text of *Die Theaterdekoration des Barock,* by P. Zucker (Rudolph Kämmerer, Berlin, 1925, 36 plates), contains the best critical history of the period to be found in condensed form; the notes are also valuable.

A particularly clear picture of the technique of stage setting, scene-shifting, and theatre-building as practised in the eighteenth century is given in a facsimile reproduction of a manuscript text-book, Jacopo Fabris' *Instruction in der Theatralischen Architectur und Mechanique* (Levin & Munksgaard, Copenhagen, 1930)—the original text and a résumé in German. The engravings of the section of † * Diderot's *Encyclopédie* illustrating theatre architecture and machinery are often detached and offered for sale separately.

La Librairie de France has published three profusely illustrated volumes: *Le théâtre à Paris au XVIIIme siècle,* by M. Aghion, and *Le livre des fêtes françaises,* by G. Mourey, which begins with the seventeenth century, as does *Les costumes de l'opéra,* by Carlos Fischer. P. L. Duchartre's *La comédie italienne (commedia dell' arte)* is complete, richly illustrated, and authoritative (same publisher).

NINETEENTH CENTURY

Die Theaterdekoration des Klassizismus (Kämmerer, Berlin, 1925, 40 plates), by P. Zucker, contains a short but important text and bibliographical notes. * *Die Musik und die Inscenierung,* by Adolphe Appia (F. Bruckmann, Munich, 1899, 18 plates), is a monument to the misuse of the German language. Appia's original manuscript in French still exists and should be published. It is high time that some American university press translated and published the light-plots at the end of this volume; they should be made required reading for university courses on dramatic production. Appia's * *La mise en scène du drame wagnérien* (L. Chailley, Paris, 1895) is the preliminary sketch for the preceding volume. His later volume, *L'œuvre d'art vivant* (Atar, Paris and Geneva, 1921), contains 20 reproductions covering his later as well as his earlier period. *Art vivant ou nature morte?* a brochure (Bottega di Poesia, Milan, 1923), contains 18 illustrations. I find these texts less important than those of Appia's earlier volumes. A pictorial record of Appia's designs from 1892 to 1926 in 56 flawless reproductions is contained in a folio † *Adolphe Appia,* privately printed in Zurich, 1929.

* *Geschichte der Meininger,* by Max Grube (M. Hesse, Berlin-Schöneberg, 1926, with 131 reproductions of drawings and 21 photographs of the acting company), is written by an important member of the Meiningen players and gives a detailed picture of their methods of staging and acting, both in performance and at rehearsal. Two charts give the repertory by plays and cities of the company's tours. Antoine's letters describing the Meiningen performances and those of contemporary French theatres, with the repertory of plays and lists of actors and authors produced by Antoine, are to be found in A. Thalasso's *Le théâtre libre* (Mercure de France, Paris, 1909). For an account of this theatre's development see A. Antoine's diary, *"Mes souvenirs" sur le théâtre libre* (A. Fayard, Paris, tenth edition, 1921), and *Antoine and the Théâtre Libre,* by S. M. Waxman (Harvard University Press, Cambridge, 1926), which includes and supplements much of the material contained in the French volumes and is a more definitive account than either.

My Life in Art, by C. Stanislavsky (Little, Brown, 1924, illustrated), includes the productions 1888-98 of the Society of Art and Literature, which developed into the Moscow Art Theatre, and continues the account of the Art Theatre's productions to the revolution of 1917 and the founding of the First Studio and the Opera Studio. An autobiography, but also among the most important expositions of modern directing.

MODERN STAGING—SINCE 1900

De luxe illustrated histories: The best picture-book to date is Léon Moussinac's folio, † *Tendances nouvelles du théâtre* (A. Levy, Paris, 1931, with 124 full-page plates in colour and photogravure, including the representative work of Continental and American designers); in each case a typical production is reproduced in its entirety by acts and scenes, with the costumes used. The reproductions, superbly printed, are superior to any that have yet appeared and the fact that all the settings of the plays chosen rather than scattered scenes are reproduced provides a valuable basis for study and comparison of modern methods not to be found in other books. American designers represented are Robert Edmond Jones, *Beyond;* Norman-Bel Geddes, *Joan of Arc, Lazarus Laughed;* Lee Simonson, *Massemensch, Marco Millions.* † The second volume of *Twentieth Century Stage Decoration,* by S. J. Hume and W. R. Fuerst (Alfred A. Knopf, New York, 1929), contains 387 plates of representative stage settings and 7 colour-plates. The work also includes a list of numerous contemporary designers, with important productions of each one.

Less expensive but well illustrated are *Das moderne Bühnenbild,* by O. Fischel (E. Wasmuth, Berlin, 1923, 8 colour-plates, 146 half-tone illustrations); *The New Spirit in the European Theatre 1914-1924,* by Huntly Carter (George H. Doran, New York, 1925); Sheldon Cheney's two volumes, *The Art Theater,* revised edition, Alfred A. Knopf, New York, 1925) and *Stage Decoration* (John Day Company, New York, 1928, 127 plates). H. K. Moderwell's * *The Theatre of To-day* (John Lane, New York, 1914, 32 illustrations) was the first and is in many ways still the simplest and clearest exposition for the general reader of the relation of recent literary tendencies, scenic design, production methods, and theatre architecture (1926 edition, John Lane, London, with introduction by John Mason Brown). K. Macgowan's *The Theatre of Tomorrow* (Boni & Liveright, New York, 1921, 8 illustrations in colour, 32 half-tone plates) is a brilliant exposition of the technical and aesthetic problems of modern stage-craft. Its development is presented, however, as a battle of the angels, with realism in the rôle of Lucifer. *Continental Stagecraft,* by K. Macgowan and R. E. Jones (Harcourt, Brace, New York, 1922), gives a first-hand picture of typical modern productions in Germany, France, and Austria—their general effect as seen from the audience as well as the theories underlying the various schools of direction. R. E. Jones's drawings help to make the volume valuable as a record of a period that has greatly influenced theatrical production in the art theatres of the United States.

Numbers 9-10, 1921 (a special number), of the Dutch art magazine

Wendingen are devoted to illustrating the International Theatre Exhibition held in Amsterdam in January and February, 1922. An English *Catalogue and Bibliography, International Theatre Exhibition,* was published by the Victoria and Albert Museum when the exhibition was shown there June-July, 1922. For the non-realistic and expressionist development of stage setting see *The Little Review,* "International Theatre Exposition, New York"— special theatre number, 1926.

THE MODERN FRENCH THEATRE

Décors de théâtre, by R. Cogniat (Chroniques du Jour, Paris, 1930), has 130 plates in colour and rotogravure of designs by French and Russian and Spanish painters, principally for ballets and experimental theatre productions in Paris, including those of Picasso, Laurencin, Derain, Dufy, Benois, Gontcharowa, etc. There is a very valuable appendix listing the names of modern French painters and productions designed by them since 1895.

THE RUSSIAN THEATRE AND THE BALLETS RUSSES

J. Gregor and R. Fülöp-Miller, † *Das russiche Theater* (Amalthea, Vienna, 1928), has 48 colour-plates and 357 half-tone plates. A complete review from the beginning of the Moscow Art Theatre to the post-revolutionary expressionism of Meyerhold, Tairov, and the Proletkult theatres. There is an illustrated chapter on the early revolutionary stages in *Geist und Gesicht des Bolshewismus* (Amalthea, Vienna, 1926), by R. Fülöp-Miller. O. Sayler's *The Russian Theatre Under the Revolution* (Little, Brown, 1920) is a well-illustrated and exciting account of how the pre-revolutionary theatres of Moscow persisted during the first six months of the Bolshevist régime 1917-18. *Inside the Moscow Art Theatre* (Brentano, New York, 1925), by the same author, was timed to coincide with the New York seasons of the Moscow Art Theatre and its studio that gave *Lysistrata* and *Carmen.* The text shows traces of Mr. Sayler's preoccupations as a press-agent of the tour. There is a valuable diagram of the organization of the Moscow Art Theatre and a number of coloured illustrations that are also to be found in the Moscow Art Studio's souvenir programme of *Carmen* and *Lysistrata.*

A number of the * Moscow Art Theatre's publications can still be picked up in Moscow, all profusely illustrated: a complete review of the Chekhov productions, a memorial volume on the twenty-fifth anniversary of the theatre, special editions of various plays, with coloured illustrations of the sets and costumes and photographs of the scenes as performed, including a portfolio in four parts of *The Revizor General,* and the First Studio production of *Turandot.* The illustrations alone are invaluable records.

The décors and costumes of the Ballets Russes can be studied in the colour-plates of W. A. Propert's † *The Russian Ballet in Western Europe, 1909-1920* (John Lane, London and New York, 1921), which includes the designs of Larionov, Golovin, Benois, and Soudekine as well as those of Bakst. Numerous *de luxe* volumes on Bakst, mostly out of print and now commanding a premium, have appeared. Some of his best work is reproduced in the 44 colour-plates of costumes in † *The Designs of Léon Bakst for the Sleeping Princess* (Benn, London, 1923). The most complete review of the settings and costumes of the Paris seasons of the Ballets Russes can be found in the * special numbers of *Comœdia illustrée* and the souvenir programmes of the performances, both illustrated in colour, which are often offered in collected form by book-dealers specializing in the modern theatre.

Das entfesselte Theater (G. Kiepenheuer, Potsdam, 1927), by A. Tairov, a German translation of the theories of the director of the Kamerny Theatre, Moscow, has illustrations from its productions.

Gontcharowa et Larionow (La Cible, Paris, 1919) has colour-plates of designs for settings and costumes of these two decorative Expressionists.

THE THEATRES OF GERMANY AND CENTRAL EUROPE

Monographs on Max Reinhardt: * *Das Deutsche Theater in Berlin* (G. Müller, Munich, 1909) is a well-illustrated pamphlet on Reinhardt's earlier productions, with contributions by William Archer, Georg Brandes, M. Maeterlinck, and a list of the repertory of the first seasons 1902-08. *Reinhardt und seine Bühne* (Eysler, Berlin, 1919) is illustrated with drawings of models, and sketches of Ernst Stern, who was Reinhardt's principal designer for a long period; it also contains diagrams of the use of the revolving stage. *Max Reinhardt,* by S. Jacobsohn (Reiss, Berlin, 1910), contains photographs of settings for *Faust, Lear, Aglavaine et Sélysette, Romeo and Juliet, The Winter's Tale. Max Reinhardt and His Theatre* (Brentano's, New York, 1924), edited by O. Sayler, is a symposium of short essays on all aspects of Reinhardt's career by Hugo von Hoffmannstahl, Hermann Bahr, Kenneth Macgowan, etc., and has one chapter by Reinhardt himself. The editor having been publicity agent for Reinhardt's American tours, the material is eulogistic rather than critical in emphasis. Pictorially the volume assembles designs in colour and photographs of productions of all of Reinhardt's periods, including those by Norman-Bel Geddes for *The Miracle. Max Reinhardt: 25 Jahre Deutsches Theater* (Piper, Munich, 1930) contains 135 plates of his productions, beginning with 1904. The supplement *Die Spielpläne Max Reinhardts 1905-1930* (Piper, Munich, 1930) gives a complete list in tabulated form of Reinhardt's productions in all his theatres, with names of the directors, scenic designers, and principal players, and opening date and number of performances. An indispensable document.

Der Szeniker Ludwig Sievert, by L. Wagner (Bühnenvolksbundverlag, Berlin, 1926), has 90 reproductions in photogravure and colour of drawings by one of the leading expressionist designers. Unfortunately no adequate monograph on Emil Pirchan has appeared to date.

Fr. Kranich's *Bühnentechnik der Gegenwart,* Vol. I (Oldenbourg, Berlin, 1929), is a profusely illustrated and technically exhaustive description of German scene-shifting and lighting apparatus.

† *Nove České Divadlo,* edited by J. Kodiček and M. Rutte (Editions Aventinum), is in three volumes, 1918-26, 1927, 1928-29. The illustrations from drawings and photographs are a particularly complete record of non-realistic, stylized productions, scenically among the most important experiments made in modern "art theatres." Some, such as *R.U.R.* and O'Neill's *The Great God Brown,* provide a very interesting basis for comparison with American productions.

Pictures of similar experiments are contained in the souvenir programmes of the Darmstadt State Theatre, 1929-30, 1930-31, published under the title *Blätter des hessischen Landestheaters.*

THE ENGLISH STAGE

Gordon Craig's * *The Art of the Theatre* (Foulis, Edinburgh and London, 1905) is a pamphlet with a cover designed by Craig and illustrations from his designs, including a photograph of the production of *Bethlehem* in 1902; preface by R. Graham Robertson. This and another dialogue and most of the illustrations are included in *On the Art of the Theatre* (Heinemann, London, 1911). *Towards a New Theatre* (Dent, London, and Dutton, New York, 1913). *Scene* has a foreword and an introductory poem by John Masefield (Oxford University Press, 1923). In *Fourteen Notes* (University of Washington Bookstore, 1931), Glenn Hughes having ventured to print some very mild criticism of "the Master" in *The Story of the Theatre* (1928), Craig favours him with 15 pages of qualifications and demurrers.

† *A Production, 1926* (Oxford University Press, 1930) is an expensive and superbly printed folio containing sketches for the production of *The Pretenders* at Copenhagen. The designs are of no great importance. The text offers an excellent, if unconscious, insight into Craig's limitations as a technician.

The Monthly Chapbook, Vol. 1, No. 2 (August, 1919), contains *Decoration in the Art of the Theatre*, a lecture by Albert Rutherston, with illustrations of his setting for Granville-Barker's production of *Androcles and the Lion*. *The Story of the Lyric Theatre, Hammersmith*, by Nigel Playfair, with an introduction by Arnold Bennett (Chatto & Windus, London, 1925), is illustrated in colour and black-and-white designs by Lovat Fraser, Sheringham, Zinkeisen, and Kapp.

THE ORIENTAL THEATRE

* *Le théâtre au Japon*, by A. Bénazet (Leroux, Paris, 1901), Annales du Musée Guimet, with a bibliography, is illustrated with line cuts; p. 269 has a drawing of the Japanese revolving stage. *Le théâtre japonais*, by A. Maybon (Laurens, Paris, 1925) is less scholarly, better illustrated. *Le théâtre chinois*, by Tchou-Kia-Kien (Brunoff, Paris, 1922), has reproductions in half-tone and colour of A. Jacovleff's drawings of the contemporary Chinese theatre. *The Chinese Drama from the Earliest Times Until To-day*, by L. C. Arlington (Kelly & Walsh, Shanghai, 1930), gives valuable illustrations in the Chinese manner of costumes, wigs, properties, etc.

THE AMERICAN THEATRE

The only complete review of contemporary American design, which also includes vaudeville and moving pictures, is † *Das amerikanische Theater und Kino*, by J. Gregor and R. Fülöp-Miller (Amalthea, Vienna, 1931, 47 colour-plates, 459 black-and-white illustrations). For the early credos and examples of the early work of Jones, Geddes, Urban, Simonson, Rosse, Peters, C. R. Johnson, and others, see the illustrated catalogue * *American Stage Designs* (Bourgeois Galleries, 1919). J. M. Brown's *Upstage* (W. W. Norton, New York, 1930) contains a critical discussion of American stage-craft in theory and in practice. Chapter 3, "Enter the Scenic Artist," concerns R. E. Jones, L. Simonson, N.-B. Geddes.

Vol. II of *Epoch: The Life of Steele Mackaye,* by Percy Mackaye (Boni & Liveright, New York, 1927), describes Mackaye's scenic innovations in connection with the spectatorium of the Chicago World's Fair, 1891-92.

MONOGRAPHS

A Project for . . . the Divine Comedy . . . , by Norman-Bel Geddes (Theatre Arts, Inc., 1924), has 40 photographs by Francis Bruguière of the model of the monumental project, with its imaginative stage lighting. *Drawings for the Theatre,* by Robert Edmond Jones (Theatre Arts, Inc., 1925), has an introduction by Arthur Hopkins and 35 plates. *Boris Aronson,* by Waldemar George (Chroniques du Jour, Paris, 1928), has designs in the Tairov tradition, some of which have been used in the Yiddish theatres in New York City.

TEXT-BOOKS AND BIBLIOGRAPHY

The best text-book to date, *Stage Scenery and Lighting,* by S. Selden and H. D. Sellman (F. S. Crofts, New York, 1930), although written for the non-professionals, is an admirable exposition of the best professional traditions. Its technical explanations are particularly concrete and clear. *Stage Lighting,* by T. Fuchs (Little, Brown, Boston, 1929), is highly technical and weak in its exposition of the interpretative use of lighting in production, but it is the only adequate analysis in English of present equipment and its possibilities. No architect's office, little theatre, or university playhouse should be without Irving Pichel's *Modern Theatres* (Harcourt, Brace, New York, 1925; enlarged from his *On Building a Theatre,* Theatre Arts Monographs, No. 1, 1920), which analyzes the essential requirements of modern theatre architecture as to both auditorium and back stage. K. Macgowan's *Footlights Across America* is a compact but exhaustive study of university and amateur theatres, with repertory lists, details of financial organization, etc., etc. (Harcourt, Brace, 1929).

The New York Public Library has published two bibliographies of its reference material compiled by W. B. Gamble: *Stage Scenery, A List of References to Illustrations Since 1900* . . . (1917) and *The Development of Scenic Art and Stage Machinery* (1920).

PERIODICAL PUBLICATIONS

An indispensable record of the development of modern American and European stage design is contained in the illustrations and text of the *Theatre Arts Magazine* founded by Sheldon Cheney, subsequently carried on by its present editor Edith Isaacs, published as a quarterly until 1924, since then as a monthly. Complete sets are now at a premium. About a hundred numbers are still available at publication price. The *Theatre Guild Magazine* has occasionally published articles and photographs of modern productions of interest to designers.

ADDENDA

Sheridan to Robertson, a Study of the Nineteenth-Century London Stage by Ernest Bradlee Watson (Harvard University Press, Cambridge, 1926—19 illustrations). An exciting book about one of the dullest periods in the English theatre, of particular interest to scenic designers in that it makes plain the "stream of life" which flows through the theatre even at its worst, the incessant interactions of public taste, literary fashions, economic and political conditions, acting traditions, and scenic technique, which keep the theatre alive even when it is not producing dramatic literature, and combine to produce changes that ultimately make possible literary and artistic innovations both in playwrighting and playgiving. Although a history of the theatre during a short and unimportant period it gives the most concrete, complete and vivid picture I know of how the theatre, in any period, lives, survives and grows.

Masks, Mimes, and Miracles, Studies in the Popular Theatre by Allardyce Nicoll (Harcourt, Brace and Company, New York, 1931—226 illustrations). An elaborately documented study of the illegitimate theatre from the days of the Greek and Roman Mimes, through the Middle Ages to the Comedia dell'Arte, valuable for its demonstration of the continuous vitality of the

543

theatre and the actor even during the long periods when there were no "legitimate" plays to perform. Required reading for theorists who identify the theatre with dramatic literature or theatre architecture.

A Method of Lighting the Stage by Stanley R. McCandless (Theatre Arts, Inc., New York, 1932—illustrated with photographs, drawings and diagrams). The clearest and simplest primer to date of the technique of modern stage lighting and the apparatus employed. The current types of lamps and their use in combination are particularly well illustrated. Unfortunately a description of the design and control of switchboards is lacking.

ADDENDA, 1963

Bernstein, Aline, Stages of the World (Theatre Arts Books, 1949).

Bieber, Margaret, The History of the Greek and Roman Theatre, (2nd Edition, Princeton University Press, 1961).

Clurman, Harold, The Fervent Years (Rev. Edition, Hill and Wang, 1957).

Davenport, Millia, The Book of Costume (2 vols. Rev. Edition, Crown, 1961).

Flanagan, Hallie, Arena (Duell, Sloan and Pearce, 1940).

Frank, Grace, The Medieval French Drama (Oxford, Clarendon Press, 1954).

Gorelik, Mordecai, New Theatres for Old (Samuel French, 1940).

Guthrie, Tyrone, A Life in the Theatre (McGraw-Hill, 1959).

Hewitt, Barnard, Theatre U. S. A. 1668-1957 (McGraw-Hill, 1959).

Hodges, C. Walter, The Globe Restored: A Study of the Elizabethan Theatre (Coward-McCann, 1954).

Hopkins, Arthur, Reference Point (Samuel French, 1948).

Houghton, Norris, Advance from Broadway (Harcourt, Brace, 1941).

Hughes, Glenn, The Penthouse Theatre (Rev. Edition, University of Washington, 1950).

Jones, Robert Edmond, The Dramatic Imagination (Rev. Edition, Theatre Arts Books, 1956).

———, The Theatre of Robert Edmond Jones (Edited by Ralph Pendleton, Wesleyan University Press, 1958).

Nicoll, Allardyce, Stuart Masques and the Renaissance Stage (Harrap, 1937).

———, World Drama from Aeschylus to Anouilh (Harrap, 1949).

Oenslager, Donald, Scenery Then and Now (Norton, 1936).

Saint-Denis, Michel, Theatre: The Rediscovery of Style (Theatre Arts Books, 1959).

544

Shoemaker, William Hutchinson, The Multiple Stage in Spain During the 15th and 16th Centuries (Princeton University Press, 1935).

Simonson, Lee, The Art of Scenic Design (Harper, 1950).

Summers, Montague, The Restoration Theatre (Kegan Paul, Trench, Trubner, 1934).

Varneke, B. V., History of the Russian Theatre, 17th-19th Century (Macmillan, 1951).

PRATICA
DI FABRICAR SCENE,
E MACHINE NE' TEATRI
DI NICOLA SABBATTINI
DA PESARO

Già Architetto del Serenissimo Duca Francesco Maria Feltrio della Rouere
Vltimo Signore di Pesaro.

Ristampata di nouo coll' Aggiunta del
Secondo Libro.
All'Illustriss. e Reuerendiss. Sig. Monsig.
HONORATO VISCONTI
Arciuescouo di Larissa della Prouincia di Romagna,
& Essarcato di Rauenna Presidente.
CON PRIVILEGIO.

In RAVENNA, Per Pietro de' Paoli, e Gio. Battista Giouannelli
Stampatori Camerali 1638. *Con licenza de' Superiori.*

NOTES AND VERIFICATIONS

PAGE 4, LINE 26: *The Theatre,* pp. 498, 541.

PAGE 9, LINE 7: For Japanese revolving stage see Bénazet's *Le Théâtre au Japon;* for Lautenschläger's elaboration of it, Hume and Fuerst's *The Twentieth Century Stage,* Vol. I.

PAGE 15, LINE 9: Cited by Waxman, *Antoine and the Théâtre Libre,* p. 133.

PAGE 16, LINE 15: From Whistler's *Ten O'Clock,* usually included in reprintings of *The Gentle Art of Making Enemies.*

PAGE 21, LINE 18: *Scene,* p. 5.

PAGE 23, LINE 22: *American Stage Designs,* Bourgeois Galleries, New York, 1919.

PAGE 24, LINE 4: *Theatre Arts Magazine,* September, 1927.

PAGE 24, LINE 17: *Continental Stagecraft,* pp. 7, 212. *Theatre of To-morrow,* p. 212.

PAGE 24, LINE 25: *The Theatre,* p. 464.

PAGE 25, LINE 11: *Continental Stagecraft,* pp. 154, 155.

PAGE 27, LINE 4: *Continental Stagecraft,* pp. 197, 208, 211.

PAGE 29, LINE 3: Rawson's translation, used in the Theatre Guild's production.

PAGE 30, LINE 28: *Attic Theatre,* pp. 64, 66.

PAGE 31, LINE 15: Cohen, *Livre de Conduite,* p. lxxviii; *Histoire de la Mise en Scène du Théâtre Religieux,* pp. 103, 176-7.

PAGE 32, LINE 10: Cited by Nicoll, *The Development of the Theatre,* p. 76.

PAGE 32, LINE 23: Bapst, *Essai sur l'Histoire du Théâtre,* p. 45.

PAGE 32, LINE 25: Bapst, *op. cit.,* p. 48.

PAGE 33, LINE 4: Mantzius, *A History of Theatrical Art* (Vol. III, pp. 76, 147 ff.), estimates that until 1599 the average payment for Shakespeare's nineteen plays was £12 apiece, and that the last seventeen plays (exclusive of theatre shares, etc.) averaged £35 per annum.

PAGE 33, LINE 7: Professor Wallace. Cited by W. J. Lawrence, *Pre-Restoration Stage Studies*, p. 252.

PAGE 33, LINE 10: Gofflot, *Le Théâtre au Collège*, pp. 213, 233.

PAGE 33, LINE 14: J. Palmer, *Molière*, p. 11: "The purchasing power of the *livre tournois* in the seventeenth century has been very variously estimated. . . . It was certainly not for any purpose less than the equivalent of five gold francs today, and for some purposes its purchasing power was considerably greater."

PAGE 33, LINE 18: *Traité sur l'art de Charpentier Théorique et Pratique publié par J. C. Kraft, architecte, et rédigé par M. A. F. Lamet* (Firmin-Didot, Paris, 1822). Copy in the Bibliothèque de l'Arsenal (Collection Rondel), Paris.

PAGE 34, LINE 17: *The Greek Theatre*, pp. 213, 216.

PAGE 35, LINE 12: Haigh, *op. cit.*, p. 344.

PAGE 35, LINE 21: Palmer, *op. cit.*, p. 41.

PAGE 35, LINE 24: Gofflot, *op. cit.*, p. 69.

PAGE 35, LINE 27: A "sacred representation" of the Passion was played annually in Rome in the sixteenth century at the Coliseum. After 1539 "an end was put to these plays in Rome because after each performance the populace sacked the Jewish quarter there." (Rolland's *Some Musicians of Former Days*, p. 40, note.)

PAGE 35, LINE 29: Cf. *Poetics* IX, XIII; Haigh, *op. cit.*, pp. 30, 348.

PAGE 49, LINE 8: Rahlenbeck, *Revue de Belgique*, 1880, cited by Gofflot, *op. cit.*, p. 71.

PAGE 51, LINE 14: *Public Opinion*, p. 81.

PAGE 52, LINE 5: *Central Italian Painters*, p. 60.

PAGE 52, LINE 10: Zucker, *Theater-Dekoration des Klassizismus*, p. 15.

PAGE 53, LINE 18: *Op. cit.*, p. 84.

PAGE 56, LINE 31: Ginzburg, *The Adventure of Science*, p. 169.

PAGE 60, LINE 7: *Florentine Painters*, p. 11. *Central Italian Painters*, pp. 96 ff.

PAGE 61, LINE 15: *Art*, p. 27.

PAGE 61, LINE 19: *Modern Painting*, pp. 150, 155.

PAGE 61, LINE 26: *The Modern Movement in Art*, p. 8.

PAGE 63, LINE 8: *On the Art of the Theatre*, p. 22.

PAGE 63, LINE 23: Text of Address before the American Society for the Advancement of Science, New York *Times,* Dec. 30, 1930.

PAGE 70, LINE 7: See Thalasso, *Le Théâtre Libre,* pp. 178 ff., for the full text of Millerand's remarks. They are equally applicable to the hypocrisy of subsequent attempts to censor *Mrs. Warren's Profession* and more recent "immoral" plays. "But how does the censor protect the public's morals? Every one knows. . . . Are we to suppose that the censor's modesty is outraged because the dialogue of a play alludes to houses of prostitution? But he permits ten or fifteen theatres every night to parade bevies of half-nude women in front of the footlights. . . . And if you want to learn how the censor protects art, you have only to glance at certain ditties sung every night in our music-halls, where there is not a trace of talent or wit, but simply obvious smut."

PAGE 77, LINE 12: Haigh, *op. cit.,* p. 74.

PAGE 77, LINE 20: The stipulation occurs in a contract form once submitted to the Guild but not used. Shaw, however, is adamant in forbidding revisions of any sort, at least in the English-speaking productions of his plays.

PAGE 78, LINE 9: *Upstage,* pp. 125-127.

PAGE 91, LINE 2: The confession occurs in an interchange of unpublished letters which I heard read by Mrs. Mansfield at a dinner given at the Town Hall Club, New York, a few years ago.

PAGE 97, LINE 10: Cited by Sayler, *The Russian Theatre Under the Revolution,* p. 210 ff.

PAGE 98, LINE 23: Performance in modern clothes by the Garrick Players, Garrick Theatre, New York, October, 1927.

PAGE 136, LINE 17: See Flickinger, *op. cit.,* p. 180, diagram of the distribution of rôles in Sophocles' *Oedipus at Colonus.*

PAGE 136, LINE 22: Flickinger, *op. cit.,* p. 66.

PAGE 137, LINE 10: Flickinger, *op. cit.,* p. 236.

PAGE 137, LINE 22: Anonymous translation of the edition illustrated by Bosschère (Liveright, New York).

PAGE 138, LINE 9: Bapst, *op. cit.,* p. 209.

PAGE 138, LINE 12: Cited by Campbell, *Scenes and Machines,* p. 186.

PAGE 143, LINE 2: For the seating capacity of Greek theatres at Athens and elsewhere see Haigh, *op. cit.,* p. 100.

PAGE 144, LINE 18: Haigh, *op. cit.,* p. 273.

PAGE 145, LINE 13: Haigh, *op. cit.,* p. 344.

PAGE 146, LINE 15: Flickinger, *op. cit.,* p. 203.

PAGE 146, LINE 18: Flickinger, *op. cit.,* p. 191.

PAGE 147, LINE 2: Cf. Haigh, *op. cit.,* p. 63, on mute characters and extras: "the story in Plutarch of a tragedian at Athens who was going to act the part of a queen and refused to perform unless the choregus supplied him with a train of female attendants dressed in expensive fashion."

PAGE 147, LINE 3: Cf. Aristotle, *Rhetoric,* III-1. "At the present day actors have greater influence on the stage than the poets."

PAGE 147, LINE 6: Haigh, *op. cit.,* p. 229.

PAGE 147, LINE 28: Haigh, *op. cit.,* p. 277 ff.

PAGE 148, LINE 13: From Nicoll's translation (*op. cit.*) of Pollux's description (pp. 41-47).

PAGE 148, LINE 28: Flickinger, *op. cit.,* p. 213.

PAGE 149, LINE 8: Cf. *The Knights,* Frere's translation, edition of 1887, p. 83; also Haigh, *op. cit.,* p. 292.

PAGE 149, LINE 11: Flickinger, *op. cit.,* p. 136.

PAGE 149, LINE 27: Flickinger, *op. cit.,* p. 222.

PAGE 150, LINE 5: Cf. Aristotle's *Poetics,* Butcher's translation, XV-5, XXV-19.

PAGE 153, LINE 2: Flickinger, *op. cit.,* p. 274.

PAGE 153, LINE 23: Zimmern, *The Greek Commonwealth,* p. 97.

PAGE 153, LINE 30: E. H. Plumptre, *Aeschylos* (D. C. Heath, Boston, 1906), Chronological Outline, p. 13.

PAGE 154, LINE 5: Haigh, *op. cit.,* p. 346.

PAGE 154, LINE 9: Cited by Decharme, *Euripides and the Spirit of his Dramas.* I am indebted to Decharme's volume for most of the passages cited from Euripides and have followed his interpretation of their contemporary significance.

PAGE 155, LINE 4: Decharme, *op. cit.,* footnote, p. 131.

PAGE 158, LINE 23: Murray, *Euripides and his Age,* p. 99.

PAGE 159, LINE 1: Cited by Murray, *op. cit.,* p. 106.

PAGE 159, LINE 14: Murray, *op. cit.,* p. 112.

PAGE 160, LINE 19: Murray, *op. cit.,* p. 123.

PAGE 162, LINE 9: Plumptre, *op. cit.,* p. 13.

PAGE 164, LINE 4: Decharme, *op. cit.,* p. 64.

PAGE 166, LINE 18: Cited by Murray, *op. cit.,* p. 77.

PAGE 167, LINE 7: Cf. Zimmern, *The Greek Commonwealth,* pp. 174, 397.

PAGE 169, LINE 23: Cheney, *op. cit.,* p. 46.

PAGE 170, LINE 4: Haigh, *op. cit.,* p. 345.

PAGE 173, LINE 17: Cohen, *Le Livre de Conduite;* see bibliography. Except where noted, the citations in this chapter are from this volume.

PAGE 180, LINE 1: Cohen, *Histoire de la Mise en Scène,* pp. 153, 155.

PAGE 181, LINE 23: Rondot, *Les Peintres de Lyon,* cited by Bapst, *op. cit.,* note, p. 66.

PAGE 183, LINE 12: In an Italian mystery, *La Creazione di Adamo ed Eva,* "the author, a canon, played Adam stark naked." In the *Spectaculum divi Francesci* "played at Naples at the beginning of the sixteenth century . . . the friar in the part of St. Francis played in a scene of seduction also unclothed." (Rolland, *op. cit.,* p. 40, note.)

PAGE 185, LINE 8: Bapst, *op. cit.,* p. 53.

PAGE 185, LINE 20: For the use of machinery and pyrotechnics in the Italian *Sacre Rappresentazione* of the sixteenth century see Rolland, *op. cit.,* pp. 37 ff. Fireworks were often set off from on high as if aureoling apostles or destroying infidels. On one occasion they set fire to the church of San Spirito in Florence. At another "sacred representation" a Paradise caught fire and God the Father was badly singed.

"There was no piece without its . . . apotheoses and mountings into heaven, without the shattering of buildings struck by thunder, and other phantasmagoria such as are to be seen in our modern fairy plays."

Animals were also used, as in France. "Signor d'Ancona [*On the Origin of the Theatre in Italy,* 1877] speaks feelingly of the two excellent lions in *S. Onofrio,* which after that saint's death, dug his grave and then took the body of their master by his feet and by his head, and reverently buried it."

PAGE 187, LINE 18: Cohen, *op. cit.*, p. 150.

PAGE 194, LINE 15: The stage directions cited are from Lancaster's edition of Laurent's and Mahelot's manuscript, pp. 86, 102, 76, 84, 83.

PAGE 197, LINE 5: Bapst, *op. cit.*, p. 194.

PAGE 197, LINE 12: Bapst, *op. cit.*, p. 196.

PAGE 197, LINE 22: Bapst, *op. cit.*, p. 200.

PAGE 198, LINE 10: Bapst, *op. cit.*, p. 204, cited from the introduction by the author, Baltharazini, to the printed edition of the play, 1582 (copy in the Bibliothèque Nationale, Paris).

PAGE 198, LINE 28: Celler, *Les Origines de l'Opéra,* p. 149.

PAGE 199, LINE 23: Gofflot, *Le Théâtre au Collège.* This and the following descriptions of French Jesuit theatricals are taken from Gofflot's volume.

PAGE 200, LINE 18: Cited by Gofflot, *op. cit.*, p. 97.

PAGE 201, LINE 20: E. Boysse, *Le Théâtre des Jésuites,* cited by Gofflot, *op. cit.*

PAGE 202, LINE 17: The prestige of Jesuit theatricals elsewhere was almost as great and they were even more elaborate. See Fülöp-Miller's *Macht und Geheimnis der Jesuiten* (p. 478) on their pageants and theatrical productions in Germany and Austria. Their college stages were outfitted with the most elaborate machines for spectacular scene-shifting. State furniture and plate was borrowed on occasion. Apparitions were sometimes achieved by the use of a magic lantern; one of the first to experiment with it was Father Kircher. Reinhardt was anticipated; for a performance of *Gottfried von Bouillon* in Munich, actors were scattered in the audience and on cue took part in the action of the play. For one pageant in 1575, also at Munich, four hundred horsemen in Roman armour were used. How long the Jesuit influence on theatrical production lasted is evinced by Goethe's favourable comment (in his *Italienische Reise*) on a production he witnessed at a Jesuit college in Regensburg.

PAGE 203, LINE 3: From Colbert's correspondence, cited by Gofflot, *op. cit.,* p. 140.

PAGE 203, LINE 17: Cited by Cohen, *Histoire de la Mise en Scène,* pp. 72, 73.

PAGE 204, LINE 16: Cited by Zucker, *Theater-Dekoration des Klassizismus*, p. 17.

PAGE 205, LINE 18: Cited by Bapst, *op. cit.*, p. 211.

PAGE 205, LINE 24: Cf. Prunières' *L'Opéra Italien en France*, p. 214 ff.

Some idea of the elaboration of Vigarani's spectacles is conveyed by the fact that Mazarin wrote during the construction of the Salle des Machines: "This summer M. Ratabon asked me for 20,000 livres for the theatre and this does not include the cost of the machines which will reach a considerable sum, nor 16,000 livres for the foundation of a large pavilion adjoining the same theatre." Vigarani's expenses were similarly prodigious. He writes of having ordered 2,000 *brasses* (over 3,500 yards) of silver gauze "to make a sea," describes a mechanical peacock, 17 yards in length, with a tail that can be spread as it walks "with the aid of a bit of mechanism in its interior," also "a silver moon placed in the middle of the stage, which opens and reveals a silver grotto." The silver, presumably silver leaf, used for *Ercole Amante*, alone cost 88,700 livres!

PAGE 205, LINE 27: Lawrence, *Elizabethan Playhouse*, 2nd series, p. 203.

PAGE 206, LINE 28: Palmer, *op. cit.*, p. 323.

PAGE 207, LINE 8: Palmer, *op. cit.*, p. 330.

PAGE 207, LINE 20: The author's translation of the epistle cited by Palmer, p. 323:

> *Illec, ainsi qu'aux Tuileries*
> *Il a les mêmes ornaments,*
> *Même éclat, mêmes agréments;*
> *Les divers changements de scène, . . .*
> *Les mers, les jardins, les déserts,*
> *Les Palais, les Cieux, les Enfers,*
> *Les mêmes Dieux, même Déesses . . .*
> *On y voit aussi tous les vols,*
> *Les aériens caracols,*
> *Les machines et les entrées,*
> *Qui furent là tant admirées.*

PAGE 209, LINE 5: Mantzius, Vol. IV, p. 228.

PAGE 209, LINE 6: Cf. Prunières, *op. cit.*, p. 104 ff. How popular spectacular scenery was in Paris during Molière's day is evinced by the continual rivalry between public theatres and those directed by Richelieu and Mazarin. Richelieu is reputed to have produced *Mirame* also in order to rival *Orpheus and Eurydice*. After Mazarin's performance of the opera *Orfeo,* the Marais company revived their piece and renamed it *Le Mariage d'Orfeo,* in order to attract the general public that could not see the legendary splendour of the Mazarin production. No sooner was *Ercole Amante* given at the Tuileries in the Salle des Machines than the Marais Theatre again revived their *Orpheus.* When Corneille's *Andromède* was being got ready by Mazarin the Marais company anticipated its opening by putting on a spectacle called *Andromède en Perse.* In 1660 they played in a *pièce à machines, La Toison d'Or,* by Corneille, staged by the Marquis de Sourdéac at his château at Neuburg. After the initial performance for a royal marriage the Marquis presented the Marais company with the scenes and machines he had devised for the play, and they performed it at their theatre in Paris, where it was a decided hit.

PAGE 209, LINE 10: The author's translation of the verses cited by Palmer, p. 329:

> *Quand j'entends le sifflet, je ne trouve jamais*
> *Le changement si prompt que je me le promets.*
> *Souvent au plus beau char le contre-poids résiste;*
> *Un Dieu pend à la corde et crie au machiniste;*
> *Un reste de forêt demeure dans la mer,*
> *Ou la moitié du ciel au milieu de l'enfer.*

PAGE 210, LINE 5: The stage direction in the edition of Molière's plays by Despois and Mesnard (1881), Vol. VI, reads: *Le théâtre, pour cet acte, doit représenter un lieu voisin des maisons de Sganarelle et de M. Robert, et peu éloigné du bois où Sganarelle façonne ses fagots.*

PAGE 213, LINE 13: Palmer, *op. cit.,* p. 327.

PAGE 213, LINE 26: Mantzius, Vol. IV, p. 105.

PAGE 217, LINE 13: *Shakespeare's England,* edition of 1926, Clarendon Press, Oxford, Vol. II, p. 254.

PAGE 218, LINE 4: Cited by W. J. Lawrence, *Pre-Restoration Stage Studies*. The citations from Lawrence, except where noted, are from this volume, Chapters IX-XI; those from Chambers from *The Elizabethan Stage*, Vol. III, Chapters XX-XXI: "Staging in the Theatres" (16th and 17th century), and Vol. I, Chapter IV: "Pageantry." Note the description of the festivities during Elizabeth's visit to Kenilworth in 1575 and Elvetham in 1571, with the fireworks and aquatic shows provided, and Chambers' comment: "I have set the Kenilworth and Elvetham entertainments side by side, partly to illustrate the permanence of the type and partly because if any actual sea-maid and fireworks gave Shakespeare a hint for Oberon's famous speech in *A Midsummer Night's Dream*, it must surely have been those which were comparatively fresh in the minds of his hearers" (p. 124).

PAGE 222, LINE 5: From a contemporary letter of Sir Henry Wotton, who attended the performance. He adds, "sufficient in truth within a while to make greatness very familiar" (*Reliquae Wottoniae*, edition of 1672).

PAGE 225, LINE 13: Cited by Gofflot, *op. cit.*, p. 69.

PAGE 228, LINE 20: *Shakespeare's England*, Vol. II, p. 316. The other citations in this part of Section 5 are from Campbell's *Scenes and Machines*.

PAGE 234, LINE 12: Chambers, *op. cit.*, Vol. I, p. 131 ff.

PAGE 239, LINE 24: L. B. Campbell, *op. cit.*

PAGE 240, LINE 19: Lawrence, "The Origin of the English Picture Stage," in *The Elizabethan Playhouse*, 2nd Series.

PAGE 242, LINE 24: Cited by Campbell, *op. cit.*

PAGE 244, LINE 19: Cited by Zucker, *Theater-Dekoration des Klassizismus*, p. 16.

PAGE 252, LINE 22: Cited by Campbell, *op. cit.*

PAGE 253, LINE 10: Translated by Foster, Bohn's Standard Library.

PAGE 253, LINE 25: For drawings, presumably for stage settings by Peruzzi, see Mariani's *Scenografia Italiana*.

PAGE 254, LINE 20: This and the following descriptions of settings at the Barberinis' theatre are cited by Rolland in *Histoire de l'Opéra en Europe*.

PAGE 256, LINE 5: Nicoll, *op. cit.*, Appendix B.

PAGE 256, LINE 25: For a description of similar but more elaborate contraptions by the Florentine engineer Cecca, see Vasari's *Lives*, translated by G. de Vere, Vol. III.

PAGE 258, LINE 7: Burckhardt, *The Renaissance in Italy*, p. 417.

PAGE 258, LINE 25: Cf. Campari, *Documents inédits sur Raphael, Gazette de Beaux Arts*, 1863.

PAGE 258, LINE 29: From Ady, *Baldassare Castiglione*.

PAGE 260, LINE 17: From Vasari, De Vere's translation, Vol. X, "The Nuptials of the Prince Don Francesco of Tuscany." The festivities involved a bewildering amount of scenery in the streets, triumphal arches, painted façades, etc., and endless pageantry of the most spectacular kind.

PAGE 261, LINE 20: Cf. Bapst, *op. cit.*, p. 475 ff.

PAGE 261, LINE 30: Zucker, *Theater-Dekoration des Baroks*, note 30, p. 24.

PAGE 262, LINE 9: Cf. Appendix of Cogniat's *Décors de Théâtre*.

PAGE 266, LINE 16: These measurements are approximate. They are based on those in *toises* (1 *toise* = 1.949 metres) in Daumont's *Parallèle de plus belles salles de Spectacles d'Italie et de la France*. An 18th century compilation.

PAGE 267, LINE 28: Cited by Macgowan, *The Theatre of To-morrow*, p. 14.

PAGE 281, LINE 9: Gilder, *Enter the Actress*, p. 275 ff.

PAGE 281, LINE 17: *Behind the Scenes with Edwin Booth*, pp. 11-12.

PAGE 283, LINE 21: For the complete texts of Antoine's open letters, see his *Souvenirs du Théâtre Libre*, pp. 192-203, and Thalasso's *Le Théâtre Libre*, p. 166.

PAGE 284, LINE 1: *My Life in Art*, p. 198.

PAGE 287, LINE 21: The descriptions of the Meiningen productions and the details of stage setting and costume are based on Grube's *Geschichte der Meininger*.

The duke also displayed another tendency characteristic of subsequent art theatres. He continually attempted to make effective in the theatre plays that were not regarded as "theatrical" or actable. He was occasionally revolutionary as well in his choice of material, as when he selected *Ghosts*, of which he gave one of the first public performances in Germany at Dresden. The police, unable to censure a reigning prince, dropped a heavy hint to Chronegk that the performance was not to be repeated. The duke then scandalized Meiningen by giving the play there at an invitation performance, which proved to be for men only, his wife and a few actresses of the company being the only women who dared to attend. Ibsen was present.

PAGE 295, LINE 10: Stanislavsky, *op. cit.*, p. 311.

PAGE 298, LINE 10: Catalogue of Matisse Retrospective Exhibition, Museum of Modern Art, New York, 1931, p. 15.

PAGE 303, LINE 3: Stanislavsky, *op. cit.*, p. 197 ff.

PAGE 309. The citations from Craig's volumes are made with the permission of his publishers in this country, E. P. Dutton & Co.

PAGE 319, LINE 26: *My Life,* p. 199 ff.

PAGE 321, LINE 11: *Op. cit.,* p. 509 ff.

PAGE 323, LINE 31: *On the Art of the Theatre,* p. 110.

PAGE 324, LINE 1: *Towards a New Theatre,* p. 81.

PAGE 324, LINE 3: *Scene,* p. 25.

PAGE 324, LINE 29: *Art of the Theatre,* p. 81.

PAGE 325, LINE 14: Bapst, *op. cit.,* pp. 17, 345.

PAGE 327, LINE 2: *Scene,* p. 23.

PAGE 327, LINE 9: Cited by Macgowan, *The Theatre of To-morrow,* p. 93.

PAGE 327, LINE 14: *On the Art of the Theatre,* p. 123.

PAGE 332, LINE 13: *Towards a New Theatre,* p. 58.

PAGE 336, LINE 27: *Fourteen Points,* p. 16.

PAGE 339, LINE 14: Translation by Gertrude Hall, *The Poems of Paul Verlaine* (Stone & Kimball, 1895).

PAGE 342, LINE 8: *A Production* (1926), p. 8.

PAGE 342, LINE 28: In the (London) *Bookman* for November, 1931, p. 42, Enid Rose says: "Of the invitations which got no further than his projected designs, one was cancelled because Mr. Shaw could not make head or tail of the designs." However, according to Miss St. John, the editor of *Ellen Terry and Bernard Shaw, a Correspondence,* as early as 1905 Shaw, on having *Caesar and Cleopatra* accepted for production by the Lessing Theatre, stipulated that Craig be retained to design the production (p. 308). According to Shaw, Craig delivered nothing but a "vague pencil memorandum on half a sheet of paper," followed by an ultimatum stating that he must be put in complete control of the production regardless of the author. It was not until then that the management of the Lessing Theatre gave up the attempt to get designs from Craig.

In the same number of the *Bookman,* Mr. Norman Marshall writes: "Miss Rose aptly compares Craig to a fiddler who lacks practice. I fail to see why Mr. Cochran or any one else should be expected to provide money for this fiddler to practise in public under the expensively ideal conditions which he stipulates. Miss Rose mentions three offers made to Mr. Craig. There have been others. When Craig was in England during the exhibition of designs for *The Pretenders* I was associated with the management which made Craig a definite offer and I had some opportunity of observing his vagueness when faced with a practical proposition."

As further testimony to Craig's present almost morbid inability to make up his mind when given an opportunity to design, the following letter from a London manager (reprinted with his permission) is relevant:

"In common with all—or at least most of us, I was hypnotized by Craig's drawings and prose in my youth. I looked on him as little short of a demi-god, and had my first bitter disillusionment in 1913 or 1914, when going to worship at his feet in Florence, I was greeted with a tirade of abuse for having used screens in Chicago. 'Screens were his property: any one else who used them was a gross plagiarist.' It was apparently irrelevant that the 'screens' I had been using were ordinary folding screens based on the Japanese plan, that have no relation to his 'screens.'

"None the less my idolatry, although somewhat tempered, persisted, so that when success (as it is called) came my way two or three years ago, one of the first things I did was to invite Craig to England (at my expense) and to offer him every facility for producing his *Hamlet* here, either with German or with English players. I made one proviso—that he should draw up a budget in advance and stick to it. I set no limit to the size of the budget, and my fellow directors and I were prepared to stretch ourselves to the utmost to give him what he needed. His tentative oral budgets varied from about £800 to (if I remember aright, and I am fairly certain that I do) over £30,000; it proved impossible to pin him to any fixed scale of expenditure or to any definite plan of operation. Finally, having grub-staked him and his assistant (not, however, to any big amount) for some weeks, and having spent a somewhat bigger sum in journeys to and from Germany, largely in his interest, the scheme was abandoned, solely because he could not or would not put it in concrete form."

PAGE 348, LINE 30: Bernard Shaw (as reported by G. W. Bishop in the London *Observer,* reprinted by the New York *Times,* Dramatic Section, Nov. 30, 1930) remarked:

"If there ever was a spoilt child in artistic Europe, that child was Teddy Craig. The doors of the theatre were wider open to him than to anybody else. He had only to come in as the others did, and do his job, and know his place, and accept the theatre with all its desperate vicissitudes, and inadequacies, and impossibilities, as the rest of us did, and the way would have been clear for all the talent he possessed. But that is not what he wanted. He wanted a theatre to play with as Irving played with the Lyceum. . . . Such theatres are not to be had. That is not what the theatre is for."

PAGE 349, LINE 20: Steichen's photograph of Craig is reproduced in the *Theatre Guild Magazine,* February, 1931.

PAGE 382, LINE 17: From *Herbert Beerbohm Tree* (Hutchinson, London), p. 243.

PAGE 387, LINE 23: New York *Evening Post,* Jan. 20, 1932: "House valued at $1,000,000 in 1929 auctioned to Emigrant Bank for $100,000. The Hudson Theatre on 44th St. east of Broadway was sold at auction today to the Emigrant Industrial Bank for $100,000. The sale came through a foreclosure proceeding brought by the bank . . . the house has not been tenanted in some time."

PAGE 389, LINE 5: Cf. the following tabulation of production expenses from "Five Little Productions and How They Grew," by Kenneth Macgowan, New York *Times,* Dramatic Section, Jan. 3, 1932:

	"Twelfth Night"	"Art and Mrs. Bottle"	"Lean Harvest"	"The Lady with a Lamp"	"Springtime for Henry"
Scenery	$ 7,739	$ 1,862	$ 6,659	$ 4,325	$ 615
Costumes	4,585	1,936	1,984	6,000	665
Dress rehearsals..	402	317	4,015	1,826	473
Properties	479	1,049	4,410	2,632	1,300
Total cost (including other items not listed here) ...	$20,865	$10,078	$24,969	$15,559	$2,931

Lean Harvest was rehearsed on a typically cramped New York stage, resulting in the "jam" and duplication of labour which adds so much to production costs. This was increased by the necessity of further rehearsals and revisions of the play on a preliminary tour out of town. Three changes of realistic interiors were required for each act, made on two turn-tables that were mechanically efficient from the start. When the handicapped crew and stage management learned to run the show, the shifts were made in 20 seconds. *Twelfth Night* and *The Lady with the Lamp* were able to utilize unit settings with resultant savings in rehearsal expense. *Springtime for Henry* represents the manager's dream: a hit (the only success of the five) with a cast of five players and one set rebuilt from old material.

PAGE 396, LINE 12: About $250,000 of Guild bonds have been retired to date. Interest on bonds has been regularly paid even during these depression years—proof that conservative business methods can be successfully applied in running a theatre, provided a management is content with less than speculator's profits.

PAGE 412, LINE 2: Municipally endowed theatres, as in Europe, are out of the question for this country. The corruption of city government is so endemic that a civic theatre would present nothing more than an outlet for a new kind of graft. We seem unable to breed civic officials with enough business integrity to run a city efficiently, let alone taste enough to run a theatre. Private endowment, however, need not extend beyond the first few years or include more than the grant of land and equipment in large cities. With proper diversification of amusements, sound management and effective co-operation with the best Broadway producers, there is no reason why privately owned civic theatres could not meet running expenses and eventually show a profit outside of New York.

PAGE 417, LINE 30: From the Annual Report of the Westchester County Recreation Commission:

The cost of carrying on the work of the Commission for the year 1930 is as follows:

From County Funds

For General Work

Salaries	$31,279.80
Wages and Fees	9,160.22
Furniture and Fixtures	1,505.73
Automobiles	1,348.66
Camp Equipment	727.58
Travel	3,947.55
Ptg., Postage and Stationery	4,711.47
Incidentals	2,495.14
Telephone	1,499.98
Office Supplies	1,000.00
Medals	589.33
Museum	388.48
Handicraft Supplies	461.03
Total	**$59,114.97**

For County Center

Salaries	$ 3,393.54
Wages and Fees	10,843.82
Telephone	765.79
Fuel, Light and Water	4,935.20
Cleaning	9,093.00
Machinery Repairs	12.99
Care of Organ	215.00
Janitors' Supplies	728.22
General Supplies	6,314.86
	$36,302.42
Less Rentals, 7½ months	10,504.43
Total	**$25,797.99**

Total from County Funds $84,912.96

Activities of Affiliated Organizations Supported by Fees, Subscriptions and Gifts

Training School for Recreation Workers	$ 167.40
Westchester Trails Association	322.32
Westchester Drama Association	611.07
Athletic Federation	578.80
School of Theatre	2,259.98
Coloured Choral Work	1,060.00
Creative Dance Class	53.15
Westchester Workshop	3,172.73
Drama Tournament	964.93
Children's Camp	5,890.41
Mothers' Camp	2,808.89
Westchester Choral Society	27,739.20
Organ Recitals	1,100.00
General	4,687.05
Total	**$51,415.93**

PAGE 428, LINE 25: *Variety,* Jan. 12, 1932, on a production of Sophocles' *Electra:* "In the modern sense it isn't a play at all, running only an hour and fifty minutes and the stage action merely extremely long speeches and soliloquies, clothed in ponderous, if resounding, language. Grand elocution but dull drama. Speeches for the most part are in blank verse."

PAGE 431, LINE 8: Cf. *A Test of the News. An Examination of the News Reports in the New York Times on aspects of the Russian Revolution,* by Charles Merz and Walter Lippmann, supplement to *The New Republic,* Aug. 4, 1920. The *Times* has since redeemed itself with Walter Duranty's dispatches, but canards from Riga about the desired collapse of the U.S.S.R. have recently been credited and printed. With the exception of an occasional exposé, our newspapers fall down most frequently when they do their own fact-finding and are at their best when the facts are found, and their importance emphasized for them. Even then they are occasionally victims of their own gullibility as in the case of the official White House summary of the Wickersham report on the Prohibition amendment, which misrepresented it as being against modification or repeal. This was given out in advance of the full text and headlined by the anti-prohibitionist press, which later could not undo the erroneous analysis they had helped to circulate. For instances of how much "news" journalists report that they know to be distorted or false, how much news they hold back which they know or believe to be true, see *The Washington Merry-Go-Round.*

For an example of typically redundant reporting see the New York *Herald Tribune* for July 2, 1931, on the return of the flyers Post and Gatty. The habit of verbosity results in faking news when there is none to report. Cf. *The New Yorker,* Nov. 21, 1931, under "The Wayward Press": "During the Laval parleys the correspondents were frankly at sea. There being nothing to report . . . it was up to the boys to sound as if each had the inside dope without actually divulging what it was. . . . Columns had to be sent in every day referring to 'unimpeachable sources' which yielded nothing, and 'it is understoods' in which no understanding was reached." Cf. *The New Republic,* March 16, 1932, apropos of the Lindbergh kidnapping: "On no day since the case opened has there been more legitimate news than could have been told in half a column of type; but the editors have proceeded on their usual theory that if the public is interested in anything it insists on reading 20,000 words a day about it however uninformative these words may be." In confirmation see "The Wayward Press," *The New Yorker,* May 7, 1932.

PAGE 432, LINE 7: Cf. Frank R. Kent, *The Nation,* March 16, 1932: "And how they [the newspaper correspondents] hung—and still hang— to that legend of his silence, of his economy in speech and his dislike to utter unnecessary words—this the most garrulous of our Presidents, whose public output of words exceeded all the rest and whose private capacity to dwell on details exceeded that of any other public man."

PAGE 432, LINE 16: Such as the Federal Trade Commission's report on propaganda by the electric power companies, which totalled 14,293 pages. Its findings were rescued for the public in Ernest Gruening's condensation, *The Public Pays.* O. H. Cheney was retained by the National Association of Book Publishers to make a survey of overproduction in the book business. He produced another volume of 150,000 words.

PAGE 444, LINE 2: In an earlier version, the play ended by two former slaves, negro "weird sisters," murdering the girl, rather than have the aristocratic tradition of their "house" violated. The melioristic ending was provided for the production staged by the Group Theatre.

PAGE 456, LINE 20: The Phipps Apartments, Long Island City. C. L. Stein, architect.

ADDENDA

PAGE 348, LINE 11: Cp. the following excerpt from an open letter by Chas. B. Cochran to *Everyman* (London) issue of Jan. 28, 1933. "I have tried to lure Mr. Craig into making a production in a London theatre. I tried honestly and sincerely to give him the facilities for showing us what he could really do. I found, as others have found before, that his acquaintance with the theatre is so nebulous and the demands he makes before he can even begin to practise his craft are so fantastically unreasonable that the project, which I should have welcomed with enthusiasm and fostered with all my energies, fell through."

INDEX

Abbey Theatre, 19
Abel's blood, in Mons production, 188
Abie's Irish Rose, 397
Abraham Lincoln, 86
Abstractions as a refuge, 134
Acharnians, The, 137, 150 ff., 169
Acis and Galatea, 341
Acoustics of masks, 143
Acting, actors: cornerstone of theatre,
75 ff.; no longer dominate, 84; Greek,
135; importance of voice in Greek
theatre, 144 ff.; Greek guild of, 147;
in mystery-plays, 188 ff.; mingling
with audience, 197, 213; Molière's
reforms, 204; Goethe on, 244; motion
and meaning, 272 ff.; as plastic ele-
ment, 306; banished by Craig, 314,
324 ff.; exalted by Craig, 342;
dwarfed in Craig's drawings, 343;
Craig dominated by psychology of,
345 ff.; in Appia's philosophy, 355,
364; importance of light to, 368;
salaries for rehearsal, 383; high salaries of, 391; praised as "restrained,"
429, 430
Action, plan of, 284 ff.
Acts of the Apostles, The, 185
Adamic, Louis, 442
Adamowsky, Adalbert, 77
Adams, Maude, 70
Adding Machine, The, 121
Addison, Joseph, 243, 244
Admiral's Men, The, 221
Aeschines, 35
Aeschylus, 21, 24, 25, 35, 49, 77, 135,
147, 149 ff., 215, 327, 407, 415
Aesthetic principles formulated by Ap-
pia, 351

Aesthetics, make-believe as, 47 ff.
Affairs of Anatol, 123
Agamemnon, 153
Aïda, 342
Aiglon, L', 67
Aglaura, 240
Alcestis (Euripides'), 138, 164,
(Gluck's) 204
Alcibiades, 156, 159
Alexander, (the Great) 145, 146;
(play) 167
Alexander's Triumph over Darius, 200,
202
Alleyn's cloak, 33
Alphonsus, 220
Amants Magnifiques, Les, 210
Amateurs: in French colleges, 199 ff.;
in English universities and schools,
229 ff.; established modern theatre,
318
Ames, Winthrop, 392, 394, 412
Amphytrion, 209
Amsterdam, exhibition of scene-designs
at, 17
Anatomy of Melancholy, 234
Anaxagoras, 163, 164
Andreiev, Leonid, 67, 73
Andromache, 154
Andromeda, 205, 555
Animals: in mystery-plays, 173, 174 ff.;
mechanical, 186; on the Renaissance
stage, 259; in *Sacre Rappresentazione,*
553
Antigone, 154, 430
Antoine, 15, 19, 70, 91, 173, 189, 272,
282, 283, 287, 289, 302, 304, 318, 386
Antony and Cleopatra, 232
Anzengruber, 81

573

LEE SIMONSON

Born New York City, June 26, 1888. His first experience of the theatre was in his late teens, seeing the classics of Lessing, Schiller and Goethe given by the German repertory company at the Irving Place Theatre, also Mansfield, not only as Beau Brummel, but as *Le Misanthrope,* and Arnold Daly as Marchbanks. Graduated from the Ethical Culture High School, 1905; Harvard, 1905–1908; BA, 1908. Took George P. Baker's then revolutionary course on contemporary playwrighting, English 47, the precursor of the present Departments of Theatre Arts at some 200 universities. Lived in Paris, 1908–1912. Studied at the Academie Julien, then at various independent academies. His first stage settings were done for the Washington Square Players, 1915. Became one of the founders of the Theatre Guild in 1919, and for 20 years was one of its directors, until his resignation in 1939. Of his Theatre Guild stage settings his favorites are those for Masefield's *The Faithful,* Shaw's *Heartbreak House,* O'Neill's *Marco Millions,* Georg Kayser's *Masse Mensch,* which he also directed. With Herbert Graf, he redid Wagner's *Nibelungen Ring* for the Metropolitan Opera Association, as well as the scenario and costumes for the American premiere of *Le Pas d'Acier* by Stravinsky.